Racing & Fo...
FLAT R...ING
GUIDE 2011

Statistics • Results
Previews • Training centre reports

Contributors: Amy Bennett, Neil Clark, Nick Deacon, Steffan Edwards, Sarah Hall, Dylan Hill, Mark Howard, Tony Jakobson, Kel Mansfield, Steve Mellish, Mark Nelson, Dave Nevison, Ben Osborne, Graham Wheldon, Richard Williams

Designed and edited by Nick Watts and Dylan Hill

Published in 2011 by Raceform,
Compton, Newbury, Berkshire RG20 6NL

Copyright © Raceform Ltd 2011

All rights reserved. No part of this publication may be reproduced, stored in a retrieval system, or transmitted in any form or by any means, electronic, mechanical, photocopying, recording, or otherwise, without prior
written permission of the publishers.

A catalogue record for this book is available from the British Library.

ISBN 978-1-906820-67-1

Printed by CPI Bookmarque, Croydon

Contents

Outlook

Editor's introduction

THE year 2010 may have lacked an equine superstar to match Sea The Stars, but it certainly produced a stunning effort on the training front. The handler in question is Henry Cecil, who marked a triumphant return to the big time on the last ever Champions Day at Newmarket when saddling Frankel to victory in the Dewhurst and Twice Over to a second successive triumph in the Champion Stakes.

Midday also did her bit for Cecil as she stormed to victory in the Nassau Stakes and the Yorkshire Oaks before just being denied a Breeders' Cup double at Churchill Downs.

It's fantastic for racing that Cecil's main patron, Khalid Abdullah, has opted to keep Midday and Twice Over in training, as well as his Derby and Arc hero Workforce, and it is only to be hoped that we see more

MIDDAY: Henry Cecil's mighty mare is back for more this season

battles between Midday and Oaks winner Snow Fairy this year. In fact you can read all about Snow Fairy's plans in Sarah Hall's brilliant interview with her trainer Ed Dunlop.

Back to Cecil, who only needs a Classic win to truly mark his comeback, one that was cruelly denied him when Jacqueline Quest was demoted in the 1,000 Guineas, ironically behind Abdullah's flying French filly Special Duty, and Frankel could be the horse to right that wrong.

His 10l victory in the Royal Lodge Stakes last year had to be seen to be believed, and he was nearly as impressive in easily landing the Dewhurst despite pulling hard.

It remains to be seen whether he has trained on, but he's sure to be a warm order for the 2,000 Guineas. And, should he clear that hurdle, the question of whether or not he stays the Derby trip will be fascinating to find out.

It was an interesting year, too, for Sir Michael Stoute, who again showed his brilliance with his handling of the seemingly fragile Workforce, who was twice beaten, in the Dante and the King George, but still proved he was the best three-year-old in training with his Derby and Arc wins.

Stoute was also desperately unlucky that his brilliant King George winner Harbinger was subsequently retired through injury just when it seemed he might have the middle-distance world at his mercy.

Otherwise, though, it was a decidedly lean year for Stoute, whose tally of 73 wins was his lowest for 15 years – meaning he's not even featured in our statistical look at the ten winningmost trainers of last year.

Workforce, though, stays in training, and Stoute will hope he has greater depth to his team – and good fortune – this time. Our ante-post expert Steffan Edwards, tipping the Stoute pair Cape Dollar and Carlton House to win Classics.

For Aidan O'Brien this year also represents something of a step into the unknown as he faces up to life after Johnny Murtagh, while it's a huge one for Godolphin's second trainer Mahmood Al Zarooni, surprisingly given Sheikh Mohammed's leading Derby hopes Dubai Prince and Casamento to look after.

You can read about all the top trainers in our brilliant training-centre reports, while, as

MAHMOOD AL ZAROONI: faces a big year after taking over leading Derby hopes Casamento anbd Dubai Prince

well as Ed Dunlop, the yard of William Knight, led by top stayer Illustrious Blue, also comes in for special attention in our trainer interviews.

On top of all that Richard Williams has sifted through last year's form book to come up with his idea of the best 30 horses to follow this season; pedigree expert Amy Bennett uncovers the best first-crop sires to follow; there's unrivalled draw analysis from Graham Wheldon; the unique views of Steve Mellish, pro punter Dave Nevison and speed guru Mark Nelson; and Dylan Hill's guide to last season's leading form.

Then there's the stats, reams and reams of winner-finding numbers detailing the top trainers and jockeys also broken down course-by-course whatever your local track.

Once again we have every base covered for a year packed with bumper profits, and don't forget to buy your copy of the *RFO* every week for the very latest news and tips.

Profiles for punters
Ed Dunlop

ED DUNLOP: has a way with the fillies as proven by Ouija Board and Snow Fairy

Profile by Sarah Hall

L A GRANGE Stables has been home to trainer Ed Dunlop since 2009 and it is an area overflowing with racing heritage. Nestled in the heart of Newmarket, it holds a rich horseracing tradition, as not only has it been home to many top-class Flat horses, it was also home to 1923 Grand National winner Sergeant Murphy.

With such a rich tapestry of racing history at La Grange it seems almost inevitable that Dunlop, the son of highly successful Arundel trainer John and brother of Lambourn trainer Harry, is the man adding to its proud past.

Veteran trainer John is something of an institution in racing. He has been training horses at Arundel for almost half a century and has won every Classic race, bar the 2,000 Guineas.

Asking Dunlop whether he would move back to Arundel, he quickly responds with a definitive "No", adding: "I don't think so, I mean my father is a tenant there and has been for over 40 years, but I think we will stay here."

And it is not hard to see why he wants to stay, as, after stints working with Nicky Henderson and the late Alex Scott and a highly successful 15 years carving out a name for himself at Gainsborough Stables, the move to La Grange has seen some great results.

Following in his father's footsteps, Dunlop has also been immensely successful in the Classic races – in his second season he trained Ta Rib to victory in the French 1,000 Guineas.

Dunlop is famed for his phenomenal success with fillies; the most well known is Ouija Board, the daughter of Cape Cross who achieved remarkable wins across the globe, notching up more than £3.5 million in prize-money by winning races such as the Breeders' Cup and the Oaks.

Dunlop reminisces: "She was a well tempered, big, attractive filly and always showed a lot of class as a two-year-old."

She was a popular filly too, once described by Dunlop as "the people's horse," with punters and racegoers applauding and cheering as she rattled up multiple wins across the world.

Dunlop's way with fillies has been richly rewarded again courtesy of his latest stable superstar, Snow Fairy.

The talented daughter of Intikhab has taken her earnings to over £2 million, with the most lucrative win being in the Group 1 Hong Kong Cup, where she took home over £900,000 in prize-money.

Preceding this run she was victorious in the Queen Elizabeth II Commemorative Cup in Kyoto where she scored in impressive style, with the eventual winning margin being 6l.

With Ouija Board there was always a plan. However, with Snow Fairy, "it was well documented that we had no route planned out at all. She was a good two-year-old but an exposed one, but the rest, as they say, is history."

Asking Dunlop the plan for Snow Fairy

SNOW FAIRY: together with proud connections following Hong Kong glory

this campaign, he jokingly replies, "We want to win as many Group 1 races as possible!"

But there is a plan. "The first aim is the World Cup meeting in March," says Dunlop. "After her spell in Dubai she will hopefully head back to Hong Kong for the Queen Elizabeth II Cup in April. If we were feeling even more ambitious after that, then there is a valuable race in Singapore."

Would he like to run her in England? "Of course, and the first logical aim for her would be something like the Prince Of Wales's Stakes or the Nassau Stakes."

So one thing's for sure, Snow Fairy will continue her globe-trotting adventures this term. "She thrives on her travels," says Dunlop, who will be accompanying her every step of the way.

Another horse getting plenty of attention is Voodoo Prince. There is a lot of hype surrounding the three-year-old, who is the first foal out of Ouija Board by Kingmambo.

"There is already a lot of pressure on the poor horse," says Dunlop. "He has been much talked about and is already in the ante-post markets."

Ouija Board has produced further offspring, including a yearling filly by Galileo.

Eddie Ahern has been secured as the stable jockey for the impending season, a move that Dunlop says has been in the pipeline for a while.

"We have been lucky having top-class jockeys riding for us over the years. But there are times when some of the horses were having different jockeys on a regular basis, and obviously the top boys are retained by owners," he explains.

"Eddie has ridden on and off for us for a long time and he is a very good rider and I am happy that he is joining us."

Although Ryan Moore will retain the ride on Snow Fairy, Ahern can look forward to riding many other top-class horses from the yard, including Native Khan, winner of the Group 3 Solario Stakes last year.

However, keep an eye out when Kieren Fallon is in the saddle as last season he had a 21 per cent strike-rate for the yard and rode Ouija Board in a number of her successes.

Impressively there were nine tracks returning a profit last term, but Dunlop reveals that his favourite is Goodwood.

"It's my favourite course for sentimental reasons, as I grew up there and spent a lot of my time going racing with my parents. It's not an ideal track to get to from Newmarket or if you get a bad draw, but we have been lucky there."

Following Dunlop's string to the all-weather tracks could prove lucrative, too, as in the 2009/2010 season, three of the four sand tracks in Great Britain returned a healthy profit.

When asked about his favourite track abroad, Dunlop smiles, "Where we win!" This is quite an extensive list, as he has notched up wins in Hong Kong, America and Japan (to name but a few), thanks to his globe-trotting fillies.

At the time of writing the figures for the 2010/2011 season are shaping up to be just as impressive, with a promising strike-rate of 63 per cent and a healthy £11.35 profit to £1 level-stakes. The Newmarket handler currently has 83 horses, so there's plenty of ammunition to go to war with.

Asking Dunlop what race he would most like to win, he immediately says the Derby, though he adds: "We have had very few runners in the Derby, as we just haven't had enough good staying colts."

However, this could all change courtesy of one of Ouija Board's progeny and I wouldn't want to be the one betting against a yard that has the power of voodoo behind it.

OUIJA BOARD: with Voodoo Prince

The horses

Al Burkaan 3yo bay/brown gelding
Medicean – Lone Look (Danehill)

He ran well to finish third on his only start at Yarmouth, finishing 3l behind Michael Bell's Margot Did, who holds some solid form, including finishing second in the Group 2 Lowther Stakes. He looks to have some ability and we will start him off in a maiden over 7f.

Baqaat 3yo bay/brown filly
Alhaarth – Hachiyah (Generous)

She was very green on her first start and then ran very well at Salisbury in a decent maiden that has since thrown out plenty of winners. I like her and she is definitely capable of winning races.

Convention 3yo bay filly
Encosta De Lago – Model Queen (Kingmambo)

She is a half-sister to David Nicholls' smart Group 1 winner Regal Parade. She is a well-bred filly and consequently was an expensive yearling. She is something of an unknown quantity but hopefully she will be high-class.

Dubai Media 4yo bay filly
Songandaprayer – Forty Gran (El Gran Senor)

She is a filly who won two for us last term. She is a mature, good-looking sort who wants fast ground. She ran at Newmarket on her last start but the ground was too soft for her. She looks to be a nice sprinter for the future. I like her and think she could be Listed class.

Fareer 5yo chestnut gelding
Bahamian Bounty – Songsheet (Dominion)

He won a Listed race over a mile at York last season and he is currently in Dubai for the carnival. He needs decent ground but he wouldn't want any extremes of going and his ideal trip is 7f up to 1m.

Haylaman 3yo bay gelding
Diamond Green – Schonbein (Shirely Heights)

This son of Diamond Green is big and immature, but won his second start at Wolverhampton over 1m. He may be able to stay a bit further, and while he is no star, he will win races.

Ho Ya Mal 3yo chestnut colt
Shamardal – Ridotto (Salse)

He is a big, backward horse who won well and travelled nicely on his only start on the all-weather last November and I'm hoping that he can go on to better things.

Kanaf 4yo bay gelding
Elnadim – Catcher Applause (Royal Applause)

He won three races for us last year and is an improving type of sprinter. He is a neat little horse and the ground is really important for him – he must have it decent. He could be on an upward spiral as he was very impressive in a 5f handicap at Sandown.

Laughing Jack 3yo bay colt
Beat Hollow – Bronzewing (Beldale Flutter)

He is a well-bred and good-looking big horse who has recently come to me from Michael Bell's yard with a tall reputation. He ran well in a decent maiden at Newmarket over a mile in October, which was won by Argocat. He has started cantering and being by Beat Hollow he should stay 1m2f and further.

Muhandis 3yo bay colt
Muhtathir – Ahdaaf (Bahri)

He ran twice last year, once on the all-weather and at Newmarket but he was a little disappointing on both starts. He has worked well at home in the past and hopefully he can win races this term.

Munaaseb 3yo chestnut gelding
Zafeen – Miss Prim (Case Law)

He has a high-class sprinting pedigree as he's a half brother to Amour Propre. He finished seventh on his racecourse debut at Yarmouth, but was very immature. He has strengthened up well and looks to have a lot of speed.

Musharakaat 3yo bay filly
Iffraaj – Gift Of Spring (Gilded Time)

She is a big, tall beautiful looking filly who won her maiden at Kempton. I am hoping that she will stay further than a mile and could be Listed/Group 3 class. Jockey Richard Hills has always liked her and she could start out this season in an Oaks trial.

Native Khan 3yo grey colt
Azamour – Viva Maria (Kendor)

He is a beautiful moving horse who won his maiden at Newmarket and then went on to score in the Solario Stakes at Sandown at the end of August last year. He came off the pace to finish fourth in the Racing Post Trophy on ground that he loathed. Ground is crucial for this horse as he simply needs very decent going. He will hopefully head to the 2,000 Guineas and I am hoping that he will stay further as his breeding would suggest. The French Derby would be an option too, if he stays, but we will see how he progresses over the next few months and take it from there. He has wintered well and we are pleased with him so far.

Red Cadeaux 5yo chestnut gelding
Cadeaux Genereux – Artisia (Peintre Celebre)

He won three last year and is a decent staying horse and one which I am hoping can contest in some of the cup races this year. He has improved enormously, has had a winter holiday and has returned to us well. He wouldn't want the going too firm and 2m is about as far as he wants to go, as he didn't quite stay in the Cesarewitch last term.

Red Lover 3yo bay filly
Azamour – Love Me Tender (Green Desert)

He was placed in a couple of maiden races last year and is a horse who travels well in his races. He wasn't quite finishing his races last year, but hopefully that was down to immaturity. He is a strong horse, has got speed, and one who would appreciate a bit of give in the ground. He is a horse who I like so hopefully he can go on this season.

Reem Star 3yo bay filly
Green Tune – Arlecchina (Mtoto)

She picked up well to win a maiden at Lingfield and ran well preceding that run at Wolverhampton where she finished second. She is by Green Tune and was always going to make a better three-year-old and I hope she will step up to be better than a handicap horse.

Rutland Boy 3yo chestnut gelding
Bertolini – Israah (Machiavellian)

He won a maiden on his second start, scoring in comfortable fashion on the all-weather at Wolverhampton and although he is no superstar, he will win more races.

Sadafiya 3yo bay filly
Oasis Dream – Nidhaal (Observatory)

A dual-winner on the all-weather and I trained her mother Nidhaal who was very fast and won a Listed race. She has a very big heart for a small filly and is a nice sort to have this year.

Satwa Royal 4yo bay gelding
Royal Applause – Dance For Fun (Anabaa)

He is a half brother to triple Group 1 winner Lush Lashes and he won his only start as a maiden on the all-weather in January. He didn't run until he was a four-year-old as he has had a few issues, but he looks to have some ability.

Sharnberry 3yo bay filly
Shamardal – Wimple (Kingmambo)

She won her maiden impressively at Lingfield on her second start and finished seventh in the Cheveley Park. Unfortunately we had problems with her for most of the season so she was difficult to train. She has a lot of speed and is talented so she could be pretty useful this term if all goes well as I think quite highly of her.

Snow Fairy 4yo bay filly
Intikhab – Woodland Dream
(Charnwood Forest)

She had phenomenal success last term after wins at home and abroad. She is hopefully going to the Dubai, where she is entered in three races – the World Cup, Sheema Classic and the Duty Free. She has been back cantering after her holiday and touch wood everything is going well with her at the moment. She will go to Dubai for a short amount of time before the race and she certainly won't be running before then. After her spell in Dubai she will hopefully head back to Hong Kong for the Queen Elizabeth II Cup in April. We are very lucky to still have her and fingers crossed she continues in good condition.

Tamareen 3yo bay colt
Bahamian Bounty – Damjanich
(Mull Of Kintyre)

He won his last two starts on a low-ish handicap mark and he has always shown talent and works well at home. He is a 7f horse who can hopefully win more races over that distance.

Tanfeeth 3yo chestnut colt
Singspiel – Nasij (Elusive Quality)

He is a colt I have always liked. He is a fine sort and a good mover who is out of Nasij, who I trained, who went on to win a Listed fillies race. He was made hot favourite on his racecourse debut at Sandown, but ran very badly and showed nothing. He came back with sore shins and coughed a lot, so we'll put a line through that run. He has done well over the winter and I think he will be a good 1m to 1m2f horse.

Wiqaaya 3yo grey filly
Red Ransom – Masaader (Wild Again)

I trained her mother Masaader who won a couple of races over 6f. She finished second at Newbury and then we put her away as I think she will be a better three-year-old.

Zarafshan 3yo bay colt
Halling – Gipsy Moth (Efisio)

An unraced colt who has always worked nicely at home and is a half-brother to William Knight's Illustrious Blue who frequently wins at Goodwood. He is a big galloping horse who I think will make a nice three-year-old.

RED CADEAUX: could be a cup horse

Profiles for punters
William Knight

WILLIAM KNIGHT: has had a meteoric rise that looks set to continue this season

Profile by Neil Clark

THE ANGMERING Park Estate in Sussex has a long and mysterious history. It is said by some that the ghost of highwayman Jack Upperton, whose dead body was hanged in a gibbet at the park's west entrance, still haunts the area.

But there is nothing mysterious or paranormal about the rise of racehorse trainer William Knight, who first started training at Lower Coombe Stables in Angmering in 2006.

Knight studied Equine Business Management at the Royal Agricultural College in Cirencester, where he obtained an honours degree.

"No one in my family worked in racing," he says, "but my father was a farmer and had some horses in training. I loved going to point-to-points."

He then worked as assistant trainer to top Flat trainers John Hills and Ed Dunlop, his time at the latter coinciding with the days of the champion filly Ouija Board and multiple Group 1 winner Lailani.

With that great experience behind him, Knight took the plunge to set up as a trainer five years ago, and it's fair to say that he hasn't looked back since.

In his first full campaign, he trained a highly respectable six turf winners, with seven more on the all-weather.

In 2008, his turf winner total rose to nine, his all-weather figure doubling to 14. He matched those totals in 2009.

Last season proved to be a real annus mirabilis. Knight's total of turf winners rose to 22, translating to an excellent 14 per cent strike-rate.

Anyone who staked a tenner on all of Knight's runners would have been rewarded by profits of £570.60, rising to £780.50 if you'd focused on his three-year-olds.

It wasn't just about the number of races Knight was winning – it was the quality of those contests too.

In April, Knight landed his first Group race when stable star Illustrious Blue, going off at odds of 16-1, landed the Group 3 Sagaro Stakes at Ascot.

Three months later, the same horse showed that was no fluke when landing the even more valuable Group 2 Goodwood Cup at Glorious Goodwood.

Other highlights of a memorable campaign included the victory of King Of Dixie (over subsequent Group 3 winner Cityscape) in a Listed race at Ascot on the six-year-old's first run for almost a year and on the same day as Illustrious Blue's Sagaro Stakes win.

Illustrious Blue finished the campaign with a highly respectable ninth in the Melbourne Cup, earning his new Australian connections £70,000 in the process.

'Blue' will now stay down under for the new campaign, but although Knight won't have the services of the horse who did so much to promote his talents, hopes are still high at Lower Coombe Stables that the yard can continue on its upward trajectory.

"We've got a nice team of horses and we're looking forward to new campaign. We'll have about 50 horses in all and about 25 two-year-olds.

"We've got an improving quality of horses, which is what we're trying to achieve.

"I've also got a very good team of staff and I'm very happy with the facilities. We have a new soft track gallop over 1m4f long, together with a five furlong polytrack gallop."

An important member of the Lower Coombe team is the highly skilled, internationally renowned vet Rob van Pelt, of the nearby Arundel Equine Hospital, who has played such a key role in the star Hungarian sprinter Overdose's return to health.

Away from training, watching other sports provides Knight's main source of relaxation.

"I like watching any sport, in particular rugby, tennis and cricket. I loved watching this winter's Ashes series – coming in on a cold winter's day and seeing the sunshine and the great action from Australia. It was fantastic."

The same word could be used to describe Knight's own meteoric rise up the training ranks, a rise which looks set to continue in the months ahead.

ILLUSTRIOUS BLUE: now departed, but seen here winning the Goodwood Cup

The horses

Bloodsweatandtears 3yo bay colt
Barathea – Celestial Princess (Observatory)

He won his maiden at Yarmouth in July and then I ran him at Sandown on ground that was too quick and it jarred him. I then put him away for the rest of the season. He's done very well over the winter and will start on a nice enough mark. He may start off in a 1m2f handicap at the Craven meeting or over 1m at Doncaster. Potentially he could be very nice. He's by Barathea so he should be okay with cut in the ground.

KING OF DIXIE: has huge ability

Forty Proof 3yo bay gelding
Invincible Spirit – Cefira (Distant View)

Won a couple of times last year – a maiden over 5f at Bath in October and a 6f handicap at Lingfield in December. He's slightly on the small side but definitely has ability – he's currently rated in the low 80s. Sprinting is his game and he'll be running in sprint handicaps.

King Of Dixie 7yo chestnut gelding
*Kingmambo – Dixie Accent
(Dixieland Band)*

He's been plagued with injuries throughout his career but has massive ability. He won a 1m Listed race at Ascot last April on his first run back for nearly a year, beating Cityscape who went on to win a Group 3 at Newmarket. He'll probably start off in a Listed race at Ascot in May. The ground is the key to him as he doesn't want it too fast or too soft.

Magical Flower 3yo bay filly
*Oasis Dream – Fancy Rose
(Joyeux Danseur)*

She ran three times last year but was still a little on the weak side. I've always liked her and she'll be running over 1m/1m2f. She'll start the campaign off on a decent mark and I'm hoping that there's races to be won with her.

Monster Munchie 3yo bay filly
Deep Impact – Muncie (Sadler's Wells)

She made her debut when a staying-on third in a 1m2f maiden at Lingfield in early February. She's very well bred – she's by Deep Impact out of a Sadlers Well's mare. She was bought in Japan as a foal and will run in races from 1m2f and 1m4f.

Oblitereight 2yo chestnut colt
Bertolini – Doctrine (Unknown)

He could be quite sharp a sharp sort and he'd definitely be one of my earliest two-year-olds.

Palace Moon 6yo bay gelding
Fantastic Light – Palace Street (Secreto)

He had a great campaign last year, finishing third in the Wokingham and second in the Bunbury Cup at Newmarket. We were going to send him over to Dubai this winter, but it had to be delayed due to sore shins. He's up to a mark of 108/109, so it's going to be difficult for him running off that mark in handicaps and therefore we're looking at Listed races or Group 3s with him. He likes top of the ground – all three of his wins have come on good to firm.

Proper Charlie 3yo bay colt
Cadeaux Genereux – Ring Of Love (Magic Ring)

Still a maiden after four runs as a juvenile but he was always going to be a better three-year-old. Sprinting is his game. He'll be out in mid-April. He doesn't want any ground extremes. Potentially he's a nice horse.

Titan Triumph 7yo bay gelding
Zamindar – Triple Green (Green Desert)

He'd been in the wilderness with a series of niggling injuries but returned to form when he dead-heated at Lingfield in January. That will have done him the world of good. We'll give him one or two more runs on the all-weather and then he'll have a break. He'll go on turf when the ground is quick enough and combine it with the all-weather.

Western Pearl 4yo bay filly
High Chaparral – Pulau Pinang (Dolphin Street)

Her owner bought her to breed from so it was pleasing to get some black type when she was third in the Noel Murless at Newmarket in September. She was always going to be a nice four-year-old. She'll be campaigned at trips ranging from 1m4f up to 2m and we may go abroad with her. She's a High Chaparral and she wants juice.

PALACE MOON (right): will be going for Listed and Group 3 events in this campaign

Two-year-olds

Filly-wise I've got a nice chestnut by Elnadim out of Photo Flash named Framed and an Alhaarth filly out of Adaya called Viola Da Gamba. Both could be good prospects. I've got a nice Bahamian Bounty colt (out of Got to Go), called Nassau Storm and another one to watch out for is Hoonose, who is a colt by Cadeaux Genereux out of Roodeye.

2011 Preview

Outlook

Ante-Post

with Steffan Edwards

2,000 Guineas

UNSURPRISINGLY the 2,000 Guineas market is dominated by **Frankel** and, whatever the international classifications might say to the contrary, he was clearly last year's standout two-year-old.

Unbeaten in four starts, not only was the style of his wins impressive, but the substance was, too.

Second time out he slammed subsequent Prix Marcel Boussac third Rainbow Springs by 13l, in the Royal Lodge at Ascot he beat subsequent Horris Hill winnner Klammer by 10l, and in the Dewhurst he overcame racing very keenly to beat Roderic O'Connor by 2l, a colt who went on to take a French Group 1 on his next start.

The form of each of his races could not have worked out any better, there are no stamina queries for him over 1m, and his pedigree suggests quick ground shouldn't bother him either.

It simply looks a question of whether he trains on and maintains his edge over his rivals.

He was certainly a very mature two-year-old, and an argument could be made that he was a bit of a bully last year and that others might have caught up with him over the winter, but there's no question that at this stage he's very much the one to beat. His price, however, very much reflects that.

Second in the lists is **Casamento**, who took the Beresford Stakes and Racing Post Trophy for Michael Halford last term.

As expected, he joined the Godolphin team in Dubai at the end of the season and will be trained by Mahmood Al Zarooni this season.

It remains to be seen whether he has more success than Saeed Bin Suroor has had in recent seasons with Godolphin's Classic prospects, but it's difficult to be too confident.

The same goes for the stable's other prospects – **Saamidd**, who looked good in his first two starts but blew out badly in the Dewhurst (ground blamed), impressive debut winner **Farhh**, and new recruit **Dubai Prince**, who looks a top-notcher in the making, but might be more of a Derby prospect.

Unbeaten National Stakes winner **PATHFORK** is very interesting, as he beat Casamento in that Group 1 race at the Curragh, and had Dewhurst third Glor Na Mara well behind.

The soft ground may have been against the latter, but Pathfork had already given him a hiding in the Futurity Stakes on fast ground before that.

The plan had been for him to go to the Breeders' Cup at the end of the season (his owners are American), but he had a little setback which meant he couldn't travel.

That could well prove a blessing with regard to his Guineas chances, and his trainer Jessica Harrington, reporting that he's "grown and developed" over the winter, has already suggested that he's likely to go straight to Newmarket without a prep.

Versatile when it comes to ground con-

STRONG SUIT (far left): flounders in the mud behind Dream Ahead in the Middle Park

ditions and a real traveller who can quicken, he'll have no trouble with 1m, and while he's by a dirt sire, his dam's a half-sister to top-class miler Spinning World, so there's nothing to worry about on that score. He looks the main danger to the favourite.

Wootton Bassett doesn't make much appeal to me. He had a tough season last year, winning five from five, including success in the Group 1 Prix Jean-Luc Lagardere, but that wasn't much of a race and he got the run of things as well.

In any case, he's not certain to head to Newmarket, as his trainer suggested after his Longchamp success that they'd look at the French and Irish Guineas as possible alternatives.

Ballydoyle's apparent lack of urgency to get their colts 100 per cent for the Guineas these days is off-putting with regard to the likes of **Roderic O'Connor** and **Zoffany**.

In recent seasons it appears that Coolmore has taken the view that the Guineas is simply the first Group 1 of a long campaign for their star three-year-olds, a race on which to build a season, as opposed to a hugely important race in itself.

In the lively expectation of hearing Aidan O'Brien declare post-race, "listen, you'd have to be pleased, he'll come on plenty for that", I'll give the Ballydoyle colts the swerve.

The forgotten horse of the race is **STRONG SUIT**. He was favourite for the Guineas in early summer following his impressive success in the Coventry, where he ran down Elzaam despite having got into all sorts of trouble, but the wheels fell off somewhat in Ireland on his next start, when perhaps a combination of easier ground and being ridden more prominently found him out.

His last run of the season came in the Middle Park at Newmarket, and while the bare form – beaten 9l into second by Dream Ahead – suggests he has a mountain to climb, I disagree, as he travelled well until asked to quicken hitting the rising ground, at which point he began to flounder in the soft ground.

Clearly the winner was very much at home in the conditions, while Strong Suit is a fast-ground horse through and through, something which is backed up by his pedigree – his sire's progeny have a seven per cent strike-rate on soft ground and 17 per cent on good to firm.

He's bred to get 1m well, his trainer Richard Hannon never hid his belief that he was his best two-year-old last year, he's reported to have wintered well, and he looks sure to be primed for the big day.

Dream Ahead got to share champion two-year-old honours with Frankel because he goes particularly well in mud and none of his rivals in the Middle Park did.

The Dewhurst probably came too soon for him afterwards, but he has a round action and is by a soft-ground sire, so quick ground on Guineas day would be a big negative. In addition, his dam was at her best over 5f, so there's a stamina question mark.

Fury is two from two and has plenty of potential, but his main target will surely be the valuable Tattersalls Millions sales race in April, and the Guineas might come too soon afterwards.

One of the most impressive debut winners last year was **Peter Martins**, and it was disappointing that injury meant that he wasn't able to showcase his talent in Group company afterwards. His trainer Jeremy

Noseda has always held him in the highest regard – the stable's Group 2 Railway Stakes winner Formosina was considered inferior to him – and it's interesting that this colt's being prepared with a view to taking in the Craven Stakes before a possible tilt at the Guineas. A mile on fast ground should be ideal, and victory in that key trial would catapult him right into the reckoning, but, annoyingly, for the time being his connections have left open the possibility of switching him to dirt (bred for the surface), and a campaign in America, so at the moment he's a risky ante-post proposition.

Dunboyne Express was a bit disappointing in the Racing Post Trophy, but the form of his Anglesey Stakes win doesn't really add up to much, as he just seemed to handle the soft ground better than his three rivals.

Head Space wasn't seen again after making an impressive debut over 5f in April. He looked a smart performer in the making that day, but his stamina would be in question if lining up for the Guineas. In contrast, **Native Khan** looks likely to be at his best beyond a mile this year.

King Torus tends to hang right, so might not be an ideal type for Newmarket. The soft surface found him out in the Prix Jean-Luc Lagardere, but a return trip for the French Guineas, granted better ground, will suit him.

2,000 Guineas

Newmarket, 30 April

	Bet365	Coral	Hills	Lads	PPower	SJames	Tote	VC
Frankel	11-10	4-5	4-5	**5-4**	Evs	11-10	4-5	Evs
Casamento	8	**10**	8	**10**	**10**	**10**	8	8
Roderic O'Connor	10	10	10	12	10	10	10	10
Pathfork	12	12	10	12	**14**	**14**	12	12
Wootton Bassett	14	14	14	12	**14**	**14**	12	**14**
Dream Ahead	16	16	12	16	16	**16**	14	16
Dubai Prince	14	14	14	-	-	**20**	-	12
Zoffany	20	16	16	16	16	16	16	**25**
Strong Suit	**25**	**25**	20	20	20	**25**	20	**25**
Saamidd	20	20	16	**25**	-	**25**	20	**25**
Fury	**33**	25	**33**	25	25	**33**	25	**33**
Peter Martins	20	20	16	25	20	**33**	25	**33**
Dunboyne Express	33	25	25	-	20	33	33	**40**
King Torus	33	33	20	-	-	**50**	40	33

each-way 1/4 odds, 1-2-3
Others on application, prices correct at time of going to press

1,000 Guineas

IN CONTRAST to the 2,000 Guineas, the first fillies' Classic lacks an outstanding favourite and looks very open.

Top of the bookies' lists is **White Moonstone**, who won each of her four starts at two, including the May Hill and Fillies' Mile, but it's not hard to pick holes in her form, and she did hang and flash her tail under pressure at Ascot.

Her pedigree suggests she might do best over further than a mile this year, although she didn't look short of speed at two.

She does have a winter in Dubai to overcome, though, so all told she's probably one to pass over at the current prices.

Disputing second-favouritism are the Marcel Boussac one-two **Misty For Me** and **Helleborine**.

The former, who was doubling her tally in Group 1 company following her win in the Moyglare Stakes, was perhaps the better suited of the two to the stamina test of 1m in soft ground at that stage of their careers.

She looks a tough filly and could well be competitive over a range of distances this year, and it's likely that whatever beats her in the Guineas will have had to battle.

Helleborine is the speedier of the two, as her pedigree would suggest (sister to high-class sprinter African Rose), but she stays a mile, and on quick ground it's easy to see her having the change of gear to reverse form with Misty For Me.

She looks a leading candidate for a trainer who has an enviable record in this race, but there is one concern, as she's a May foal, and a filly that young hasn't won the race in over 20 years.

It's not as if they haven't tried either. Just in the last two renewals we've had a couple of well-fancied May foals, in the shape of Rainbow View and Seta, bomb out.

Perhaps there's something in the theory that the race comes too soon in the year for them.

Another who fails on that stat is **Havant**, who won both her starts last year by clear margins and was particularly impressive in the Oh So Sharp Stakes.

Her pedigree suggests she'll be at her best over middle distances this year, but she could still be a big runner in the Guineas, especially if she gets the bit of ease in the ground which she seems to like.

The filly she beat in the Oh So Sharp, **Look At Me**, is interesting, as she's really bred for the job, being by Danehill Dancer out of a sister to Henrythenavigator.

She showed a smart turn of foot on her debut and, while she found Havant too good at Newmarket, things could be different if the pair meet again in the Guineas, as the

1,000 Guineas							Newmarket, 1 May	
	Bet365	Coral	Hills	Lads	PPower	SJames	Tote	VC
White Moonstone	7	5	7	7	7	6	6	5
Misty For Me	8	6	7	8	6	8	6	7
Helleborine	9	7	8	8	10	8	8	8
Havant	9	8	10	12	12	10	10	9
Memory	10	10	8	10	12	12	10	12
Hooray	14	14	16	12	16	16	16	16
Zoowraa	16	16	14	16	16	16	16	-
Theyskens' Theory	-	16	12	14	12	16	14	-
Laughing Lashes	20	16	20	20	16	20	16	20
Exemplify	20	-	12	-	16	16	16	20
Together	25	25	20	20	14	20	16	25
Soraaya	25	20	25	33	25	25	20	25
Chrysanthemum	25	20	25	25	-	25	20	20
Cape Dollar	25	-	33	20	25	33	-	33
each-way 1/4 odds, 1-2-3								
Others on application, prices correct at time of going to press								

O'Brien filly is the one likeliest to be at her best over 1m.

Of the speedier types who contested the big 6f races last year, it was **Hooray** who took Group 1 honours in the Cheveley Park Stakes.

That didn't look a great race, though, and there has to be a doubt about her getting 1m this year given the speed she shows.

For all that she improved as the season went on, it's also hard to forget how she and subsequent Princess Margaret winner Soraaya were both put firmly in their place by **Memory** in the Cherry Hinton Stakes earlier in the campaign.

Richard Hannon's filly overcame a lot of trouble in running that day and still produced a devastating turn of foot to win easily.

She was disappointing in the Moyglare Stud Stakes afterwards, which coincided with the stable's least successful period of the

campaign, but a return to the sort of form she showed at Newmarket would make her a big threat in the Guineas, with a strong-run race on quickish ground ideal.

Her pedigree suggests a mile should be within her range, although clearly she doesn't lack zip.

Zoowraa, who impressed in going 2-2 last season, including success in the Listed Radley Stakes, doesn't have much size about her so there's some question over whether she'll train on. She's also left the now-retired Michael Jarvis and joined the Godolphin stable, to be trained by Mahmood Al Zarooni, which could be argued to be a negative.

Theyskens' Theory had the run of things when winning the Prestige Stakes and looked to be beaten fair and square in the Fillies' Mile.

Sent to the Breeders' Cup afterwards to

WHITE MOONSTONE: beats Together and Theyskens' Theory at Ascot last season

CAPE DOLLAR: edges home in the Rockfel and adds strength to the Stoute team

contest the Juvenile Fillies, she could only finish sixth there, but given that dirt racing is what she's bred for I still expect her campaign this year to be mainly geared around targets in the US.

I expect Freddie Head's **Moonlight Cloud** and **Pontenuovo**, who's now trained by Roger Charlton, to be aimed at the French Guineas, while **Handassa**, who won a backend Curragh maiden impressively and could be anything, might need a bit more time, so it wouldn't be a surprise to see her connections wait for the Irish Guineas.

Fast ground would be a concern for **Chrysanthemum**, and in any case the form of her Weld Stakes win doesn't stack up to much, and the same can be said for **Kissable**, who is very much bred to appreciate some juice in the ground.

Laughing Lashes shouldn't have any trouble with fast ground on pedigree but whether she'll appreciate running down into the Dip at Newmarket is another question.

Together was up there with the best of her generation last year, but she had a busy time of it and didn't always look the most straightforward.

She drifted left in the closing stages of the Debutante Stakes, and did so to even more dramatic effect in a valuable sales race at Newmarket in the autumn, a manoeuvre that undoubtedly cost her the race. We might already have seen the best of her.

The Rockfel is always a race to take note of when it comes to the Guineas. Since it was upgraded to a Group 2 race in 1998 it's produced five winners and three runners-up, and that record might have been enhanced further in 2010 had Music Show not been drawn on the wrong side.

Much like in 2009, three came clear from the rest of the field in last year's renewal, with **CAPE DOLLAR** just edging out Cochabamba and **I LOVE ME**.

The winner, a daughter of Cape Cross out of a Kingmambo mare, probably won despite the easy ground, as everything about her screams fast-ground filly.

Her pedigree also suggests improvement for 1m is a given, while it's no bad thing to have notched up valuable experience of the Rowley Mile.

She doesn't have a great deal to find with the market leaders on collateral form, and while the betting suggests she's the Stoute stable's number two behind Havant, that could all change very quickly in the event of a dry spring. At the prices she's certainly

I LOVE ME: big price for Guineas glory

worth a punt.

No-one should fall off their chairs if **Cochabamba**, trained by Roger Teal, runs a big race in the Guineas, although of more interest is the filly who finished one place behind her in the Rockfel, I Love Me.

Andrew Balding's filly, who ran out a shock winner of a valuable sales race on her debut and ran a cracker from a poor draw in a similar event next time, travelled strongly and was last off the bridle in the Rockfel.

She only went down narrowly, and perhaps the fact that it was her third start in the space of a month found her out, but she has the size to improve greatly from two to three and looks a big player in an open year, especially as she has plenty of course form.

By Cape Cross out of a mare who won the Fillies' Mile on good to firm, it's hard to imagine her not improving for fast ground.

The only concern would be her connections being lured towards another crack at a valuable sales race held in April, rather than having her peak for the Guineas, but as those races are over the less-than-ideal distances of 6f and 1m2f, I expect the Classic to be her main aim.

Majestic Dubawi isn't one to write off, despite being a shock winner of the Firth Of Clyde Stakes, as she progressed a long way in a short space of time and remains open to plenty of improvement.

She showed a surprising amount of speed last year, but as a daughter of Dubawi out of a Singspiel mare she should relish the step up to 1m.

There are a couple of Irish maiden winners to keep an eye on.

The John Oxx-trained **Alanza** didn't make her debut until September, and perhaps the Guineas will come a bit quick for her, but if she does make the trip to Newmarket the hint should be taken as her trainer is not in the habit of tilting at windmills, and she looked out of the top draw on her debut at Listowel.

The same can also be said of **Zaminast**, who took a Galway maiden that her trainer Dermot Weld targets (previous winners include Group 1 scorers Dance Design and Market Booster) in impressive style, and as a half-sister to Famous Name she has the pedigree to go to the top.

Oaks

WITH the favourites around the 10-1 mark, this is another race without a strong market leader, and as a result it's probably worth having a crack at a couple at decent prices.

Havant boasts obvious claims. She impressed in winning both starts at two over 7f, and as a half-sister to Leadership, who won a Group 1 over 1m4f, and Tuscan Gold, who's won over as far as 2m, she shouldn't have any trouble with the Oaks trip. Indeed she should relish it.

With Epsom in mind, her possible need for some ease in the ground is a slight concern – it was quite quick last year on the Friday, and a course record was set by Workforce the following day – but the course tries to ensure that it's no worse than good for the first day of the meeting these days, so it'll help her cause if they water.

White Moonstone, who went 4-4 at two, has a chance of staying 1m4f, although there is speed on her dam's side. She has to overcome the winter trip to Dubai, though, and although Godolphin have Mahmood Al Zarooni in charge of the Classic hopefuls now, only time will tell whether that switch will improve their fortunes.

The Ballydoyle challenge is led by **Misty For Me**, who improved for the step up to 1m at two and is expected to be able to challenge in the Guineas and Oaks this year.

Although by Galileo, her dam is a half-sister to Fasliyev, so there's a good mix of speed and stamina in her pedigree, and she looks sure to be a major player, although she's priced accordingly.

At bigger odds, the extremely well bred **WONDER OF WONDERS**, by Kingmambo out of Oaks runner-up All Too Beautiful, herself a sister to Galileo and Sea The Stars, gives the stable a fine second string.

She really took the eye when running on

MORNING CHARM (left): gives owner George Strawbridge plenty of Oaks options

Oaks

Epsom, 3 June

	Bet365	BlSq	Hills	Lads	PPower	SJames	Tote	VC
Havant	10	10	8	8	10	10	10	10
White Moonstone	10	8	7	10	8	10	10	10
Misty For Me	12	10	12	10	8	10	8	10
Rainbow Springs	16	-	-	14	-	16	-	16
Elas Diamond	20	20	-	16	-	20	-	16
Chrysanthemum	16	20	20	20	14	20	16	16
Wonder Of Wonders	25	-	-	25	20	16	-	20
Together	25	-	12	-	-	25	-	25
Morning Charm	20	20	-	20	25	25	-	20
Kissable	25	-	25	-	-	25	-	25
Blue Bunting	20	-	-	16	-	25	25	25
All Time	-	-	-	-	-	33	-	33
Izzi Top	33	-	-	-	-	33	-	33
Devastation	-	-	-	33	-	40	-	40

each-way 1/4 odds, 1-2-3
Others on application, prices correct at time of going to press

for second behind a more experienced filly on her debut in a Leopardstown maiden, and has bundles of improvement in her. Right now she boasts a strikingly similar profile to Remember When, who finished third for the yard in last year's Oaks.

Spin should get the trip all right, but she bombed out badly when sent off odds-on for a Listed event on her final start last year so has a bit to prove, while **Together** has prospects of staying 1m4f, but it's arguable her half-brother by Montjeu, Jan Vermeer, was at his best over slightly shorter.

Rainbow Springs was well held in third behind Misty For Me in the Marcel Boussac, but she was much less experienced (second start) than the O'Brien filly going into the race, and in the circumstances it wasn't a bad effort.

I just wonder whether the slightly shorter distance of the Prix de Diane will be her target rather than the Oaks, especially as her owner has another, possibly more suitable Epsom candidate in the shape of **Morning Charm**. As a half-sister to St Leger winner Lucarno by Derby winner North Light, stamina is not going to be a problem for her.

The same owner could also be represented by **Midnight Caller**, although she'll have to bounce back from a disappointing show in the May Hill.

Elas Diamond didn't achieve a great deal when running away with a poor maiden second time out, but she built on it, finishing runner-up to Godolphin's Blue Bunting in a 1m Listed race next time. By Danehill Dancer out of that high-class mare Ela Athena, she has decent prospects of getting 1m4f.

Blue Bunting herself looks nailed-on to get the Oaks trip, and probably the St Leger distance too, as she's a half-sister to a winner at beyond 2m1f. She needed all of 1m last year and looks just the type to do better at three, but she's another that has spent the winter in Dubai.

Chrysanthemum looks more of an Irish Oaks prospect than an Epsom sort to me, and the same can be said for **Kissable**, who was always putting in her best work at the finish of her races last year and promises to appreciate a step up to middle distances this time around.

In contrast, Jessica Harrington's **Bible Belt** probably wants better ground, so it's not out of the question that she might travel over.

The Doncaser maiden John Gosden sent out **Devastation** to win last October has thrown up one or two Oaks candidates in recent years.

In 2005 Time On, who went on to take the Cheshire Oaks the following year, finished third, in 2007 subsequent Lingfield Oaks Trial winner Miracle Seeker also finished third, and in 2009 Gosden himself saddled Gertrude Bell to finish second, and she went on to take the Cheshire Oaks and fifth place at Epsom.

Devastation is the second foal of top-class miler Attraction, but the fact that she's by Montjeu means she has genuine prospects of getting 1m4f this year. She idled in front when winning at Doncaster, but that doesn't diminish the impression left by her stable-mate **IZZI TOP**, who finished second to her in the race.

Very much the second string both in the betting and on jockey bookings, she was green and given the kindest of introductions but, despite finding some trouble in running, kept on strongly under a hand ride to finish just half a length down. It was a really eyecatching run against some more experienced fillies, and she clearly has bags of potential.

The third, fourth and eighth have given the form some substance by winning maidens since and, given her pedigree – she's a half-sister by Pivotal to Rock N Roll Ransom, who earlier this year won over 1m3f in Dubai – there has to be a good chance she'll get the Oaks distance. Her dam, who won the Prix de l'Opera, is a half-sister to Opera House and Kayf Tara, so the stamina is there on the distaff side.

My only concern would be fast ground, as her dam, although twice a winner on quick ground, appreciated a bit of dig, while her sire's stock generally like to get their toe in as well. However, in a bid to prevent injuries at the track Epsom now have a habit of putting quite a lot of water down, and I'd be surprised if she couldn't cope with genuinely good ground.

Primevere is an interesting wildcard, having taken the eye when successful in a backend Kempton maiden. Well regarded by her trainer Roger Charlton, she has a good chance of staying the Oaks trip, but an outing in one of the trials will tell us more.

The Rockfel winner **Cape Dollar** strikes me more as a Guineas candidate, for all that there is stamina on her dam's side, and perhaps of more interest from that race is **Nabah**, who ran particularly well considering she'd only made her debut five days earlier.

She's got the pedigree to suggest she'll thrive over middle distances this year, and one would imagine that Clive Brittain will campaign her with the Oaks in mind.

JOHN GOSDEN: had an eyecatching one-two in a Doncaster fillies' maiden last October

PICTURE EDITOR (left): could be Henry Cecil's main hope if Frankel misses the gig

Derby

WHILE he doubted his ability to get the Derby trip last year, it would no doubt be difficult for Henry Cecil to resist the temptation to send **Frankel** for the Derby should he win the 2,000 Guineas first.

On paper the pedigree is more than en couraging with regards to 1m4f, as he's closely related to Bullet Train, who took the Lingfield Derby Trial last year. However, he tended to race very keenly in his races last year and didn't look short of speed, so perhaps his trainer's belief that the colt takes more after his dam, who was a sprinter, is worth bearing in mind.

If he fails to make the line-up it doesn't necessarily mean that the stable will be without a runner as Cecil has more than one other interesting candidate.

Picture Editor looked good when winning his first two starts and, while the bubble burst somewhat in the Zetland Stakes, his trainer thought he was over the top there. He's still a promising type and his pedigree suggests he'll have no trouble getting 1m4f.

Specific Gravity ran away with a Nottingham maiden in October and it wouldn't be a surprise to see him follow in the footsteps of his half-brother Linda's Lad and stake his claim to a place in the Derby field by taking one of the recognised trials.

It's also quite possible that a candidate will emerge from the unraced brigade at Warren Place.

There are several with attractive pedigrees such as **Midsummer Sun**, a half-brother to Midday, and **Late Telegraph**, who's by

Montjeu out of a half-sister to Irish Oaks winner Moonstone, but the biggest buzz has been about **World Domination**, who's out of the Oaks winner Reams Of Verse. He is quoted at no bigger than 25-1 for the Derby, and while that sort of price about a horse yet to see a racecourse is for the dreamers, the yard does have previous in the shape of Commander In Chief.

Godolphin look to have a strong hand, led by the two Shamardal colts who raced in Sheikh Mohammed's colours for Irish trainers last year.

Dubai Prince, previously with Dermot Weld, looked a special horse when taking the Killavulan Stakes last backend, and he's bred to improve as he steps up to middle distances this year. His dam won at up to 1m5f, so the Derby trip should be right up his street, but he has a turn of foot as well, and were it not for the concern over him having had to winter in Dubai for his new

yard he'd be a strong fancy.

Casamento has the stronger form of the two at the moment, having already bagged the Group 1 Racing Post Trophy, but his stamina for the Derby trip looks less assured on pedigree, and the same questions regarding the switch of stable apply to him as well.

French Navy, who was trained by Andre Fabre last year but is another now with Godolphin, isn't sure to stay 1m4f on pedigree and so the French Derby, over slightly shorter, looks a far more suitable target for him.

Genius Beast has the right pedigree, being out of Irish Oaks winner Shawanda, but **Farhh** is more exciting. A son of Pivotal out of that tough German middle-distance mare Gonbarda, he has that mix of speed and stamina in his pedigree which could just see him develop into a major player.

As usual the Ballydoyle stable is well rep-

RECITAL: looks a surefire stayer but is unproven on ground quicker than heavy

Derby

Epsom, 4 June

	Bet365	Coral	Hills	Lads	PPower	SJames	Tote	VC
Frankel	5	**6**	7-4	5	3	5	3	4
Dubai Prince	**12**	**12**	10	0	**12**	**12**	**12**	**12**
Casamento	10	**12**	10	**12**	10	**12**	10	10
Roderic O'Connor	**12**	10	10	10	10	**12**	10	**12**
Seville	12	12	12	10	**14**	**14**	10	**14**
Carlton House	**16**	12	12	14	·16	14	**16**	**16**
Recital	**16**	**16**	14	**16**	14	14	**16**	12
World Domination	20	**25**	**25**	**25**	**25**	20	**25**	20
Picture Editor	20	**25**	16	-	12	**25**	**25**	16
Long Live The King	-	-	-	-	**25**	**25**	**25**	**25**
Sea Moon	25	**33**	25	25	20	25	20	20
Saamidd	25	25	20	-	-	**33**	25	25
Mantoba	**33**	-	-	**33**	-	**33**	-	**33**
French Navy	20	**40**	25	-	-	**33**	-	**40**

each-way 1/4 odds, 1-2-3

Others on application, prices correct at time of going to press

resented in the ante-post lists, and if recent years are any guide they could well have several runners on the day itself.

Picking between their likely candidates isn't easy, although **Roderic O'Connor** clearly boasts the best form of the lot at the moment having finished runner-up to Frankel in the Dewhurst and then comfortably taken the Criterium International next time out.

While that win in France came in heavy ground, a quicker surface wouldn't be as much of a concern as the Derby trip, for like Frankel he's the result of a Galileo-Danehill cross, and most have tended to find success at up to 1m2f and not beyond.

Seville looks solid on paper as his form ties in with some of the best from last year – second to Dubai Prince first time up and second to Casamento in the Racing Post Trophy –and he's also bred to make a much better three-year-old over middle distances. Another by Galileo, his dam won three times over the Derby distance and he could well be the stable's best chance.

A runaway winner of the Criterium de Saint-Cloud over 1m2f in heavy ground last backend, **Recital** shouldn't have any stamina concerns. He's by Montjeu and is a brother to a Prix Ganay winner, but he has to prove he can be as effective on a quicker surface.

Apache begins the year a maiden but there was plenty to like about his debut effort when he was very green, and this brother to Cheshire Oaks winner Perfect Truth could yet earn a place on the team bus.

An impressive 9l winner of a Newbury maiden second time out, the Queen's **CARLTON HOUSE** is by the Dubai World Cup winner Street Cry out of a 1m2f Group 2 winner, and he's a half-brother to Friston Forest, who stayed 2m, so it would be something of a surprise if stamina for the Derby trip was an issue for him.

The form of his maiden win is already working out, with the runner-up Yaseer, rated by his trainer Marcus Tregoning as his best juvenile, winning easily next time, and he must hold sound claims for the stable responsible for last year's winner Workforce.

Originally 25-1 after he won his maiden, the 16-1 available now isn't quite as generous, but he's clearly Sir Michael Stoute's number one hope, will be trained with the race in mind and couldn't be in better hands, so it's hard to quibble.

The well-related **Sea Moon** is a potential second-string for the stable, but he's only looked workmanlike so far and will need to step up considerably to be a realistic contender.

Native Khan is fairly interesting. He found the ground softer than ideal in the Racing Post Trophy but still ran a creditable race, and his pedigree gives hope that he'll get the Derby trip, but perhaps connections will be tempted by the intermediate distance at Chantilly.

Maxios, a half-brother to Arc winner Bago, has already been earmarked to return in the Prix Noailles, a traditional trial for the Prix du Jockey-Club, so it's unlikely he'll travel over, while **Notable Graduate**, who's closely related to Refuse To Bend and is a half-brother to Melbourne Cup winner Media Puzzle, might find himself targeted at the Irish Derby, along with the John Oxx-trained **Adilapour**.

The likes of **Zoffany**, **Saamidd**, **Dunboyne Express** and **Pathfork** look likely non-stayers to me, but John Gosden has a couple of interesting maidens, namely **Nathaniel** and **Thimaar**, who could yet be players.

Nathaniel, who was unlucky to bump into Frankel on his debut and Picture Editor second time out, shouldn't have any trouble staying 1m4f, but might just lack the change of gear required, while Thimaar shaped with plenty of promise on his debut and is another whose stamina isn't really in question, as he's out of a mare from the family of Salsabil.

Recommended Bets

2,000 Guineas

2pts Pathfork 14-1
(Paddy Power, Stan James)

1pt Strong Suit 25-1
(generally available)

1,000 Guineas

1pt Cape Dollar 33-1
(generally available)

1pt I Love Me 44-1
(32Red)

Oaks

1pt Wonder Of Wonders 25-1
(Bet365, Ladbrokes)

1pt Izzi Top 33-1
(generally available)

Derby

2pts Carlton House 16-1
(generally available)

ADILAPOUR (nearest): may head for the Curragh rather than Epsom

Outlook's
Horses to Follow

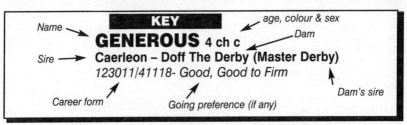

KEY

Name → **GENEROUS** 4 ch c ← *age, colour & sex*
← *Dam*
Sire → **Caerleon – Doff The Derby (Master Derby)**
123011/41118- Good, Good to Firm
↗ ↗ ↑ *Dam's sire*
Career form *Going preference (if any)*

ADILAPOUR 3 b c
Azamour – Adelfia (Sinndar)
1-

Won his only race as a two-year-old, a 1m Gowran Park maiden in September, beating 14 others. The ground was yielding and he looked as though he had a bit to learn. With Azamour as his sire and Sinndar and Night Shift as his grandsires he has a great pedigree and it is no surprise that he has a Derby entry. The Aga Khan's jockey Johnny Murtagh has a colt to look forward to.

John Oxx, Currabeg

AFSARE 4 b c
Dubawi – Jumaireyah (Fairy King)
2111-

Unraced at two, he won three out of four as a three-year-old, culminating with his Hampton Court Stakes win at Royal Ascot. The third horse in that 1m2f Listed race was Wigmore Hall, who won the John Smith's Cup on his next start. He met with a setback after Ascot but is fine now and has options at the highest level from 1m to 1m4f. Perhaps Luca Cumani might even send him over to America for the Arlington Million.

Luca Cumani, Newmarket

ALAYIR 3 b g
Azamour – Alaya (Ela-Mana-Mou)
33-

Made his debut in a Curragh maiden in October and ran as though he needed it. Later that month he came third again, this time in a Navan maiden over a mile which looked quite hot. He might well have won it but for being blocked, and he finished with a nice turn of foot. The early Classics are off the agenda as he has been gelded but he should have no difficulty picking up Group prizes like the Irish St Leger.

John Oxx, Currabeg

AWAIT THE DAWN 4 b c
Giant's Causeway – Valentine Band (Dixieland Band)
11-

This late-developing four-year-old should be a force in Group races over 1m2f this season, a department in which Aidan O'Brien has a strong hand already with Cape Blanco and So You Think. The colt demolished his rivals on his final start, the Group 3 Kilternan Stakes at Leopardstown, beating South Easter by 9l. He was due to run in the Champion Stakes at Newmarket before he became a late withdrawal. He's still unexposed and it's a matter of conjecture as to whether he's Group 1 standard. The chances are he probably is.

Aidan O'Brien, Ballydoyle

BANKSTERS BONUS 3 b g
Big Bad Bob – Heroine (Sadler's Wells)
13-

Beat an Aidan O'Brien hotpot (Apache) on his debut when scoring at 20-1 in a 1m Curragh maiden in October. He couldn't follow up in a Listed race next time when never at home on the soft ground. He still managed third behind Tiz The Shot, however, and he's a good-looking gelding who should make his mark over middle distances.

Jessica Harrington, Kildare

BIBLE BELT 3 br f
Big Bad Bob – Shine Silently (Bering)
413-

Won a 7f Roscommon fillies' maiden on soft to heavy where Jessica Harrington nearly withdrew her because of the ground. She won in style, too, pulling 5l clear and the third horse (Emerald Ring) franked the form by scoring by 7l a month later. She came third behind Chrysanthemum in a 7f Group 3, the CL Weld Park Stakes at the Curragh, on her final start but she was only beaten two heads and she may have found the trip too sharp. Harrington thinks enough of her to be considering the Oaks and she should do well over a trip.

Jessica Harrington, Kildare

CASTLES IN THE AIR 6 b g
Oasis Dream – Dance Parade (Gone West)
100310006-

This is a solid 6f/7f handicapper who is likely to win his fair share and quite possibly pop up at a big price in a heritage handicap somewhere down the line. His two wins last year were at 6-1 and 14-1, the first in a Pontefract handicap and the second in the International heritage handicap at Ascot in July when he beat 20 others. Trained by Richard Fahey and owned by Jim McGrath, we can rest assured that his targets will be carefully chosen. Fahey carried all before him last season and more of the same can be expected this term.

Richard Fahey, Malton

CHATTEL HOUSE 3 b f
Aussie Rules – Starring Role (Glenstal)
83-

This could be an interesting filly. A mediocre eighth on her debut at the Curragh in June, it was a different story next time out at Leopardstown when she came third to Why in a 7f maiden. She was given quite an easy time of it by Johnny Murtagh once it was clear she was going to make third place and Murtagh probably had the future in mind. A daughter of Aussie Rules, who won the French 2,000 Guineas, she is a half-sister to six winners.

David Wachman, Tipperary

CHRYSANTHEMUM 3 b f
Danehill Dancer – Well Spoken (Sadler's Wells)
11-

Made her debut in a Listed race in which eight of the ten runners were previous winners. She upstaged them all when bolting up by two and a half lengths at 25-1. She then went on to win the CL Weld Park Stakes over 7f from Wild Wind and Bible Belt by two heads. It was a good effort considering the trip was on the sharp side. She's well bred, with her dam a half-sister to 7f/1m winner Pure Illusion who is out of the 6f Group 3 2yo winner Saintly Speech.

David Wachman, Tipperary

CITYSCAPE 5 ch h
Selkirk – Tantina (Distant View)
4211-

This lightly raced horse (he has nine starts under his belt) has matured into a Group player. His finest hour came in the Group 3 Joel Stakes over a mile at Newmarket in October, his final race of 2010. He beat the Lincoln winner Penitent by 7l with many decent types in behind. This race represented a change of plan by Roger Charlton who originally had the Cambridgeshire in mind for Cityscape but pulled him out because of the soft ground. Actually, a little bit of cut seems to help him but he also has winning form on good ground.

Roger Charlton, Beckhampton

DEVASTATION 3 b f
Montjeu – Attraction (Efisio)
21-

Touched off by a short-head on her debut at Nottingham, she made no mistake at Doncaster in October when beating her stablemate Izzi Top and 15 others next time out. She has a pedigree to die for being by Montjeu out of the Mark Johnston-trained Attraction, who won the 1,000 Guineas. Distances of more than 1m will suit and she surely has a decent future. Owned, like Attraction, by the Duke of Roxburghe, she's run so far on good to soft and good ground. A little bit of dig seems sure to bring out the best in her.

John Gosden, Newmarket

DUBAI PRINCE 3 b c
Shamardal – Desert Frolic (Persian Bold)
11-

Dermot Weld sent him out to make a winning debut in a 1m Gowran Park maiden beating Seville (went on to be second in the Racing Post Trophy) by a length. He then won the Group 3 Killavullan Stakes over 7f, the same race that Weld trained Grey Swallow to win. He couldn't have been more impressive and it was no surprise that his owner, Sheikh Mohammed, decided to transfer him to Godolphin. Mahmood Al Zarooni is the trainer entrusted with this potential 2,000 Guineas horse.

Mahmood Al Zarooni, Newmarket

ELUSIVE PIMPERNEL 4 b/br c
Elusive Quality – Cara Fantasy (Sadler's Wells)
15-

Looked an interesting prospect when second to St Nicholas Abbey in the Racing Post Trophy and also when winning the Craven Stakes. A disappointing fifth in the 2,000 Guineas, he met with a setback when being prepared for the Prix du Jockey-Club. He is recovered now and was out cantering before Christmas so he will be one of the most forward of John Dunlop's horses, ready for an early start. Expect his first race to be over 1m, after which distances of up to 1m2f will surely be on the agenda.

John Dunlop, Arundel

FLYING CROSS 4 b c
Sadler's Wells – Ramruma (Diesis)
139-

Was trained in Ireland last year by Aidan O'Brien and won a small race at Tipperary before going on to be third in the Irish St Leger behind Sans Frontieres. Switched to John Gosden, he ran ninth in the 2m Group 1 Prix Royal-Oak at Longchamp on soft ground and was below his best. He clearly has plenty of stamina, being out of Henry Cecil's great Oaks winner Ramruma ,and it will be interesting to see how Gosden, a master trainer of older horses, campaigns him.

John Gosden, Newmarket

FURY 3 b c
Invincible Spirit – Courting (Pursuit Of Love)
11-

Kieren Fallon, in a recent interview, said that this was the three-year-old he was looking forward to most for the 2011 Flat season. This is hardly surprising given the way that the Cheveley Park-owned colt picked his way through a large field to land the £500,000 Tattersalls Millions 2YO Trophy. Fallon felt he could have won from any draw (he was 24 of 27) and was impressed with how he handled the soft ground. William Haggas has the 2,000 Guineas in his sights, which may be a tad ambitious, but Group prizes should come his way.

William Haggas, Newmarket

HAVANT 3 b f
Halling – Louella (El Gran Senor)
11-

After her win in a minor Newmarket maiden, Sir Michael Stoute uppod Havant to the Group 3 Oh So Sharp Stakes over 7f in October which she won easily, under hands and heels, from the Aidan O'Brien-trained Look At Me. What was surprising was the speed she showed for one with so much stamina on her dam's side. This means that both the 1,000 Guineas and the Oaks are options. Our own Morning Mole is a big believer in this filly too.

Sir Michael Stoute, Newmarket

HIGH CONSTABLE 4 b g
Shamardal – Abbey Strand (Shadeed)
12-

Looked promising enough when winning a modest maiden at Wolverhampton and then stepped up to be second in a 7f handicap at Newbury's Greenham meeting. The race, often a good pointer to the Britannia Handicap, contained a host of subsequent winners including Rebel Soldier who won the Gordon Stakes. The Queen's High Constable met with a setback subsequently but is now apparently ready to rock and roll.

Roger Charlton, Beckhampton

LAUGHING LASHES 3 gr f
Mr Greeley – Adventure (Unbridled's Song)
2212-

Laughing Lashes may not be the most straightforward of fillies with her tail-swishing and her need to be held up late, but she sure is useful. Runner-up to Together in a Leopardstown Group 3, she then won the Group 2 Debutante Stakes at the Curragh beating Misty For Me and Together. She was second to Misty For Me on her final start, the Group 1 Moyglare Stakes but was far from disgraced on ground that was a bit quick for her. She will head to the 1,000 Guineas at Newmarket with every chance.

Jessica Harrington, Kildare

MORIARTY 3 b c
Clodovil – Justice System (Criminal Type)
8211-

After coming second in a Newbury maiden, he won York's Convivial Stakes, run for the first time over 7f. After that he won the Haynes, Hanson & Clark Stakes, an influential race won in the past by Shergar, Rainbow Quest and Shahrastani. In addition Authorized came third in it in 2006. Like so many good horses trained by Richard Hannon, Moriarty does not have a fancy pedigree. Indeed he cost just 52,000 guineas as a yearling, but that doesn't matter to Hannon, who has done so well previously with unfashionably bred types.

Richard Hannon, East Everleigh

MOTRICE 4 gr f
Motivator – Entente Cordiale (Affirmed)
52111332-

She's been kept in training with Cup races in mind. Her third in the 2m Doncaster Cup won by Samuel, and her second in the 2m2f Jockey Clup Cup behind Tastahil entitle her to respect in Group races over a distance and Sir Mark Prescott will not be wasting her entries. He knows the family well having trained her half-sister Foreign Affairs.

Sir Mark Prescott, Newmarket

NAQSHABBAN 3 b g
Street Cry – Reem Three (Mark Of Esteem)
1-

The winner of a 7f backend maiden at Leicester on good to soft. What was impressive about this victory was the way he quickened up a second time after he looked like being beaten. He's closely related to Afsare (also in these lists) and is a gelding. With lots of improvement in him, he could pick up a handicap or two in true Cumani style.

Luca Cumani, Newmarket

PATHFORK 3 b c
Distorted Humor – Visions Of Clarity (Sadler's Wells)
111-

Three wins from three starts – all at the Curragh over 7f. The first was a maiden, the second the Group 2 Futurity Stakes (won by such luminaries as St Jovite, Giant's Causeway, Hawk Wing and New Approach) and the third the Group 1 National Stakes. In the last race he beat Casamento by a head and that one went on to land the Racing Post Trophy subsequently. His trainer has mentioned the Leopardstown Guineas Trial on March 27 but he now seems more likely to go straight to Newmarket for the 2,000 Guineas.

Jessica Harrington, Kildare

PETER MARTINS 3 ch c
Johannesburg – Pretty Meadow (Meadowlake)
1-

The winner of his only race, a 7f novice on Newmarket's July course in mid-summer, this good-looking colt was clearly ready for his debut and was sent off 2-1 favourite. He tracked the leaders and, once given the office by Frankie Dettori, impressed with the way he stretched his legs and came home 5l in front of some youngsters from top yards. He's likely to go for a Classic, possibly the 2,000 Guineas at Newmarket, or alternatively Group 1 races in France. Wherever he goes though, you must keep a close eye on him as he has the potential to go right to the very top.

Jeremy Noseda, Newmarket

RECITAL 3 b c
Montjeu – Dibenoise (Kendor)
11-

Was one of four Aidan O'Brien-trained horses making their debuts in a 1m Navan maiden in October and was the choice of Johnny Murtagh. It was the same Navan maiden won by Fame And Glory and he, too, came home first. The Montjeu colt went on to win the Group 1 Criterium de Saint-Cloud over 1m2f the following month in heavy ground. It was an easy 5l victory and he was handed a 16-1 quote for the Derby. As a half-brother to a Prix Ganay (1m2f) winner he is pretty much guaranteed to stay 1m4f, though there should also be plenty of 1m2f races on his agenda.

Aidan O'Brien, Ballydoyle

RIEN NE VA PLUS 3 b f
Oasis Dream – Sought Out (Rainbow Quest)
6-

Sixth in a backend Newmarket maiden on her only start, this filly picks herself on breeding alone. She's a Ballymacoll Stud product, a half-sister to Derby winner North Light and the very useful Researched and Cover Up – a winner of the Queen Alexandra at Royal Ascot. The maiden she ran in was just a sighter and we can expect considerably better this season.

Sir Michael Stoute, Newmarket

RITE OF PASSAGE 7 ch g
Giant's Causeway – Dahlia's Krissy (Kris S)
1-

Dermot Weld will aim to win the Ascot Gold Cup for the second time with this ex-hurdler. Last year he won the Ascot race at 20-1 and it was his only run that season. Don't be surprised if he again goes to Ascot without a prep. This year it's possible that he will take in a few other races afterwards, including the Melbourne Cup. He's only had ten races in his life so there could be plenty left in the tank. Weld decided to shelve a hurdling campaign with him this winter in order to keep him fresh for the Flat

Dermot Weld, Curragh

SEVILLE 3 b c
Galileo – Silverskaya (Silver Hawk)
212-

Second to Dubai Prince on his debut, he then took the same conditions race at Tipperary that High Chaparral did. His final appearance was when running-up Casamento in the Racing Post Trophy, the only horse to give the winner a race. On breeding he should stay 1m4f and quotes of 12-1 for the Derby are not fanciful. O'Brien also has Recital for that race, but he regularly goes into the Epsom race mob-handed so it wouldn't be a huge surprise if he didn't run the two together. In fact, he will probably have more!

Aidan O'Brien, Ballydoyle

SO YOU THINK 5 b/br c
High Chaparral – Triassic (Tights)
111113-

The great Australian trainer Bart Cummings was reportedly unhappy to lose So You Think to Coolmore but at least Irish eyes are smiling. This is a brilliant 1m2f horse who won four Group 1s over roughly that distance last season before sheer class enabled him to finish third in the 2m Melbourne Cup. One of those races was the Cox Plate, Australia's premier weight-for-age contest, which he was winning for the second time. Aidan O'Brien trained his sire to win the Derby and will use all his considerable skills to draw the best out of So You Think.

Aidan O'Brien, Ballydoyle

ZAMINAST 3 b f
Zamindar – Fame At Last (Quest For Fame)
1-

This Khalid Abdullah-owned filly won her one and only start at the Galway Festival in July, a 7f maiden on good ground. It was a reasonable field and among the 15 beaten horses were three from Ballydoyle. Dermot Weld, who was winning this maiden for the 12th time since 1990, said that the filly was slightly green. We can expect plenty of improvement from this half-sister to Famous Name.

Dermot Weld, Curragh

ZOFFANY 3 b c
Dansili – Tyranny (Machiavellian)
1161113-

Zoffany's record of five from seven speaks volumes. The only times he was beaten came at the highest level, first the Coventry and then the Group 1 National Stakes. It's also worth remembering he was on the go from April to September so he can be excused a blip. His big moment came when landing the Group 1 Phoenix Stakes, beating good yardstick Glor Na Mara by half a length. He's Classic material.

Aidan O'Brien, Ballydoyle

RFO's top 12 to follow

Afsare	**Recital**
Await The Dawn	**Rite Of Passage**
Dubai Prince	**Seville**
Havant	**So You Think**
Motrice	**Zaminast**
Pathfork	**Zoffany**

Outlook

Pedigrees for punters with Amy Bennett

THE PROFILE of a good sire of two-year-olds often comes down to some simple factors – precocity, speed and numbers. It is rare to see a Derby winner siring a juvenile winner at Royal Ascot or the winner of the Brocklesby Stakes on the first day of the Flat season.

If a sire was himself a precocious speedy type his progeny have higher chance of following in his mould, and to make an impact a stallion must have attracted a good number of mares.

AMADEUS WOLF
Mozart – Rachelle (Mark Of Esteem)

A precocious talent from the sole crop of the top-class sprinter Mozart, Amadeus Wolf debuted successfully in May and went on to triumph in the Group 2 Gimcrack and the Group 1 Middle Park.

Winless at three in the notoriously competitive sprint division, he was Group 1-placed three times, however, and returned at four to score in the Group 2 Duke of York Stakes.

Amadeus Wolf stands at the Irish National Stud alongside the like of Invincible Spirit who sired a record-breaking number of winners from his first crop.

By a speedy sire from the all-conquering Danehill line, he is out of a dam who won over 1m in Italy, and is from the family of successful US sires Awesome Again and Storm Creek.

Amadeus Wolf's first crop of over 60 live foals averaged 22,443gns at the yearlings sale, with seven making £50,000 or more, but they proved popular with agents and trainers alike at all the major European sales.

The year 2011 sees the debut of runners by the Derby winners Authorized, Lawman, Street Sense and Sir Percy, and the outstanding middle-distance performers Dylan Thomas, Manduro and Rail Link.

All have an excellent chance of siring talented runners, but it is unlikely that middle-distance talent will beget early speed.

The six sires listed below were all talented performers at two, with several training on to be top racehorses at three and beyond, and all are worthy of note as their first crops make their racecourse debuts.

One to watch - unnamed colt
Amadeus Wolf – Princess Mood (Muhtarram)

Bought by McKeever Bloodstock for 50,000gns at Tattersalls October Yearling Sale Book 1. This colt is a half-brother to the smart sprinter Kingsgate Prince from a family that has produced talented performers in Germany and France.

COCKNEY REBEL
Val Royal – Factice (Known Fact)

For a dual Guineas winner, Cockney Rebel garnered surprisingly little fanfare when he retired to stud.

He showed smart form to win his juvenile debut in July and went on to finish a very close third to Vital Equine in the Group 2 Champagne Stakes. He got his revenge the following year when defeating that rival in the 2,000 Guineas and went on to frank the form with a comfortable win in the Irish 2,000 Guineas.

His dam was a precocious type, winning over 5f at two, while Val Royal, although not an early type, also had plenty of speed at up to a mile with his biggest win coming in the Breeders' Cup Mile.

Cockney Rebel does not have a large first crop but his 21 yearlings who sold at public auction in 2010 averaged 27,671gns, finding support from all the right people.

One to watch – unnamed colt

Cockney Rebel – Forest Fire (Never So Bold)

Bought by Clive Cox for 30,000gns at Tattersalls October Yearling Sale Book 1. This colt is a half-brother to Presvis (Sakhee), a Group 1 winner in Hong Kong and a multiple stakes winner in Dubai, from a smart family in Scandinavia.

DARK ANGEL
Acclamation – Midnight Angel (Machiavellian)

Dark Angel may have retired at the end of his two-year-old season, but he had already clocked an impressive juvenile record and with nine starts under his belt he raced more than many of his contemporaries.

Dark Angel debuted in April and took a valuable sales race at York in August. He triumphed by a head in the Group 2 Mill Reef and two weeks later returned to win the Group 1 Middle Park, but found the extra furlong of the Group 1 Dewhurst a trip too

far, confirming his sprint credentials.

Dark Angel was bred to be fast, being a son of the high-class sprinter Acclamation, who was crowned leading first crop sire in 2007 and is an excellent source of speed.

While Midnight Angel was herself unraced, she has produced five winners in all, including another stakes winner, and is herself out of a useful sprinter.

Dark Angel's first crop of around 90 foals were well received at the yearling sales, and his progeny are now with trainers such as Barry Hills, Richard Hannon, Richard Fahey, Dermot Weld and Michael Bell.

One to watch - unnamed colt

Dark Angel – Kelsey Rose (Most Welcome)

Bought by Blandford Bloodstock for 105,000gns at Tattersalls October Yearling Sale Book 1. This colt is a half-brother to the smart filly Puff, winner of last season's Group 3 Fred Darling Stakes, from a family that has shown both speed and precocity.

EXCELLENT ART
Pivotal – Obsessive (Seeking The Gold)

Excellent Art's top-class record at three over 1m makes it is easy to forget that he was also an early two-year-old, making a winning

EXCELLENT ART (nearest to us): slugs it out with Duke Of Marmalade at Ascot

debut in April. He went on to win the Listed National Stakes in May, finished a good third in the Group 1 Prix Morny in August, and won the Group 2 Mill Reef Stakes.

At three he scored in the Group 1 St James's Palace Stakes and notched up a hat-trick of narrow defeats in Group 1s including the Sussex Stakes, Queen Elizabeth II Stakes and the Breeders' Cup Mile.

Pivotal has an outstanding record as a sire and is represented by two successful sire sons in Kyllachy and Captain Rio. Obsessive was best at around 1m2f so Excellent Art can pass along stamina as well as speed to his progeny.

Excellent Art has over 90 juveniles in his first crop, and top buyers were keen on them at all levels of the yearling market.

One to watch - Imperial Order

Excellent Art – Sao Gabriel (Persian Bold)

Bought by Sir Robert Ogden for £75,000 at

THREE VALLEYS: former Coventry winner

Doncaster Premier Yearling Sale. This colt, in training with Richard Hannon, is an intriguing mixture of speed and stamina. Excellent Art should provide a good turn of foot while his unraced dam is from the family of the Oaks winner Love Divine and her St Leger-winning son Sixties Icon.

THREE VALLEYS
Diesis – Skiable (Niniski)

Three Valleys was a top juvenile, winning the Group 3 Coventry Stakes by 8l and beaten just a head when second in the Group 1 Dewhurst Stakes. He was also first past the post in the Middle Park only to be disqualified later.

Transferred to race in the US, he was twice Grade 1-placed at 1m and also added a Grade 2 and Grade 3 to his tally.

Three Valleys will have been well supported by his owner/breeder Juddmonte, and is an attractive stallion for breeders, being competitively priced and from the outstanding family of leading sire Dansili.

Three Valleys is also bred along similar lines to Diesis' leading stallion son Halling, being out of a mare by a son of Nijinsky.

His progeny returned some good prices at auction for their breeders, with the highest priced selling for 85,000gns. His trainer Roger Charlton is among those to have taken charge of one of his first crop.

One to watch – unnamed colt

Three Valleys – Alexander Duchess (Desert Prince)

Bought by Kern/Lillingston Association for 24,000gns at Tattersalls October Yearling Sales Book 2. This colt is a half-brother to a triple two-year-old winner in Scarlet Rocks, and is out of a winning sister to the Listed winner Jadalee and half-sister to the high-class mare Grace O'Malley, from the family of Sir Percy.

TEOFILO
Galileo – Speirbhean (Danehill)

Teofilo blazed a trail through his juvenile career, winning all five of his starts including two at Group 1 level and all over 7f, but his career was curtailed by injury and he was retired without racing at thre.

His career highlights included two defeats of Holy Roman Emperor in Group 1 contests, first in the National Stakes and then the Dewhurst.

Galileo already has a remarkable record at stud, and Teofilo's dam was a useful enough performer at a mile, although her own siblings showed some talent at up to 1m2f.

It was no surprise at all to see 22 of Teofilo's progeny garnering six-figure sums at the yearling auctions, and although John Ferguson, agent for Sheikh Mohammed at whose Darley stud Teofilo stands, accounted for several of those, plenty of other notable buyers got in on the action including Sir Robert Ogden, who bought the most pricey, at auction in France.

One to watch – You Don't Love Me
Teofilo – Alleluia (Caerleon)

Bought by Badgers Bloodstock for 100,000gns at Tattersalls October Yearling Sale Book 1. This filly – who was in training with Michael Jarvis so will now be in the care of his former assistant Roger Varian – is a three-parts sister to the top-class stayer Allegretto, who captured the Group 1 Prix Royal-Oak, as well as the Goodwood Cup and Henry II Stakes during an illustrious career. She hails from one of the best families in the Stud Book, with other recent successes including Aussie Rules, Midas Touch, Yesterday and Quarter Moon.

TEOFILO: some notable buyers have been snapping up his progeny at the sales

POETRY IN MOTION: Frankel goes down to the start prior to his Dewhurst victory

Newmarket by Aborigine

HENRY CECIL has handled an abundance of smart horses over the years so when he says that **Frankel** is probably the best colt he has had since one of his earliest Classic winners – the 1976 2,000 Guineas hero Wollow – it will pay to sit up and take notice.

The Galileo colt started off with a smooth maiden win on the July course followed by a Doncaster conditions cakewalk.

He then showed himself in his true colours, rounding the season off with fluent wins in the Group 2 Royal Lodge and Group 1 Dewhurst Stakes.

Cecil has been delighted with the progress he has made over the winter months and as he takes his racing so well he could give him a sharpener in the Greenham at Newbury on his way to Newmarket. The Derby could then follow if his work indicates that 1m4f is within his powers.

Twice Over has won the Champion Stakes for the last two seasons and Cecil tells me that will again be his end-of-season objective.

In the meantime he tackles the Dubai World Cup at Meydan, and the way he has been working suggests that he will have a great chance of erasing the memory of his disappointing effort in that race in 2010 – even though he had anything but a clear run.

There are many promising individuals lurking among the impeccably bred three-year-olds at Warren Place, but the one who should be singled out for mention is the once-raced **Arizona Jewel**.

By the up-and-coming sire Dansili, she was backward when third to Aneedah at Yarmouth in October but has come on in leaps and bounds during the winter and is a very exciting prospect.

SIR MICHAEL STOUTE lost his champion trainer's crown to Richard Hannon last year but in his brilliant Derby winner **Workforce** he has a horse capable of landing races like the King George and the Coronation Cup to take him back near the top this year.

After his below-par run behind the now-retired Harbinger in the King George, he bounced back to win the Prix de l'Arc de Triomphe.

Stoute then wisely decide to withdraw him from his Breeders' Cup engagement at the eleventh hour because of the fast ground.

This typical Stoute pragmatism always protects his stars and should bring rich rewards as Workforce looks a far stronger and more mature individual this year.

ED DUNLOP handled the dual Oaks winner Ouija Board brilliantly, and though it looked as if she would be a once-in-a-lifetime filly, he has managed to unearth another jewel in **Snow Fairy**.

The daughter of Intikhab also won the Oaks and the Irish Oaks and her efforts on the international stage in the autumn contributed handsomely to Dunlop's pension funds!

She picked up Group 1s in Japan and Hong Kong to round her year off on a high. It was the speed that won her the Oaks and the Hong Kong Cup that gives Dunlop many options from the 1m2f of the Dubai World Cup to the 1m4f of the Coronation Cup at Epsom.

MICHAEL BELL's mercurial star Sariska has been retired to the paddocks, but keep an eye open for the unexposed sprinter **Gramercy** at a lower level, while **Mokalif** will come into his own when stepped up in trip.

Gitano Hernando has been *MARCO BOTTI*'s flag bearer over the last couple of seasons and will again ensure the up and coming Italian hits the headlines.

GITANO HERNANDO: seen here winning at Dundalk. He will be back for more

MASKED MARVEL: big things are expected of John Gosden's colt this season

Don't forget Botti also has a way with fillies having landed a juvenile fillies' Pattern race in virtually every season since he started training.

It is early days yet but an unnamed two-year-old Motivator filly who is a half-sister to the Newsells Park Stud's smart performer Strawberrydaiquiri is giving all the right vibes. Look out for her.

Botti also feels that both his all-weather winners **Ekasin** and **Acclamazing** can build on their early form and go on to bigger and better things on grass.

WILLIAM HAGGAS has attracted quite a following among punters as they know he can ready a horse for a big race like **Penitent**, who won the Lincoln last season.

He has a highly promising three-year-old filly in **Shuhra**, whose debut third to Istishaara at Nottingham augured well for the future. **Lord Of The Hills** and **Beaten Up** are two other three-year-olds likely to make an impact.

WILLIAM JARVIS had a relatively quiet time in 2010 but hit the deck running on the all-weather early this year and the momentum should keep going through to the Flat season proper.

He holds out particularly high hopes for **Qushchi**, who made a winning in the familiar Howard De Walden colours at Newmarket. She has continued to progress through the winter and the aim will be to make her

a Pattern winner to enhance her paddocks value.

JOHN GOSDEN's star filly Dar Re Mi is now at stud but he has a trio of horses that should be winning races at the right level.

In the premier league **Tazeez**, third to stable-companion Debussy in the Arlington Million and the winner of his final two starts last season, will ply his trade successfully at home and abroad.

Masked Marvel and **Izzi Top** could also earn themselves mentions in despatches in due course.

CHRIS WALL has the Lockinge Stakes at Newbury as his stable star **Premio Loco**'s first main objective in Britain after he returns from a trip to the Godolphin Mile in Dubai.

Wall's gift of improving handicappers could again be seen to good effect, with the three-year-old pair **Midnight Rider** and **Moonlight Mystery** leading the way.

Among Newmarket's younger trainers *DAVID SIMCOCK* is tipped for the top and gained his first Group 1 success, when he won the Prix Morny with the speedy **Dream Ahead**.

Forget his fifth behind Frankel in the Dewhurst as Simcock admits he may have gone back to the well too quickly and he still believes Dream Ahead could trouble Frankel in the 2,000 Guineas.

My own feeling is that his turn of foot will see him make his mark in the top sprinters

IMPERIAL GUEST (middle): can keep George Margarson's flag flying high

around Europe. Simcock also has another money-spinner in **Bushman**, who has overcome his early aversion to faster ground now that he is a stronger individual.

MARK TOMPKINS has a couple of fillies who are set to earn their keep during the summer.

Mark and his wife Angie run the Dullingham Stud just outside Newmarket and their home bred **Brushing** has already earned herself a future at stud with her win in the Galtres at the trainer's favourite track of York. The shrewd Yorkshireman reckons there is more in the tank, and along with progressive **Kathleen Frances** they can keep the Tompkins banner flying.

Former jockey *PAUL D'ARCY* sent out the 2003 Irish 2,000 Guineas winner Indian Haven and though he has nothing of that calibre in his current team he holds out high hopes for **Edinburgh Knight**.

Early in the season he was working so well that he was heavily backed on his reappearance and justified support with wins at Lingfield and Wolverhampton.

After a couple of poor runs it a decided to geld him and towards the end of the year he started recapturing his sparkle.

D'Arcy reckons he is well handicapped and the plan is to continue on the sprint route with big races like the Portland Handicap

at Doncaster and the Ayr Gold Cup possible targets.

Keep an eye open for stable-companion **Night Lily**. She has already contributed to her keep with four wins and D'Arcy believes there are more handicaps in her as she attempts to move into Listed class in due course.

GEORGE MARGARSON soldiers on with a small team and he appears to have found another handicapper to follow in the footsteps of his prolific winner Young Mick, who ran many of his best races at Ascot.

This is **Imperial Guest**, who could also make his mark at Ascot as he will be trained with the Wokingham Handicap at the royal meeting as his main target. His gallops suggest he has improved and is ahead of the handicapper.

JULIA FEILDEN had her best ever season in 2010 and the stable star **Spirit Of Sharjah** can continue to advertise the former amateur rider's talents.

Though his main recent successes have been in all-weather Listed races, don't forget he won one of these events on grass at Goodwood as a two-year-old.

Feilden has a way with the rejects of other stables, and appears to have picked up another bargain basement buy with the ex-Khalid Abdullah filly **Sail Home**.

She showed good form in France without winning but won at Southwell on her second attempt over here and she has scope for further improvement.

JAMES EUSTACE has done us several good turns on previous previews and the one he singled out for us on this occasion is **Scottish Star**. Owned and bred by his long time-patron Jeff Smith, this daughter of Kirkwall is expected to build on the promise she has been showing on the gallops.

ALAN BAILEY has done brilliantly since returning to HQ from Cheshire and **Outpost**, a son of Rock Of Gibraltar, has been slow to come to hand but looks as if he has the ability to start making up for lost time.

TOM KEDDY's **Star Danser** gives the impression that he has as yet untapped potential and could be aimed at one of the big three-year-old sales races at Newmarket in the spring.

Hot off the Heath

Outpost
Scottish Star
Star Danser

Genuine inside info straight from the trainers!

Big price winners all the way with

Tony Jakobson

To subscribe to Tony's daily tips, text
RFOJAKO to UK: 84080/ROI: 57856

Online every morning at 9am

0904 088 8321

Ireland
by Jerry M

REMARKABLY *AIDAN O'BRIEN* failed to train a single juvenile winner in Britain last year, but there were enough positive signs at the end of the season to suggest he has some top-class three-year-old colts to go to war with this year as Roderic O'Connor chased home Frankel in the Dewhurst before winning a Group 1 in France, Recital also won at the top level at Saint-Cloud and Seville finished second in the Racing Post Trophy.

Seville may well prove the best prospect of that trio. Second to Dubai Prince in a red-hot maiden on his debut, he was an impressive winner next time at Tipperary, where Hawk Wing, High Chaparral and Dylan Thomas all won their first races for O'Brien, before just being touched off by Casamento at Doncaster.

Seville was caught out by the winner's turn of foot but stayed on strongly all the way to the line and promises to be much better when stepped up to 1m4f. It's telling that the two horses to have beaten him, Dubai Prince and Casamento, have both moved to Godolphin this winter with no guarantee of how they will come back, and Seville looks likely to be the leading Ballydoyle hope come the Derby.

Roderic O'Connor looks O'Brien's main 2,000 Guineas contender, but he could come into his own after the Newmarket Classic, possibly over further.

He stepped up on a promising debut third to win his maiden at the Curragh in June and then returned from a lengthy absence to easily beat all bar Frankel in the Dewhurst.

Having got the run of the race in front on both those occasions, he showed some versatility when landing a fairly strong Criterium International at Saint-Cloud with a tremendous burst of speed turning for home, and having won on heavy going and good to firm all ground clearly comes alike to him.

More worrying, though, was the fact that

SEVILLE: hacked up at Tipperary before a fine second in the Racing Post Trophy

he wandered all over the track at Saint-Cloud even though it was already his fourth start and, while he handled the Rowley Mile in the Dewhurst, that came in a six-runner affair and he could just struggle to keep a true line in the Guineas. The St James's Palace Stakes or the Coral-Eclipse could be more up his street.

Recital has more to prove having won only a very modest Group 1 at Saint-Cloud two weeks after Roderic O'Connor's success, but he's clearly another hugely promising colt guaranteed to stay at least the Derby trip.

The Montjeu colt showed speed and stamina to come from last to first over 1m2f on heavy ground on only his second start, having also won well on good going at Navan on his debut. It would be no surprise to see him end up in the St Leger.

O'Brien's other colt for the backend was **Master Of Hounds**, the first choice of former stable jockey Johnny Murtagh in the Racing Post Trophy and a fair third behind Casamento and Seville.

It's been said that Murtagh had a habit of choosing the wrong Ballydoyle colt, but when it comes to its two-year-olds the yard always takes a long-term view with jockey bookings and that suggests Master Of Hounds will come good this year.

There were eyebrows raised when Murtagh picked Zoffany over Samuel Morse in the Coventry Stakes last year, seemingly vindicated when Zoffany disappointed, but look at how that pair turned out over the rest of the campaign.

Similarly, O'Brien's faith in Master Of Hounds should pay off. Though he took four runs to get off the mark, he was twice beaten by smart horses in Dunboyne Express (by a short-head) and Roderic O'Connor and he stayed on in eyecatching fashion at Doncaster, looking sure to do better over further.

It was therefore no surprise that he found fast ground over 1m at Churchill Down too quick for him when sixth at the Breeders' Cup. He's crying out for 1m2f and, being out of O'Brien's Oaks fifth Silk And Scarlet, could even be another Derby type.

As for **Zoffany**, he did brilliantly to land the Phoenix Stakes over 6f even though the trip looked to be very much on the short side

for him as he took an age to get going before showing a stunning turn of foot.

He's certainly much better than he showed on soft ground in the National Stakes on his final start and is likely to join Roderic O'Connor in races like the 2,000 Guineas and the St James's Palace Stakes, while there is enough stamina in his dam's pedigree to suggest 1m2f will be well within his compass as well.

For a dark horse you could do worse than follow **Apache**, who looked greener than Banksters Bonus when beaten by a head in a Curragh maiden in October over 1m and has a real middle-distance pedigree. He could well blossom at some stage this year.

O'Brien also hit the crossbar in Britain with his juvenile fillies last year as **Together** finished second in the Fillies' Mile and then threw away victory in the Tattersalls Fillies 800 at Newmarket by swerving across the track, not the first time she has shown that worrying trend.

However, O'Brien knows he has an even better filly at home in **Misty For Me**, who landed a Group 1 double in the Moyglare Stud Stakes and the Prix Marcel Boussac.

Those two wins capped a progressive campaign in which Misty For Me got better with every run and she seems sure to improve again, particularly when stepped up in trip. She is set to start in the 1,000 Guineas before moving on to Epsom, which probably represents her best chance of Classic glory, but this tough filly is likely to be a standing dish in all the top fillies' races over a range of trips.

Wonder Of Wonders is another lively Oaks prospect. Beaten half a length on her only start at Leopardstown over an inadequate 7f in October, she was also very green that day and has a terrific pedigree for middle distances being by Kingmambo out of Oaks second All Too Beautiful.

Fame And Glory will again lead Ballydoyle's assault on the top older prizes. Last year was another solid one for Fame And Glory, who won two more Group 1 races to make it four in total during his career, but there was a sense of a missed opportunity as he was put away for a second unsuccessful crack at the Arc, a race that really seems too sharp for him.

RITE OF PASSAGE: again has the Ascot Gold Cup as his objective for the year

Give him a long straight in which to gallop his rivals into submission and Fame And Glory is desperately tough to beat, whether over 1m2f or 1m4f, and the Coronation Cup, in particular, looks tailor-made for him.

Cape Blanco and Jan Vermeer give O'Brien more strength in depth over middle distances. **Cape Blanco** won twice at the top level last year, including the Irish Derby, but he looked even better when dropped to 1m2f for the Irish Champion Stakes, blasting a high-class field into submission from the front. Races like the Prince of Wales's Stakes and the Juddmonte International at York, where he has already won over course and distance in the Dante, are likely to be on his agenda.

Jan Vermeer was never right last year after a rushed preparation for the Derby. He went on to finish third in the Irish Derby and the Grand Prix de Paris but was then put away for the year, with O'Brien convinced a long break would see him come back a much better four-year-old.

The Ballydoyle operation are never afraid to send a four-year-old well up in trip to tackle the Ascot Gold Cup. Last year it brought out

a career-best performance in the unfortunate Age Of Aquarius and the next top stayer could be **Midas Touch**, who was good enough to finish second in the Irish Derby and the St Leger while always looking capable of going much further.

O'Brien has also achieved great success with Australian imports Haradasun and Starspangledbanner in recent years and he has another exciting new arrival in **So You Think**. The five-year-old signed off his career in Australia with an honourable third in the Melbourne Cup, but he did all his winning last year from 7f to 1m2f, including four Grade 1 victories in a row, and he has a vast number of options.

The wild-card in the camp, of course, is **St Nicholas Abbey**, who missed nearly all of last season with muscular problems but remains a fine prospect from 1m2f to 1m4f if he bounces back to form.

DERMOT WELD finished second to O'Brien in the trainers' table last year but just got the better of him in the Ascot Gold Cup with **Rite Of Passage**, whose campaign will be geared towards a repeat win.

Rite Of Passage hadn't even run on the

Flat 18 months ago, but after winning the November Handicap at Leopardstown by eight lengths and not quite hitting the heights over hurdles, he was kept back for the Flat and duly fought off Age Of Aquarius.

It was a remarkable effort for only his third Flat start and there should be more to come, even though he took so long to get over Ascot that he hasn't been seen since.

Casual Conquest, for whom thoughts of a novice hurdling campaign were put on hold for another winter, is likely to return after missing last year through injury and should join **Famous Name** in pursuing decent middle-distance prizes.

If there is a horse who can match the Classic success of Bethrah, it may well be **Zaminast**, who won her only start at Galway in July. It took a long time for the penny to drop that day as she turned for home only fifth yet still won what was a hot maiden with the third and fourth winning next time out.

JESSICA HARRINGTON is more well known for her handling of jumps superstars such as Moscow Flyer, but she had a terrific season on the Flat with 30 wins, crowned by Group 1 glory for **Pathfork**.

Pathfork's big day came in the National Stakes when he took his unbeaten record to three, all over 7f at the Curragh, even though jockey Fran Berry said that he never enjoyed the soft ground having previously won the Futurity on good to firm. He came back into training early this year and the 2,000 Guineas is looming.

Laughing Lashes also gives Harrington plenty to look forward to in the top fillies' races after she found only Misty For Me too good in the Moyglare.

KEVIN PRENDERGAST has a similarly exciting bunch of three-year-olds. **Dunboyne Express** may just have had his limitations exposed in the Racing Post Trophy when fourth, but **Snow Watch**, who won his last two starts in terrific style, is one to watch and it's just a shame he had to be gelded last year, ruling him out of the Classics.

Handassa also caught the eye when easily landing a gamble in her maiden at the Curragh in October. She could well be good enough to run in a Guineas.

JOHN OXX was always likely to suffer a comedown after the retirement of Sea The

PATHFORK: with Jessica Harrington

Stars and duly had a quiet year. It remains to be seen whether he has any horse capable of taking him back to the top table this year, but **Alanza** certainly has potential. She produced a remarkable performance on her only start at Listowel in September, coming from 15 lengths off the pace turning for home to win comfortably, and looks smart.

DAVID WACHMAN and *JIM BOLGER* also have very nice fillies on their hands. Wachman thought enough of **Chrysanthemum** to throw her in at Listed level for her debut over 1m at the Curragh, but she won easily at 25-1 and then followed up in a Group 3 when dropped down to 7f. She has plenty of speed and should stay at least 1m2f.

Bolger still has every faith in **Hurricane Havoc**, who was disappointing when put up in grade following a maiden win at Roscommon, lastly when a well-beaten sixth in the Rockfel, but she's clearly capable of much better than that.

Invincible Irish

Misty For Me
Seville
So You Think

Berkshire by Downsman

THE 2011 Flat season is with us and revolution is in the air! It has to be said that many trainers have not exactly embraced the wholesale alterations to the fixture list brought about by the BHA's Racing For Change programme, but one trainer setting a fine example is *ROGER CHARLTON*.

It is hard to remember a more economically depressed time for the sport we all love. Prize-money is now a joke, and this, together with spiralling transport, bedding and horse-feed costs, could see many trainers on the breadline, or worse still bankrupted out of the game.

Charlton, though, took positive steps to keep the wolf from the door, and enjoyed a highly successful 2010 campaign, thanks of course to a good crop of horses, but also to a more aggressive marketing approach, led by a new aesthetically pleasing and highly informative website.

Charlton did well with all the generations last year but was particularly adept at placing his unexposed three-year-olds as several improved steadily throughout the year and managed to run up healthy win-to-run ratios.

Once again he has a healthy mix of older horses and three-year-olds, backed up by an increased number of two-year-olds – a great effort given the shortage in money

ROGER CHARLTON: stans with his stable star Genki who can win more sprints

CLOWANCE: the six-year-old mare should be up to winning again in good company

supply at the moment!

The most exciting prospect for the new season, is a new acquisition from France, bought by billionaire Swede Bjorn Neilsen.

Pontenuovo ended the season as the third highest rated three-year-old filly in Europe, and boasts a highly creditable third to Dream Ahead in the Group 1 Prix Morny, among her juvenile exploits during her first season.

Charlton has been delighted with the progress she has made during the darker months and is targeting her at the 1,000 Guineas trial at Newbury in April, before a possible tilt at a Classic.

Whatever heights Pontenuovo scales, many at Beckhampton believe **Primevere** will be able to match her.

There was much talk throughout the summer about this filly, and it was a major surprsie to all who had party to this imformation that she went off a 16-1 shot on her debut at Kempton in September.

There were stories of Beckhampton staff dancing around the stone circle at the nearby Avebury World heritage site after she won, displaying a smart turn of foot.

Primevere has not grown that much during the winter, but connections are not in the least bit worried about that because she has thickened out and strengthened up substantially.

Of the colts, pride of place must go to **Al Kazeem**, the impressive winner of a maiden at Newbury towards the end of the season.

Although ground conditions were soft, he should handle a sounder surface and he is another three-year-old causing a real stir among the staff.

Cry Fury is somewhat less exposed having seen action only once, and he did not set any rivers alight on that occasion.

But he has always shown a bit at home and is expected to leave that performance behind sooner rather than later.

Sergeant Troy, **Waterborne** and **Korithi** should also win their share of races, and one unraced colt to note is **Hundred Sen**. He has a presence about him and good things are expected.

Charlton always does well with his older horses and 2011 promises much, with old stalwarts like **Genki**, **Clowance** and **Cityscape** back and ready to add to their Pattern haul.

Border Patrol will be looking to make up for lost time after he missed much of last season. He has strengthened up well after a gelding operation and looks sure to do well in mile events, and possibly 1m2f.

Bated Breath, a brother to Cityscape, did well in his debut season, winning two three-year-old handicaps after his maiden win.

He indicated with his final effort in a Listed race that he should be able to hack it at that level this term, and given his lack of miles on the clock, he should improve further.

Charlton's neighbour BRIAN MEEHAN took the trophy for landing the most important victory of any local trainer in 2010 when he won his second Breeders' Cup Turf with **Dangerous Midge**.

It was a remarkable training effort from the Manton handler and a great reward for a typically bold decision to send a horse with very limited experience at Group 3 level, let alone the highest level, for a high-profile race.

Dangerous Midge won in great style and he will bid to give his trainer a flying start to the season with a trip to the Dubai World Cup meeting in March.

Like Charlton, Meehan has plenty of older horses around. **Field Day** improved steadily during her three-year-old season and should add more significant black type to her name, and a handicapper to look out for is **Signor Verdi**.

Although a winner of his debut at Kempton, he took his time to really find his feet but added a handicap at Thirsk in midsummer to his tally before returning at the backend to run a fair fifth at Newmarket. He should progress again.

Arguably the star performer among the Meehan three-year-olds last season was **Lady Of The Desert**.

Bred to be very speedy, she is by Rahy out of the brilliant Cheveley Park Stakes winner Queen's Logic, but she began the season attempting to win a Classic and looked a shade unlucky when a very close fifth in the French 1,000 Guineas.

Connections bowed to the inevitable eventually, however, and she showed that sprinting was very much her game in the closing weeks of the campaign.

Having finished second to Markab in the Group 1 Sprint Cup at Haydock, she won the valuable Diadem Stakes at Ascot later the same month before finishing an unlucky

second to Gilt Edge Girl in the Prix de l'Abbaye at Longchamp just eight days later.

She has done well and all the top sprints will be on her agenda this term.

Meehan once again more than held his own with his two-year-olds and plenty is expected once again from **Titus Mills** and **Waiter's Dream**. The latter may make his debut at Meydan in March.

Earl Of Leitrim ended a very successful first season with a Listed win and he should more than pay his way in sprint events, especially when the ground is on the easy side.

Brevity, the winner of the Listed Dick Poole Stakes at Salisbury on her final start, could tread a similar path.

Meehan is unusually strong in the three-year-old maiden department, and expect two Hamdan Al Maktoum-owned colts **El Muqbil** and **Muqtarrib**, to win sooner rather than later. Both boast very good placed form in high class maidens in the second half of the season.

Dean Swift is likely to ply his trade at a little lower level, but he should pay his way, and both **Red Eyes** and **Red Inca** should get on the scoresheet.

Marie Rose showed promise on her only outing as a juvenile, and an intriguing new acquisition is the former Gay Kelleway-trained **Catfish**, a decisive winner of a Newmarket maiden last summer.

The three-year-old this correspondent is most looking forward to seeing, however, is the unexposed **Warneford**. A bit weak last season, he looks better than his two outings so far suggests.

BARRY HILLS did not manage to scale the heights of 2009 last season, and he seemed less than pleased with the overall form of his team for most of the summer and autumn.

However, every cloud has a silver lining and the cunning old fox has plenty of talented, unexposed talent to draw on during the weeks ahead.

Failasoof is typical of a number of the Hills three-year-old colts. A big rangy son of Dynaformer, he paid a visit to one of his trainer's favourite hunting grounds for his first appearance – the all-weather at Kempton – snd showed a fair amount of potential. He

SERIOUSLY QUICK: that's Lady Of The Desert who made her mark sprinting last year

always showed plenty in his work and must improve as the season progresses.

Slumber showed little on his only outing at Newbury, but he was on the weak side and looks a different specimen now. He looks the sort to come to hand early, and could head for a maiden at the Newmarket Craven meeting.

Moqaraat is another well made son of Dalakhani and will build on his only only run as a juvenile, as should **Ektibaas**, who was seventh on his debut at Newmarket.

Special mention, however, should be made of the once-raced **Canna**. He finished fourth of 17 on his sole visit to the track so far, and is expected to do well over further. A son of High Chaparral, he holds a Derby entry.

Edmaaj and **Commended** saw action on three occasions during their first season and would look slightly more exposed than some of their stablemates, but remember the team were not at their best during the second half of the season and they start the season on attractive handicap marks.

The same could apply to **Early Applause**, who was in action during he opening weeks of the season but remained a maiden after five attempts, despite a cracking effort in a valuable nursery at the Doncaster St Leger meeting.

Quality does not show with the same abundance among the fillies as that as their male counterparts, but hopes are high that the unraced **Rougette**, a daughter of Red Ransom, could enjoyed a highly fruitful first season.

Cheque Book, the winner of her only start at Chester before injury struck, looks to have plenty of potential and a note must be made of the Bath winner **Yasmeena**. She is out of Hills' top-class sprinter La Cucaracha, and

HEDDWYN (far right): could be Royal Ascot-bound if he goes the right way

looks sure to progress.

Pride of place among the older horses is shared by **Ransom Note** and **Redwood**.

Ransom Note developed into a top class handicapper last season and connections are looking for an elevation to Listed and Group 3 company this season. A determined try at 1m2f is also on the agenda.

Redwood was not the easiest to place last season but he managed a win on home turf before enjoying highly lucrative trips to Canada and Hong Kong which included a Grade 1 win and two placed efforts. He will be on his travels again this season, as will the sprinter **Swilly Ferry**.

Before all that, however, we have one of Hills' favourite races, the Lincoln. Mud-lover **Gunner Lindley** is being primed and looks to have done well again during the winter.

MARCUS TREGONING suffered last season once again, but he has a handful of three-year-olds to look out for in what will be something of a rebuilding campaign.

Yasmeer followed a cracking debut effort with a win on the Kempton all-weather and he could make into a Classic trial horse.

Atraaf won his only start as a juvenile and is another well liked by his trainer. He could also be seen during the spring, along with the filly **Hawaafez**. She shaped well on her debut effort and was another to chalk up her first success on the all-weather.

Of the older horses, Tregoning singled out **Heddwyn** as a handicapper to follow. Not unfancied despite his 50-1 starting price when breaking his duck at Windsor, he might be aimed at one of the Royal Ascot handicaps if things go his way in the spring.

Berkshire's Best

Canna
Lady Of The Desert
Primevere

The North by Borderer

THE 2010 Flat campaign proved to be a record-breaking one for *RICHARD FAHEY*. The Malton handler sent out 165 winners with his prize-money surpassing £2 million. While there were numerous highlights along the way, pride and place must go to unbeaten juvenile **Wootton Bassett**.

The Iffraaj colt collected two valuable sales races at York and Doncaster before showing he can mix it at the highest level by capturing the Group 1 Jean-Luc Lagardere at Longchamp on Arc day by two and a half lengths. The 2,000 Guineas is understandably his first port of call and he shouldn't be underestimated.

Another Fahey-trained juvenile from last year who we almost certainly haven't seen the best of yet is **Alben Star**.

A dual winner at Musselburgh and Ayr, he may have lost his unbeaten record at York at the backend but remains a potentially smart individual. Don't be surprised if he returns to the Knavesmire in June for the Reg Griffin Memorial Handicap over 6f.

Our Joe Mac won a competitive 1m handicap at Haydock and came mighty close to securing a decent event at Chester in May.

However, the four-year-old spent most of the season being thwarted by the prevailing fast ground. Much better with plenty of give underfoot, he steel a major pot granted his favoured conditions.

He has reportedly done very well during

ALBEN STAR (right): remains a smart prospect for the season ahead

JUKEBOX JURY: back in training and likely to win more middle-distance races

the winter and is Lincoln-bound.

Corsican Run went through the sales ring or 175,000gns as a yearling and is bred to be useful being a half-brother to Steinbeck.

Runner-up on his debut at Thirsk, the son of Medicean made amends at Beverley next time. Officially rated 75, there will be a lot of disappointed people at Musley Bank if he can't take advantage of such a lenient-looking mark.

MARK JOHNSTON fared even better than his North Yorkshire counterpart last term with 218 winners.

His Royal Ascot winners Monterosso and Rainfall may have spent the winter in sunnier climes but plenty of firepower remains at Kingsley House Stables.

Jukebox Jury won the Jockey Club Stakes at Newmarket in May and, while he disappointed in the Coronation Cup, he was far from disgraced in Germany in mid-summer. Absent for the second half of the season, he is back in training now and will continue to run in middle-distance Group races.

This time last year, **Awzaan** was being touted as a possible Guineas winner having won the Mill Reef and Middle Park Stakes as a juvenile.

Unfortunately, things didn't go to plan during his three-year-old following a lacklustre display on the Rowley Mile.

Third at Haydock and Newbury on his comeback runs having spent most of the summer on the sidelines, he needs to bounce back but is kept in training in the hope he does just that.

Greyfriarschorista was a three-time winner on the all-weather but proved he is equally adept on the turf by finishing third in the Britannia Stakes at Royal Ascot.

Rated 98, he was considered good enough to contest the 2,000 Guineas and there could be a big handicap in him this season, with the Royal Hunt Cup appealing as a likely target.

Sergeant Ablett looked a horse with bright future when disposing of a field of maidens at Newcastle on his debut.

A half-brother to a former stablemate Drill Sergeant, he was slightly disappointing thereafter but he is not too harshly treated off 89 and could develop into a King George V Handicap prospect at the Royal meeting. He will have no trouble staying 1m4f.

That event also looks a realistic target for Leicester maiden winner **Sadler's Risk**.

Well beaten in one of the Newmarket sales race at the backend, he produced a gutsy display at the Midlands track to fend off the late challenge of the potentially high-class Sea Moon. It will be a major surprise if the Sadler's Wells colt canıt win races off his allocated mark of 82.

TIM EASTERBY was responsible for 98 winners, which is a career best since taking over the reins from his legendary father Peter.

Hamish Mcgonagall did his bit as usual winning three times and performing with distinction in Group races. He may be a six-year-old but he will continue to run well in conditions races.

Deauville Flyer won twice at York in May and June before enduring a luckless run in the Northumberland Plate.

Never quite right during the second part of the year, his trainer feels there is room for improvement this season. Expect to see him at the Knavesmire once more with a return to Gosforth Park likely, too.

Among the three-year-old ranks, hopes are high that **Mariachi Man** will develop into a fair sort. A winner at Ripon and Newmarket, he was runner-up at Doncaster in a nursery and has thrived during the off-season. He is a fine prospect and capable of winning a valuable prize this year.

Stablemate **Cocktail Charlie** never quite lived up to expectations having made an

DEAUVILLE FLYER: not quite right at the end of last season but ready to go now

impressive start to his career when making a winning debut at Ripon in the spring.

Although narrowly touched off at both York and Musselburgh, he suffered with sore shins for much of the year and can be forgiven a below par run at Ripon over 6f last time.

He may prove best over the minimum trip and could be about to make up for lost time and realise his undoubted potential.

DAVID NICHOLLS claimed yet another Ayr Gold Cup with **Redford** producing a career-best on only his third start for the sprint king.

The former Michael Bell and Kevin Ryan-trained gelding was given a confident ride by Frankie Dettori before powering clear in the final furlong.

Reappearing a week later, he won another prestigious handicap at Ascot, this time over an extra furlong. Rated 111, it will clearly be much tougher during his six-year-old career but who's to say he won't develop into a Pattern sprinter? It wouldn't be the first time Dandy has converted a handicapper into a Group performer.

Victoire De Lyphar chased home his stablemate at Ayr in September and looks a sprinter with a big future. Having collected the Reg Griffin Memorial Handicap at York in June, he came close to winning the Stewards' Cup consolation next time.

Much depends on his official rating at the time but the four-year-old looks tailor-made for the Wokingham Handicap at Royal Ascot. One suspects his future lies in Group races later on, though.

Magic Casement is unbeaten in two starts having won a Chester nursery in devastating fashion.

The Proclamation gelding scored by 7l and, not surprisingly, the handicapper reacted granting him a mark of 104. Effective over 6f and 7f, he is another possible for the Reg Griffin Memorial given Dandy's excellent record in the race.

Two horses who joined Tall Trees Stables halfway through last year but remain open to improvement are **Al Muheer** and **Courageous**.

Al Muheer ran well at Ascot and Goodwood before disappointing at York's Ebor Festival. Previously handled by Clive Brittain, he invariably runs well at Ascot and could be ideal for either the Victoria Cup or Buckingham Palace at the royal fixture.

Courageous was a smart juvenile when under the guidance of Bryan Smart and he only ran twice for his new trainer.

Having performed well at Haydock over the minimum trip, he narrowly missed out in the Ayr Bronze Cup in September. Favourably treated on his past form, he can win a big prize for his new connections.

Sweet Lightning proved a shrewd acquisition out of Willie Muir's yard for *MICHAEL DODS* and owner Andrew Tinkler.

A winner at both Chester's May Festival and York's Ebor meeting, he is a useful performer over 1m2f with some ease underfoot.

Below par in the Cambridgeshire, he has run two good races at Meydan during the winter including when runner-up in February. Higher in the ratings, he can win another good prize back on home soil.

Another Dods-trained runner who sports the red, white and blue silks of Tinkler is impressive Ayr winner **Well Sharp**.

A colt by Selkirk, he spreadeagled his field before disappointing in testing conditions in the Group 3 Horris Hill Stakes next time.

Held in high regard by the Piercebridge trainer, he is rated 82 and looks capable of winning his share of three-year-old handicaps during 2011.

Dods' near neighbour Alan Swinbank had his best ever season numerically with 52 winners.

Boss's Destination may have only contributed one winner to that tally but he remains a well-handicapped four-year-old.

Owned by Kirkby Lonsdale-based George Bell, he broke his duck in a 1m2f maiden at Newcastle before running well in a competitive Ripon handicap. Given time off during the second-half of the season, he has reportedly strengthened and could be one for the Cumberland Plate at Carlisle in June.

Northern rocks

*Alben Star
Sadler's Risk
Victoire De Lyphar*

The West by Hastings

RICHARD HANNON enjoyed yet another cracking campaign in 2010 and thoroughly deserved being named Flat Trainer of the Year by racing scribes at the Derby Awards.

His Wiltshire yards at Everleigh and Herridge boast nearly 200 horses and amassed 210 winners – 166 on turf – yielding almost £3million in total prize-money in Britain alone last year. With the awesome Paco Boy off to stud, it's on the broad shoulders of star turns like **Canford Cliffs** and **Dick Turpin** to keep shining at the highest level.

Given the considerable talent coming through to back up those established names, Hannon can look forward to another memorable summer.

Pick of a typically strong juvenile crop last year was **King Torus** – the highest-rated of four Hannon youngsters good enough to feature in the International Classifications.

He's related to winners and stepped up on an impressive maiden success with a tenacious effort to deny Ecliptic in the Group 2 Superlative Stakes over 7f at Newmarket in July.

He turned on the style when unleashing an electric burst of speed to go clear under a 3lb penalty in the Vintage at Glorious Goodwood soon after.

It was more a case of being found out by much deeper ground than the step up to Group 1 level when a tiring seventh behind Wootton Bassett in the Prix Jean-Luc Lagardere at Longchamp. Granted a better surface, he remains a likely contender for top prizes.

Another held in high regard by top connections is **Strong Suit**, who represents good each-way value in the 2,000 Guineas for leading owner Julie Wood. He more than lived up to his positive homework when clocking a good time in landing the odds in a Newbury maiden.

STRONG SUIT (right): cuts down Elzaam

However, his true potential shone through when recovering from significant interference to make up a 3l deficit in the final furlong to chin the classy Elzaam on the line in the Coventry at Royal Ascot.

Although turned over at short odds in the Group 1 Phoenix at the Curragh next time, he was only just worried out of it in third behind the smart Zoffany on ground slower than ideal. His potent turn of foot was once again blunted by taxing underfoot conditions when no match for the top-class Dream Ahead in the Middle Park at Newmarket.

He's bred to stay 1m and Hannon believes he'll be stronger mentally this year. Provided the ground doesn't deteriorate, expect a good deal better from Strong Suit on the eagerly awaited return to Headquarters.

Hannon also has a lively player in the 1,000 Guineas with ace filly **Memory**. She was another to dig deep at the royal meeting when mastering a 22-strong field in the Albany over 6f.

She then made it three from three when quickening to land the spoils a shade cosily in the Cherry Hinton over the same trip at Newmarket. It was merely a bad day at the office when she was never going at any stage in a flop at the Curragh in August.

She's better judged by her previous successes, is bred to stay further and remains a leading Classic hope.

The talented **Libranno** could well emerge as Hannon's representative off a mark of 112 in the Free Handicap.

Having made all in both the July Stakes at Newmarket and the Richmond at Goodwood, the classy trail-blazer was made favourite for the Prix Morny at Deauville.

However, he couldn't repel the likes of Dream Ahead in that Group 1, fading to a respectable sixth, beaten just under 4l.

He'd probably gone over the top for the season when again beaten favourite in the Mill Reef at Newbury. Although he possesses a high cruising speed, there are some stamina influences on his dam's side and even bigger things are expected of him at three.

Cai Shen and **Eucharist** are others expected to thrive, albeit at a lower level. The former proved a ready Sandown maiden success was no one-off when following up, despite still showing signs of greenness

under pressure, in a 1m novice event at Salisbury. He possesses a willing attitude and should stay 1m2f.

Eucharist also made big strides on her rookie campaign. Having posted a fourth win when overcoming a troublesome passage to land a valuable nursery off 88 at Doncaster when last seen, she might well be up to successfully graduating into Listed company as a three-year-old.

Hannon's **Energizing** made a belated debut when running well above market expectations (50-1) in second at Kempton in December and wasted little time going one better when easily converting there a fortnight later. Being a May foal, he looks sure to continue progressing with age and experience, and should make a smooth transition to grass. At the very least, he can develop into a useful handicapper.

Angel's Pursuit is a genuine Pattern-race performer on his day and retained the ability to win off a lofty all-weather mark at Kempton in December. He'll likely go to the Dubai Carnival at Meydan before adding to his British tally over the summer.

The reliable **Royal Exchange** stepped up significantly to complete a hat-trick, despite

LIBRANNO: a useful two-year-old for the Hannon team last season

ATTRTACTED TO YOU: ought to do well

the bit slipping through his mouth early, in a Listed event at Salisbury (1m, soft) in August and only just failed to claw back the front pair in a Group 3 at Newmarket next time.

He's equally effective on fast ground and, having finished in the money on all starts, he represents an attractive betting proposition if kept to a realistic grade.

Attracted To You, a close relation to dual Listed-class winner Super Motiva, is yet another Hannon three-year-old expected to take higher order this summer. She created a favourable impression when, despite refusing to settle mid-race, she plugged on promisingly to finish under 3l off the winner in sixth at Goodwood in July.

Despite being brod to want further, she once again showed plenty of pace when pulling clear of subsequent Cornwallis third Darajaat over 6f at Newbury – a maiden that's produced a few high-class performers over the years – the following month. She's bound to settle with age, and will benefit once upped to 7f and beyond on her second campaign.

Pausanias is part-owned by Sir Alex Ferguson and looked a shrewd purchase for the Red Devils manager when second in a bid to retain his unbeaten record in a Group 3 over 1m at Ascot. There's plenty of size

about the colt and should make into an even better three-year-old once filling that ample frame. He's versatile regarding ground preference and should stay further in time.

Hannon's pair **Humdrum** and **Census** are among those expected to prove a headache for the handicapper. Humdrum silenced any doubts regarding her attitude when wearing down Show Rainbow to open the account in a Chester maiden and appreciated a step up to 1m when all out to defy a mark of 76 at Doncaster. She's consistent and embarks on her second season off a feasible mark.

The Queen should enjoy success from her promising **General Synod**. The half-brother to four winners up to 1m2f held a Racing Post Trophy entry for a time and went close to justifying market confidence when beating all bar the $1m purchase Treasury Devil, who's franked the form since, over 7f at Newbury. Although a subsequent fifth at Sandown marked a step back, he should return with a maiden win before going on to better things.

ROD MILLMAN has enjoyed over 400 winners and £4million in prizemoney since setting up his dual-purpose yard at The Paddocks in Devon.

He should enjoy another fruitful campaign from **Galatian**, who got his act together when finishing strongly to land fair sprint handicaps at Leicester and Goodwood when last seen. He can continue to improve with age, has relatively few miles on the clock and acts on any ground.

RON HODGES' decision to up **Sula Two** in trip proved a masterstroke. The shrewd Somerset trainer saddled the progressive filly to net her third win in an open 2m1f handicap at Bath in October. We've yet to see the best of her and, with that in mind, has the potential to continue defying the handicapper as a four-year-old.

Best of the West

Canford Cliffs
Galatian
Pausanias

The South by Southerner

WHY *JOHN DUNLOP* has not been made a Knight of the Realm for services to racing is one of the great mysteries. The master of Castle Stables' training career spans six decades and the 3,500-plus winners he's saddled include 16 Classics in Britain and Ireland.

The only British Classic to have eluded Dunlop so far is the 2,000 Guineas and he had high hopes of adding the Newmarket contest to his CV with **Elusive Pimpernel** last season.

However, after winning the Group 3 Craven Stakes over the Rowley Mile on his seasonal bow, the American-bred colt found the pedestrian early gallop of the 2,000 Guineas itself against him last May and his powerful late finish only carried him into fifth place behind surprise winner Makfi.

He then suffered a setback on the eve of the race when strongly fancied for the Prix du Jockey-Club and wasn't seen out again last term.

There's no doubt that Elusive Pimpernel is a top-class colt and he can make up for lost time this season with races like the Coral-Eclipse at Sandown and the Juddmonte International at York obvious targets.

As usual Castle Stables houses several

ELSUIVE PIMPERNEL: the seldom seen kid will be returning this season

lightly raced three-year-olds who should win races in the months to come.

It was disappointing that **Yair Hill** wasn't able to get off the mark last year but he should win races.

A full brother to former stable stalwart Jedburgh, who won seven times and earned over £166,000 in prize-money, he finished a never-nearer seventh to Native Khan in a traditionally strong 7f maiden at Newmarket's July Cup meeting and chased home Godolphin's highly regarded Saamidd in a similar heat at Newbury on his next start.

The Selkirk colt finished third at Goodwood and second at Leicester when a well backed favourite for maidens on his other two runs.

Misk Khitaam should be well worth watching. The American-bred colt failed to make much impact on his debut when down the field in the 7f maiden won by Baptist at Newbury in September but he clearly benefited from the experience as he came from another parish when a strong-finishing fifth to Loving Spirit in a 7f Newmarket maiden two weeks later on his only other start.

As a close relative of Give Notice, who was a very smart stayer and winner of the 2m4f Group 1 Prix Du Cadran for the stable nine years ago, **Knightly Escapade** is going to be suited by a thorough test of stamina.

The chestnut son of Sakhee, another former Dunlop star, lived up to his breeding when eighth to Auden in a 1m two-year-old maiden at Newmarket on his sole outing last year. He was slowly away and very green on the Rowley Mile but was getting the hang of things in the closing stages and kept on to be less than 6l adrift of the winner crossing the line.

Elrasheed was another to have just one run as a juvenile. A half-brother to Dunlop's smart stayer Akmal, the Red Ransom colt finished seventh in a 1m maiden at Newmarket in August.

He never managed to be competitive on the July course but to be beaten 13l when sent off an unfancied 25-1 shot wasn't without promise as it wasn't just any old maiden but the one won by Frankel!

Even less was expected of **Abbakhan** when he made his debut in and he was allowed to start at 40-1.

Therefore, connections were delighted when he stayed on in good style to finish a never-nearer eighth, beaten just 5l behind subsequent Tattersalls Millions winner Fury in a 7f Newbury maiden run on good to firm going in September.

The grey failed to build on that when well down the field in a 1m Newbury maiden the following month but the ground was good to soft that day.

Mountain Range stayed on well to open his account at the fourth time of asking in a 1m nursery at Windsor in October. The High Chaparral gelding will appreciate a stiffer test of stamina this year and should have no trouble adding to his laurels.

Beatrice Aurore has scope and is expected to develop into a smart filly this year. She was not hard pressed to land a 1m Newmarket maiden in September second time out last year and has been given an entry in the Irish Oaks.

Korngold should make up into a decent middle-distance handicapper. The Dansili colt had three runs over 7f last season and, although he never finished closer than ninth, each time he was noted staying on in good style at the finish.

The Redoute's Choice colt **Maraheb** should pay his way this term. He finished fifth in well contest 7f maiden at Newbury and York last autumn.

Muzdahi made a pleasing start to his career when third in a Newmarket maiden in June. He was sent off 5-2 favourite for a 7f York maiden a month later but could finish only tenth to Samurai Sword. He shouldn't be too harshly judged on that effort as he was badly hampered approaching the final furlong.

Hot Spice should also pay his way in handicap company. The Kodiac gelding showed little on his first starts last year but there was definite promise when he made late headway to be sixth in a 7f Leicester maiden in October on his third and final appearance as a youngster.

The Alhaarth filly **Masaraat** got up in the final stride to win a 1m maiden at Bath in August on the second of her two starts last year and she should should improve when tacking 1m2f and further this term.

ROGER TEAL: trains Cochabamba

Tameen is a similar sort. The Shirocco filly won a 1m Nottingham maiden on her third and final juvenile outing and 1m4f should be well within her compass this year.

Istihaara also won a 1m Nottingham maiden third time out last term. By Kingmambo, she is not sure to stay much further but she should pick up more races this year.

The Nayef filly **Mafateng** shouldn't prove difficult to place to advantage in the months to come. She revealed plenty of ability when staying on nicely to be a close fifth to Pandorea in a 7f maiden at Salisbury last October on her only appearance as a two-year-old.

Dunlop used the same race to introduce **Tanassuq** and she too showed a good deal of promise in finishing fourth.

The American-bred filly's siblings include the top class Bahri and Bahhare and, while unlikely to emulate their exploits, Dunlop shouldn't have any trouble finding her suitable opportunities.

Dunlop's neighbour *WILLIAM KNIGHT* sent out a record 34 winners last year and is a young trainer going places.

Knight does particularly well with older horses such as **King Of Dixie**, who won the Listed Paradise Stakes at Ascot in the spring, and the six-year-old **Palace Moon**, who was beaten just a neck by St Moritz in the Bunbury Cup at Newmarket in July, just needs a little leniency from the handicapper to get his head back in front.

The three-year-olds **Magical Flower**, who ran with promise on all three of her juvenile starts, and Yarmouth maiden winner **Bloodsweatandtears** should also add to Knight's tally this year.

Pullborough-based *AMANDA PERRETT's* **Pivotman** and Inimitable Romanee are a couple of lightly raced three-year-olds that could do well this season.

The first-named ran out an easy 4l winner of a 1m Salisbury maiden on easy ground in September from the Sir Michael Stoute-trained Carlton House, who was subsequently an impressive Newbury winner.

The chestnut colt was disappointing when beaten over 17l in fifth in the Houghton Stakes at Newmarket in October on quicker going on his only other start last year but he should be given the chance to show that was not his form.

Inimitable Romanee is a half-sister to the stable's fine servant Classic Vintage and she followed a promising fourth to Azameera in a 7f Salisbury maiden in September on her first appearance by romping away with a 1m maiden at Bath in October.

ROGER TEAL has done a brilliant job with the six-year-old **Steele Tango**, who's been running well in Dubai this year and earned over £250,000 for his lucky owners The Thirty Acre Racing Partnership.

Teal's big hope for this season is the filly **Cochabamba**. She won a 6f Lingfield maiden first time out and competed with considerable credit in some high class juvenile fillies races subsequently.

She chased home Theysken's Theory in the 7f Group 3 Prestige Stakes in August and concluded her campaign by running Cape Dollar to half a length in the 7f Group 2 Rockfel Stakes at Newmarket in October.

As a daughter of Prix de l'Arc de Triomphe and King George winner Hurricane Run, there's every chance she will train on this season.

Southern stars

Elusive Pimpernel
Inimitable Romanee
Korngold

The Midlands
by John Bull

SATURDAY September 18, 2010, is a day that Staffordshire handler *ED MCMAHON* (nor indeed your correspondent) will ever forget having been at Newbury to see two of his horses, **Temple Meads** and **Astrophysical Jet**, run in Group races.

At 2.30, the former lined up in the Group 2 Mill Reef Stakes. On his previous run, in the Gimcrack Stakes at York, Temple Meads had been allowed to run too free and failed to see home the 6f trip. But at Newbury, there was to be no mistake.

Held up in the rear by jockey Richard Mullen, the Avonbridge colt moved up menacingly 2f out and soon powered clear

of the filed to record an impressive success.

Just over an hour later, Astrophysical Jet lined up in the Group 3 Dubai World Trophy.

Again the filly was held up and again she came with a strong run at the business end of affairs to land the 5f event.

In just over 70 minutes, McMahon had won two Group races. *John Bull* was lucky enough to be with the Tamworth trainer that afternoon – which was not only McMahon's most memorable day in his six-year training career but one of the best days in Midlands Flat racing in recent years.

But McMahon's annus mirabilis was still not over. At Ascot in early October, Electric Waves, who earlier in the summer had

ASTROPHYSICAL JET: gets up close home for a famous win at Newbury last season

landed a Listed race at Newbury, stayed on strongly at the finish to win the Group 3 Cornwallis Stakes.

Although the two-year-old was later sold to race abroad, McMahon will still have the services of his other Group winners from 2010 for the new campaign and hopes are high that they can land more top races.

"Temple Meads is likely to start off in the Group 2 Duke of York stakes at York in May where he'll have a 3lb penalty for his Group 2 win, but three-year-olds get 10lb from older horses.

"Then, all being well, he'll run at Royal Ascot in the King's Stand or the Golden Jubilee, or maybe even the Jersey Stakes, where of course he'd just be against his age group.

"With Astrophysical Jet, we'll be aiming at the Group 1 sprints. We gave her a break after she won at Newbury in September as we didn't want to bottom her out and we decided to wait for the Abbaye for one more year.

"She'll start off in the Palace House at the Guineas meeting, and then she could run into Temple Meads at Royal Ascot, though we'll try to keep the two apart as much as we can.

"She'd go for the Nunthorpe all being well and her end-of-season target would be the Abbaye, but going-wise she wouldn't want it too soft."

McMahon looks to have an abundance of riches in the sprinting stakes as in addition to Temple Meads and Astrophysical Jet, he'll also have the services of a rejuvenated **Noble Storm**, who could yet make an impact at Group level.

"He had a virus and a bug and took a while to get over it. But at the end of the season he was returning to his best and finished off winning very nicely in a conditions stakes at Southwell," McMahon says.

"He stays a full horse – we decided not to cut him. We'll keep him to 5f conditions races and gradually work him up in class, rather than putting him in the deep end to begin with."

The four-year-old **Venutius** rose 17lb in the handicap after a great early-summer run during which he won a 1m handicap at Haydock in June and twice finished a close-up second at Newmarket.

He found life difficult after that, rising to a mark of 92, but watch out for him winning again when the handicapper shows him some leniency and he gets his favoured fast ground.

Regarding his three-year-olds McMahon hopes the John Fretwell-owned **Iron Range**, an impressive 5l winner of a 6f maiden at

NOBLE STORM (left): his trainer believes he could still make an impact at Group level

Ayr in September, can build on the promise he showed in his only run as juvenile.

"He'll be out early doors" McMahon says. "I think he'll be effective at distances from 6f to 7f and even get 1m. We'll be looking at conditions and Listed races with him. He likes a bit of cut."

Indian Ballad did really well as a juvenile, winning four of his last five races and finishing second on the other occasion. He'll start the campaign off a mark of 88 and McMahon hopes there'll be more to come.

"He'll start in handicaps and we'll see if he can exploit his mark. It makes sense to see how far we can go in handicaps before stepping him up in grade."

McMahon will have team of around 24 two-year-olds for the new campaign. "I've got a nice Dutch Art filly who I got at Tattersalls and an Aussie Rules who is a bit quick and could be a late developer. I've also got a full sister to Cartimandua, who won two Listed races for us."

MARK BRISBOURNE is a trainer whose record with cheaply bought purchases is second to none.

The Shropshire handler proved that again last year with £800 purchase **Belle Royale**, who as a two-year-old won four times last season (including a hat-trick in the first three weeks of August) and finished second on a further five occasions.

Overall Belle Royale won £30,881 in prize-money – not a bad return on the initial investment! And Brisbourne believes there'll be further success to come with the Val Royal filly.

"She'll start the season off a mark of 85 and she'll be running in three-year-old fillies handicaps. Her first main target will be Chester's May meeting – she won twice at the Roodee last summer. She's a tough filly and can improve further."

The five-year-old **Lord Of The Dance** won on the turf at Chepstow last summer and then won two further races on the all-weather before Christmas.

"'He's had a wind operation and a nice holiday and will be back in May.

"He reminds me of Roman Maze who was a great servant for us in that he's got speed but also stamina – he's won at 7f and over 1m1f. I think he'll be one to follow."

Brisbourne is also predicting a profitable campaign for the four-year-old **Market Puzzle**.

"Up to now he's only won a seller at Ripon and he's only rated in the 50s. But I think he's a different animal this year.

"He hasn't run since August, when he was a staying-on fourth in a 1m2f handicap at Ayr, and I think the break – the first real break he's had in his career – has done him the world of good.

"I see him as a real 1m2f horse, but I think he'll stay a bit further too. The thing is that he must have good ground – if it's soft he may as well stay at home."

Veteran Kinnersley trainer *JOHN SPEARING* believes that **Hawk Moth**, winner of a 7f handicap at Wolverhampton in October, but beaten in his other five starts as a juvenile, will improve a lot as a three-year-old this season.

"He was very backward last year. I think he's strengthened up a lot over the winter and we'll see a different horse now."

The Hawk Wing gelding will start the campaign off in the low/mid 60s and we can expect his trainer to exploit his current rating.

Whitecrest is another three-year-old who Spearing believes can improve on his juvenile form.

"She was knocking on the door last year, placed in four of his six races without winning. I'm hopeful she can get off the mark and then go on from there."

Talented dual-purpose **Rajeh** will once again combine runs on the Flat with hurdling. His Flat rating has risen to the high 80s and will need to drop a few pounds to start winning again, but watch out for him if he lines up in the 0-85 handicap at Pontefract in May which he won last year at odds of 12-1.

Midlands magic

Astrophysical Jet
Lord Of The Dance
Temple Meads

Outlook

Morning Mole
by Steve Mellish

Star horses should help to ensure a stellar Flat season

THE next few years look sure to be very tough ones, as racing tries to survive in recession-hit Britain. Prize-money at laughable levels will threaten the livelihoods of most who work in the sport and, sadly, it's likely that many will go under.

Certainly, it's hard to see how the fixture list, in anything like its present form, can remain – and nor should it.

The economic climate will force the sport to cut its cloth in order to survive. I suspect racing will do badly out of the forthcoming sale of the Tote and, hard as I look, I can't make out the cavalry riding over the horizon to save us.

Ultimately, though, it's the horses that make the sport so exciting and on a more positive note, there is much to look forward to on the Flat in 2011, with so many top horses remaining in training.

The magnificent Goldikova will continue to strut her stuff as a six-year-old; multiple Group 1 winners Twice Over and Midday come back for more; spectacular Derby winner Workforce and top miler Canford Cliffs

– arguably, the best two three-year-olds of last season – will be competing as older horses, and then there is Frankel to look forward to.

Few juveniles in my memory have caused as much excitement as this son of Galileo. Unbeaten in four starts, and barely extended in two of them, he's already an ultra-warm favourite for the 2,000 Guineas and rightly so.

Henry Cecil, his trainer, hasn't attempted to dampen people's enthusiasm and, if things go to plan, there will be a big crowd at Newmarket on the first Saturday in May hoping to witness his coronation as an equine great.

On the jockey front, people who enjoyed last season's epic contest for the jockeys' title could be in for a repeat with last year's duellists Paul Hanagan and Richard Hughes locking horns with Ryan Moore and a resurgent Kieren Fallon.

Ashbrittle 4yo gelding
3/2131- (Ralph Beckett)

This lightly raced gelding appeals as one to make his mark in staying handicaps this season.

His best effort to date came on his final start at Doncaster when taking a competitive handicap over the St Leger trip.

He'd never previously run over further than 1m4f, and he clearly relished every yard of the new distance, staying on strongly to get on top in the closing stages.

A 4lb rise is more than fair and with just five runs under his belt he's open to further improvement, particularly when he gets the chance to run over 2m-plus. To date, his best efforts have come with cut in the ground – he's yet to encounter a sound surface – and only time will tell whether such conditions are important to him. That caveat aside, he appeals strongly as a stayer to follow.

Bourne 5yo gelding
4044/11- (Luca Cumani)

Rather like Ashbrittle, what we have here is a progressive gelding with not many miles on the clock.

He was successful on both of his starts in 2010 – 1m2f handicaps at Nottingham in May and Doncaster in October.

On each occasion, he was a narrow winner and it was only close home that he got on top but that doesn't tell the whole story as he looked to have a fair bit in hand.

Running style and breeding suggest Bourne will be better still when returned to 1m4f or more and he could improve considerably this term when upped in trip.

Given his trainer's record in the race, it would be no surprise to see him develop into an Ebor horse.

Cityscape 5yo colt
212/20/4211- (Roger Charlton)

This is a bit of a speculative pick. Not that there's any doubt about his ability, it's just that he ended 2010 under a bit of a cloud after reportedly suffering an injury.

Let's hope he makes a speedy recovery as his final performance at Newmarket last season fully justifies his inclusion in this list.

He'd shown useful form several times prior to Newmarket, but his trouncing of Penitent and Co in the Joel Stakes is the day he came of age as a top-notcher.

He received an official rating of 119 after this romp but that looks a huge underestimation of what he achieved.

The second and third had marks of 114 and 110 respectively and Cityscape almost certainly ran to a figure in the mid-120s.

This is Group 1 country and it was no surprise to hear his trainer nominate the Lockinge as a possible target in 2011.

If he is able to return to his best he'll be threat to anything in the top mile races.

CITYSCAPE: looked good when beating Penitent at Newmarket last season

HAVANT: The Mole likes her a lot and will be supporting her in the 1,000 Guineas

Havant 3yo filly
11- (Sir Michael Stoute)

Havant made quite an impression in her two starts at Newmarket as a juvenile.

First time out she took a maiden in great style by 5l then a couple of months later she took the step up into Pattern company in her stride.

All bar one of her nine opponents that day was more experienced than her and several were proven in Pattern class but she brushed them aside with ease, storming clear to win going away by over 3l.

There's plenty of stamina in her pedigree and she could well develop into an Oaks filly in time.

However, she doesn't want for speed and, if things go smoothly over the winter period, she'll surely have a tilt at the 1,000 Guineas first.

At this stage, there's nothing I would rather back and I'm looking forward to her.

Lyric Street 3yo colt
3- (Luca Cumani)

Lyric Street ran a race full of promise on his sole start at two in a backend Newmarket maiden.

A bit green early and slightly outpaced in the Dip, he ran on in good style in the final furlong to grab third close home.

Given his breeding – he's by the Arc winner Hurricane Run and out of the 1m4f Group 1 winner Elle Danzig – a slowly run race over 7f was never going to see him at his best.

Add to that the patient way in which his trainer brings horses along, and it's virtually certain that much better will be seen of this colt as a three-year-old.

He's entered in the Derby and certainly has good prospects of staying the trip.

Whether he proves up to that class only time will tell but a maiden over 1m2f or more looks his for the taking.

racing & football outlook

CELEBRATIONS...

This guy has just backed a winner on the Mole line. You can too.

THE MOLE LINE
0906 911 0230
With Steve Mellish

Calls cost £1/min all times. Outlook Press, Raceform House, Compton, Berks RG20 6NL

Outlook

Dave Nevison

Read Dave's diary every week in the RFO

Why Hanagan can win the title again this year

EVEN a 40-1 winner like Paul Hanagan doesn't last forever and I am saddened by the fact that my life doesn't seem to have materially altered since that fantastic victory. Maybe I should stop spending it as soon as I get hold of any…but she was probably worth it!

As I mentioned in the weekly column last autumn, I still didn't get that the bookies are really not rating his chances of following up this year and at prices ranging from 7-1 to 10-1 I think he is worth a small interest again this year.

It is hardly as if his guv'nor Richard Fahey is going to be lacking in horses this time around and how he manages to keep his handicappers in a winning frame of mind marks him down as something a bit special. Fahey himself could be an outside bet for the trainers' championship in the next couple of seasons.

It doesn't look as though Fahey will be winning the Guineas, however, as good though Wootton Bassett undoubtedly is, he does not look to be in the same league as Frankel, who looked an absolute machine when tearing a part a top class field in the Dewhurst .

The 5-4 for the 2,000 Guineas has killed the market but after those performances how can you put anything up against him at this stage?

It looks like we might need the big box of Kleenex when Henry Cecil leads in another Guineas winner.

On the less obvious and back on the subject of northern handicappers, one young horse that I thought would definitely pay his way next season was Tim Easterby's **Mariachi Man**, who shows an extremely tough attitude to win and get beaten just a short head in his last two starts in nurseries.

Good and soft ground come alike to him and he looks like he will stay at least 1m2f with Nashwan on the dam's side. One of those early Haydock handicaps looks a good target before the Dante meeting at York.

From the same stable **Deauville Flyer** looked a horse that was massively on the up in mid-summer when upped in trip but the big targets did not go well for him.

It could possibly be a blessing as he has dropped a few pounds after an initial hike and he will be a much stronger horse this year.

The Chester Cup looks a probable first target and then he will probably follow the Northumberland Plate/Ebor/Cesarewitch route and one of those might come his way.

Andrew Balding had some good two-year-olds last season that he was bringing on very steadily but **Desert Law** certainly looked one of the more promising when breaking his maiden in good style the day before Champions Day at Newmarket. This one may end

ARCTIC COSMOS: comes clear of his field to win the St Leger for John Gosden

up a handicapper rather than a Group contender but he impressed with the way he picked up in the Dip on this occasion and he looks a horse with a future.

One that didn't manage to break his maiden last term but wont take long in the spring is **El Muqbil** who looks a useful staying prospect for Brian Meehan.

Hopefully he won't be pitched too highly by his trainer who still has a tendency to stick them in high but a Royal Ascot handicap might well be the thing for him.

Tazahum was a brute when I saw him at Kempton in the autumn and looked as though he would improve massively for the run, which probably explains why he went off at 10-1. However, he belied those odds and ran out an impressive winner which was hugely annoying.

He then went to Ascot for a conditions stakes event and was well supported against Group-class performers.

However, it was a really wet day and although the ground was given as officially good, I am convinced it was patchy and he ended up getting beaten by three and a half lengths at a 25-1 shot.

He is better than that and his half-brother was still winning races when he was seven so that bodes well for his progession. He could be a horse for something like one of the Chester Derby trials early doors.

Another three-year-old who I missed at a big price as a juvenile is David Elsworth's **Seattle Drive**, who looked a picture on his debut at Newmarket.

I was covering the meeting for Racing UK

at the time and don't usually bet when on the box. At 33-1 he was a very bad miss and showed great purpose when he passed every horse in the last couple of furlongs to win this modest affair in good style.

Although beaten twice since then, he improved with each run and he, too, looks a horse who will definitely win a couple of races, possibly up to Listed company.

Putting up a Leger winner who is blinkered is fraught with danger as often these types are campaigned over the wrong trip in the later races and very few successfully go back to 1m4f.

If John Gosden does the right thing with **Arctic Cosmos** he could have a really wonderful stayer on his hands given the way he was improving last summer.

The blinkers definitely helped but it could have been immaturity and it would not surprise me to see him working okay without them this season. Hopefully he will take the staying route.

On the jockey front this year there may not be a Buick on the scene but two have hugely impressed me. One is Julie Burke, who is a serious young rider and will rattle thorugh her claim pretty quickly provided the prejudice about girl riders does not hold her back.

George Challoner is in the right place to be a champion at Richard Fahey's and will definitely get opportunities for his own stable. He is showing all the right signs to me and if he heeds the advice of Hanagan and Fahey he wont be claiming 7lb for too much longer.

Time Test *with Mark Nelson*

Phenomenal Frankel is set to storm the Classic scene

THERE'S only one place to start when casting an eye over the 2011 Classic generation for 2011 and that's with Frankel. Unbeaten in four starts as a juvenile at 7f and 1m, he's the first two-year-old to record a Time Test figure above 70 since New Approach in 2007, and he later went on to win the Derby, the Irish Champion and the Champion Stakes at Newmarket, not to mention placed efforts in both Guineas and the Juddmonte International.

Frankel won his maiden on soft ground but had no problem coping with faster conditions at Doncaster, where, despite the small field, he returned a suitably impressive time on the stopwatch.

He slammed the subsequent Horris Hill winner by ten lengths in the Royal Lodge, and was even more impressive on the clock when rounding off his campaign in the Dewhurst where he recorded a personal best, bettering figures I have awarded to top juveniles such as Teofilo and Holy Roman Emperor in the past.

While I much prefer to take on favourites where I can, the clock could not be more impressed with Frankel, and his position at the head of the market for both the Guineas and Derby is well deserved.

Next best of the colts is **Roderic O'Connor** after he chased home Frankel at Newmarket, although he may be slightly flattered by his proximity to the winner as he undoubtedly had the run of the race from the front.

Aidan O'Brien's charge subsequently bagged a Group 1 success at Saint-Cloud on heavy ground and will reportedly head to Newmarket for another crack at Frankel in the 2,000 Guineas.

Just 1lb below Roderic O'Connor on my figures is stablemate **Recital**. With Henry Cecil expressing doubts over Frankel for the Derby, Recital may prove to be the one for Epsom.

I like the fact that, unlike Roderic O'Connor, who had four starts at two, Recital has been lightly raced with just two outings to date and has yet to taste defeat.

His dam was by a French Guineas winner and his sire, Montjeu, was responsible for Derby winner Motivator. Recording a speed figure of 67 on just his second racecourse appearance marks him out as a potential star, and while this is still 10lb below Frankel, there's clearly plenty of room for improvement at three.

It's never easy trying to second-guess the pecking order at Ballydoyle, but with doubts surrounding Frankel for the Derby, a small each-way investment on Recital at double-figure odds for the Epsom showpiece may not prove too far wide of the mark.

The Irish challenge by no means stops there either. **Pathfork** has a creditable speed figures following his duel with Casamento in the National Stakes, when I really liked his attitude.

A minor setback prevented him from building on this figure, so although he's a little way adrift of the very best on my figures, I'll be surprised if he's not a deal better than his current number suggests.

Casamento franked the National Stakes form by winning both subsequent starts, although he didn't really progress on the clock and he might be one to take on at short prices early in 2011 for new trainer Mahmood Al Zarooni.

Glor Na Mara has yet to win a race but his efforts on the stopwatch suggest he's no mug. He's seen the backend of Pathfork on more than one occasion, though, and was no match for Frankel in the Dewhurst so he might be difficult to place this term.

Another member of the home team that must not be forgotten is the Richard Fahey-trained **Wootton Bassett**.

Unbeaten in five starts up to 7f, his speed figures progressed all season, culminating in a career-best at Longchamp where he landed his first Group 1.

I see no reason why he shouldn't get 1m, but he had several hard races last term and I wonder if he can keep progressing at three, which he will need to do, if he is to prove a realistic threat to Frankel in the Guineas.

In summary, there could be a huge gulf between Frankel and the other colts this year. The main threat from Ireland may prove to be Pathfork, with Recital the fancy for Derby honours if Henry Cecil's potential superstar side-steps the gig.

As in recent years, the juvenile fillies proved to be much of a muchness.

Not since Finsceal Beo have we had a filly to get really excited about, her Time Test figure of 74 in the Prix Marcel Boussac an outstanding juvenile performance. In recent seasons, we've had to be content with the top fillies recording figures around the 60 mark and 2010 was no different.

In **Hooray**, we at least had one filly who proved much the best on the clock from an early stage having improved massively once racing from the front.

Her effort in the Lowther Stakes marked her out as a top performer and she didn't let followers down when she won twice more, including the Cheveley Park on her final start. On the downside, her speed figures

would not be insurmountable for a progressive three-year-old this term, her trainer voiced doubts at an early stage as to her ability to train on at three, and there are also stamina fears to allay too.

The lack of an outstanding talent in the fillies' division reflects why it's nearly double-figure odds the field, in both the Oaks and the 1,000 Guineas. Come the day of the first fillies' Classic it might pay to look for a lightly raced type that has yet to show her full potential on the clock.

Of the rest of those near the top of the market, **Misty For Me** has the best Time Test figure thanks to her win in the Moyglare Stud Stakes last August. A bruised foot prevented her building on that effort in the Fillies' Mile, but she did return to land the Prix Marcel Boussac.

So, although she's yet to excel on the clock, she is a dual Group 1 winner, effective over 1m and is likely to stay further.

She makes more appeal than **White Moonstone**, despite that one's unbeaten record at two. Godolphin's filly was good enough to win the Fillies' Mile, but the time wasn't anything special and she's only a light-framed sort, so I'd have reservations at three until she's proved herself on the stopwatch.

Another unbeaten filly near the top of the Classic markets is Sir Michael Stoute's **Havant**. Her five-length maiden success told us little, as the time was slow, and her rivals have done very little to advertise the form,

HOORAY: best filly but no superstar

but she created a very impressive visual impression when winning the Oh So Sharp Stakes at Newmarket in October.

Although her speed figure for that effort was still only modest, it was at least a step forward on the clock and it's safe to assume she should be capable of much better.

Memory was all the rage early in the season last year, yet she was another filly who failed to impress to any great extent on the stopwatch. It was impressive to watch her win slowly-run races with a decent turn of foot, but the winning times were poor and her bubble was burst in the Moyglare.

Looking down the others in my list of top juveniles from last year, **Cape Dollar** might prove to be overpriced in the Guineas.

The stable is also responsible for Havant, but Cape Dollar achieved more on the clock last year, with figures nicely on an upward curve. She'll definitely get the mile this year and, at a price, might be worth a small each-way interest.

With things very much up in the air, though, I'd tread very carefully with the fillies in the early part of the season. It may pay to give Hooray a chance, but I'll keep an eye on the figures of anything having a prep race prior to the Guineas meeting. I'll keep you posted each week in the RFO.

Top two-year-old colts of 2010

	Horse	Speed rating	Distance in furlongs	Going	Track	Date achieved
1	**Frankel**	**77**	**7**	**GD**	**Newmarket**	**Oct 16**
2	Roderic O'Connor	69	7	GD	Newmarket	Oct 16
3	Recital	67	10	HY	Saint-Cloud	Nov 13
4	Wootton Bassett	67	7	VS	Longchamp	Oct 3
5	Glor Na Mara	65	7	GD	Newmarket	Oct 16
6	Pathfork	64	7	SF	Curragh	Sep 11
7	Casamento	64	7	SF	Curragh	Sep 11
8	Dream Ahead	64	6	SF	Newmarket	Oct 1
9	Waiter's Dream	64	7	GD	Newmarket	Oct 16
10	Zoffany	63	6	YD	Curragh	Aug 8

Top two-year-old fillies of 2010

	Horse	Speed rating	Distance in furlongs	Going	Track	Date achieved
1	**Hooray**	**62**	**6**	**GS**	**Newmarket**	**Oct 1**
2	Electric Waves	60	5	GS	Ascot	Oct 9
3	Meow	60	5	GF	Curragh	Aug 21
4	Ladie's Choice	59	5	GF	Curragh	Aug 21
5	Margot Did	58	6	GD	York	Aug 19
6	Maqaasid	57	5	GF	Ascot	Jun 16
7	Cape Dollar	56	7	GS	Newmarket	Oct 16
8	Moonlit Garden	56	5	GF	Curragh	Aug 21
9	Ladies Are Forever	55	5	GF	Ascot	Jun 16
10	Cochabamba	54	7	GS	Newmarket	Oct 16

Going key: F = firm, GF = good to firm, GD = good, Gs = good to soft, S = soft, H = heavy.

Review of 2010

Outlook

News Diary

by Richard Williams

January

12 The World Thoroughbred Rankings are released and it's enough to briefly awaken Flat aficianados from their mid-winer hibernation. Needless to say Sea The Stars is head and shoulders above the other three-year-olds with a rating of 136, seven places ahead of Rip Van Winkle on 129 and eight ahead of Fame And Glory on 128. Goldikova has top rank among the older horses, her Breeders' Cup and Prix Jacques Le Marois wins being highlights of 2009. But it is with an eye to the future that Flat fans really perk up, especially those holding ante-post vouchers about St Nicholas Abbey for the 2,000 Guineas and Derby. His impressive turn of foot in the Racing Post Trophy earns him a rating of 124, four points above his nearest rival, Godolphin's Passion For Gold. It is the fifth year running that Ireland has provided the top juvenile.

16 Leading owner Sir Robert Ogden increases his team of Flat horses and adds four new names to his roster of trainers. Dermot Weld, Richard Fahey, Brian Meehan and Sir Michael Stoute have taken two-year-olds, bringing Ogden's total number of horses to 22. Jeremy Noseda is still his main trainer, though, with nine in his care.

20 William Buick is appointed stable jockey to John Gosden. The 21-year-old, who was joint champion apprentice in 2008, has gone from riding his first winner to becoming retained rider for one of the most powerful yards in Britain in a little more than three years. However, the move means that Jimmy Fortune is now looking for a new job. Fortune missed out on the winning ride on Raven's Pass in the 2008 Breeders' Cup Classic and also stepped aside to allow Frankie Dettori to ride Gosden's horses in the 2009 Breeders' Cup at Santa Anita. Gosden says: "We remain friends and have no argument but it is time to move on. There is no reason why Jimmy shouldn't ride for us in the future." The appointment means that Buick ends his close association with Andrew Balding.

21 Andrew Balding asks Jimmy Fortune to take over from William Buick. Fortune says: "I've had quite a few offers and I'm really flattered by the response. Andrew has just lost a good jockey but I really haven't had time to think about it. I'm going to take a couple of weeks out and think about whether I want to take a job or go freelance."

27   Terry Mills, one of Epsom's best trainers, dies at the age of 71 after a lengthy battle with cancer. The master of Loretta Lodge made his fortune as a waste disposal and demolition tycoon. He bought his first lorry at the age of 22 when demobbed from the army and had a fleet of 150 by the time he sold his company, A & J Bull, in the late 1990s. He bought his first horse from the profits he made digging out the gravel pits at Kempton before taking out a licence to train in 1993. Probably his most famous horse

was Where Or When, who won the Queen Elizabeth II Stakes in 2002. Other Group winners were Bobzao, who won the Hardwicke, and Mitcham, who won the King's Stand. His son and assistant Robert is expected to take over.

28   It's the first day of the Dubai Carnival at its new venue Meydan. Estimated to have cost $2 billion, the grandstand alone has a crowd capacity of 60,000. The surface on the all-weather track is Tapeta, the formula for which was invented by former trainer Michael Dickinson. There are 10,000 undercover spaces for parking. The prize-money for Dubai World Cup night comes in at $10 million, the 1m2f World Cup itself being worth $6 million.

February

21   Khalid Abdullah's racing manager Teddy Grimthorpe rules out Workforce from the Derby, saying: "We see him more as a 1m/1m2f horse. Both he and Treble Jig are in good shape and will be entered for the 2,000 Guineas next week." The 20-1 fourth favourite for the Derby went into many a notebook when hammering subsequent Tattersalls Timeform Million winner Oasis

Dancer by 6l on his sole juvenile start at Goodwood. He is by King's Best, whom Workforce's trainer Sir Michael Stoute trained to win the 2,000 Guineas ten years earlier. Despite most of King's Best's progeny excelling at distances of 1m or shorter, Workforce had been widely expected to be supplemented for the big race at Epsom on April 6.

March

19   Steinbeck, a 9-1 chance for the 2,000 Guineas, meets with a setback and is unlikely to run in the Classic, says Aidan O'Brien. Bookmakers react to the news by shortening up his stablemate St Nicholas Abbey to 2-1.

20   Kieren Fallon is punched by an owner at Lingfield Park after the second race. David Reynolds, the joint-owner of beaten favourite The Scorching Wind and the third-placed Seek The Fair Land, is escorted off the track. The incident happens in the unsaddling area where Fallon is talking to the connections of his mount Elna Bright. Elna Bright's owner Peter Crate also receives a glancing blow to the cheek. Fallon says: "He came

up behind me when I was unsaddling but I'm all right. He hits like a girl." Crate recalls the incident thus: "I was standing looking at my horse's injured leg and he came in like a whirlwind and landed a punch from behind on Kieren, smashing him in the face. He caught me a glancing blow as he swung and both he and Brett Johnson got in between him and Kieren." Reynolds later explains: "I believe Kieren Fallon impeded my horse thus resulting in injuring his own horse and in the heat of the moment I slapped him. I'm very embarrassed by my actions and apologise to the owner and the trainer but not to Mr Fallon. He has cost me the prize-money and a substantial gamble."

23 Sheikh Mohammed appoints a new trainer for his Godophin horses, Mahmood Al Zarooni. The former assistant to Saeed Bin Suroor takes charge of seven of Godolphin's 20-strong squad for World Cup night which is just three days away. Al Zarooni is also to have his own set-up at Newmarket, Moulton Paddocks situated a mile away from Bin Suroor's Goldolphin stables. He will call upon the services of jockey Ahmed Ajtebi while Bin Suroor will continue to retain Frankie Dettori.

27 Two big races, one at Doncaster worth £77,000 to the winner, and one at Meydan in Dubai worth £3,700,000 to the winner. The former race, the famous Lincoln Handicap goes to Penitent, trained by William Haggas and ridden by Johnny Murtagh. The World Cup is won by Gloria De Campeao, trained by Frenchman Pascal Bary and ridden by Brazilian TJ Pereira. Although British runners can only finish fifth and sixth, both of them collect more prize-money than Penitent. Channel 4's coverage of the event is marred somewhat when the programme closes before the result of the photo finish to the World Cup is known. The Sheema Classic, a 1m4f event run on turf and worth £1,800,000 to the winner, falls to the John Gosden-trained Dar Re Mi. The five-year-old mare, who is owned by Lord Lloyd-Webber, is ridden by William Buick who has a dream start to his new job.

April

5 Peter Walwyn announces his intention to place Windsor House Stables on the market. Situated just off Lambourn's high street, the property consists of a six-bedroom Georgian house, a cottage, 50 boxes and an equine swimming pool. Walwyn started off training there 50 years ago, then moved to Seven Barrows before moving back to Windsor House having swapped stables with Nicky Henderson.

14 Greville Starkey dies at his home outside Newmarket at the end of an eight-year battle with cancer. The 70-year-old won the 1978 Derby on Shirley Heights but it was an incident in the same race eight years later that he will possibly be best remembered for, the defeat of Dancing Brave. His rollcall of big-race victories included winning both the Oaks and Sussex Stakes twice, and the Eclipse Stakes and Gold Cup three times apiece. He also won the 2,000 Guineas and partnered Star Appeal to a shock victory in the Prix de l'Arc de Triomphe in 1975. He rode for John Oxley for eight years and for Henry Cecil for four years but it was his association with Guy Harwood that delivered the most success. Together they were a major force at the top end of British racing. Starkey was a great mimic and was known as The Barker because of his ability to imitate a Jack Russell. Meanwhile, the recession has had a knock-on effect on racing's finances. The Levy Board announces that there will be cuts of £4.6 million to prize-money in the second half of 2010, a revision of its original budget.

23 The Sangster family buy a share in the 2,000 Guineas hope Inler. Harry Findlay remains the largest shareholder in the Red Ransom colt who is trained by John Best. Guy Sangster says: "Harry has kept us abreast of all the Inler news from before his first run last year. When we enquired about taking a share this week he came back to us with an offer that was simply too good to refuse. His enthusiasm is infectious."

25 The latest edition of the Sunday Times Rich List indicates that racing's wealthiest supporters have come through the recession unscathed. Indeed, several have prospered during the downturn. A number of independent bookmakers and racehorse owners see a significant increase in their fortunes. New entries to the list include owners James and Fitriani Hay, whose worth is valued at £200 million. Betfred boss Fred Done and his brother Peter see their combined worth climb by £150 million to £660 million. Topping the racing list, and now ranked in fifth place among Britain's richest, are

David and Simon Reuben whose portfolio of interests include Northern Racing and Arena Leisure, owners of more than a third of Britain's racecourses. The value of the brothers' assets soared 121 per cent to £5.532bn. Betting shop punters throughout the land breathe a sigh of relief.

28   The Racing For Change-inspired experiment to dispense with fractional odds at Ascot on a Wednesday afternoon results in a drop in turnover for those on-course bookmakers offering decimal prices. On a day when Ascot's decision to offer free admission to its Grandstand enclosure (another RFC-inspired idea) was richly rewarded with nearly 20,000 racegoers visiting the track, four bookmakers allow themselves to be used as guinea pigs by offering decimal odds on the seven races. Bookmaker Martyn Verrall, one of the 'pigs', claims his two pitches were nearly 80 per cent down on forecast turnover (allowing for the increase in crowd numbers). He says: "If I'm trying to compete with my fractional colleagues, it's a no-brainer. They will wipe the floor with me every time." Still, the rookie racegoers enjoy themselves, a certain Alfie Panchal from Staines exclaiming: "There's nothing I can think of that I haven't enjoyed." That's good news then.

May

2/3   It's Guineas weekend at Newmarket and the story of the 2,000 version is as much about the demise of the much-heralded St Nicholas Abbey as it is about the 33-1 winner from France, Makfi. The former finishes sixth with Aidan O'Brien blaming the slow early pace which he says turned the second half of the race into a sprint. St Nicholas Abbey is pushed out in the Derby betting from 6-4 to 4-1. Makfi is a bargain horse, bought for 26,000gns after being considered surplus to requirements at Marcus Tregoning's yard by advisers to Hamdan Al Maktoum, who bred him at his Shadwell Stud. The sheikh's racing manger Angus Gold admits to having made a mistake. "It was obviously not my finest moment," says Gold. "Marcus had never been able to get a decent run with the horse because he was always being stopped and held up by little niggling problems. This was one that slipped through the net." The drama in the colt's Classic cannot match that of its fillies' counterpart, the 1,000 Guineas. The filly first past the post, 66-1 shot Jacqueline Quest, is relegated to second place following a stewards' inquiry and Special Duty, owned by Khalid Abdullah and trained by Criquette Head-Maarek is awarded the prize. Jacqueline Quest is adjudged to have interfered with Special Duty and to have come off a straight line when she and her jockey Tom Queally duelled through the final furlong. The result is a blow for trainer Henry Cecil and the quadriplegic owner Noel Martin. Cecil takes it with good grace, saying: "I'm please for Criquette and the Prince but I would obviously rather have won. Maybe I'll get my own back at Royal Ascot." It would have been Cecil's seventh win in the 1,000 Guineas but instead it is Head-Maarek's fourth win in the Classic. It is also the first time French horses have brought off the 2,000/1,000 double.

4   Racing For Change's intiative of organising a week of free racing can only be described as a resounding success if attendance figures are anything to go by. The percentage increases per course are Ascot 133 per cent, Goodwood 59, Huntingdon 387, Kempton 180, Nottingham 414, Sedgefield 66, Towcester 28 and Wolverhampton 102. Note that Towcester would have been free anyway. Kempton managing director Amy Starkey says: "What we will probably do is make People's Day an annual event here, whereby we will offer free admission."

10   British bookmakers are smarting from a payout of more than £1 million after gambles were landed on three horses, two trained by master punter Barney Curley, with defeat for a fourth preventing one of the most spectacular coups in betting history. Irish layers are said to have taken an even bigger hit. The fourth leg of the gamble is Sommersturm who fails to justify odds of 1-3 at Wolver-

hamptoi i. The two Curley-trained horses are Agapanthus, a 2-1 from 7-1 shot who scores at Brighton, and Savaronola, an 11-10 from 5-1 shot who stays on well at Wolverhampton.

18   The betting for the jockeys' title suggests that Ryan Moore is a shoo-in. He is a general 1-4 shot while Kieren Fallon is 5-1 with William Hill. With two weeks to the Derby, the same firm offer 7-4 about St Nicholas Abbey.

25   Having put aside £61m for prize-money in 2011, the Levy Board now plan to hand over £48 million, a drop of more than 20 per cent. It's further bad news for owners and racing as a whole.

28   Jan Vermeer shoots to the head of the Derby betting, ousting stablemate St Nicholas Abbey after a lacklustre workout causes turmoil in the ante-post market. A statement from Ballydoyle indicates that Johnny Murtagh will delay his choice of rides until halfway through Derby week. Gallinule Stakes winner Jan Vermeer is now 5-2 from 5-1 with Paddy Power while his stablemate is 3-1.

June

1   Aidan O'Brien rules out St Nicholas Abbey from the Derby, citing a muscle injury. Kieren Fallon is booked to ride Al Zir for Saeed Bin Suroor.

2   A planning application for the development of Lord Derby's Hatchfield Farm on Newmarket's Fordham Road is rejected at an extraordinary meeting of Forest Heath District Council. The 12 councillors are unanimous in turning down Lord Derby's plans to build up to 1,200 homes. Members of the Save Historic Newmarket Action Group, Tattersalls, Godolphin, Darley and most HQ trainers including John Gosden and his wife Rachel Hood are delighted. The last-named says: "We have campaigned long and hard for this result to protect unique, historic Newmarket. We would like to thank our new MP Matt Hancock for all he has done to live up to his campaign promise to save Newmarket from destruction." However, it emerges that Lord Derby is likely to appeal.

4/5   It's an Oaks/Derby double for Ryan Moore, who rides Snow Fairy to victory for Ed Dunlop in the fillies' Classic and Workforce in the Derby for Sir Michael Stoute. Snow Fairy is Moore's first Classic and a second Oaks for Dunlop after Ouija Board six years earlier. Workforce, owned by Khalid Abdullah, gives Stoute his fifth Derby and the seven-length margin is the third biggest in the history of the race. The time smashes Lammtarra's 1995 course record by nearly a second.

23   The Levy Board announces another cut in prize-money for 2010, chopping off £2.1 million from August 1 onwards. This is because of the dramatic drop in money coming in to British racing from the levy on bookmakers' gross profits.

27   With the best part of five months of the Flat season still to run, bookmakers have Ryan Moore as 1-3 favourite to retain his champion jockey crown. He is neck and neck with Paul Hanagan (8-1) on 68 winners while Richard Hughes (8-1) is two behind on 66. Kieren Fallon is out to 12-1 in the betting.

29   With Ryan Moore suspended, Paul Hanagan rides a treble at Hamilton and pulls seven clear of Moore. He is cut to 7-2 by Paddy Power.

30   The BHA is poised to axe around 250 of its meetings from the fixture list in 2011 as a response to rapidly falling income received by the Levy Board from the betting industry's gross profits. The bidding process that has been in place for the last five years is to be scrapped. The only exceptions to the cuts will be the 16 BHA-owned fixture slots granted to Ffos Las as a new racecourse. If the 2011 programme emerges with the forecast 1,240 meetings, the total would be the smallest since 2002. While racecourse proprietors, trainers and owners greet the news with dismay, it should be remembered that many punters have long thought that there is too much horseracing.

July

9   Richard Hughes is so determined not to miss Glorious Goodwood through suspension that he decides to take the week off. He says: "I've totted up 15 days now so I'm looking at more days if I reach the trigger point. A lot of us are picking up one or two-day bans for what used to get just a caution. They say 'it's only a day' or 'it's only two days' but they add up."

24   There's a new equine champion on the scene – Harbinger. His 11-length victory in the King George And Queen Elizabeth Stakes at Ascot under French pilot Olivier Peslier marks him down as something special as he beats two Derby winners, Workforce and Cape Blanco, as well as Youmzain. He is owned by a 12-person Highclere Thoroughbred Racing syndicate and triained by Sir Michael Stoute, whose Workforce proves a damp squib in the race. Not only does Harbinger post the widest margin victory ever recorded for the race, he shatters the track record.

26/27   It's a week of two festivals, Glorious Goodwood in Britain and the Galway Festival in Ireland. The focus is on Richard Hannon at the first location and Dermot Weld at the second. It doesn't take Weld long to strike, in fact he wins the opening race on the first day with Force Of Habit. On day two he wins four races with Universal Truth, Easy Mate, Zaminast and Parlour. Meanwhile back in Britain, The Richard Hannon/Richard Hughes combination land a double on the first day of Goodwood, Zebedee taking the Molecomb Stakes and Martyr landing a 1m6f handicap. Hannon would go on to saddle nine winners at the Sussex venue, all of them ridden by Richard Hughes. Weld would proceed to rack up 11 winners in west Ireland, beating his personal best of ten which he achieved in 1993, 1994, 1998, 2001 and 2008. This is the 26th time he is leading trainer at the meeting and to mark this achievement he is made an honourary member of the Galway Race Committee.

August

7   Harbinger fractures a cannonbone at exercise on the Limekilns and becomes a longshot for the Prix de l'Arc de Triomphe. It's devastating news for the syndicate members who own him. He is operated on at an equine hospital and is expected to make a full recovery.

10   There is a revision in the forecast reduction in meetings for 2011. While a few months ago it looked as though there would be 250 fewer meetings, now it appears there may be a reduction of 140. Discussions may have saved 97 winter twilight fixtures. As a concession to cost-saving, the 2011 twilight meetings are likely to attract a much-reduced basic daily rate of Levy Board prize-money. Each meeting could lose around £10,000. The big bookmakers welcome the news but perhaps someone should tell them that punters aren't exactly salivating at the prospect of being served

up more dross at a weird time of day.

11   Paddy Power make Paul Hanagan 8-13 to wrest the jockeys' title away from Ryan Moore who is sidelined with a bruised wrist sustained after a fall at Windsor. The champion is not even in second place, that position being held by Richard Hughes who is five ahead of Moore but 11 behind Hanagan.

14   At the Deauville sales one man (or at least the representatives of one man) is notable by his absence. That man is Hamdan Al Maktoum who the year before had been the leading buyer. The vacuum he leaves is partly filled by Sir Robert Ogden who spends €910,000 on four yearlings. Sheikh Mohammed is also relying more and more on homebreds rather than purchases for his racing operation. His representative John Ferguson buys just one yearling, a €360,000 son of Shamardal which is a big reduction

on his spending the previous year. Ferguson says: "As we saw at Saratoga, we're in a different world and we have to be realistic. I can't see that the market will be much different at Tattersalls and Goffs."

15   Newbury defends its decision to combine the CGA Hungerford Stakes fixture with an after-racing concert that alienated some traditional racegoers and prompted Barry Hills to leave midway through the meeting calling the whole thing a disgrace. Around 30,000 customers give Newbury a modern-day record attendance with the majority of those present there because of Westlife. This was a considerably larger figure than the 17,500 that watched Denman land his second Hennessy Gold Cup. Hills claims that most of the crowd weren't racing people, but Newbury's managing director Stephen Higgins counters: "We cannot offer good prize-money if we aren't making a profit. We will talk to our stakeholders, including trainers, owners and annual members but we must attract new people and post-racing concerts are a good way of doing that."

27   John McCririck's second spell in a Big Brother household (his first was in 2005) is going rather well. He is in an affable mood, even trying to rekindle the relationship of divorced housemates Preston and Chantelle. However his habit of wandering around at night in his Y-fronts is somewhat worrying.

September

11   William Buick and John Gosden combine to win their first domestic Classic, the St Leger with Arctic Cosmos. Buick bides his time on the 12-1 shot and makes his challenge two furlongs out to beat Midas Touch by two lengths. "He took a pull because he thought he was going too well," says the Newmarket trainer. "He knows this is a bloody long straight. I've seen people go for it here and die at the furlong pole." The colt is part-owned by Gosden's wife Rachel Hood who is having a year to remember having already scuppered Lord Derby's plans to concrete over a large part of Newmarket town.

14   Paul Hanagan returns from suspension to deal with a new threat to the jockey's title in the shape of Richard Hughes, Ryan Moore having ruled himself out of the race. Hughes, who was cut to 7-2 by Paddy Power the previous day, is pledging to pull out all the stops and is only 13 behind Hanagan. "I have had a three-day ban which I would say cost me five or six winners," says Hanagan. "That's why I have always said there is a long way to go and it is still very open. I am definitely not counting my chickens."

15   A decision on the future of the Tote moves a step closer when John Penrose, the Coalition's minister responsible for gambling, says he is launching a process to set a value for the pool betting monopoly. A team of accountants and lawyers working for the government's advisers Lazards moves in to the Tote's Wigan offices. One estimate of how much the Tote will fetch is £200 million, but that is half the amount mooted when the Tote was almost sold off three years earlier in 2007. However BHA chief executive Nic Coward disputes that the government owns the Tote, a body set up in 1928. This is reflected in an official statement from Penrose which says that the sale will recognise the support the Tote currently provides to the racing industry.

22   The British Flat season will have a different look to it in 2011 with the BHA approving a revamped Champions Day fixture at Ascot on October 15, despite protests from the French racing authorities. The French objection is that the fixture is two weeks after Arc weekend which could leave Longchamp with fewer stars than it is used to hosting. Protests from British racegoers focus on the moving of the Champion Stakes from Newmarket to Ascot, where it will be run on the same card as the Queen Elizabeth II Stakes. The Champion Stakes has a long history and has been run at Newmarket since 1877. From 2011 the equivalent fixture will be run a week before the Ascot meeting and will be billed

as Future Champions Day because of its emphasis on two-year-old racing. The Dewhurst Stakes and the Middle Park Stakes will be highlights. Ascot will also play host to two other races associated with Newmarket, the 2m Jockey Club Cup and the 1m4f Group 2 Pride Stakes for fillies and mares. There will be at least £3 million prize-money for the Ascot card. In a further piece of news the BHA reveals the finalised fixture list for 2011. It transpires that far fewer fixtures will be lost than was feared. Only 23 have been cut.

October

3   A great day at Longchamp for Britain when Workforce, ridden by Ryan Moore, lands the Prix de l'Arc de Triomphe to give Sir Michael Stoute his first winner of the race. The Newmarket man had left it until the Thursday before the race to confirm Workforce as a definite runner having been worried about his condition. The result fills a glaring gap in his trophy cabinet. "It's the ambition of any trainer to win the Arc," he says. "We've had a good crack at it. A lot of my horses have run very well but we've never quite hammered it. The King George haunted me. Ryan didn't give him the best of rides. He felt his tactics were wrong. On reflection I felt we had trained this big, immature horse too hard for the race." With an Oaks and Derby already under his belt in 2010, things have got even better for Stoute's stable jockey. On the same card another milestone is passed when Goldikova, the Freddie Head-trained mare, wins her 11th Group 1 breaking a European record for Group/Grade 1 wins. She is cut to 6-4 to follow up in the Breeders' Cup Mile.

7   Richard Hughes insists that the jockeys' title race is not over despite losing his appeal against a six-day ban.

22   The world's leading betting exchange, Betfair, makes its debut on the London stock market and the shares are floated at £13, valuing the company at £1.39 billion. At the end of the day the shares trade at £15.50, a rise of 19 per cent on the initial offering. However there are a few raised eyebrows when it emerges that a company that BHA chairman Paul Roy co-founded and chairs, New Smith, is now a major stakeholder in Betfair. Roy has regularly criticised Betfair for not contributing enough to horseracing.

November

2   Such is his antipathy to the revamping of the autumn fixture list proposed by Racing for Change and then ratified by the BHA, Jim McGrath resigns from the BHA in protest. He says he sees no merit in the rejigging of a four-week period based around a Champions Day at Ascot on October 15, describing it as "complete nonsense". He adds: "I found it very hard to agree with the suggested changes which will make British racing worse and weaker. How does running the Middle Park and Dewhurst on the same day make things better? There is no merit in the proposals. I've not heard one convincing argument for them." Meanwhile, with four days racing left in the British Flat season Richard Hughes is trailing Paul Hangan – 183 to 186. However Richard Hannon secures the Flat trainers' championship.

6   With 191 winners to his name, Paul Hanagan becomes champion jockey on the last day of the season. He beats Richard Hughes by two and says: "I can't believe it. I have so many people to thank, Richard Fahey mainly."

8   Johnny Murtagh resigns as stable jockey to Aidan O'Brien. Murtagh's agent releases a short statement thanking the Coolmore team and O'Brien for their support but doesn't spell out the reasons for his resignation. He was retained jockey at Ballydoyle since the start of the 2008 Flat season.

Outlook

Group 1 review
by Dylan Hill

For two-year-old Group 1s, see 'Two-year-olds of 2010', page 97

---

1 StanJames.com 2,000 Guineas Stakes (1m)
Newmarket May 1 (Good To Firm)
1 **Makfi** 3-9-0   Christophe-Patrice Lemaire
2 **Dick Turpin** 3-9-0   Ryan Moore
3 **Canford Cliffs** 3-9-0   Richard Hughes
33/1, 16/1, 12/1. 1¼l, ½l. 19 ran. 1m 36.35s (M Delzangles).

All the pre-race hype was about **St Nicholas Abbey**, but instead a new golden generation of milers emerged as **Makfi** saw off the Richard Hannon pair of **Dick Turpin** and **Canford Cliffs**, with the trio farming six Group 1 wins between them before the end of the season. Never previously tried above Group 3 level, French raider Makfi travelled well throughout and produced a telling turn of foot to overhaul Dick Turpin, while Canford Cliffs also cruised into contention but didn't have enough left to match the winner's finishing burst having pulled hard early. **Xtension** ran a solid race in fourth ahead of **Elusive Pimpernel** and St Nicholas Abbey, who both stayed on well having been outpaced.

2 StanJames.com 1,000 Guineas Stakes (Fillies) (1m)
Newmarket May 2 (Good To Soft)
2d **Jacqueline Quest** 3-9-0   Tom Queally
1 **Special Duty** 3-9-0   Stephane Pasquier
3 **Gile Na Greine** 3-9-0   K J Manning
66/1, 9/2F, 25/1. nse, hd. 17 ran. 1m 39.66s (Mme C Head-Maarek).

Huge controversy as **Special Duty** was awarded the race after an enquiry which saw first-past-the-post **Jacqueline Quest** demoted to second. Jacqueline Quest had edged out the favourite by a nose but carried her across the track in the final furlong, leaving little doubt that Special Duty was the better filly, although both were given a big helping hand by a huge

draw bias which saw the first five come from a small group on the stands' side. **Music Show** proved best of those on the far side in sixth, but even she struggled to shake off **Rumoush**, who would soon require much further, marking this out as an extremely moderate renewal.

3 totesport.com Lockinge Stakes (1m)
Newbury May 15 (Good To Firm)
1 **Paco Boy** 5-9-0   Richard Hughes
2 **Ouqba** 4-9-0   Richard Hills
3 **Lord Shanakill** 4-9-0   Tom Queally
8/11F, 16/1, 9/1. ¾l, 3½l. 9 ran. 1m 37.31s (R Hannon).

Paco Boy managed a third Group 1 win in successive seasons as he cruised to a remarkably easy victory in a weak contest. Paco Boy was always going supremely well and only needed to be pushed out in the final 50 yards to ease past **Ouqba**, who failed to make the grade later in the season, while **Lord Shanakill** was well below his best even in third.

4 Abu Dhabi Irish 2,000 Guineas (1m)
Curragh May 22 (Good To Firm)
1 **Canford Cliffs** 3-9-0   Richard Hughes
2 **Free Judgement** 3-9-0   K J Manning
3 **Viscount Nelson** 3-9-0   P J Smullen
9/4F, 25/1, 20/1. 3l, 1½l. 13 ran. 1m 37.64s (R Hannon).

Canford Cliffs got things right on his second crack at 1m as he ran out a comprehensive winner. Settling much better off a true gallop, Canford Cliffs was still cruising as he edged forward in the closing stages and he burst clear in the final furlong to thrash **Free Judgement** and **Viscount Nelson**, with **Steinbeck** staying on for fourth from the disappointing **Xtension**.

5 Etihad Airways Irish 1,000 Guineas (Fillies) (1m)
Curragh May 23 (Good To Firm)
1 **Bethrah** 3-9-0   P J Smullen

GOLDIKOVA (right): gets back on the Group 1 trail with victory in the Queen Anne

2 **Anna Salai** 3-9-0   Ahmed Ajtebi
3 **Music Show** 3-9-0   Ryan Moore
16/1, 15/2, 3/1F. hd, nk. 19 ran. 1m 37.49s
(D K Weld).

A blanket finish saw the first five separated by less than 1l, with 16-1 shot **Bethrah** coming out on top. Progressive in lesser company, Bethrah produced a strong late run to deny **Anna Salai**, while **Music Show**, favourite having been given no chance by the draw at Newmarket, still just came up short in third ahead of the Ballydoyle pair **Remember When** and **Lillie Langtry**, making her seasonal debut.

6 **Tattersalls Gold Cup (1m2f110yds)**
       Curragh May 23 (Good To Firm)
1 **Fame And Glory** 4-9-0   J Murtagh
2 **Recharge** 4-9-0   C D Hayes
3 **Chinese White** 5-8-11   P J Smullen
8/15F, 25/1, 6/1. 7l, nk. 6 ran. 2m 13.57s
(A P O'Brien).

The 2009 Irish Derby hero **Fame And Glory**, twice denied further success by Sea The Stars in 2009, added another overdue Group 1 win as he ruthlessly destroyed his rivals. Pacemaker **Dixie Music** set up the race perfectly and Fame And Glory galloped clear from before the 2f pole, with smart mare **Chinese White** among those beaten out of sight, while **Cutlass Bay** kicked off his bitterly disappointing campaign for Godolphin in fifth.

7 **Investec Coronation Cup (1m4f10yds)**
       Epsom June 4 (Good)
1 **Fame And Glory** 4-9-0   J Murtagh
2 **Sariska** 4-8-11   Jamie Spencer
3 **High Heeled** 4-8-11   William Buick

5/6F, 5/2, 25/1. 1½l, 1¼l. 9 ran. 2m 33.42s
(A P O'Brien).

A quickfire double for **Fame And Glory**, who faced far stiffer competition with dual Classic heroine **Sariska** and both placed horses from the 2009 Arc up against him but proved well up to the task. Taking over from pacemaker **Dixie Music** 3f out, Fame And Glory was soon joined by Sariska but powered clear once hitting top gear while Sariska also stayed on well to hold off another filly, **High Heeled**, for second. **Youmzain** and **Cavalryman** both ran decent races without ever being able to land a blow.

8 **Investec Oaks (Fillies) (1m4f10yds)**
       Epsom June 4 (Good)
1 **Snow Fairy** 3-9-0   Ryan Moore
2 **Meeznah** 3-9-0   Ted Durcan
3 **Remember When** 3-9-0   J Murtagh
9/1, 25/1, 8/1. nk, 2l. 15 ran. 2m 35.77s
(E A L Dunlop).

A modest renewal was lit up by a magical performance from **Snow Fairy**, who looked in an impossible position for much of the race but showed great speed to find a succession of gaps and got up in the final 50 yards. Snow Fairy just denied another strong finisher in **Meeznah**, who was demoted several months later for failing a dope test, with **Remember When** in third and a 4l gap back to **Rumoush**. However, with that one hampered at a key stage and **Akdarena** failing to stay in sixth, the overall form proved extremely modest and several fillies were beaten much further next time out by Hibaayeb in the Ribblesdale.

9 Investec Derby (1m4f10yds)
Epsom June 5 (Good To Firm)

1	**Workforce** 3-9-0	Ryan Moore
2	**At First Sight** 3-9-0	J A Heffernan
3	**Rewilding** 3-9-0	Frankie Dettori

6/1, 100/1, 9/2. 7l, ½l. 12 ran. 2m 31.33s
(Sir Michael Stoute).

Workforce proved head and shoulders above his rivals as he stormed to a sensational win. Racing for only the third time, Workforce produced an electrifying turn of foot to chase down the runaway leader **At First Sight** and simply powered further and further clear, pointing the way to a crack at the top all-aged 1m4f prizes. At First Sight proved hugely flattered by his second place having been gifted a big cushion in front, but the form stood up well otherwise with **Rewilding** staying on well in third ahead of the Aidan O'Brien pair **Jan Vermeer** and **Midas Touch**, while **Al Zir** and **Coordinated Cut** were next ahead of the subsequent German Derby hero **Buzzword**.

10 Queen Anne Stakes (1m)
Ascot June 15 (Good)

1	**Goldikova** 5-8-11	Olivier Peslier
2	**Paco Boy** 5-9-0	Richard Hughes
3	**Dream Eater** 5-9-0	Jimmy Fortune

11/8F, 11/4, 50/1. nk, 3¼l. 10 ran. 1m 37.74s
(F Head).

Goldikova made only her second appearance in Britain a winning one as she just held off the fast-finishing **Paco Boy** in a thrilling finish despite not quite showing the sparkle that would later see her break Miesque's all-time Group 1 record and land a third successive Breeders' Cup Mile. Goldikova struck for home 2f out but seemed to idle in front and was nearly caught close home by Paco Boy, leading many to suggest the runner-up was unlucky, though he later finished behind Goldikova three times to show that he wasn't quite in the great mare's league. **Dream Eater** stuck on well for third, while **Rip Van Winkle** badly needed his first run of the season in sixth.

11 King's Stand Stakes (5f)
Ascot June 15 (Good)

1	**Equiano** 5-9-4	Michael Hills
2	**Markab** 7-9-4	Pat Cosgrave
3	**Borderlescott** 8-9-4	Neil Callan

9/2, 14/1, 16/1. 1½l, nk. 12 ran. 59.00s
(B W Hills).

Equiano became the first British winner since 2004 as big Australian hope **Nicconi** could manage only fourth. Back to his 2008-winning form for the first time since moving to Barry Hills from Spain, Equiano broke well and made all the running as he comfortably shook off **Markab** and **Borderlescott** for a hugely impressive win. Nicconi endured a troubled passage from the rear but at least stayed on past the disappointing favourite **Kingsgate Native** in sixth.

12 St James's Palace Stakes (1m)
Ascot June 15 (Good)

1	**Canford Cliffs** 3-9-0	Richard Hughes
2	**Dick Turpin** 3-9-0	Ryan Moore
3	**Hearts Of Fire** 3-9-0	Jimmy Fortune

11/4J, 5/1, 33/1. 1l, ¾l. 9 ran. 1m 39.55s
(R Hannon).

Newmarket form was turned on its head as **Canford Cliffs** confirmed his improvement with a tremendous win over **Dick Turpin** while **Makfi** was a hugely disappointing seventh. Canford Cliffs again settled well and produced a typically strong late burst to cut down Dick Turpin in the final 100 yards, though whether he would have beaten an on-song Makfi, who was found to be suffering from a throat infection and bounced back to turn over the mighty Goldikova and Paco Boy in the Prix Jacques le Marois, will never be known. **Hearts Of Fire** and **Siyouni** also ran good races to finish ahead of the American challenger **Noble's Promise**.

13 Prince of Wales's Stakes (1m2f)
Ascot June 16 (Good To Firm)

1	**Byword** 4-9-0	Maxime Guyon
2	**Twice Over** 5-9-0	Tom Queally
3	**Tazeez** 6-9-0	Tadhg O'Shea

5/2F, 11/2, 40/1. ½l, ¾l. 12 ran. 2m 5.35s
(A Fabre).

The progressive **Byword** took a fairly soft first step up to Group 1 level in his stride as he just held off the fast-finishing **Twice Over**. Byword was always well placed and made a decisive move 2f out, with Twice Over the only hold-up horse able to even remotely challenge him, and he would duly put the record straight under a better-judged ride in the Juddmonte International at York. The front-running **Tazeez** managed to hold on to third ahead of **Stimulation** and German raider **Wiener Walzer**.

14 Gold Cup (2m4f)
Ascot June 17 (Good To Firm)

1	**Rite Of Passage** 6-9-2	P J Smullen
2	**Age Of Aquarius** 4-9-0	J Murtagh
3	**Purple Moon** 7-9-2	Kieren Fallon

20/1, 8/1, 12/1. nk, 6l. 12 ran. 4m 16.92s
(D K Weld).

A new era for the stayers with Yeats out of the way and none of the field having ever run in the race before, and **Rite Of Passage** became an unlikely champion on only his third ever Flat start. With connections only encouraged to race on the Flat at the end of 2009 after a promising bumper campaign, Rite Of Passage's stamina won the day as he edged past **Age Of**

Aquarius in a thrilling battle after the runner-up, sadly retired after picking up an injury at Goodwood next time, had briefly quickened clear turning for home. The pair pulled 6l clear of **Purple Moon** with the rest of the field well strung out, including patent non-stayers **Ask** and **Manifest**.

15 Coronation Stakes (Fillies) (1m)
Ascot June 18 (Good To Firm)
1 **Lillie Langtry** 3-9-0   J Murtagh
2 **Gile Na Greine** 3-9-0   K J Manning
3 **Jacqueline Quest** 3-9-0   Tom Queally
7/2F, 25/1, 6/1. 1¼l, 2¼l. 13 ran. 1m 39.69s
(A P O'Brien).

The first authoritative performance by a three-year-old filly over a mile as **Lillie Langtry** produced a tremendous run in the straight to cut down **Gile Na Greine** and win going away. Much improved for her return at the Curragh, Lillie Langtry picked up well to comfortably see off the long-time leader, who had been given the run of the race in front as she reversed Newmarket form with **Jacqueline Quest** in third, while **Music Show**, again done few favours by a wide draw, ran creditably enough in fourth.

16 Golden Jubilee Stakes (6f)
Ascot June 19 (Good To Firm)
1 **Starspangledbanner** 4-9-4   J Murtagh
2 **Society Rock** 3-8-11   Pat Cosgrave
3 **Kinsale King** 5-9-4   Kieren Fallon
13/2J, 50/1, 8/1. 1¾l. hd. 24 ran. 1m 12.57s
(A P O'Brien).

A much stronger international flavour than the King's Stand with six countries represented and Aidan O'Brien even relied on an Aussie import, **Starspangledbanner**, to win. Starspangledbanner broke well and made virtually all, staying on strongly from the youngster **Society Rock**, who led the British challenge with distinction by holding off American raider **Kinsale King** for third. **Fleeting Spirit** was best on the far side in fourth and would almost certainly have been second with a more favourable draw, with **War Artist** and **Varenar** next in that group.

17 Audi Pretty Polly Stakes (Fillies & Mares) (1m2f)
Curragh June 26 (Good To Firm)
1 **Chinese White** 5-9-9   P J Smullen
2 **Flying Cloud** 4-9-9   Frankie Dettori
3 **Akdarena** 3-8-11   K J Manning
4/1, 3/1, 5/1. 1¼l, shd. 9 ran. 2m 3.84s
(D K Weld).

Chinese White put Ireland's younger generation in their place as she battled to a narrow victory on her final appearance before retirement. Placed only once in four previous attempts at the top level, Chinese White was still best placed to overhaul **Akdarena** in the

final furlong as her brave attempt to make all came short in the final furlong, with **Flying Cloud** also staying on late into second. **Remember When** could never throw down a challenge and was beaten just over 7l in fourth.

18 Dubai Duty Free Irish Derby (1m4f)
Curragh June 27 (Good To Firm)
1 **Cape Blanco** 3-9-0   J Murtagh
2 **Midas Touch** 3-9-0   C O'Donoghue
3 **Jan Vermeer** 3-9-0   J A Heffernan
7/2, 9/2, 4/1. ½l, 1½l. 10 ran. 2m 28.68s
(A P O'Brien).

Aidan O'Brien put a string of disappointments for his big Derby hopes behind him as he saddled the first three, with French Derby flop **Cape Blanco** leading the way. **Midas Touch** and **Jan Vermeer** also showed they were much better than their Epsom form, but neither could match the pace of Cape Blanco, who had been unbeaten prior to Chantilly and produced a strong run down the outside to win well. The form was solid with the fourth, **Monterosso**, having put **At First Sight** in his place when winning at Royal Ascot and again finishing clear of the Derby second, though with just 3l sepa-rating the first four none of the principals would trouble the very best at this trip.

19 Coral-Eclipse (1m2f7yds)
Sandown July 3 (Good To Firm)
1 **Twice Over** 5-9-7   Tom Queally
2 **Sri Putra** 4-9-7   Philip Robinson
3 **Viscount Nelson** 3-8-10   J Murtagh
13/8F, 33/1, 4/1. ½l, ½l. 5 ran. 2m 4.64s
(H R A Cecil).

Having looked an unlucky loser at Royal Ascot, **Twice Over** confirmed he was still on the upgrade at the age of five as he eased to a far cosier win than the eventual margin would indicate. Driven straight to the front with none of the quintet likely to force the pace, Twice Over kicked clear turning for home and was soon in complete command before seemingly idling as **Sri Putra** narrowed the gap. **Viscount Nelson**, disappointingly the only three-year-old in the field, at least upheld Classic form having been beaten just as comfortably by Canford Cliffs in Ireland, but **Dar Re Mi** was well below her best.

20 Etihad Airways Falmouth Stakes (Fillies & Mares) (1m)
Newmarket July 7 (Good To Firm)
1 **Music Show** 3-8-10   Richard Hughes
2 **Spacious** 5-9-5   Kieren Fallon
3 **Rainfall** 3-8-10   Frankie Dettori
13/2, 9/1, 15/2. 2l, ¾l. 8 ran. 1m 36.76s
(M R Channon).

Out of luck earlier in the season, **Music Show** took the chance to finally show her true colours as she ran out a ready winner. **Spacious** perhaps failed to turn the race into a sufficient test in front, but either way Music Show showed a hitherto unseen turn of foot to quickly put the contest to bed in the final furlong, quickening away from Spacious with **Rainfall** a good third. **Strawberrydaiquiri**, who had just beaten the runner-up at Royal Ascot, would have been in a similar position again but for being badly hampered, but **Lillie Langtry** was well below-par in fifth and **Special Duty** flopped having pulled muscles.

21 Darley July Cup (6f) Newmarket July 9 (Good To Firm)

1	**Starspangledbanner** 4-9-5	J Murtagh
2	**Equiano** 5-9-5	Michael Hills
3	**Alverta** 7-9-2	Tye Angland

2/1F, 12/1, 66/1. nk, ¾l. 14 ran. 1m 9.81s (A P O'Brien).

A wonderful battle between Royal Ascot winners **Starspangledbanner** and **Equiano**, with Starspangledbanner's stamina just proving decisive in the end. Hard ridden to stay close to Equiano for much of the way, Starspangledbanner finally wore him down in the final furlong to prove himself a real champion, in spite of subsequent failures, as the pair proved too good for Australian mare **Alverta** and the back-to-form **Kingsgate Native**. **Fleeting Spirit** was slightly below-par in fifth as **Varenar** got much closer than he had at Royal Ascot, with connections blaming the fast ground, while **Society Rock** got going too late in seventh.

22 Darley Irish Oaks (Fillies) (1m4f) Curragh July 18 (Good To Yielding)

1	**Snow Fairy** 3-9-0	Ryan Moore
2	**Miss Jean Brodie** 3-9-0	William Buick
3	**Lady Lupus** 3-9-0	J P O'Brien

7/2, 33/1, 66/1. 8l, ¾l. 15 ran. 2m 34.87s (E A L Dunlop).

A far more comprehensive victory for **Snow Fairy**, who was helped by some below-par performances down the field but still underlined her clear superiority over her rivals. Snow Fairy was always going well and quickened clear in supreme fashion, thrashing the Godolphin second string **Miss Jean Brodie** and mudlark **Lady Lupus** with Epsom runner-up **Meeznah** only fourth. **Remember When** was again disappointing, while favourite **Hibaayeb** failed to act on the ground.

23 King George VI and Queen Elizabeth Stakes (1m4f)

Ascot July 24 (Good)

1	**Harbinger** 4-9-7	Olivier Peslier
2	**Cape Blanco** 3-8-9	C O'Donoghue
3	**Youmzain** 7-9-7	Richard Hughes

4/1, 9/2, 12/1. 11l, 3¼l. 6 ran. 2m 26.78s (Sir Michael Stoute).

An outstanding performance from **Harbinger** as he inflicted the largest winning margin in the race's history on what had looked a strong field. **Workforce** and **Cape Blanco** formed the strongest three-year-old challenge for many years, and while Workforce was clearly well

STARSPANGLEDBANNER (right): holds off Equiano for a memorable sprint double

below his best, seemingly set alight by chasing the strong early pace, it's hard to imagine he would have had a chance against the brilliant winner as Harbinger, who was always travelling ominously well, quickened away from his rivals in a matter of strides and powered relentlessly clear – the Arc was surely there for the taking but for injury. Cape Blanco seemed to run his race and did well to hold off **Youmzain** for second, while French filly **Daryakana** also edged in front of the out-of-sorts Derby winner.

24 Sussex Stakes (1m)
Goodwood July 28 (Good To Firm)
1 **Canford Cliffs** 3-8-13   Richard Hughes
2 **Rip Van Winke** 4-9-7   Ryan Moore
3 **Premio Loco** 6-9-7   George Baker
4/6F, 9/4, 17/2. nk, 3¼l. 7 ran. 1m 37.44s
(R Hannon).

A vintage clash of the generations with **Canford Cliffs** completing a Group 1 hat-trick against **Rip Van Winkle**. The 2009 winner made a terrific bid to follow up, kicking past his pacemaker into a clear lead at the furlong pole and finishing further in front of the solid fifth **Dream Eater** than fellow big guns Goldikova and Paco Boy had managed in the Queen Anne, yet he still could never seriously inconvenience Canford Cliffs, who quickened past

him in a matter of strides and was immediately eased for an astonishingly cosy victory. **Premio Loco** ran a cracker in third ahead of **Beethoven** and Dream Eater.

25 Blue Square Nassau Stakes (Fillies & Mares) (1m1f192yds)
Goodwood July 31 (Good To Firm)
1 **Midday** 4-9-6   Tom Queally
2 **Stacelita** 4-9-6   Christophe Soumillon
3 **Antara** 4-9-6   Frankie Dettori
15/8F, 9/2, 8/1. 1¼l, 1l. 7 ran. 2m 7.25s
(H R A Cecil).

A second successive win in the race for the brilliant **Midday**, who won rather more comfortably than the margin suggests given she tried to pull herself up having roared into the lead 2f out before summoning another telling burst of speed to see off French filly **Stacelita**. **Antara** ran a fine race as she reversed previous form with **Strawberrydaiquiri**, who seemed to see out the trip on her first crack at 1m2f despite coming up in short in fourth.

26 Juddmonte International Stakes (1m2f88yds)
York August 17 (Good)
1 **Rip Van Winke** 4-9-5   J Murtagh
2 **Twice Over** 5-9-5   Tom Queally
3 **Byword** 4-9-5   Maxime Guyon

RIP VAN WINKLE (left): swoops late to deny Byword (centre) and Twice Over (right)

7/4F, 6/1, 11/4. ½l, ¾l. 9 ran. 2m 8.58s
(A P O'Brien).

Running over 1m2f for the first time since his
brilliant second to Sea The Stars in the 2009
Eclipse, **Rip Van Winkle** relished every yard
of the trip as he got up late to deny **Twice Over**
in a thrilling battle. Rip Van Winkle took time
to respond having been asked for his effort 3f
out but finally produced a sustained surge in
the final 150 yards to nail the unfortunate Twice
Over, who had turned the tables on his Royal
Ascot conqueror **Byword** by getting the better of a protracted duel in the straight. The first
three were 4l clear of **Cavalryman**, while **Dick
Turpin** was unable to settle on his first attempt
at the trip in fifth.

27 Darley Yorkshire Oaks (Fillies &
Mares) (1m4f)
York August 19 (Good)
1 **Midday** 4-9-7   Tom Queally
2 **Snow Fairy** 3-8-11   Richard Hughes
3 **Eleanora Duse** 3-8-11   Olivier Peslier
11/4, 5/2, 25/1. 3l, 2l. 8 ran. 2m 30.53s
(H R A Cecil).

A vintage clash of the generations suffered an
early blow when **Sariska** refused to race, but
the older fillies still held sway as **Midday** ran
out a tremendous winner from **Snow Fairy**.
Midday left her rival behind with a stunning turn
of foot approaching the final furlong, and even
though Snow Fairy had no answer to such brilliance, she still seemed to run up to her best
in second, beating a back-to-form **Meeznah**
more comfortably than she had at Epsom as
the Oaks runner-up was run out of third by the
progressive **Eleanora Duse**. That quartet
pulled a whopping 8l clear of **Flying Cloud**.

28 Coolmore Nunthorpe Stakes (5f)
York August 20 (Good To Firm)
1 **Sole Power** 3-9-9   W M Lordan
2 **Starspangledbanner** 4-9-11   J Murtagh
3 **Piccadilly Filly** 3-9-6   Eddie Creighton
100/1, 6/4F, 100/1. 1¼l, 1¼l. 12 ran. 57.14s
(Edward Lynam).

A colossal upset as Irish rag **Sole Power**, who
had broken the course record at Dundalk earlier
in the season before disappointing in his last
three races, landed the spoils at 100-1. The
result was even more remarkable given that four
of the first five in the market were in-form multiple
Group 1 winners, but only **Starspangledbanner**
ran anywhere near his best and he just found
the drop to 5f against him whereas Sole Power
proved all speed as he picked up the trail-
blazing **Rose Blossom** at the furlong pole and
won going away. **Piccadilly Filly** and **Prime
Defender** also stayed on past the early leader
to place the form in a fairly modest light, while

SOLE POWER: shock Nunthorpe winner

Equiano badly missed the break, **Kingsgate
Native** had one of his frequent off-days and
Borderlescott was well below-par.

29 Coolmore Fusaichi Pegasus Matron
Stakes (Fillies & Mares) (1m)
Leopardstown September 4 (Good)
1 **Lillie Langtry** 3-8-12   J Murtagh
2 **Spacious** 5-9-3   Kieren Fallon
3 **Music Show** 3-8-12   F M Berry
7/2, 11/4, 2/1F. nk, 1¼l. 6 ran. 1m 39.68s
(A P O'Brien).

Lillie Langtry bounced back to form to confirm
herself the best three-year-old filly in Europe
over a mile, though she still had to pull out all
the stops to see off **Spacious**. The runner-up
made a typically bold bid for an elusive Group
1 as she struck for home early, but Lillie Langtry
tracked her move and just proved stronger in
the final furlong. **Music Show** came up short
in third, while **Bethrah**, returning from a break,
briefly threatened in the straight before fading
into fifth.

30 Tattersalls Millions Irish Champion
Stakes (1m2f)
Leopardstown September 4 (Good)
1 **Cape Blanco** 3-9-0   J A Heffernan
2 **Rip Van Winke** 4-9-7   J Murtagh
3 **Twice Over** 5-9-7   Tom Queally
6/1, 8/11F, 100/30. 5½l, shd. 6 ran. 2m 3.89s
(A P O'Brien).

MARKAB (left): the progressive sprinter was too strong for the filly Lady Of The Desert

A strongly-run 1m2f proved the key to unlocking **Cape Blanco**'s potential as he romped to a wide-margin win, though it remains to be seen whether he will prove quite as effective when not allowed his own way in front. Cape Blanco was soon well clear of his rivals, setting a searching gallop, and he showed few signs of stopping as a quality field, led by **Rip Van Winkle** and **Twice Over**, could never get close. That pair ran close to York form, though the proximity of **Beethoven** and **Sea Lord** suggests neither had fully recovered from those exertions.

31 Betfred Sprint Cup (6f)
Haydock September 4 (Good To Firm)

1	**Markab** 7-9-3	Pat Cosgrave
2	**Lady Of The Desert** 3-8-12	M Dwyer
3	**Genki** 6-9-3	Steve Drowne

12/1, 9/1, 20/1. 1¼l, 1l. 13 ran. 1m 9.40s (H Candy).

Seemingly much improved when second in the King's Stand and far more at home over 6f, **Markab** made a nonsense of his 12-1 odds to land a thoroughly merited Group 1 win. Markab made all on the stands' side and did best of the six in that group by more than 5l, while **Lady Of The Desert**, who hadn't quite made the grade over 1m, proved she was a top-class filly down in trip with a win in the Diadem and a fine second over an inadequate 5f in the Abbaye to follow. **Genki** became the latest handicapper to graduate to Pattern class in third ahead of the infuriating **Kingsgate Native**, who was doing all his best work at the death despite having previously looked best over 5f, while **Starspangledbanner** was well below his best in fifth.

32 Ladbrokes St Leger (1m6f132yds)
Doncaster September 11 (Good)

1	**Arctic Cosmos** 3-9-0	William Buick
2	**Midas Touch** 3-9-0	C O'Donoghue
3	**Corsica** 3-9-0	Joe Fanning

12/1, 13/2, 40/1. 1¾l, nse. 10 ran. 3m 3.12s (J H M Gosden).

A searching test of stamina, seemingly for the benefit of red-hot favourite **Rewilding**, instead played into the hands of **Arctic Cosmos**, who had plenty to find on the form book on two placed efforts in lesser Pattern company but relished stepping up in trip and proved too strong for his rivals. **Corsica** set a fierce gallop for Rewilding, who had easily beaten runner-up **Midas Touch** in the Great Voltigeur, but he was soon struggling and failed to even pass his pacemaker as Arctic Cosmos produced a withering run down the outside to see off Midas Touch. Oaks winner **Snow Fairy** was ridden with exaggerated waiting tactics to get the trip but could produce only a brief effort when pressed, finishing fourth, and with neither of the form horses showing their best Arctic Cosmos still has plenty to prove at the top level.

33 The Irish Field St Leger (1m6f) Curragh September 11 (Soft)

1 **Sans Frontieres** 4-9-11   Olivier Peslier
2 **Profound Beauty** 6-9-8   P J Smullen
3 **Flying Cross** 3-9-0   J Murtagh
13/8F, 5/2, 7/1. ¾l, 1¾l. 8 ran. 3m 10.36s (J Noseda).

A desperately poor contest for the top level, but **Sans Frontieres** had the best form following a pair of Group wins over slightly shorter and managed to make his class pay, showing far too much speed for the solid mare **Profound Beauty** inside the final furlong.

34 Queen Elizabeth II Stakes (1m) Ascot September 25 (Good To Soft)

1 **Poet's Voice** 3-8-13   Frankie Dettori
2 **Rip Van Winke** 4-9-3   J Murtagh
3 **Red Jazz** 3-8-13   Michael Hills
9/2, 11/4, 40/1. nse, ½l. 8 ran. 1m 39.76s (Saeed Bin Suroor).

A surprise result as **Poet's Voice**, a former leading juvenile bouncing back from a disappointing spring, just touched off the 2009 winner **Rip Van Winkle** with favourite **Makfi** flopping in fifth. Rip Van Winkle had the race run to suit with pacemaker **Air Chief Marshal** ensuring a true test, but he was short of his best when asked to assert in the straight, even struggling to shake off **Red Jazz** and seeing **Beethoven** finish a couple of lengths closer in fourth than he had in the Sussex Stakes, and that allowed Poet's Voice to cut him down with a terrific turn of foot from the rear. Red Jazz still produced a much-improved effort in third, franked by his subsequent Challenge Stakes win.

35 Kingdom of Bahrain Sun Chariot Stakes (Fillies & Mares) (1m) Newmarket October 2 (Soft)

1 **Sahpresa** 5-9-2   Christophe Soumillon
2 **Strawberrydaiquiri** 4-9-2   Ryan Moore
3 **Rainfall** 3-8-13   Frankie Dettori
9/2, 5/1, 6/1. 1¾l, 1l. 11 ran. 1m 38.80s (Rod Collet).

French raider **Sahpresa** won the race for the second successive year as she exposed the shortcomings of the domestic fillies with a comprehensive victory. The globetrotting mare was always going well as she cut down her rivals and quickened clear in the final furlong, easily seeing off **Strawberrydaiquiri**, who ran a fine race in second ahead of **Rainfall**. **Music Show** again failed to confirm the promise of her Falmouth win in a disappointing fourth, followed by the staying-on **Aviate**, but **Spacious** and **Seta** were well below-par.

36 Qatar Prix De L'Arc De Triomphe (1m4f) Longchamp October 3 (Very Soft)

1 **Workforce** 3-8-11   Ryan Moore
2 **Nakayama Festa** 4-9-5   Masayoshi Ebina
3 **Sarafina** 3-8-8   Gerald Mosse
6/1, 22/1, 12/1. hd, 2½l. 19 ran. 2m 35.30s (Sir Michael Stoute).

Workforce confirmed his status as a truly vintage Derby winner as he fought hard to land a tremendous victory over Japanese raider **Nakayama Festa**. There were plenty of hard-luck stories in a rough race, but Workforce, taught to settle better since his Ascot flop, looked in as much trouble as any of his rivals as he turned for home with a wall of horses in front of him and showed great speed to quicken through the gaps before staying on strongly when pressed throughout the final furlong. **Sarafina** was the most unlucky horse in the race as she finished with a tremendous rattle in third having been forced to make her move from miles back, while **Behkabad** and **Fame And Glory** were next having had little luck in running but lacked Workforce's speed in recovering. **Youmzain** and **Cape Blanco** were among the also-rans.

37 Emirates Airline Champion Stakes (1m2f) Newmarket October 16 (Good To Soft)

1 **Twice Over** 5-9-3   Tom Queally
2 **Vision D'Etat** 5-9-3   Olivier Peslier
3 **Debussy** 4-9-3   William Buick
7/2, 3/1F, 10/1. 1¾l, ¾l. 10 ran. 2m 8.54s (H R A Cecil).

Twice Over bounced back to form in brilliant fashion as he stormed to a second successive win in the race. Always lying handy off a muddling pace, Twice Over struck decisively for home 2f out and comfortably held off old rival **Vision D'Etat**, who had beaten Twice Over into fourth in a tight finish to the 2009 Prince of Wales's Stakes but could never get on terms this time as he just shook off **Debussy** and **Gitano Hernando** for second. **Poet's Voice** was stepped up in trip after his QEII win but failed to settle and faded into ninth.

Group 1 index

All horses placed or commented on in our Group 1 review section, with race numbers

Outlook

Two-year-olds of 2010
by Dylan Hill

1 bluesq.com National Stakes (Listed) (5f6yds)

Sandown May 27 (Good To Firm)
1 **Dinkum Diamond** 2-9-0   Dane O'Neill
2 **Chilworth Lad** 2-9-0   Ryan Moore
3 **Cape To Rio** 2-9-0   Richard Hughes
9/4, 6/1, 11/8F. 1¼l, hd. 6 ran. 1m 1.88s
(H Candy).

A decent early-season contest with the first three having won four of their previous five starts between them and pulling more than 3l clear of the rest, and **Dinkum Diamond** proved best of the lot as he stayed on strongly to beat **Chilworth Lad** and **Cape To Rio**.

2 Investec Woodcote Stakes (Listed) (6f)

Epsom June 5 (Good To Firm)
1 **High Award** 2-9-0   J Murtagh
2 **Dubawi Gold** 2-9-0   Phillip Makin
3 **Premier Clarets** 2-9-0   Paul Hanagan
7/1, 5/2F, 11/2. 1½l, hd. 9 ran. 1m 9.23s
(T Stack).

Epsom is always a tough test for a juvenile and Irish raider **High Award** coped best as he stayed out of trouble with more talented juveniles suffering behind, most notably **Approve**, who had no luck in running and finished an eyecatching fourth.

3 Coolmore Stud Fillies' Stakes (Group 3) (6f)

Naas June 7 (Good To Firm)
1 **Radharcnafarraige** 2-8-12   K J Manning
2 **Emerald Ring** 2-8-12   W M Lordan
3 **Juliet Capulet** 2-8-12   J A Heffernan
2/1F, 10/1, 25/1. 3l, 2½l. 8 ran. 1m 10.43s
(J S Bolger).

An excellent performance from **Radharcna-farraige**, who booked her Royal Ascot ticket as she was the only filly to race up with a strong gallop who was able to keep up the momentum, running her rivals into the ground. In contrast **Geesala**, among the most precocious British

fillies having already won a Listed race at Beverley, dropped out to finish last.

4 Coventry Stakes (Group 2) (6f)

Ascot June 15 (Good)
1 **Strong Suit** 2-9-1   Richard Hughes
2 **Elzaam** 2-9-1   Richard Hills
3 **Roayh** 2-9-1   Frankie Dettori
15/8F, 3/1, 22/1. nse, 2½l. 13 ran. 1m 14.29s
(R Hannon).

A slightly misleading race in retrospect with the first four failing to win in 12 subsequent attempts at Pattern level, though **Strong Suit** and **Elzaam** still created big enough impressions to suggest both could be worth further chances. Elzaam looked to have won the race with an impressive turn of foot at the furlong pole, but Strong Suit, having been short of room, flew home to get up on the line with the pair 2¹/₂l clear of **Roayh**. There was a further gap back to **Samuel Morse**, while Ballydoyle first string **Zoffany** was a disappointing sixth.

5 Windsor Castle Stakes (Listed) (5f)

Ascot June 15 (Good)
1 **Marine Commando** 2-9-3 Paul Hanagan
2 **Petronius Maximus** 2-9-3   J Murtagh
3 **Excello** 2-8-12   Ian Mongan
9/2, 20/1, 14/1. nk, nse. 14 ran. 1m 1.09s
(R A Fahey).

This race attracted an unusually small field, but **Stone Of Folca** still went off much too fast in front and set the race up for a pair of clearly inferior rivals as **Marine Commando** came with a late run and just held the even faster-finishing **Petronius Maximus**, both falling well short of expectations later.

6 Queen Mary Stakes (Group 2) (Fillies) (5f)

Ascot June 16 (Good To Firm)
1 **Maqaasid** 2-8-12   Richard Hills
2 **Meow** 2-8-12   J Murtagh
3 **Ladies Are Forever** 2-8-12   Tom Eaves
9/4F, 7/2, 10/1. nk, nk. 18 ran. 59.17s

(J H M Gosden).

The market called this perfectly as favourite **Maqaasid** did well to quicken past chief rival **Meow** and **Ladies Are Forever**, but the draw was still the key factor as the first four astonishingly came from the highest four stalls in exact draw order and none of those involved proved particularly special. The trio pulled 5l clear of **Serena's Pride** with **Moonlit Garden** best of those drawn low in seventh, but even she proved overrated, twice beaten favourite at Listed level in her next two starts.

7 Norfolk Stakes (Group 2) (5f)
Ascot June 17 (Good To Firm)
1 **Approve** 2-9-1   Eddie Ahern
2 **Reckless Reward** 2-9-1   Ryan Moore
3 **Excel Bolt** 2-9-1   Tom Eaves
16/1, 16/1, 7/1. 1¼l, ½l. 12 ran. 1m 0.14s
(W J Haggas).

Dropping back to 5f for the last time after an unlucky fourth in the Woodcote, **Approve** produced a remarkable performance as he put a decent field of speedsters to the sword. Approve produced a strong late run past **Reckless Reward** and **Excel Bolt**, while **Stone Of Folca**, benefiting from a more patient ride, finished a good fourth with class act **Zebedee**, who went off too fast, and **Dinkum Diamond** next to give the form a solid look.

8 Albany Stakes (Group 3) (Fillies) (6f)
Ascot June 18 (Good To Firm)
1 **Memory** 2-8-12   Richard Hughes
2 **Margot Did** 2-8-12   Hayley Turner
3 **Tiz My Time** 2-8-12   Kieren Fallon
15/2, 7/1, 16/1. hd, 2½l. 22 ran. 1m 13.70s
(R Hannon).

An excellent contest as **Memory** just got the better of **Margot Did** with the pair pulling clear of several useful rivals. Memory was slowly away and behind early, but she showed her class by collaring the runner-up close home, Margot Did having comfortably shaken off **Tiz My Time** and favourite **Radharcnafarraige** with the likes of **Crying Lightening** and **Hooray** in the chasing pack.

9 Chesham Stakes (Listed) (7f)
Ascot June 19 (Good To Firm)
1 **Zaidan** 2-9-3   Seb Sanders
2 **Sonning Rose** 2-8-12   Alan Munro
3 **Casper's Touch** 2-9-3   Kieren Fallon
7/1, 12/1, 9/1. 3l, ¾l. 12 ran. 1m 27.51s
(C E Brittain).

A runaway win for **Zaidan**, who came through to lead well over a furlong out and stayed on strongly with seven previously unbeaten horses strung out behind him, though the class horse of the race, **King Torus**, saw his chance

badly compromised by a poor draw and could manage only fourth. Useful filly **Sonning Rose** did well to claim second ahead of American raider **Casper's Touch**.

10 totesport.com Empress Stakes (Listed) (Fillies) (6f)
Newmarket June 26 (Good To Firm)
1 **Khor Sheed** 2-8-12   Kieren Fallon
2 **Shoshoni Wind** 2-8-12   Jamie Spencer
3 **Imperialistic Diva** 2-8-12   Ted Durcan
3/1, 5/2F, 7/1. 1l, nk. 7 ran. 1m 13.23s
(L M Cumani)

A highly promising effort from **Khor Sheed**, who won with great authority over an admittedly moderate runner-up in **Shoshoni Wind**, and despite failing to live up to expectations when twice tried at Pattern level, she again suggested she was still capable of winning in a higher grade when landing a sales race at Newmarket later in the year.

11 Ladbrokes.com Railway Stakes (Group 2) (6f)
Curragh June 27 (Good To Firm)
1 **Formosina** 2-9-1   Ryan Moore
2 **Samuel Morse** 2-9-1   J Murtagh
3 **Clondinnery** 2-9-1   K Latham
7/2, 5/2F, 7/2. shd, nk. 7 ran. 1m 10.77s
(J Noseda).

Formosina became the first British winner since 1996 as he took advantage of an unusually modest Ballydoyle challenge with only Coventry fourth **Samuel Morse** running for Aidan O'Brien. Formosina was short of room for much of the race but finished well to pip Samuel Morse, while Listed winner **Clondinnery** was third ahead of **Chilworth Lad** and **High Award**.

12 Irish Thoroughbred Marketing Cherry Hinton Stakes (Group 2) (Fillies) (6f)
Newmarket July 7 (Good To Firm)
1 **Memory** 2-8-12   Richard Hughes
2 **Soraaya** 2-8-12   Ryan Moore
3 **Hooray** 2-8-12   Seb Sanders
5/4F, 10/1, 9/2. ¾l, ½l. 7 ran. 1m 12.44s
(R Hannon).

Memory followed up her Royal Ascot victory with an equally impressive win despite its narrow margin. With no room until the final 100 yards, Memory produced a devastating turn of foot to cut down her rivals once in the clear, easily beating **Soraaya** and **Hooray**, who still did well to reverse Albany form with **Radharcnafarraige**, and marking herself out as a truly top-class juvenile filly.

13 TNT July Stakes (Group 2) (6f)
Newmarket July 8 (Good To Firm)
1 **Libranno** 2-8-12   Ryan Moore
2 **Neebras** 2-8-12   Frankie Dettori

3 **Elzaam** 2-8-12   Richard Hills
10/1, 100/30, 4/7F. ¾l, 3¼l. 5 ran. 1m 11.37s
(R Hannon).

A surprise result as **Libranno** made all the running while the expected challenges of **Elzaam**, who scoped badly after the race, and the equally disappointing **Approve** both failed to materialise. Libranno still proved a decent winner, though, having quickened well when pressed by **Neebras**, who didn't run again all season.

14 32Red.com Superlative Stakes (Group 2) (7f)
Newmarket July 9 (Good To Firm)
1 **King Torus** 2-9-0   Richard Hughes
2 **Ecliptic** 2-9-0   Ahmed Ajtebi
3 **Klammer** 2-9-0   Shane Kelly
7/2, 5/1, 6/1. nk, 2¼l. 6 ran. 1m 26.24s
(R Hannon).

A thrilling finish saw **King Torus** just hold off the seemingly unlucky **Ecliptic**, who swerved badly right at the furlong pole and nearly got back up. Even with Ecliptic not seen again, the form looks decent as the pair pulled 2¹/₄l clear of **Klammer**, though the race came too soon for the disappointing **Formosina** in sixth.

15 Silver Flash Stakes (Group 3) (Fillies) (7f)
Leopardstown July 15 (Good)
1 **Together** 2-8-12   J Murtagh
2 **Laughing Lashes** 2-8-12   F M Berry
3 **Kissable** 2-8-12   C D Hayes
9/10F, 4/1, 7/1. 1l, 1¾l. 8 ran. 1m 28.65s

(A P O'Brien).

A terrific clash between three very smart fillies, with **Together** showing a fine turn of foot to lead the way. The trio had a fair rival in **Highly Composed** well beaten in fourth even though **Laughing Lashes** and **Kissable** looked slightly unlucky in running, as both would prove by finishing in front of Together later in the season.

16 Rose Bowl Stakes (Listed) (6f8yds)
Newbury July 16 (Good)
1 **Al Aasifh** 2-9-0   Frankie Dettori
2 **Cape To Rio** 2-9-0   Ryan Moore
3 **Sir Reginald** 2-9-0   Kieren Fallon
2/1F, 5/2, 5/1. ½l, 6l. 8 ran. 1m 15.74s
(Saeed Bin Suroor).

A strongly-run 6f saw a decent field well strung out, but surprisingly the form worked out badly as **Al Aasifh** and **Cape To Rio**, who pulled 6l clear of the subsequent Gimcrack third **Sir Reginald**, failed to make a mark, with the winner twice particularly disappointing though surely capable of better.

17 Weatherbys Super Sprint (5f34yds)
Newbury July 17 (Good)
1 **Temple Meads** 2-8-6   Richard Mullen
2 **Bold Bidder** 2-7-13   L-P Beuzelin
3 **Move In Time** 2-8-6   Tom Eaves
5/1, 22/1, 22/1. 1l, ½l. 24 ran. 1m 3.55s
(E S McMahon).

The usual fiercely competitive cavalry charge produced a remarkable winner in **Temple**

KING TORUS (right): takes advantage of Ecliptic's waywardness in the Superlative Stakes

ZEBEDEE (nearest): cheekily lands the Molecomb at Glorious Goodwood

Meads, who was the least experienced runner in the field with just one previous run and came from stall one in a race favouring those drawn high yet wore down his rivals to win going away.

18 Jebel Ali Stables & Racecourse Anglesey Stakes (Group 3) (6f63yds)
Curragh July 18 (Yielding)
1 **Dunboyne Express** 2-9-1 D P McDonogh
2 **Samuel Morse** 2-9-1   J Murtagh
3 **Rudolf Valentino** 2-9-1   J A Heffernan
9/2, EvensF, 12/1. 8l, 2l. 4 ran. 1m 18.97s
(Kevin Prendergast).

A modest contest with **Samuel Morse** good enough to be sent off just 11-10 and running a flat race in second, but **Dunboyne Express** still marked himself out as a useful prospect as he drew well clear when quickening to the front having been scrubbed along earlier.

19 Weatherbys Bloodstock Insurance Star Stakes (Listed) (7f16yds)
Sandown July 22 (Good To Firm)
1 **Lily Again** 2-8-12   Jamie Spencer
2 **Cochabamba** 2-8-12   Jack Mitchell
3 **Crying Lightening** 2-8-12   Martin Dwyer
9/2, 5/1, 5/2J. 1l, hd. 8 ran. 1m 31.71s
(P F I Cole).

A competitive Listed race even without any major stars in the field, with **Lily Again** following her Cherry Hinton fifth with a gusty win. **Crying Lightening**, another who had previously come up just short in Pattern company, was third, split by the more progressive **Cochabamba**.

20 Korean Racing Authority Tyros Stakes (Group 3) (7f)
Leopardstown July 22 (Yielding)
1 **Zoffany** 2-9-1   J Murtagh
2 **High Ruler** 2-9-1   J A Heffernan
3 **Jolie Jioconde** 2-8-12   C D Hayes

1/7F, 9/1, 14/1. 2l, ½l. 4 ran. 1m 32.61s
(A P O'Brien).

A simple task for **Zoffany**, who had rebuilt his reputation with a Listed win following his Royal Ascot flop and eased to another impressive victory despite having little to beat with pacesetting stablemate **High Ruler** able to stick on for second.

21 Jaguar XK Winkfield Stakes (Listed) (7f)
Ascot July 24 (Good)
1 **Toolain** 2-9-2   Philip Robinson
2 **Galtymore Lad** 2-9-2   Tony Culhane
3 **Premier Clarets** 2-9-2   Ryan Moore
11/4F, 9/1, 4/1. ¾l, 2l. 8 ran. 1m 29.72s
(M A Jarvis).

An extremely strong contest for the grade with **Galtymore Lad** and **Premier Clarets** going on to perform well against Group 1 winner Wootton Bassett in sales races, saying much for the quality of **Toolain**. The giant colt quickened up well despite looking like he had plenty more to learn, hanging left under pressure having earlier swerved and unseated his rider on his debut.

22 Princess Margaret Abu Dhabi Stakes (Group 3) (Fillies) (6f)
Ascot July 24 (Good)
1 **Soraaya** 2-8-12   Ryan Moore
2 **Margot Did** 2-8-12   Hayley Turner
3 **Perfect Tribute** 2-8-12   Luke Morris
3/1, 2/1F, 14/1. ½l, 2l. 11 ran. 1m 14.86s
(M R Channon).

Both second to Memory in their previous starts, **Soraaya** and **Margot Did** fought out a tremendous battle with Soraaya just wearing down her rival in the final 50 yards in a strong contest. **Perfect Tribute** ran a cracker in third, with

Imperialistic Diva, who stepped up hugely on her previous third to Khor Sheed, and **Sweet Cecily** hot on her heels.

23 Betfair Molecomb Stakes (Group 3) (5f)

Goodwood July 27 (Good)

1	**Zebedee** 2-9-0	Richard Hughes
2	**Stone Of Folca** 2-9-0	Jimmy Quinn
3	**Choose Wisely** 2-9-0	Neil Callan

2/1F, 4/1, 33/1. nk, hd. 12 ran. 58.49s (R Hannon).

Zebedee left his Norfolk form well behind as he reversed those placings with **Stone Of Folca** and had plenty in hand to boot. This time ridden from off the pace, having also benefited from a change in tactics to win a Listed event at Sandown prior to Goodwood, Zebedee ate up the ground instantly when asked to quicken and won very cosily, though those behind were generally a modest bunch.

24 Veuve Clicquot Vintage Stakes (Group 2) (7f)

Goodwood July 28 (Good To Firm)

1	**King Torus** 2-9-3	Richard Hughes
2	**Stentorian** 2-9-0	Frankie Dettori
3	**Major Art** 2-9-0	Ryan Moore

11/4, 8/1, 5/1. 6l, shd. 7 ran. 1m 27.13s (R Hannon).

A comprehensive victory for **King Torus**, who kept out of trouble in a rough race as he tracked the leader **Stentorian** before bounding clear in hugely impressive fashion. That said, his task was made easier by a real barging match behind as Stentorian stuck on for second and the well-backed favourite **Crown Prosecutor** was worst affected, still moving up to challenge before fading into sixth.

25 Tanqueray Richmond Stakes (Group 2) (6f)

Goodwood July 30 (Good)

1	**Libranno** 2-9-3	Richard Hughes
2	**The Paddyman** 2-9-0	Philip Robinson
3	**Roayh** 2-9-0	Frankie Dettori

5/4F, 4/1, 9/1. 1¼l, 1¼l. 6 ran. 1m 11.48s (R Hannon).

Richard Hannon completed a remarkable clean sweep of the two-year-old Group races for the second successive summer festival, with **Libranno** matching King Torus in winning at Newmarket and Goodwood. Libranno wasn't quite as impressive as his stablemate in a fairly modest contest, though, as he again made all and held off **The Paddyman**.

26 Coolmore Hurricane Run Stakes (Listed) (7f100yds)

Tipperary August 6 (Good)

1	**Snow Watch** 2-9-1	D P McDonogh

2	**Triple Eight** 2-9-1	P J Smullen
3	**Jackaroo** 2-9-1	J Murtagh

7/2, 10/1, 4/6F. 2½l, 1½l. 5 ran. 1m 35.67s (Kevin Prendergast).

A desperately weak contest with **Jackaroo**, already a beaten favourite in the Chesham, clearly vastly overhyped and runner-up **Triple Eight** having failed to beat a single horse in two previous attempts at this sort of grade, but **Snow Watch**, disappointingly not seen out again, still looked hugely impressive as he put the race to bed quickly and pulled clear with plenty more still in the tank.

27 German-Thoroughbred.com Sweet Solera Stakes (Group 3) (Fillies) (7f)

Newmarket August 7 (Good To Soft)

1	**White Moonstone** 2-8-12	Frankie Dettori
2	**Crying Lightening** 2-8-12	Martin Dwyer
3	**Khor Sheed** 2-8-12	Kieren Fallon

11/4J, 7/1, 11/4J. 1¼l, 3½l. 9 ran. 1m 27.02s (Saeed Bin Suroor).

White Moonstone pointed the way to bigger things as she overcame greenness to land a straightforward victory, always looking well on top despite edging left. **Crying Lightening**, whose limitations had already been exposed, stuck on for second, while **Khor Sheed** pulled far too hard to get the trip and faded into third.

28 Keeneland Debutante Stakes (Group 2) (Fillies) (7f)

Curragh August 8 (Yielding)

1	**Laughing Lashes** 2-8-12	F M Berry
2	**Misty For Me** 2-8-12	J A Heffernan
3	**Together** 2-8-12	J Murtagh

5/1, 8/1, 6/4F. 1l, 3l. 9 ran. 1m 24.49s (Mrs John Harrington).

An impressive performance from **Laughing Lashes**, who stepped up on her previous second behind **Together** as the favourite could manage only third. Laughing Lashes stayed on strongly to beat the progressive **Misty For Me**, while Together ruined her chance by hanging badly left but still left a pair of Listed winners in **Seedarn** and **Lily Again** behind.

29 Keeneland Phoenix Stakes (Group 1) (6f)

Curragh August 8 (Yielding)

1	**Zoffany** 2-9-1	J Murtagh
2	**Glor Na Mara** 2-9-1	K J Manning
3	**Strong Suit** 2-9-1	Richard Hughes

3/1, 12/1, 4/9F. ½l, shd. 7 ran. 1m 11.29s (A P O'Brien).

Zoffany produced a remarkable burst of speed in the final furlong to cut down **Glor Na Mara** and **Strong Suit** for a fine victory. Zoffany looked well beaten at the furlong pole but finally found his stride and quickened between his rivals in a matter of strides to suggest he would have had far more in hand over further. The bare form was only fair, though, with Strong Suit possibly left in front too long and both placed horses beaten much further in subsequent Group 1 attempts.

30 Bathwick Tyres St Hugh's Stakes (Listed) (5f34yds)
Newbury August 13 (Good)
1 **Electric Waves** 2-8-12 Richard Mullen
2 **Sweet Cecily** 2-8-12 Richard Hughes
3 **The Thrill Is Gone** 2-8-12 Neil Callan
10/1, 7/2, 25/1. 1¼l, ¾l. 12 ran. 1m 3.02s
(E S McMahon).

A highly competitive contest with the first three doing well to pull 5l clear of the pack and **Electric Waves** hinting at the fireworks to come in the Cornwallis with an impressive victory. However, little went right for hot favourite **Hooray** as she flopped in sixth.

31 Matalan Stakes (registered as the Washington Singer Stakes) (Listed)
(7f) Newbury August 14 (Good To Soft)
1 **Janood** 2-9-0 Frankie Dettori
2 **Slim Shadey** 2-9-0 Liam Keniry
3 **Sensei** 2-9-0 Richard Hughes
2/1, 9/1, 9/2. 1¾l, 3½l. 4 ran. 1m 28.82s
(Saeed Bin Suroor).

A desperately poor performance from Chesham winner **Zaidan**, seemingly unsuited by the soft ground, left **Janood** with a straightforward task, and though he did things well enough two disappointing subsequent efforts leave him with plenty to prove to live up to this.

32 Sportingbet.com Acomb Stakes (Group 3) (7f)
York August 17 (Good)
1 **Waiter's Dream** 2-9-0 Kieren Fallon
2 **Silvertrees** 2-9-0 P J McDonald
3 **Timothy T** 2-9-0 Frankie Dettori
5/2, 8/1, 9/1. 4½l, 1l. 7 ran. 1m 24.82s
(B J Meehan).

Four impressive maiden winners filled the first four places, but only **Waiter's Dream** looked even remotely up to Pattern level as he won virtually unchallenged, racing prominently throughout and easily drawing clear with the aid of the rail while **Silvertrees** was left toiling in second.

33 Irish Thoroughbred Marketing Gimcrack Stakes (Group 2) (6f)
York August 18 (Good)
1 **Approve** 2-9-1 Eddie Ahern
2 **Crown Prosecutor** 2-8-12 Martin Dwyer
3 **Sir Reginald** 2-8-12 Frankie Dettori
8/1, 15/2, 14/1. ¾l, 2½l. 11 ran. 1m 11.67s
(W J Haggas).

Approve put a couple of below-par efforts behind him as he fulfilled the promise of his Royal Ascot win by defying a 3lb penalty. Approve needed all of the 6f trip to wear down **Crown Prosecutor** after that one had won a seemingly decisive battle with the front-running **Temple Meads**, who failed to get home in the final furlong and lost third to **Sir Reginald**, while **Premier Clarets** was also close up in fifth.

34 Julia Graves Roses Stakes (Listed) (5f)
York August 18 (Good)
1 **New Planet** 2-9-0 Kieren Fallon
2 **Pabusar** 2-9-0 Jim Crowley
3 **Julius Geezer** 2-9-0 Richard Kingscote
17/2, 5/1, 28/1. nk, 2½l. 13 ran. 58.93s
(J J Quinn).

A strong Listed contest as **New Planet** and **Pabusar**, both impressive winners on their previous starts, took a step up in grade in their stride and pulled well clear of **Julius Geezer**, with **Bathwick Bear** and **Black Moth**, first and third at the same level at Ripon next time, among those behind. Molecomb third **Choose Wisely** was best of those on the far side in fifth though probably wouldn't have quite troubled the principals even with a better draw.

35 Jaguar Cars Lowther Stakes (Group 2) (Fillies) (6f)
York August 19 (Good)
1 **Hooray** 2-8-12 Seb Sanders
2 **Margot Did** 2-8-12 Hayley Turner
3 **Rimth** 2-8-12 Jamie Spencer
11/1, 100/30, 4/1. ¾l, 2¼l. 8 ran. 1m 10.14s
(Sir Mark Prescott).

Hooray found the key to her potential as she produced a much-improved effort to beat **Margot Did** with the Queen Mary winner **Maqaasid** a disappointing fourth. Hooray was allowed to make the running and stayed on strongly to hold Margot Did, who was again left unrewarded for arguably her best ever performance as the pair pulled clear of **Rimth** and Maqaasid with **Imperialistic Diva** left behind in fifth in a strong renewal.

36 Galileo European Breeders Fund Futurity Stakes (Group 2) (7f)
Curragh August 21 (Good To Firm)
1 **Pathfork** 2-9-1 F M Berry
2 **Glor Na Mara** 2-9-1 K J Manning
3 **Samuel Morse** 2-9-1 J Murtagh
10/11F, 2/1, 8/1. 1½l, 2½l. 7 ran. 1m 23.45s
(Mrs John Harrington).

Gambled into odds-on despite facing Phoenix Stakes runner-up **Glor Na Mara**, **Pathfork** lived up to his billing as he retained his unbeaten record in commanding fashion. Pathfork took up the running early and was always well on top of Glor Na Mara, who still ran a good race with **Samuel Morse** well beaten in third

37 Grangecon Stud Stakes (Listed) (5f) Curragh August 21 (Good To Firm)

1	**Meow** 2-8-12	J Murtagh
2	**Ladie's Choice** 2-8-12	B A Curtis
3	**Moonlit Garden** 2-8-12	P J Smullen

4/6F, 10/1, 4/1. nk, ¾l. 6 ran. 58.36s
(David Wachman).

Meow became only the second runner from the Queen Mary to win subsequently but still made hard work for herself given most of the field, including **Moonlit Garden**, were well held on the form book as she just held off **Ladie's Choice** to make all the running.

38 Alexis Catchpole Celebration Solario Stakes (Group 3) (7f16yds)
Sandown August 21 (Good To Firm)

1	**Native Khan** 2-9-0	Eddie Ahern
2	**Measuring Time** 2-9-0	Richard Hughes
3	**Surrey Star** 2-9-0	Liam Keniry

6/5F, 6/1, 20/1. ½l, ½l. 6 ran. 1m 29.19s
(E A L Dunlop).

An impressive win from **Native Khan**, who made rapid headway to cruise into the lead at the furlong pole and appeared to be idling as he was ridden out for victory, going on to prove he was certainly much better than some relatively modest rivals. **Measuring Time** let the form down when a beaten favourite behind the well exposed filly Singapore Lilly next time at Listed level, while the seemingly regressive **Roayh** was a disappointing fourth.

39 Darley Prix Morny (Group 1) (6f) Deauville August 22 (Good)

1	**Dream Ahead** 2-9-0	William Buick
2	**Tin Horse** 2-9-0	Thierry Jarnet
3	**Pontenuovo** 2-8-10	Stephane Pasquier

8/1, 33/1, 8/1. 1½l, nk. 11 ran. 1m 9.60s
(D M Simcock).

While several more established British hopes came up short, most notably the disappointing favourite **Libranno**, **Dream Ahead** still landed the spoils for the raiders. Having hacked up in a Nottingham maiden on his only previous start, Dream Ahead showed a tremendous turn of foot to quicken clear of a trio of French horses in scintillating fashion, though **Tin Horse** got closer in second than he did to Wootton Bassett later in the campaign and the French are often more backward than their British counterparts at this stage of the season.

40 Chichester Observer Prestige Stakes (Group 3) (7f)
Goodwood August 28 (Soft)

| 1 | **Theyskens' Theory** 2-9-0 | Martin Dwyer |

NATIVE KHAN: wins the Solario

| 2 | **Cochabamba** 2-9-0 | Jack Mitchell |
| 3 | **Cape Dollar** 2-9-0 | Kieren Fallon |

11/10F, 11/1, 4/1. 1¼l, ½l. 7 ran. 1m 28.90s
(B J Meehan).

A fairly straightforward step up to Pattern level for **Theyskens' Theory**, who comfortably made all the running and strongly suggested there was plenty more in the tank. **Cochabamba** stuck on well to take second with **Cape Dollar** just coming up short, while **Sonning Rose** struggled on soft ground in seventh.

41 Moyglare Stud Stakes (Group 1) (Fillies) (7f)
Curragh August 29 (Good To Firm)

1	**Misty For Me** 2-8-12	J A Heffernan
2	**Laughing Lashes** 2-8-12	F M Berry
3	**Kissable** 2-8-12	C D Hayes

10/1, 7/2, 12/1. 1l, nk. 12 ran. 1m 24.56s
(A P O'Brien).

Misty For Me maintained her progress to turn around previous form with **Laughing Lashes** and confirm herself top of the pile in Ireland while favourite **Memory** ran well below-par. Misty For Me made the running and proved strong enough in the closing stages despite a persistent challenge from Laughing Lashes, while **Together** produced a much more balanced performance on fast ground but could still manage only fourth with **Kissable** also getting in the mix. That quartet pulled 5l clear of **Wild Wind**, who was beaten just a head in a Group 3 next time, though Memory clearly wasn't herself as she never figured in sixth.

42 Go And Go Round Tower Stakes (Group 3) (6f)
Curragh August 29 (Good)

1 **Dingle View** 2-8-12   Cathy Gannon
2 **Glor Na Mara** 2-9-1   K J Manning
3 **Big Issue** 2-9-1   Richard Hughes
22/1, 4/5F, 11/4. hd, 2l. 9 ran. 1m 12.89s
(P D Evans).

Glor Na Mara was unable to break his duck despite dropping in grade as he was a below-par second, though he ran into a vastly under-rated rival in British filly **Dingle View**, who had been progressive over 5f and relished the step up in trip as he made all and just outfought the favourite. The pair pulled 2l clear of **Big Issue** with several decent yardsticks behind.

43 European Breeders' Fund Dick Poole Fillies' Stakes (Listed) (6f)
Salisbury September 2 (Good To Firm)

1 **Brevity** 2-8-12   Martin Dwyer
2 **Rimth** 2-8-12   Jamie Spencer
3 **Margot Did** 2-8-12   Hayley Turner
10/1, 100/30, 11/10F. nse, nk. 8 ran. 1m 13.37s
(B J Meehan).

The drop to Listed level failed to bring a change in fortunes for the seemingly unwilling **Margot Did**, who also ran into a very strong bunch of rivals for the grade. **Brevity** proved the best of them as she edged out the subsequent Cheveley Park second **Rimth** to suggest that she's a smart prospect, while **Sweet Cecily** was a close fourth.

44 totepool Sirenia Stakes (Group 3) (6f)
Kempton September 4 (Standard)

1 **Hooray** 2-9-2   Seb Sanders
2 **Reckless Reward** 2-9-0   Richard Hughes
3 **Signs In The Sand** 2-9-0   Frankie Dettori
5/2, 7/1, 7/4F. 3¾l. 6l. 5 ran. 1m 11.50s
(Sir Mark Prescott).

Another impressive all-the-way win for **Hooray**, who was far too good for the colts even under a penalty. The opposition wasn't up to much, however, with **Reckless Reward** failing to follow up his good second in the Norfolk while **Signs In The Sand** ruined his chance by pulling hard.

45 Peter Willett Stakes (registered as the Stardom Stakes) (Listed) (7f)
Goodwood September 7 (Good)

1 **Titus Mills** 2-9-0   Martin Dwyer
2 **Big Issue** 2-9-0   Richard Hughes
3 **Surrey Star** 2-9-0   Liam Keniry
5/6F, 5/2, 7/1. ½l, 2½l. 5 ran. 1m 29.36s
(B J Meehan).

A seemingly high-class effort from **Titus Mills**, who made the running and found more when strongly pressed close home by **Big Issue** with the pair pulling well clear of **Surrey Star**. He has questions to answer after his subsequent Racing Post Trophy flop, though, with Surrey Star possibly failing to run to form in third.

46 Weatherbys Insurance £300,000 2-Y-O Stakes (6f110yds)
Doncaster September 9 (Good)

1 **Wootton Bassett** 2-8-9   Paul Hanagan
2 **Galtymore Lad** 2-8-6   Kieren Fallon
3 **Premier Clarets** 2-8-3   Jimmy Quinn
2/1F, 11/2, 28/1. 1l, 1½l. 21 ran. 1m 17.99s
(R A Fahey).

A remarkable carbon copy of the big sales race at York's Ebor meeting as **Wootton Bassett**, who had beaten **Galtymore Lad** on that occasion, defied an 8lb swing in the weights to deny the same horse again with a performance clearly worthy of a much higher grade. The unbeaten colt was always prominent and got stronger and stronger as the race went on, pointing to his subsequent step up in trip, though the bare form was still very strong with

BREVITY (second right): just edges a tight battle at Salisbury in the Dick Poole

Premier Clarets, receiving 6lb, well beaten in third despite running close to Gimcrack form with **Sir Reginald**, a good fifth also carrying maximum weight.

47 **Polypipe Flying Childers Stakes (Group 2) (5f)**

Doncaster September 10 (Good)
1 **Zebedee** 2-9-0   Richard Hughes
2 **Dinkum Diamond** 2-9-0   Dane O'Neill
3 **New Planet** 2-9-0   Ryan Moore
100/30F, 6/1, 7/2. nk, ¾l. 12 ran. 59.42s
(R Hannon).

The unofficial 5f juvenile championship went to **Zebedee**, who won with his customary panache even against much stronger opposition. Switched early to get plenty of cover, Zebedee put the race to bed quickly when asked to quicken and won cosily as **Dinkum Diamond**, producing a career-best effort in second, closed the gap late ahead of **New Planet**. The rest finished in a heap, with 66-1 shot **Black Moth** beating **The Thrill Is Gone** to fourth and **Electric Waves** bitterly disappointing in seventh, though Irish fillies **Ladie's Choice** and **Meow**, who reportedly lost her action, were detached as they filled the last two places.

48 **Keepmoat May Hill Stakes (Group 2) (Fillies) (1m)**

Doncaster September 10 (Good)
1 **White Moonstone** 2-8-12   Frankie Dettori
2 **Al Madina** 2-8-12   Tom Eaves
3 **Musharakaat** 2-8-12   Richard Hills
8/11F, 66/1, 16/1. 5l, 1¼l. 7 ran. 1m 38.73s
(Saeed Bin Suroor).

White Moonstone took another step up the ladder as she romped to victory, destroying the field with her turn of foot and powering clear in the final furlong. **Musharakaat** was beaten marginally further than when fifth behind White Moonstone in the Sweet Solera, but the presence of Chesham second **Sonning Rose**, back to her best returned to good ground, and **Lily Again** showed the progress both had made since Newmarket with more to come from the winner in the Fillies' Mile.

49 **Neptune Investment Management Champagne Stakes (Group 2) (7f)**

Doncaster September 11 (Good)
1 **Saamidd** 2-8-12   Frankie Dettori
2 **Approve** 2-9-1   Eddie Ahern
3 **Waiter's Dream** 2-8-12   Kieren Fallon
5/6F, 9/2, 9/4. 2¼l, ½l. 6 ran. 1m 26.32s
(Saeed Bin Suroor).

A spectacular performance from **Saamidd**, who built on an impressive debut win by putting two smart rivals in **Approve** and **Waiter's Dream** to the sword and won eased down. Approve, stepping up to 7f for the first time, saw out the

trip well but was simply left behind by the winner's turn of foot, with Waiter's Dream and the well-beaten fourth, **Karam Albaari**, both going on to uphold the form at Group 1 level to suggest Saamidd remains a colt of serious potential even after his Dewhurst flop.

50 **boylesports.com Vincent O'Brien National (Group 1) (7f)**

Curragh September 11 (Soft)
1 **Pathfork** 2-9-1   F M Berry
2 **Casamento** 2-9-1   D P McDonogh
3 **Zoffany** 2-9-1   J Murtagh
2/1, 11/1, 6/4F. hd, 5l. 9 ran. 1m 27.95s
(Mrs John Harrington).

An eagerly-awaited clash between **Pathfork** and **Zoffany** never materialised with Zoffany well below his best on soft ground, but Pathfork also appeared ill at ease in the conditions and still knuckled down to produce a superb performance to beat **Casamento**. Pathfork made the decisive move 2f out when taking over from the front-running Casamento and was then all out to hold on as the runner-up fought back, the pair pulling well clear of Zoffany and **Samuel Morse**, who was among the few proven in the conditions. **Glor Na Mara** and **Janood** were both beaten out of sight.

51 **Irish Field Blenheim Stakes (Listed) (6f)**

Curragh September 11 (Soft)
1 **Longhunter** 2-9-1   D P McDonogh
2 **Katla** 2-8-12   W J Lee
3 **Emperor Hadrian** 2-9-1   J Murtagh
3/1J, 11/2, 3/1J. shd, 2½l. 8 ran. 1m 15.48s
(Kevin Prendergast).

A good Listed contest as the first two pulled well clear of a couple of useful yardsticks in **Emperor Hadrian** and **Queen Of Spain**, with **Longhunter**, twice below-par after an impressive winning debut, bouncing back to form to hold off the filly **Katla**, who was a six-length winner at this level at York next time.

52 **Zenith Ltd Refurbishment Specialists Harry Rosebery Stakes (South Ayrshire Cup) (Listed) (5f)**

Ayr September 17 (Good)
1 **Arctic Feeling** 2-9-3   Paul Hanagan
2 **Krypton Factor** 2-9-3   Seb Sanders
3 **The Thrill Is Gone** 2-8-12   Phillip Makin
8/1, 7/4F, 5/2. nk, 1½l. 9 ran. 59.35s
(R A Fahey).

A strange result as **Arctic Feeling**, found out on several other starts in a similar grade, just saw off the fast-improving **Krypton Factor** to land a surprise win, while **The Thrill Is Gone**, who failed to uphold Flying Childers form with the winner having been too keen early, was below her best in third.

53 Laundry Cottage Stud Firth of Clyde Stakes (Group 3) (Fillies) (6f)
Ayr September 18 (Good)
1 **Majestic Dubawi** 2-8-12   Chris Catlin
2 **Ragsah** 2-8-12   Frankie Dettori
3 **Barefoot Lady** 2-8-12   Paul Hanagan
22/1, 100/30, 6/1. 1l, hd. 10 ran. 1m 12.01s
(M R Channon).

A competitive contest which saw **Majestic Dubawi** follow up an impressive maiden win at Bath, marking her out as a smart prospect with the runner-up **Ragsah** going on to take fourth in the Cheveley Park. That said, hot favourite **Rimth** found all sorts of trouble and was heavily eased in seventh, with a line through Ragsah suggesting she may well have won given a clear run.

54 Dubai Duty Free Mill Reef Stakes (Group 2) (6f8yds)
Newbury September 18 (Good To Firm)
1 **Temple Meads** 2-9-1   Richard Mullen
2 **Formosina** 2-9-4   Ryan Moore
3 **Crown Prosecutor** 2-9-1   Martin Dwyer
4/1, 8/1, 3/1. 1¾l, ½l. 7 ran. 1m 11.73s
(E S McMahon).

The only race in which **Temple Meads** managed to settle over 6f all season and he duly showed his rich potential with a comfortable victory. Temple Meads was held up and made steady headway before being driven clear in the final furlong, proving his York running all wrong with Gimcrack second **Crown Prosecutor**, who could manage only third this time behind **Formosina**. **The Paddyman** was a close fourth ahead of a below-par **Libranno**.

55 Juddmonte Royal Lodge Stakes (Group 2) (Colts & Geldings) (1m)
Ascot September 25 (Good To Soft)
1 **Frankel** 2-8-12   Tom Queally
2 **Klammer** 2-8-12   Kieren Fallon
3 **Treasure Beach** 2-8-12   J Murtagh
30/100F, 11/1, 11/2. 10l, ¾l. 5 ran. 1m 41.73s
(H R A Cecil).

Frankel confirmed his arrival as a top-class colt as he produced an astonishing turn of foot to thrash a field far more worthy than the cynics would soon try to suggest. Held up off a modest pace, Frankel pulled his way to the front turning for home without coming off the bridle before powering further and further clear to a remarkable winning margin. Runner-up **Klammer** already had solid form and would later win the Horris Hill, while even **Slim Shadey**, who finished last of five, was a fair yardstick, the pair split by a couple of potential Ballydoyle improvers, marking Frankel's effort out as the outstanding juvenile performance of a strong year for the colts.

56 Meon Valley Stud Fillies' Mile (Group 1) (1m)
Ascot September 25 (Good To Soft)
1 **White Moonstone** 2-8-12 Frankie Dettori
2 **Together** 2-8-12   J Murtagh
3 **Theyskens' Theory** 2-8-12   Ryan Moore
4/5F, 5/1, 9/4. nk, 1¼l. 5 ran. 1m 42.75s
(Saeed Bin Suroor).

Just five runners but the cream rose to the top as three exciting prospects fought out the finish and **White Moonstone** rubber-stamped her credentials as Britain's leading juvenile filly with a gutsy win. Held up in last, White Moonstone produced a powerful run down the outside and really knuckled down to see off **Together** and the front-running **Theyskens' Theory** while suggesting she may have even more to come back on better ground. Together benefited from an extra furlong but still finished close enough to point to the superiority of the top Irish fillies with Theyskens' Theory their only serious rival in a race lacking strength in depth.

57 C.L. Weld Park Stakes (Group 3) (Fillies) (7f)
Curragh September 26 (Yielding To Soft)
1 **Chrysanthemum** 2-8-12   W M Lordan
2 **Wild Wind** 2-8-12   J Murtagh
3 **Bible Belt** 2-8-12   F M Berry
7/2, 11/4F, 5/1. hd, hd. 11 ran. 1m 28.96s
(David Wachman).

A Listed winner on her only previous start, **Chrysanthemum** confirmed herself a hugely exciting prospect by running out a determined winner over **Wild Wind**, who seemed to improve on her Moyglare fifth to push her close. **Bible Belt** and **Quiet Oasis** also finished in the mix as the quartet pulled 7l clear of subsequent Listed winner **Katla**, with Quiet Oasis's fair seventh in the Breeders' Cup Juvenile Fillies Turf giving a further nod to the form.

58 Juddmonte Beresford Stakes (Group 2) (1m)
Curragh September 26 (Yielding To Soft)
1 **Casamento** 2-9-1   P J Smullen
2 **Mawaakef** 2-9-1   D P McDonogh
3 **Robin Hood** 2-9-1   J A Heffernan
4/6F, 7/2, 12/1. 4l, 2½l. 7 ran. 1m 43.52s
(M Halford).

Casamento enjoyed a straightforward opportunity to go one better than the National Stakes as he romped to victory over **Mawaakef**, impressively seeing out the extra furlong to point the way to the Racing Post Trophy though not required to come out of first gear.

59 Somerville Tattersall Stakes (Group 3) (7f)
Newmarket September 30 (Soft)
1 **Rerouted** 2-8-12   Michael Hills

HOORAY: makes all in the Cheveley Park for a comprehensive triumph

2 **Surrey Star** 2-8-12   Kieren Fallon
3 **Royal Exchange** 2-8-12 Richard Hughes
8/1, 11/2, 9/4F. shd, ½l. 7 ran. 1m 26.06s
(B W Hills).

A narrow win for the progressive **Rerouted**, who had been only fourth off 89 in a nursery on his previous start but would soon hold his own at Group 1 level at Saint-Cloud, though the bare form of this race still looks modest for the grade. **Surrey Star** was just touched off despite having twice been a well-beaten third at a similar level, while **Royal Exchange**, who got going all too late dropping down in trip, was turned over at odds-on in a very weak Listed race at Pontefract next time and **The Paddyman** found the step up to 7f and good to soft ground too taxing on his stamina as he faded into fourth.

60 Sakhee Oh So Sharp Stakes (Group 3) (Fillies) (7f)
Newmarket October 1 (Good To Soft)
1 **Havant** 2-8-12   Ryan Moore
2 **Look At Me** 2-8-12   J Murtagh
3 **Khawlah** 2-8-12   Frankie Dettori
11/2, 100/30F, 7/2. 3¼l, 1¾l. 10 ran. 1m 28.74s
(Sir Michael Stoute).

A comprehensive victory for **Havant**, who seemed green throughout but drew well clear in the final furlong. It remains to be seen whether she beat any decent rivals, though, with the next three all stepping up from maiden wins, including the fourth, **Ladyanne**, who was beaten much further by Zoowraa next time, while **Lily Again**, regressive near the end of a

long season, and **Cochabamba** were below their best.

61 Adnams Cheveley Park Stakes (Group 1) (Fillies) (6f)
Newmarket October 1 (Good To Soft)
1 **Hooray** 2-8-12   Seb Sanders
2 **Rimth** 2-8-12   William Buick
3 **Maqaasid** 2-8-12   Richard Hills
7/2F, 11/1, 8/1. 4½l, 1¼l. 11 ran. 1m 14.09s
(Sir Mark Prescott).

A race badly weakened by the absence of likely hot favourite Memory, and **Hooray** took full advantage as she maintained her sharp upward curve by spreadeagling a competitive field, quickly taking up her customary position in front and simply galloping her rivals into submission. Nonetheless, she was flattered slightly as the ground (changed to soft immediately after the race) didn't suit many of her opponents, most notably her old rival **Margot Did** and **Wild Wind**. **Rimth** did well to beat the rest comfortably, ahead of **Maqaasid** and **Ragsah**, while **Sharnberry** caught the eye in seventh having paid the price for laying up with the pace.

62 Shadwell Middle Park Stakes (Group 1) (6f)
Newmarket October 1 (Soft)
1 **Dream Ahead** 2-8-12   William Buick
2 **Strong Suit** 2-8-12   Richard Hughes
3 **Approve** 2-8-12   Ryan Moore
5/4F, 7/2, 9/1. 9l, shd. 8 ran. 1m 14.28s
(D M Simcock).

A devastating victory for **Dream Ahead**, who

was always travelling supremely well and simply left his rivals for dead in the final furlong as he relentlessly powered further and further clear. Those behind had looked a strong bunch beforehand to boot, with **Strong Suit** holding off **Approve** for second, but with **Temple Meads** unable to be restrained after his saddle slipped and the thoroughly exposed 100-1 shot **Foghorn Leghorn** just 1½l behind Strong Suit in fifth, it remains to be seen whether this was truly a superstar performance.

63 £500,000 Tattersalls Millions 2YO Trophy (7f)
Newmarket October 2 (Soft)
1 **Fury** 2-9-3   Kieren Fallon
2 **Pisco Sour** 2-9-3   Jimmy Fortune
3 **Formosina** 2-9-3   Ryan Moore
11/2J, 14/1, 7/1. 1¾l, 1¼l. 27 ran. 1m 27.43s
(W J Haggas).

A strong renewal of this hugely valuable sales event saw a hugely impressive performance from **Fury**, who had won only a Newbury maiden but quickened up well and easily beat **Pisco Sour**. Class act **Formosina** was admittedly unlucky not to finish closer having badly missed the break after staying on into third, while **Measuring Time** came up short in fourth and **Janood** again disappointed in ninth.

64 £300,000 Tattersalls Millions 2YO Fillies' Trophy (7f)
Newmarket October 2 (Soft)
1 **Masaya** 2-9-0   Tom Queally
2 **Tale Untold** 2-9-0   Richard Hughes
3 **Together** 2-9-0   J Murtagh
20/1, 9/1, 13/8F. shd, nk. 20 ran. 1m 27.56s
(C E Brittain).

This race revolved all around Fillies' Mile second **Together**, who was the clear form pick but already unsuited by the drop back in trip even before throwing away victory by drifting across the entire width of the track in the final furlong. That suggests the form needs treating with caution as just 1l covered the first five, led by the gutsy front-runner **Masaya**, while **Tale Untold** had been receiving 6lb when just touched off by **Khor Sheed** in another sales race and the fifth, **I Love Me**, wasn't helped by the draw, doing by far the best of those drawn low.

65 totepool Two-Year-Old Trophy (Listed) (6f)
Redcar October 2 (Good To Soft)
1 **Ladies Are Forever** 2-7-12   S De Sousa
2 **Codemaster** 2-8-6   Dane O'Neill
3 **Ballista** 2-8-6   Richard Kingscote
3 **Krypton Factor**   Seb Sanders
3/1F, 7/2, 33/1, 6/1. 1¼l, nk. dht. 22 ran. 1m 12.60s
(G R Oldroyd).

A straightforward win for **Ladies Are Forever**, who was hugely favoured by the weights if running at her best after a long absence since the Queen Mary and duly beat **Codemaster**. **Krypton Factor** came out by far the best at the weights as he dead-heated for third, while **Dingle View** made the running but was soon struggling over a shorter trip, finishing sixth.

66 Total Prix Marcel Boussac – Criterium Des Pouliches (Group 1) (Fillies) (1m)
Longchamp October 3 (Very Soft)
1 **Misty For Me** 2-8-11   J Murtagh
2 **Helleborine** 2-8-11   Stephane Pasquier
3 **Rainbow Springs** 2-8-11   William Buick
3/1, 10/11F, 16/1. 1l, 3l. 8 ran. 1m 42.50s
(A P O'Brien).

A great clash between Moyglare winner **Misty For Me** and France's big hope **Helleborine**, and Misty For Me battled to a game victory to confirm herself an outstanding juvenile and underline the strength of the Irish fillies in general. Helleborine, odds-on having won each of her three races, looked set to land the spoils when quickening to lead at the furlong pole, but Misty For Me fought back superbly and won going away, with the pair pulling 3l clear of the only other British challenger **Rainbow Springs**.

67 Prix Jean-Luc Lagardere (Grand Criterium) (Group 1) (7f)
Longchamp October 3 (Very Soft)
1 **Wootton Bassett** 2-9-0   Paul Hanagan
2 **Maiguri** 2-9-0   Johan Victoire
2 **Tin Horse** 2-9-0   Thierry Jarnet
4/1, 16/1, 6/1. 2½l, dht. 9 ran. 1m 23.00s
(R A Fahey).

Wootton Bassett completed a memorable unbeaten campaign as he made virtually all the running to land an admittedly modest renewal with little other high-class foreign representation. Wootton Bassett could barely have won any easier, though, making a decisive move with more than 2f still to run and never looking in any danger thereafter, while **Maiguri** dead-heated with **Tin Horse** for second and **King Torus** was the big disappointment of the race in seventh.

68 Sodexo Prestige Cornwallis Stakes (Group 3) (5f)
Ascot October 9 (Good To Soft)
1 **Electric Waves** 2-8-11   Richard Mullen
2 **Move In Time** 2-9-0   Tom Eaves
3 **Darajaat** 2-8-11   Richard Hills
7/1, 25/1, 10/1. 2¼l, shd. 14 ran. 1m 1.21s
(E S McMahon).

A terrific performance by **Electric Waves**, arguably the best by a juvenile over 5f all season, as she put a poor showing in the Flying Childers behind her by leaving a wealth of useful sprinters strung out behind. Electric Waves was in front before halfway and stayed on strongly to comfortably choke off **Move In Time**, who left his previous form behind in second, with **Dinkum Diamond**, **Pabusar**, **Cape To Rio** and **Arctic Feeling**, the first two admittedly below-par, among those well beaten. **Anadolu**, just too good for the overrated Moonlit Garden when winning a Listed event at Tipperary, was only ninth as the top Irish sprinters continued to struggle in Britain.

69 Jaguar XJ Autumn Stakes (Group 3) (1m)
Ascot October 9 (Soft)
1 **Abjer** 2-9-0 — Richard Hills
2 **Pausanias** 2-9-0 — Richard Hughes
3 **Dux Scholar** 2-9-0 — Ryan Moore
33/1, 9/1, 7/2. 1¾l, ½l. 8 ran. 1m 44.84s (C E Brittain).

A tough race to assess, with **Abjer** running out a shock winner and favourite **Toolain** not getting a clear run in fourth, but Abjer still won well enough to look like he was victorious on merit with **Dux Scholar**'s subsequent Horris Hill second suggesting he's a decent prospect. The 33-1 shot stayed on strongly in the final furlong to wear down Dux Scholar, who couldn't quite get home in the conditions and lost second close home to **Pausanias**.

70 Coral Rockingham Stakes (Listed) (6f)
York October 9 (Soft)
1 **Katla** 2-8-10 — W J Lee
2 **Barefoot Lady** 2-8-9 — Paul Hanagan
3 **Carrignavar** 2-8-9 — E J McNamara
5/1, 11/4F, 11/1. 6l, nk. 7 ran. 1m 17.94s (J F Grogan).

The mud helped to make **Katla**'s trip from Ireland worthwhile as she revelled in conditions disliked by many of her opponents, though the manner of victory brooked little room for argument as she stormed clear of favourite **Barefoot Lady** for a wide-margin win.

71 Lanwades & Staffordstown Studs Stakes (Listed) (Fillies) (1m)
Curragh October 10 (Yielding To Soft)
1 **Gemstone** 2-8-12 — J Murtagh
2 **Rising Wind** 2-8-12 — C D Hayes
3 **Hurricane Havoc** 2-8-12 — K J Manning
7/1, 4/1, 2/1F. 1¼l, nk. 10 ran. 1m 46.48s (A P O'Brien).

Gemstone bounced back from a series of disappointing efforts to confirm the promise of an early-season maiden win over Kissable as she made virtually all the running, though a line through the fourth, **Luxurious**, who was beaten 7l by Chrysanthemum on her previous start when that filly was making her debut, suggests this was moderate form.

72 Dubai Dewhurst Stakes (Group 1) (Entire Colts & Fillies) (7f)
Newmarket October 16 (Good To Soft)
1 **Frankel** 2-9-1 — Tom Queally
2 **Roderic O'Connor** 2-9-1 — J Murtagh
3 **Glor Na Mara** 2-9-1 — K J Manning
4/6F, 25/1, 33/1. 2¼l, 2¾l. 6 ran. 1m 25.73s (H R A Cecil).

This race was never likely to quite live up to its billing, but **Frankel** did his bit with another

ABJER: stays on past apparent non-stayer Dux Scholar in the Autumn Stakes at Ascot

superb performance to confirm his status as champion two-year-old while fellow big guns **Dream Ahead** and **Saamidd** flopped. Keen in the early stages after a hefty bump, Frankel made his customary rapid headway to take over from **Roderic O'Connor** 2f out and was always doing enough to win comfortably, while the front-running second also ran a cracker having previously won only a Curragh maiden as he kept up the gallop to easily beat the back-to-form **Glor Na Mara**. **Waiter's Dream** was just a head adrift in fourth, his performance suggesting Saamidd would have been second on his Champagne form, but he was last of the sextet this time, possibly finding the ground too soft, while the race may have come too soon for the equally disappointing Dream Ahead.

73 Rockfel Stakes (Group 2) (Fillies) (7f) Newmarket October 16 (Good To Soft)

1 **Cape Dollar** 2-8-12   Ryan Moore
2 **Cochabamba** 2-8-12   Jack Mitchell
3 **I Love Me** 2-8-12   Jimmy Fortune
7/2, 12/1, 9/4F. ½l, hd. 10 ran. 1m 26.91s (Sir Michael Stoute).

A modest renewal with only fair Pattern form on show and none of the maiden winners making the step up, but **Cape Dollar** at least improved on her previous performances to reverse Goodwood placings with **Cochabamba**

and land a determined victory. **I Love Me** seemed to run her race in third ahead of the outsider **Nabah**, though the latter finished only a little closer at Listed level next time to deliver a further blow to the form.

74 Racing Post Trophy (Group 1) (1m) Doncaster October 23 (Good)

1 **Casamento** 2-9-0   Frankie Dettori
2 **Seville** 2-9-0   C O'Donoghue
3 **Master Of Hounds** 2-9-0   J Murtagh
2/1F, 8/1, 15/2. ¾l, 2l. 10 ran. 1m 37.03s (M Halford).

The Irish dominated with the British big guns having all gone for the Dewhurst, but the superiority of the first two still pointed to a strong renewal as **Casamento** got the better of **Seville** with several decent yardsticks trailing in their wake. Casamento made his move early when hitting the front 2f out and picked up again when strongly pressed by Seville, possibly winning a shade cosily in the end, while the runner-up did well to pull 2l clear of a second unexposed Aidan O'Brien contender, **Master Of Hounds**, in third. **Native Khan** was by far the best of the home challenge in fourth, staying on past the slightly disappointing **Dunboyne Express** having been outpaced, and that pair were also nicely clear of **Karam Albaari**, **Toolain** and **Zaidan**. **Titus Mills** ran no sort of race and was last of the ten runners.

CASAMENTO (nearest): sees off Seville at Doncaster to earn his move to Godolphin

75 TheBettingSite.com Stakes (registered as the Doncaster Stakes) (Listed) (6f)
Doncaster October 23 (Good)
1 **Earl Of Leitrim** 2-9-1   Shane Kelly
2 **Night Carnation** 2-8-10   Franny Norton
3 **Galtymore Lad** 2-9-1   Kieren Fallon
11/1, 25/1, 11/10F. ½l, 1½l. 8 ran. 1m 11.79s
(B J Meehan).

A competitive Listed contest which saw progressive pair **Earl Of Leitrim** and **Night Carnation** step up on successful maiden efforts to dominate the finish, Earl Of Leitrim just proving stronger than the filly having initially looked outpaced. **Galtymore Lad** wasn't at his best in third, but **Cape To Rio** and Cornwallis eighth **Invincible Ridge** were both well beaten while **Signs In The Sand** pulled too hard and faded into sixth.

76 John Smith's Extra Smooth Stakes (registered as the Horris Hill Stakes) (Group 3) (7f)
Newbury October 23 (Good To Soft)
1 **Klammer** 2-8-12   Jamie Spencer
2 **Dux Scholar** 2-8-12   Ryan Moore
3 **Elzaam** 2-8-12   Richard Hills
6/1, 7/2F, 9/2. nse, nk. 10 ran. 1m 28.21s
(Jane Chapple-Hyam).

Klammer finally got his head in front at Pattern level after several decent efforts in defeat as he just proved good enough to beat **Dux Scholar** in a thrilling three-pronged battle, with **Elzaam** also shaping well on his first start for more than three months out. The trio pulled well clear of **Madawi** with **Big Issue** and **Surrey Star** also behind.

77 John Moore And Biddestone Stud Memorial Stakes (registered as the Radley Stakes) (Listed) (Fillies) (7f)
Newbury October 23 (Good To Soft)
1 **Zoowraa** 2-8-12   Philip Robinson
2 **Flood Plain** 2-8-12   William Buick
3 **Sweetie Time** 2-8-12   Jamie Spencer
3/1F, 8/1, 20/1. 3¼l, 1¾l. 14 ran. 1m 30.52s
(M A Jarvis).

A spectacular victory from **Zoowraa**, who showed a superb turn of foot to hit the front before drawing well clear of the field. While nearly all of her rivals were totally unproven at this level, the few who did hold reasonable Listed form were all beaten out of sight to suggest the form is strong, with **Flood Plain**, slightly less favoured by the draw, also producing an excellent effort in second.

78 JRA Killavullan Stakes (Group 3) (7f) Leopardstown October 25 (Good To Firm)
1 **Dubai Prince** 2-9-1   P J Smullen

2 **Warning Flag** 2-9-1   J Murtagh
3 **Park Avenue** 2-9-1   C O'Donoghue
4/9F, 4/1, 12/1. 3½l, 1¾l. 8 ran. 1m 28.13s
(D K Weld).

A hugely promising performance from **Dubai Prince** as he put a pair of fair yardsticks firmly in their place with a telling turn of foot turning for home, staying on strongly to win going away. **Warning Flag** had beaten **Park Avenue** in an admittedly modest Listed event at Dundalk and slightly extended his superiority over the third but was still left well behind by the winner.

79 European Breeders' Fund Bosra Sham Fillies' Stakes (Listed) (6f)
Newmarket October 29 (Good To Soft)
1 **Sweet Cecily** 2-8-12   Richard Hughes
2 **Question Times** 2-8-12   Jack Mitchell
3 **Sharnberry** 2-8-12   Ryan Moore
5/1, 14/1, 7/2. ½l, ½l. 8 ran. 1m 15.81s
(R Hannon).

Sweet Cecily earned a richly deserved win after several fine efforts in top company as she battled well to shake off **Question Time**, while **Sharnberry**, clearly better than her Cheveley Park seventh when she paid the price for chasing Hooray, still came up just short in third.

80 bet365.com E B F Montrose Fillies' Stakes (Listed) (1m)
Newmarket October 30 (Good To Soft)
1 **Blue Bunting** 2-8-12   Ahmed Ajtebi
2 **Elas Diamond** 2-8-12   Ryan Moore
3 **Whisper Louise** 2-8-12   Micky Fenton
10/1, 7/4F, 14/1. 1l, nse. 11 ran. 1m 41.65s
(Mahmood Al Zarooni).

A decent Listed contest, with the running of **Nabah** in fifth placing the form close to the Rockfel, and **Blue Bunting** proved best of several fillies stepping up in class as she outstayed her main rival **Elas Diamond** to point to a bright future over further.

81 Criterium International (Group 1) (1m)
Saint-Cloud October 31 (Heavy)
1 **Roderic O'Connor** 2-9-0   J Murtagh
2 **Salto** 2-9-0   Olivier Peslier
3 **Maiguri** 2-9-0   Johan Victoire
5/2, 14/1, 9/1. 1½l, 5l. 10 ran. 1m 45.70s
(A P O'Brien).

Still looking extremely green as he wandered far from a true line in the straight, **Roderic O'Connor** nonetheless underlined his top-class credentials and paid yet another handsome compliment to Frankel with an impressive victory. Roderic O'Connor kicked clear turning for home and was always well in command despite allowing **Salto** to get closer than he really merited, though he was still 5l clear of

Maiguri, beaten much further than in the Lagardere, and **Rerouted** in a close battle for third. Unbeaten favourite **French Navy** disappointed in fifth, while **Pisco Sour** and **Abjer** could never land a blow.

82 Royal College Of Surgeons Race Against Breast Cancer Eyrefield Stakes (Listed) (1m1f)
Leopardstown October 31 (Soft)
1 **Tiz The Shot** 2-9-1   D P McDonogh
2 **Obligation** 2-9-1   J A Heffernan
3 **Banksters Bonus** 2-9-1   F M Berry
6/1, 8/11F, 3/1. 1l, 6l. 5 ran. 2m 2.93s
(Kevin Prendergast)

A moderate race on paper with the first two having taken a combined eight attempts to win their maidens, but **Tiz The Shot** at least showed he was progressive by outstaying odds-on favourite **Obligation** to avenge an earlier

83 defeat to him with the pair 6l clear of the rest.

Criterium De Saint-Cloud (Group 1) (1m2f)
Saint-Cloud November 13 (Heavy)
1 **Recital** 2-9-0   J Murtagh
2 **Bubble Chic** 2-9-0   Stephane Pasquier
3 **Prairie Star** 2-9-0   Anthony Crastus
3/1, 7/1, 5/2F. 5l, 2l. 10 ran. 2m 24.80s
(A P O'Brien)

Not as strong as the Group 1 won by Roderic O'Connor at the same track, but **Recital** still put his name forward as an exciting middle-distance prospect with a comprehensive win. Having won a maiden on his debut at Navan, Recital quickened up well from the rear and stayed on relentlessly to pull clear of **Bubble Chic**, who reversed previous Group 3 form with **Prairie Star**, the only previous Pattern winner in the field, with that one 6l clear of the rest.

Two-year-olds index

All horses placed or commented on in our two-year-old review section, with race numbers

Trainer Statistics

Mark Johnston

It says a lot about Johnston's success that he may just feel disappointed about last year, when he fell five short of his 2009 total of 216 despite sending out significantly more runners.

Even so, it's hard to argue with a second successive 200 tally for the master of Middleham.

By month – 2010

	Overall			Two-year-olds			Three-year-olds			Older horses		
	W-R	%	£1	W-R	%	£1	W-R	%	£1	W-R	%	£1
January	14-38	37	-0.90	0-0	-	+0.00	11-25	44	+3.16	3-13	23	-4.05
February	17-51	33	+1.35	0-0	-	+0.00	16-38	42	+7.85	1-13	8	-6.50
March	10-75	13	-29.67	0-0	-	+0.00	10-52	19	-6.67	0-23	-	-23.00
April	18-108	17	-23.88	0-1	-	-1.00	14-77	18	-18.25	4-30	13	-4.63
May	21-166	13	-58.76	0-7	-	-7.00	12-108	11	-50.51	9-51	18	-1.25
June	19-190	10	-94.82	1-19	5	-10.50	10-116	9	-62.07	8-55	15	-22.25
July	42-229	18	+23.67	3-29	10	-11.75	30-156	19	+26.86	9-44	20	+8.56
August	29-186	16	-13.04	5-41	12	-7.38	17-100	17	-2.00	7-45	16	-3.67
September	22-214	10	-92.13	8-58	14	-10.25	10-113	9	-63.75	4-43	9	-18.13
October	12-134	9	-58.13	5-62	8	-38.00	5-55	9	-16.00	2-17	12	-4.13
November	3-38	8	-28.25	2-28	7	-22.25	1-7	14	-3.00	0-3	-	-3.00
December	4-29	14	-2.50	1-15	7	-8.50	3-10	30	+10.00	0-4	-	-4.00

2009

	Overall			Two-year-olds			Three-year-olds			Older horses		
	W-R	%	£1	W-R	%	£1	W-R	%	£1	W-R	%	£1
January	11-36	31	+7.21	0-0	-	+0.00	6-23	26	-7.05	5-13	38	+14.25
February	10-35	29	+0.70	0-0	-	+0.00	9-25	36	+6.95	1-10	10	-6.25
March	17-62	27	+3.49	0-1	-	-1.00	11-38	29	+9.50	6-23	26	-5.01
April	18-98	18	-18.79	0-3	-	-3.00	17-64	27	+11.46	1-31	3	-27.25
May	20-125	16	-34.22	6-25	24	+11.18	9-61	15	-32.40	5-39	13	-13.00
June	38-180	21	+23.16	9-42	21	-7.78	24-98	24	+34.94	5-40	13	-4.00
July	27-187	14	-27.73	7-58	12	-26.47	14-94	15	-28.76	6-35	17	+27.50
August	26-177	15	-20.51	14-65	22	-0.26	9-79	11	-19.25	3-33	9	-1.00
September	20-141	14	-23.34	12-69	17	-25.09	6-53	11	+5.00	2-19	11	-3.25
October	14-122	11	-47.51	9-62	15	-14.26	5-44	11	-17.25	0-16	-	-16.00
November	9-32	28	+15.72	5-21	24	-0.41	3-8	38	+7.13	1-3	33	+9.00
December	6-32	19	-17.34	6-19	32	-4.34	0-6	-	-6.00	0-7	-	-7.00

2008

	Overall			Two-year olds			Three-year-olds			Older horses		
	W-R	%	£1	W-R	%	£1	W-R	%	£1	W-R	%	£1
January	8-48	17	-21.53	0-0	-	+0.00	8-39	21	-12.53	0-9	-	-9.00
February	10-42	24	+3.59	0-0	-	+0.00	9-38	24	-2.41	1-4	25	+6.00
March	12-56	21	-20.35	0-0	-	+0.00	10-45	22	-17.23	2-11	18	-3.13
April	13-82	16	-9.86	0-2	-	-2.00	12-64	19	+4.14	1-16	6	-12.00
May	17-125	14	-57.85	3-18	17	-11.83	11-89	12	-42.02	3-18	17	-4.00
June	9-132	7	-53.00	0-28	-	-28.00	7-88	8	-21.50	2-16	13	-3.50
July	25-170	15	+12.62	8-36	22	+6.62	14-110	13	-20.00	3-24	13	+26.00
August	12-126	10	-21.88	5-45	11	+1.88	6-65	9	-15.75	1-16	6	-8.00
September	21-130	16	-14.29	15-68	22	-4.29	5-52	10	-5.00	1-10	10	-5.00
October	17-145	12	-34.89	12-81	15	-1.89	4-50	8	-27.00	1-14	7	-6.00
November	13-49	27	+15.42	11-27	41	+28.17	1-17	6	-14.25	1-5	20	+1.50
December	7-40	18	+1.90	4-23	17	-6.10	3-13	23	+12.00	0-4	-	-4.00

By race type – 2010

	Overall			Two-year-olds			Three-year-olds			Older horses		
	W-R	%	£1	W-R	%	£1	W-R	%	£1	W-R	%	£1
Handicap	133-988	13	-281.76	5-53	9	-29.50	93-635	15	-140.03	35-300	12	-112.23
Group 1,2,3	7-34	21	+12.63	0-4	-	-4.00	4-20	20	+0.88	3-10	30	+15.75
Maiden	59-367	16	-92.40	20-189	11	-69.13	34-163	21	-30.97	5-15	33	+7.70

2009

	Overall			Two-year-olds			Three-year-olds			Older horses		
	W-R	%	£1	W-R	%	£1	W-R	%	£1	W-R	%	£1
Handicap	111-719	15	-74.98	11-72	15	-14.00	68-417	16	-57.76	32-230	14	-3.21
Group 1,2,3	5-31	16	-0.75	3-12	25	+3.25	2-6	33	+9.00	0-13	-	-13.00
Maiden	89-396	22	-14.09	47-236	20	-36.35	40-155	26	+20.06	2-5	40	+2.20

2008

	Overall			Two-year-olds			Three-year-olds			Older horses		
	W-R	%	£1	W-R	%	£1	W-R	%	£1	W-R	%	£1
Handicap	85-647	13	-116.39	13-67	19	-2.92	60-473	13	-107.48	12-107	11	-6.00
Group 1,2,3	3-37	8	+0.00	2-14	14	+12.00	1-6	17	+5.00	0-17	-	-17.00
Maiden	63-389	16	-60.55	37-215	17	-6.28	26-172	15	-52.27	0-2	-	-2.00

By jockey – 2010

	Overall			Two-year-olds			Three-year-olds			Older horses		
	W-R	%	£1	W-R	%	£1	W-R	%	£1	W-R	%	£1
Joe Fanning	84-542	15	-148.45	9-87	10	-38.00	59-332	18	-58.38	16-123	13	-52.07
Greg Fairley	39-297	13	-65.46	4-66	6	-31.50	24-170	14	-34.37	11-61	18	+0.40
Frankie Dettori	22-103	21	-24.71	0-3	-	-3.00	14-77	18	-31.59	8-23	35	+9.88
Kieren Fallon	15-58	26	+16.50	2-18	11	-2.00	10-29	34	+6.50	3-11	27	+12.00
R Ffrench	12-147	8	-83.72	3-26	12	-4.50	8-83	10	-43.97	1-38	3	-35.25
Richard Hills	7-53	13	-9.59	2-9	22	-2.50	2-28	7	-19.59	3-16	19	+12.50
S De Sousa	6-29	21	+2.23	2-10	20	-4.38	4-17	24	+8.60	0-2	-	-2.00
Adrian Nicholls	5-30	17	+4.58	0-6	-	-6.00	4-20	20	+4.58	1-4	25	+6.00
Andrew Elliott	4-16	25	+21.00	0-3	-	-3.00	3-11	27	+19.00	1-2	50	+5.00
Paul Hanagan	3-4	75	+4.63	1-2	50	+1.50	2-2	100	+3.13	0-0	-	+0.00
Neil Callan	3-13	23	+0.00	0-0	-	+0.00	2-9	22	-1.00	1-4	25	+1.00
Tadhg O'Shea	2-23	9	-16.25	2-15	13	-8.25	0-8	-	-8.00	0-0	-	+0.00
Alan Munro	1-1	100	+16.00	0-0	-	+0.00	1-1	100	+16.00	0-0	-	+0.00
Ryan Moore	1-2	50	+7.00	0-0	-	+0.00	1-2	50	+7.00	0-0	-	+0.00
Eddie Ahern	1-3	33	+1.00	0-0	-	+0.00	1-2	50	+2.00	0-1	-	-1.00

2009

	Overall			Two-year-olds			Three-year-olds			Older horses		
	W-R	%	£1	W-R	%	£1	W-R	%	£1	W-R	%	£1
Joe Fanning	69-371	19	-40.06	23-110	21	-19.63	33-188	18	-38.42	13-73	18	+17.99
Greg Fairley	67-325	21	-23.95	23-106	22	-3.60	34-143	24	+7.65	10-76	13	-28.00
R Ffrench	30-229	13	-66.82	7-70	10	-38.26	21-111	19	+11.19	2-48	4	-39.75
Richard Hills	13-33	39	+29.04	6-11	55	+18.49	6-16	38	+12.80	1-6	17	-2.25
J-P Guillambert	13-61	21	+39.63	4-18	22	+0.63	5-28	18	+14.00	4-15	27	+25.00
Tadhg O'Shea	6-26	23	-3.69	2-7	29	+5.50	4-17	24	-7.19	0-2	-	-2.00
Jimmy Quinn	3-9	33	+8.25	0-1	-	-1.00	2-6	33	+8.00	1-2	50	+1.25
Robert Winston	3-10	30	+0.69	2-4	50	+3.44	1-5	20	-1.75	0-1	-	-1.00
Jimmy Fortune	2-8	25	+27.00	0-1	-	-1.00	0-0	-	+0.00	2-7	29	+28.00
Andrew Mullen	2-13	15	-2.25	0-4	-	-4.00	1-7	14	+0.50	1-2	50	+1.25
Neil Callan	2-17	12	-6.50	0-7	-	-7.00	2-9	22	+1.50	0-1	-	-1.00

By jockey – 2008

	Overall			Two-year-olds			Three-year-olds			Older horses		
	W-R	%	£1	W-R	%	£1	W-R	%	£1	W-R	%	£1
Joe Fanning	57-371	15	-95.46	19-103	18	-5.96	30-220	14	-79.88	8-48	17	-9.63
Greg Fairley	50-324	15	-38.86	13-79	16	+8.75	36-208	17	-20.61	1-37	3	-27.00
R Ffrench	16-110	15	+1.74	11-45	24	+8.24	4-53	8	-13.50	1-12	8	+7.00
J-P Guillambert	10-61	16	-8.00	2-17	12	-7.50	5-34	15	-17.00	3-10	30	+16.50
Darryll Holland	8-42	19	+14.90	3-15	20	+1.40	4-20	20	+12.50	1-7	14	+1.00
Robert Winston	7-29	24	+19.57	2-5	40	+3.13	5-21	24	+19.45	0-3	-	-3.00
Frankie Dettori	3-18	17	+0.88	1-9	11	-6.13	2-7	29	+9.00	0-2	-	-2.00
Richard Hills	3-37	8	-28.13	3-17	18	-8.13	0-17	-	-17.00	0-3	-	-3.00
J Murtagh	2-3	67	+21.00	1-2	50	+13.00	1-1	100	+8.00	0-0	-	+0.00
Franny Norton	1-2	50	+8.00	0-0	-	+0.00	1-2	50	+8.00	0-0	-	+0.00
Miss A Deniel	1-2	50	+13.00	0-0	-	+0.00	1-1	100	+14.00	0-1	-	-1.00

By course – 2007-2010

	Overall			Two-year-olds			Three-year-olds			Older horses		
	W-R	%	£1	W-R	%	£1	W-R	%	£1	W-R	%	£1
Ascot	22-227	10	-51.62	5-35	14	-7.92	12-113	11	-25.45	5-79	6	-18.25
Ayr	11-121	9	-80.67	7-61	11	-39.47	4-43	9	-24.20	0-17	-	-17.00
Bath	11-40	28	-2.08	3-17	18	-6.63	7-19	37	+4.54	1-4	25	+0.00
Beverley	35-149	23	+17.83	12-40	30	+24.74	18-91	20	-7.91	5-18	28	+1.00
Brighton	11-36	31	+39.07	5-16	31	+10.00	5-14	36	+14.07	1-6	17	+15.00
Carlisle	5-41	12	-27.05	2-14	14	-8.80	3-20	15	-11.25	0-7	-	-7.00
Catterick	28-130	22	-2.61	12-53	23	+1.87	11-59	19	-12.22	5-18	28	+7.75
Chepstow	7-23	30	+10.75	1-9	11	-6.13	3-10	30	+11.63	3-4	75	+5.25
Chester	14-109	13	-30.25	1-16	6	-12.50	10-66	15	-12.25	3-27	11	-5.50
Doncaster	18-168	11	-59.32	6-62	10	-19.92	9-66	14	-10.38	3-40	8	-29.03
Epsom	10-86	12	-39.10	2-17	12	-3.50	6-48	13	-27.10	2-21	10	-8.50
Ffos Las	7-29	24	+1.50	1-4	25	+4.00	2-15	13	-8.13	4-10	40	+5.63
Folkestone	3-23	13	-5.63	1-6	17	+5.00	1-15	7	-11.00	1-2	50	+0.38
Goodwood	25-161	16	+78.70	4-38	11	-4.50	14-80	18	+41.20	7-43	16	+42.00
Hamilton	44-192	23	+22.00	14-48	29	+11.80	24-114	21	+18.70	6-30	20	-8.50
Haydock	17-172	10	-79.88	4-49	8	-28.25	10-95	11	-45.97	3-28	11	-5.67
Kempton (AW)	43-294	15	-94.28	8-77	10	-27.88	28-164	17	-61.72	7-53	13	-4.68
Leicester	26-104	25	+39.05	12-43	28	+30.36	11-51	22	-3.80	3-10	30	+12.50
Lingfield	2-17	12	-8.00	1-4	25	+1.50	1-12	8	-8.50	0-1	-	-1.00
Lingfield (AW)	64-330	19	-82.06	10-69	14	-29.80	45-199	23	-38.83	9-62	15	-13.43
Musselburgh	26-128	20	-11.25	7-37	19	-10.82	16-75	21	+5.20	3-16	19	-5.63
Newbury	13-80	16	-8.88	6-30	20	+8.53	5-32	16	-8.67	2-18	11	-8.75
Newcastle	21-125	17	-46.29	8-41	20	-10.25	9-61	15	-25.79	4-23	17	-10.25
Newmarket	16-164	10	-69.03	4-35	11	-16.40	9-84	11	-26.25	3-45	7	-26.38
Newmarket (J)	17-143	12	-10.25	2-40	5	-27.38	11-85	13	+8.13	4-18	22	+9.00
Nottingham	9-98	9	-49.25	5-42	12	-9.75	3-45	7	-31.75	1-11	9	-7.75
Pontefract	17-144	12	-49.07	5-37	14	-17.65	11-81	14	-15.42	1-26	4	-16.00
Redcar	19-122	16	+19.19	8-54	15	+2.88	11-61	18	+23.31	0-7	-	-7.00
Ripon	12-123	10	-68.57	2-30	7	-22.83	8-77	10	-35.48	2-16	13	-10.25
Salisbury	2-13	15	-5.88	1-1	100	+1.63	1-7	14	-2.50	0-5	-	-5.00
Sandown	14-157	9	-49.57	6-39	15	+5.75	6-92	7	-57.32	2-26	8	+2.00
Southwell	1-3	33	-0.25	0-0	-	+0.00	1-2	50	+0.75	0-1	-	-1.00
Southwell (AW)	58-224	26	+19.97	9-50	18	-19.08	38-122	31	+34.01	11-52	21	+5.04
Thirsk	17-112	15	+15.47	5-30	17	+16.75	12-73	16	+7.72	0-9	-	-9.00
Warwick	8-55	15	+6.46	2-20	10	-4.00	4-31	13	+5.13	2-4	50	+5.33
Windsor	5-43	12	-4.00	2-9	22	+4.00	3-26	12	+0.00	0-8	-	-8.00
Wolves (AW)	71-348	20	-43.16	23-109	21	+2.26	42-189	22	-32.17	6-50	12	-13.25
Yarmouth	6-80	8	-39.63	1-37	3	-31.50	4-32	13	-0.63	1-11	9	-7.50
York	10-164	6	-84.50	5-45	11	-6.50	3-74	4	-50.00	2-45	4	-28.00

Ten-year summary

	Wins	Runs	%	Win prize	Total prize	£1 Stake
2010	211	1458	14	£1,657,512.68	£2,419,718.15	-377.04
2009	216	1227	18	£1,747,013.96	£2,843,943.25	-139.14
2008	164	1145	14	£1,345,669.48	£2,070,937.14	-200.11
2007	161	998	16	£1,188,791.46	£1,651,628.48	-122.33
2006	158	1005	16	£1,245,722.50	£1,868,197.71	-87.83
2005	141	885	16	£1,118,373.15	£1,864,674.04	-80.25
2004	119	799	15	£1,726,950.89	£2,437,676.95	-156.74
2003	139	758	18	£1,410,772.78	£2,049,041.43	-5.49
2002	134	748	18	£1,639,288.85	£2,302,133.87	-62.35
2001	116	771	15	£1,338,475.06	£1,808,895.93	-29.07

RAINFALL: wins the Jersey Stakes to help Mark Johnston to another great Royal Ascot

Richard Hannon

Though one short of Johnston's tally for the whole of 2010, Hannon topped the list that really matters as he won the trainers' championship for the first time since 1992.

A 16% strike-rate went a long way towards securing the prize, with Paco Boy and Canford Cliffs helping.

By month – 2010

	Overall			Two-year-olds			Three-year-olds			Older horses		
	W-R	%	£1	W-R	%	£1	W-R	%	£1	W-R	%	£1
January	1-12	8	-10.56	0-0	-	+0.00	1-6	17	-4.56	0-6	-	-6.00
February	2-11	18	+4.00	0-0	-	+0.00	2-8	25	+7.00	0-3	-	-3.00
March	8-31	26	+3.91	1-1	100	+3.50	4-18	22	-4.59	3-12	25	+5.00
April	22-96	23	+2.42	10-21	48	+15.00	8-56	14	-11.31	4-19	21	-1.28
May	33-194	17	-6.74	15-61	25	+17.32	14-97	14	-5.04	4-36	11	-19.02
June	31-187	17	-4.45	15-70	21	-6.90	16-88	18	+31.45	0-29	-	-29.00
July	44-205	21	+15.76	29-104	28	+12.99	10-72	14	+0.87	5-29	17	+1.90
August	21-189	11	-91.46	15-105	14	-48.46	5-58	9	-26.00	1-26	4	-17.00
September	28-206	14	-57.88	21-134	16	-25.00	5-50	10	-24.39	2-22	9	-8.50
October	17-145	12	-10.37	12-91	13	-18.37	2-40	5	-30.00	3-14	21	+38.00
November	1-44	2	-41.90	1-26	4	-23.90	0-12	-	-12.00	0-6	-	-6.00
December	2-21	10	-6.33	1-15	7	-13.33	1-5	20	+8.00	0-1	-	-1.00

2009

	Overall			Two-year-olds			Three-year-olds			Older horses		
	W-R	%	£1	W-R	%	£1	W-R	%	£1	W-R	%	£1
January	3-30	10	-10.00	0-0	-	+0.00	2-26	8	-11.00	1-4	25	+1.00
February	1-20	5	-16.50	0-0	-	+0.00	1-11	9	-7.50	0-9	-	-9.00
March	8-35	23	+26.13	0-2	-	-2.00	5-22	23	+21.25	3-11	27	+6.88
April	12-91	13	-29.77	4-19	21	-8.64	3-48	6	-26.76	5-24	21	+5.63
May	30-169	18	+1.59	15-56	27	+5.76	10-75	13	+7.95	5-38	13	-12.13
June	25-180	14	-20.29	15-73	21	+20.37	8-81	10	-34.00	2-26	8	-6.67
July	30-224	13	-68.61	17-120	14	-34.49	9-75	12	-33.38	4-29	14	-0.75
August	35-211	17	+16.81	19-115	17	+25.50	12-75	16	-3.78	4-21	19	-4.92
September	19-190	10	-55.55	12-117	10	-62.05	7-51	14	+28.50	0-22	-	-22.00
October	14-157	9	-28.07	10-99	10	-5.57	3-46	7	-19.50	1-12	8	-3.00
November	8-47	17	-6.00	6-28	21	+5.00	1-13	8	-9.50	1-6	17	-1.50
December	3-17	18	-3.33	0-12	-	-12.00	3-3	100	+10.67	0-2	-	-2.00

2008

	Overall			Two-year-olds			Three-year-olds			Older horses		
	W-R	%	£1	W-R	%	£1	W-R	%	£1	W-R	%	£1
January	1-20	5	-3.00	0-0	-	+0.00	1-17	6	+0.00	0-3	-	-3.00
February	3-20	15	-12.83	0-0	-	+0.00	3-15	20	-7.83	0-5	-	-5.00
March	10-43	23	-10.40	0-0	-	+0.00	7-27	26	-2.13	3-16	19	-8.27
April	18-104	17	-20.28	3-14	21	+0.50	8-65	12	-23.38	7-25	28	+2.59
May	26-182	14	-51.78	15-58	26	+3.06	6-89	7	-53.75	5-35	14	-1.09
June	28-189	15	-21.29	15-80	19	-22.29	8-79	10	-25.50	5-30	17	+26.50
July	32-196	16	+1.18	18-112	16	-5.18	12-66	18	+12.85	2-18	11	-6.50
August	22-182	12	-39.53	13-118	11	-29.35	6-45	13	-16.93	3-19	16	+6.75
September	22-185	12	-53.67	15-115	13	-19.12	5-49	10	-23.05	2-21	10	-11.50
October	14-172	8	-30.13	10-104	10	+2.38	1-45	2	-37.00	3-23	13	+4.50
November	9-76	12	-28.75	5-49	10	-20.00	3-21	14	-7.75	1-6	17	-1.00
December	4-37	11	-13.13	0-25	-	-25.00	1-8	13	+3.00	3-4	75	+8.88

By race type – 2010

	Overall			Two-year-olds			Three-year-olds			Older horses		
	W-R	%	£1	W-R	%	£1	W-R	%	£1	W-R	%	£1
Handicap	69-611	11	-111.50	17-119	14	-18.58	37-349	11	-86.67	15-143	10	-6.25
Group 1,2,3	15-66	23	-0.80	9-32	28	+10.46	4-18	22	+0.92	2-16	13	-12.17
Maiden	79-436	18	-72.52	64-358	18	-67.94	15-78	19	-4.58	0-0	-	+0.00

2009

	Overall			Two-year-olds			Three-year-olds			Older horses		
	W-R	%	£1	W-R	%	£1	W-R	%	£1	W-R	%	£1
Handicap	73-631	12	-123.28	9-124	7	-55.17	49-363	13	-26.19	15-144	10	-41.92
Group 1,2,3	11-86	13	+36.07	6-35	17	+35.86	1-29	3	+0.00	4-22	18	+0.21
Maiden	60-410	15	-86.46	57-356	16	-46.12	3-54	6	-40.34	0-0	-	+0.00

2008

	Overall			Two-year-olds			Three-year-olds			Older horses		
	W-R	%	£1	W-R	%	£1	W-R	%	£1	W-R	%	£1
Handicap	63-624	10	-196.42	11-146	8	-66.79	34-347	10	-120.79	18-131	14	-8.83
Group 1,2,3	11-86	13	-7.39	4-45	9	-4.00	3-15	20	+2.20	4-26	15	-5.59
Maiden	65-429	15	-83.08	57-348	16	-29.35	8-81	10	-53.73	0-0	-	+0.00

By jockey – 2010

	Overall			Two-year-olds			Three-year-olds			Older horses		
	W-R	%	£1	W-R	%	£1	W-R	%	£1	W-R	%	£1
R Hughes	113-556	20	-84.63	64-235	27	-14.57	37-232	16	-54.01	12-89	13	-16.05
Pat Dobbs	31-244	13	-89.18	19-122	16	-27.87	10-92	11	-43.31	2-30	7	-18.00
Ryan Moore	28-123	23	+34.39	20-71	28	+14.99	3-30	10	-6.75	5-22	23	+26.15
Jimmy Fortune	8-89	9	-16.33	2-45	4	-39.56	5-29	17	+34.73	1-15	7	-11.50
Dane O'Neill	5-31	16	-6.36	4-17	24	-1.86	1-8	13	+1.50	0-6	-	-6.00
F McDonald	4-55	7	-11.25	3-33	9	+8.50	1-21	5	-18.75	0-1	-	-1.00
Patrick Hills	4-64	6	-34.33	1-20	5	-18.27	3-32	9	-4.06	0-12	-	-12.00
Richard Mullen	2-7	29	+24.88	0-3	-	-3.00	2-3	67	+28.88	0-1	-	-1.00
Pat Cosgrave	2-11	18	+22.00	1-8	13	+18.00	1-3	33	+4.00	0-0	-	+0.00
Charles Eddery	2-22	9	-13.00	0-3	-	-3.00	2-12	17	-3.00	0-7	-	-7.00
Fergus Sweeney	1-2	50	+3.50	1-1	100	+4.50	0-1	-	-1.00	0-0	-	+0.00
Greg Fairley	1-2	50	+6.00	1-2	50	+6.00	0-0	-	+0.00	0-0	-	+0.00
Martin Dwyer	1-3	33	+0.50	0-2	-	-2.00	0-0	-	+0.00	1-1	100	+2.50
Liam Keniry	1-4	25	+13.00	0-2	-	-2.00	0-0	-	+0.00	1-2	50	+15.00
David Probert	1-5	20	+4.00	1-2	50	+7.00	0-3	-	-3.00	0-0	-	+0.00

2009

	Overall			Two-year-olds			Three-year-olds			Older horses		
	W-R	%	£1	W-R	%	£1	W-R	%	£1	W-R	%	£1
R Hughes	96-475	20	+35.53	54-201	27	+78.07	28-196	14	-26.82	14-78	18	-15.71
Pat Dobbs	32-253	13	+2.22	13-119	11	-15.96	16-107	15	+26.43	3-27	11	-8.25
Ryan Moore	17-160	11	-63.41	12-91	13	-28.41	3-50	6	-35.00	2-19	11	+0.00
Dane O'Neill	10-86	12	-33.88	4-36	11	-20.88	4-30	13	-1.50	2-20	10	-11.50
Patrick Hills	7-59	12	+7.10	0-21	-	-21.00	6-24	25	+33.10	1-14	7	-5.00
Franny Norton	4-20	20	-4.80	4-16	25	-0.80	0-4	-	-4.00	0-0	-	+0.00
Jimmy Fortune	4-66	6	-34.92	4-29	14	+2.08	0-20	-	-20.00	0-17	-	-17.00
Jim Crowley	3-11	27	-0.63	1-4	25	-1.13	1-5	20	-1.00	1-2	50	+1.50
Steve Drowne	3-35	9	+14.00	1-21	5	-2.00	1-10	10	+5.00	1-4	25	+11.00
S Whitworth	2-5	40	+5.00	1-3	33	+0.50	0-0	-	+0.00	1-2	50	+4.50
Jamie Spencer	2-9	22	-0.25	0-3	-	-3.00	2-6	33	+2.75	0-0	-	+0.00

By jockey – 2008

	Overall			Two-year-olds			Three-year-olds			Older horses		
	W-R	%	£1	W-R	%	£1	W-R	%	£1	W-R	%	£1
R Hughes	80-497	16	-67.32	44-214	21	+28.61	25-196	13	-79.52	11-87	13	-16.41
Ryan Moore	37-234	16	-35.90	17-124	14	-47.36	7-72	10	-36.30	13-38	34	+47.76
Pat Dobbs	20-172	12	-35.60	14-89	16	+16.90	4-65	6	-43.00	2-18	11	-9.50
Dane O'Neill	11-72	15	-9.50	6-39	15	-3.00	3-28	11	-12.75	2-5	40	+6.25
Jimmy Fortune	8-42	19	+25.00	5-21	24	+23.50	1-10	10	-2.50	2-11	18	+4.00
Patrick Hills	7-76	9	-27.71	0-29	-	-29.00	6-40	15	-1.71	1-7	14	+3.00
Eddie Ahern	6-34	18	+7.75	3-18	17	-3.75	2-11	18	+9.00	1-5	20	+2.50
Hadden Frost	5-41	12	-6.25	0-5	-	-5.00	3-24	13	+1.50	2-12	17	-2.75
Charles Eddery	4-29	14	+5.88	0-6	-	-6.00	4-17	24	+17.88	0-6	-	-6.00
Hayley Turner	2-8	25	-3.55	0-1	-	-1.00	2-7	29	-2.55	0-0	-	+0.00
Jim Crowley	2-11	18	+14.00	1-8	13	+9.00	1-3	33	+5.00	0-0	-	+0.00

By course – 2007-2010

	Overall			Two-year-olds			Three-year-olds			Older horses		
	W-R	%	£1	W-R	%	£1	W-R	%	£1	W-R	%	£1
Ascot	17-259	7	-108.38	7-112	6	-66.21	4-80	5	-61.00	6-67	9	+18.83
Ayr	0-4	-	-4.00	0-2	-	-2.00	0-1	-	-1.00	0-1	-	-1.00
Bath	19-135	14	-44.23	11-80	14	-33.18	2-40	5	-32.30	6-15	40	+21.25
Beverley	3-7	43	+1.61	3-6	50	+2.61	0-1	-	-1.00	0-0	-	+0.00
Brighton	18-72	25	+23.54	11-44	25	-1.21	4-22	18	+7.50	3-6	50	+17.25
Carlisle	0-1	-	-1.00	0-0	-	+0.00	0-1	-	-1.00	0-0	-	+0.00
Catterick	0-2	-	-2.00	0-2	-	-2.00	0-0	-	+0.00	0-0	-	+0.00
Chepstow	14-88	16	-25.81	7-33	21	-9.49	6-48	13	-13.65	1-7	14	-2.67
Chester	9-47	19	-10.71	7-26	27	-1.21	1-12	8	-8.00	1-9	11	-1.50
Doncaster	23-134	17	+64.08	10-75	13	-1.43	6-31	19	+44.50	7-28	25	+21.00
Epsom	9-83	11	-46.53	3-27	11	-22.03	5-34	15	-13.50	1-22	5	-11.00
Ffos Las	3-20	15	-5.89	0-9	-	-9.00	3-7	43	+7.12	0-4	-	-4.00
Folkestone	15-68	22	-4.88	9-28	32	+15.01	5-35	14	-19.39	1-5	20	-0.50
Goodwood	60-417	14	-35.38	38-190	20	+29.86	15-146	10	-39.73	7-81	9	-25.50
Hamilton	1-3	33	-0.13	0-0	-	+0.00	1-3	33	-0.13	0-0	-	+0.00
Haydock	14-76	18	-30.94	6-33	18	-13.50	6-28	21	-6.60	2-15	13	-10.84
Kempton (AW)	82-633	13	-189.52	38-281	14	-97.53	37-259	14	-18.59	7-93	8	-73.40
Leicester	15-97	15	-3.98	12-56	21	+14.52	3-33	9	-10.50	0-8	-	-8.00
Lingfield	15-70	21	+9.99	9-38	24	+12.58	6-27	22	+2.42	0-5	-	-5.00
Lingfield (AW)	63-448	14	-112.56	21-147	14	-47.61	28-205	14	-67.24	14-96	15	+2.29
Newbury	52-470	11	-163.61	34-273	12	-88.12	15-140	11	-27.97	3-57	5	-47.52
Newcastle	0-3	-	-3.00	0-1	-	-1.00	0-1	-	-1.00	0-1	-	-1.00
Newmarket	31-275	11	-39.30	18-136	13	+23.30	4-96	4	-72.00	9-43	21	+39.50
Newmarket (J)	40-205	15	+11.47	26-152	17	+26.12	11-85	13	-18.05	3-28	11	+3.40
Nottingham	14-83	17	-13.74	6-42	14	-16.29	6-31	19	+8.75	2-10	20	-6.20
Pontefract	2-28	7	-14.00	1-16	6	-11.00	1-9	11	+0.00	0-3	-	-3.00
Redcar	0-1	-	-1.00	0-1	-	-1.00	0-0	-	+0.00	0-0	-	+0.00
Ripon	1-2	50	-0.43	1-1	100	+0.57	0-0	-	+0.00	0-1	-	-1.00
Salisbury	53-356	15	-70.55	24-163	15	-58.17	24-153	16	-3.62	5-40	13	-8.75
Sandown	39-283	14	-7.96	22-122	18	+12.69	11-122	9	-17.63	6-39	15	-3.03
Southwell (AW)	1-7	14	-2.00	0-2	-	-2.00	1-4	25	+1.00	0-1	-	-1.00
Thirsk	0-2	-	-2.00	0-1	-	-1.00	0-1	-	-1.00	0-0	-	+0.00
Warwick	12-67	18	+4.58	7-35	20	+6.45	3-23	13	-14.88	2-9	22	+13.00
Windsor	77-472	16	-61.56	35-210	17	-39.51	28-190	15	-22.39	14-72	19	+0.33
Wolves (AW)	22-114	19	+35.81	9-50	18	+6.39	9-44	20	+20.92	4-20	20	+8.50
Yarmouth	2-10	20	-0.43	0-6	-	-6.00	2-4	50	+5.57	0-0	-	+0.00
York	6-63	10	-23.50	3-30	10	-11.50	1-11	9	-7.00	2-22	9	-5.00

Ten-year summary

	Wins	Runs	%	Win prize	Total prize	£1 Stake
2010	210	1341	16	£2,054,058.90	£3,218,574.92	-203.61
2009	188	1371	14	£1,751,642.04	£2,814,384.49	-193.61
2008	189	1406	13	£1,884,767.33	£2,982,090.39	-283.60
2007	148	1075	14	£1,192,346.67	£2,083,975.15	-178.25
2006	127	1067	12	£1,043,024.26	£1,753,310.04	-261.41
2005	145	1261	11	£1,209,719.79	£2,030,928.02	-282.57
2004	113	1201	9	£795,942.69	£1,464,125.73	-235.21
2003	122	1031	12	£1,028,947.30	£1,688,075.94	-271.73
2002	121	1099	11	£928,854.33	£1,731,689.28	-394.70
2001	112	1180	9	£862,584.65	£1,430,473.86	-496.38

FREE AGENT: a welcome royal winner for Richard Hannon at York in July

Richard Fahey

Fahey has increased his winning tally in nine of the last ten seasons and another superb campaign saw him close in on Johnston and Hannon with a mighty 181 winners.

That doesn't even include Wootton Bassett's breakthrough Group 1 win in France last October.

By month – 2010

	Overall			Two-year-olds			Three-year-olds			Older horses		
	W-R	%	£1	W-R	%	£1	W-R	%	£1	W-R	%	£1
January	5-40	13	-12.65	0-0	-	+0.00	1-5	20	-3.27	4-35	11	-9.38
February	3-23	13	-9.25	0-0	-	+0.00	2-7	29	+1.25	1-16	6	-10.50
March	10-51	20	+10.83	3-5	60	+7.45	1-9	11	-6.13	6-37	16	+9.50
April	20-96	21	+27.15	3-12	25	-2.52	3-32	9	-21.88	14-52	27	+51.55
May	19-168	11	-78.68	4-18	22	-5.25	7-67	10	-30.55	8-83	10	-42.88
June	21-160	13	-68.69	11-41	27	+10.82	5-46	11	-25.09	5-73	7	-54.42
July	26-178	15	-62.16	15-57	26	-4.41	2-42	5	-30.13	9-79	11	-27.63
August	20-177	11	-25.45	11-65	17	+21.60	3-45	7	-22.00	6-67	9	-25.05
September	24-185	13	-55.40	11-57	19	-2.75	5-42	12	-12.00	8-86	9	-40.65
October	13-139	9	+1.83	5-41	12	+4.50	2-36	6	-22.00	6-62	10	+19.33
November	12-75	16	-1.88	9-25	36	+32.63	0-18	-	-18.00	3-32	9	-16.50
December	8-64	13	+0.80	3-15	20	+6.50	2-13	15	+11.00	3-36	8	-16.70

2009

	Overall			Two-year-olds			Three-year-olds			Older horses		
	W-R	%	£1	W-R	%	£1	W-R	%	£1	W-R	%	£1
January	5-37	14	+60.17	0-0	-	+0.00	1-7	14	+6.00	4-30	13	+54.17
February	2-23	9	-17.00	0-0	-	+0.00	0-4	-	-4.00	2-19	11	-13.00
March	7-36	19	+8.63	0-1	-	-1.00	1-9	11	-6.13	6-26	23	+15.75
April	14-75	19	+20.60	1-5	20	-2.90	3-21	14	-10.50	10-49	20	+34.00
May	25-148	17	-8.08	4-22	18	-1.50	8-38	21	+2.34	13-88	15	-8.92
June	32-151	21	+83.53	5-33	15	-14.50	12-36	33	+96.63	15-82	18	+1.40
July	24-158	15	+17.86	5-40	13	-24.42	9-48	19	+32.66	10-70	14	+9.63
August	16-155	10	-100.97	3-40	8	-28.59	6-52	12	-36.10	7-63	11	-36.28
September	26-152	17	+31.13	11-51	22	+19.63	4-30	13	-8.50	11-71	15	+20.00
October	12-97	12	-2.63	5-38	13	-14.63	2-15	13	+14.50	5-44	11	-2.50
November	0-32	-	-32.00	0-9	-	-9.00	0-5	-	-5.00	0-18	-	-18.00
December	2-42	5	-36.00	0-9	-	-9.00	0-9	-	-9.00	2-24	8	-18.00

2008

	Overall			Two-year-olds			Three-year-olds			Older horses		
	W-R	%	£1	W-R	%	£1	W-R	%	£1	W-R	%	£1
January	1-27	4	-22.67	0-0	-	+0.00	0-1	-	-1.00	1-26	4	-21.67
February	2-13	15	-6.13	0-0	-	+0.00	0-1	-	-1.00	2-12	17	-5.13
March	4-38	11	-1.25	0-1	-	-1.00	1-6	17	+1.00	3-31	10	-1.25
April	10-79	13	-41.50	1-2	50	+2.50	3-23	13	-10.88	6-54	11	-33.13
May	17-131	13	+20.83	3-14	21	+39.00	5-33	15	+4.83	9-84	11	-23.00
June	19-142	13	-39.13	5-21	24	+13.38	3-41	7	-27.00	11-80	14	-25.50
July	22-149	15	-16.13	3-31	10	-21.84	7-42	17	-5.46	12-76	16	+11.17
August	10-127	8	-70.38	3-36	8	-21.00	4-30	13	-0.13	3-61	5	-49.25
September	11-112	10	-52.09	3-31	10	-18.88	2-28	7	-14.00	6-53	11	-19.22
October	10-103	10	-45.22	4-35	11	-14.47	2-26	8	-10.50	4-42	10	-20.25
November	7-37	19	+0.88	3-11	27	+5.75	2-9	22	+2.38	2-17	12	-7.25
December	0-13	-	-13.00	0-4	-	-4.00	0-3	-	-3.00	0-6	-	-6.00

By race type – 2010

	Overall			Two-year-olds			Three-year-olds			Older horses		
	W-R	%	£1	W-R	%	£1	W-R	%	£1	W-R	%	£1
Handicap	95-925	10	-238.11	19-93	20	+30.53	23-272	8	-136.22	53-560	9	-132.42
Group 1,2,3	1-28	4	-19.00	0-15	-	-15.00	1-3	33	+6.00	0-10	-	-10.00
Maiden	43-227	19	-20.63	37-164	23	+28.80	4-55	7	-45.33	2-8	25	-4.10

2009

	Overall			Two-year-olds			Three-year-olds			Older horses		
	W-R	%	£1	W-R	%	£1	W-R	%	£1	W-R	%	£1
Handicap	101-740	14	+62.49	8-56	14	-20.63	31-205	15	+50.13	62-479	13	+32.98
Group 1,2,3	2-16	13	+9.00	0-9	-	-9.00	0-1	-	-1.00	2-6	33	+19.00
Maiden	30-200	15	-18.15	23-145	16	-28.01	7-50	14	+14.86	0-5	-	-5.00

2008

	Overall			Two-year-olds			Three-year-olds			Older horses		
	W-R	%	£1	W-R	%	£1	W-R	%	£1	W-R	%	£1
Handicap	73-688	11	-235.88	4-41	10	-14.00	23-188	12	-64.08	46-459	10	-157.79
Group 1,2,3	2-15	13	-7.75	0-5	-	-5.00	0-0	-	+0.00	2-10	20	-2.75
Maiden	24-150	16	+40.40	18-108	17	+22.07	6-42	14	+18.33	0-0	-	+0.00

By jockey – 2010

	Overall			Two-year-olds			Three-year-olds			Older horses		
	W-R	%	£1	W-R	%	£1	W-R	%	£1	W-R	%	£1
Paul Hanagan	101-567	18	-90.33	42-150	28	+3.93	19-155	12	-63.25	40-262	15	-31.02
Tony Hamilton	17-152	11	-24.54	7-38	18	+15.38	4-54	7	-34.63	6-60	10	-5.29
Lee Topliss	16-136	12	-24.13	4-20	20	+2.88	4-25	16	+5.50	8-91	9	-32.50
Barry McHugh	9-116	8	-58.43	7-37	19	+11.88	1-32	3	-25.50	1-47	2	-44.80
G Chaloner	4-12	33	+22.30	1-2	50	+7.00	2-6	33	+18.00	1-4	25	-2.70
Paul Mulrennan	3-28	11	-16.38	2-13	15	-4.13	0-6	-	-6.00	1-9	11	-6.25
Tom Eaves	3-33	9	-14.13	3-13	23	+5.88	0-8	-	-8.00	0-12	-	-12.00
Jack Mitchell	2-10	20	+17.00	1-2	50	+15.00	0-2	-	-2.00	1-6	17	+4.00
Miss P Tutty	2-11	18	+12.00	0-0	-	+0.00	0-0	-	+0.00	2-11	18	+12.00
Jimmy Quinn	2-21	10	-3.00	1-6	17	+3.00	0-6	-	-6.00	1-9	11	+0.00
Frederik Tylicki	2-26	8	-21.42	0-1	-	-1.00	1-8	13	-6.17	1-17	6	-14.25
M Jeziorek	2-29	7	-13.13	0-3	-	-3.00	0-5	-	-5.00	2-21	10	-5.13
Adam Carter	1-1	100	+8.00	0-0	-	+0.00	0-0	-	+0.00	1-1	100	+8.00
Hayley Turner	1-1	100	+16.00	1-1	100	+16.00	0-0	-	+0.00	0-0	-	+0.00
Ian Mongan	1-1	100	+3.50	0-0	-	+0.00	0-0	-	+0.00	1-1	100	+3.50

2009

	Overall			Two-year-olds			Three-year-olds			Older horses		
	W-R	%	£1	W-R	%	£1	W-R	%	£1	W-R	%	£1
Paul Hanagan	74-493	15	+44.08	19-128	15	-46.86	24-129	19	+61.27	31-236	13	+29.68
Frederik Tylicki	32-162	20	+48.03	6-35	17	+12.00	5-26	19	+0.28	21-101	21	+35.75
Tony Hamilton	31-208	15	-34.28	7-55	13	-29.30	12-61	20	+9.60	12-92	13	-14.58
Barry McHugh	6-48	13	+5.50	0-1	-	-1.00	0-8	-	-8.00	6-39	15	+14.50
Jamie Moriarty	5-30	17	-3.50	0-3	-	-3.00	0-8	-	-8.00	5-19	26	+7.50
Miss P Tutty	3-11	27	+11.00	0-0	-	+0.00	0-0	-	+0.00	3-11	27	+11.00
Mrs V Fahey	2-12	17	+1.75	0-0	-	+0.00	1-1	100	+2.75	1-11	9	-1.00
Lee Topliss	2-29	7	-21.60	0-4	-	-4.00	1-6	17	+0.00	1-19	5	-17.60
David Allan	1-1	100	+4.00	0-0	-	+0.00	0-0	-	+0.00	1-1	100	+4.00
Martin Lane	1-1	100	+2.75	1-1	100	+2.75	0-0	-	+0.00	0-0	-	+0.00
Cathy Gannon	1-2	50	+3.00	0-1	-	-1.00	1-1	100	+4.00	0-0	-	+0.00

By jockey – 2008

	Overall			Two-year-olds			Three-year-olds			Older horses		
	W-R	%	£1	W-R	%	£1	W-R	%	£1	W-R	%	£1
Paul Hanagan	60-447	13	-64.81	16-91	18	+30.66	18-120	15	+4.63	26-236	11	-100.09
Jamie Moriarty	15-127	12	-28.04	2-25	8	-12.75	3-21	14	-7.25	10-81	12	-8.04
Tony Hamilton	15-144	10	-68.68	5-42	12	-22.47	2-39	5	-29.13	8-63	13	-17.08
Frederik Tylicki	11-73	15	-2.25	0-7	-	-7.00	3-18	17	-1.00	8-48	17	+5.75
Barry McHugh	8-71	11	-33.50	2-10	20	+2.00	1-15	7	-12.00	5-46	11	-23.50
Kerrin McEvoy	2-3	67	+5.50	0-0	-	+0.00	1-1	100	+1.50	1-2	50	+4.00
Lance Betts	1-1	100	+6.50	0-0	-	+0.00	1-1	100	+6.50	0-0	-	+0.00
Dale Gibson	1-31	3	-26.50	0-3	-	-3.00	0-7	-	-7.00	1-21	5	-16.50
Andrea Atzeni	0-1	-	-1.00	0-0	-	+0.00	0-1	-	-1.00	0-0	-	+0.00
Andrew Elliott	0-1	-	-1.00	0-0	-	+0.00	0-0	-	+0.00	0-1	-	-1.00
Brian Toomey	0-1	-	-1.00	0-0	-	+0.00	0-0	-	+0.00	0-1	-	-1.00

By course – 2007-2010

	Overall			Two-year-olds			Three-year-olds			Older horses		
	W-R	%	£1	W-R	%	£1	W-R	%	£1	W-R	%	£1
Ascot	5-86	6	+17.50	1-16	6	-10.50	1-10	10	+57.00	3-60	5	-29.00
Ayr	44-244	18	+10.10	16-65	25	+0.08	9-53	17	+4.63	19-126	15	+5.40
Bath	0-5	-	-5.00	0-0	-	+0.00	0-2	-	-2.00	0-3	-	-3.00
Beverley	37-265	14	-84.41	9-56	16	-23.38	16-86	19	-16.04	12-123	10	-45.00
Brighton	1-2	50	+0.63	0-0	-	+0.00	0-1	-	-1.00	1-1	100	+1.63
Carlisle	21-122	17	-6.63	4-32	13	-19.71	8-36	22	+15.96	9-54	17	-2.88
Catterick	16-116	14	-39.26	8-45	18	-13.72	1-27	4	-22.00	7-44	16	-3.54
Chester	14-129	11	-15.42	2-25	8	-4.75	2-47	4	-34.17	10-57	18	+23.50
Doncaster	24-241	10	-60.27	9-59	15	+21.65	3-49	6	-33.92	12-133	9	-48.00
Epsom	3-37	8	-25.34	1-3	33	+0.75	2-8	25	-0.09	0-26	-	-26.00
Folkestone	0-2	-	-2.00	0-0	-	+0.00	0-1	-	-1.00	0-1	-	-1.00
Goodwood	2-79	3	-60.50	0-15	-	-15.00	0-18	-	-18.00	2-46	4	-27.50
Hamilton	42-193	22	+4.35	8-33	24	+19.52	9-56	16	-17.67	25-104	24	+2.50
Haydock	17-192	9	-83.16	6-46	13	-12.77	3-67	4	-53.59	8-79	10	-16.79
Kempton (AW)	7-108	6	-58.75	0-17	-	-17.00	2-31	6	-19.75	5-60	8	-22.00
Leicester	5-49	10	-5.63	0-12	-	-12.00	2-22	9	-9.63	3-15	20	+16.00
Lingfield (AW)	12-97	12	-32.87	7-12	58	+33.00	1-18	6	-9.50	4-67	6	-56.37
Musselburgh	23-180	13	-82.63	8-25	32	+4.20	4-45	9	-28.64	11-110	10	-58.20
Newbury	2-40	5	-11.50	0-6	-	-6.00	0-4	-	-4.00	2-30	7	-1.50
Newcastle	31-197	16	-33.87	11-42	26	+0.90	9-58	16	-12.63	11-97	11	-22.15
Newmarket	1-60	2	-43.00	1-14	7	+3.00	0-10	-	-10.00	0-36	-	-36.00
Newmarket (J)	2-52	4	-39.50	1-12	8	-7.50	1-19	5	-11.00	0-21	-	-21.00
Nottingham	7-54	13	-3.03	1-13	8	-6.00	4-24	17	-0.63	2-17	12	+3.00
Pontefract	23-172	13	-4.44	5-37	14	+1.85	6-52	12	-9.13	12-83	14	+2.83
Redcar	30-178	17	-13.53	10-61	16	+2.83	10-58	17	-2.32	10-59	17	-14.05
Ripon	18-174	10	-64.50	5-48	10	-20.50	5-54	9	-21.38	8-72	11	-22.63
Salisbury	0-9	-	-9.00	0-2	-	-2.00	0-3	-	-3.00	0-4	-	-4.00
Sandown	1-19	5	-15.00	0-4	-	-4.00	1-4	25	+0.00	0-11	-	-11.00
Southwell	0-9	-	-9.00	0-0	-	+0.00	0-5	-	-5.00	0-4	-	-4.00
Southwell (AW)	42-272	15	-21.84	5-33	15	-9.68	6-49	12	+16.60	31-190	16	-28.77
Thirsk	19-126	15	-5.09	7-34	21	+14.78	5-42	12	-12.50	7-50	14	-7.38
Warwick	2-22	9	-5.50	1-5	20	+6.00	0-4	-	-4.00	1-13	8	-7.50
Windsor	2-9	22	+4.50	0-2	-	-2.00	1-3	33	+1.50	1-4	25	+5.00
Wolves (AW)	40-399	10	-27.86	7-72	10	-35.90	6-112	5	-63.38	27-215	13	+71.42
Yarmouth	6-24	25	+7.75	1-7	14	-4.25	1-7	14	-2.00	4-10	40	+14.00
York	42-368	11	-31.06	12-80	15	-19.65	11-69	16	+34.50	19-219	9	-45.92

Ten-year summary

	Wins	Runs	%	Win prize	Total prize	£1 Stake
2010	181	1356	13	£1,325,389.94	£2,075,925.44	-273.54
2009	165	1106	15	£1,123,057.39	£1,657,128.68	+25.22
2008	113	971	12	£753,492.30	£1,247,043.13	-285.77
2007	85	926	9	£643,994.08	£1,132,827.97	-327.77
2006	87	734	12	£677,880.08	£1,098,407.35	-98.05
2005	79	768	10	£487,562.61	£802,151.94	-131.29
2004	77	649	12	£504,814.42	£740,641.01	-53.26
2003	50	466	11	£346,111.20	£526,707.78	-134.77
2002	46	370	12	£403,128.23	£505,931.06	+30.38
2001	26	377	7	£121,143.25	£219,483.85	-176.79

WOOTTON BASSETT: a real money-spinner for Richard Fahey last year

Kevin Ryan

To Ryan's enormous credit he secured a third century in four years despite a reduction in his number of runners for the fourth successive year.

A 13% strike-rate helped Ryan to reach the milestone, with particularly good results during the winter months on the all-weather.

By month – 2010

	Overall			Two-year-olds			Three-year-olds			Older horses		
	W-R	%	£1	W-R	%	£1	W-R	%	£1	W-R	%	£1
January	10-32	31	-3.93	0-0	-	+0.00	3-5	60	+6.95	7-27	26	-10.88
February	7-33	21	-0.79	0-0	-	+0.00	4-10	40	+11.08	3-23	13	-11.88
March	4-47	9	-33.03	0-2	-	-2.00	0-18	-	-18.00	4-27	15	-13.03
April	9-61	15	+9.88	2-11	18	+5.50	4-23	17	+13.00	3-27	11	-8.63
May	17-112	15	-2.58	6-34	18	-5.58	6-28	21	+21.88	5-50	10	-18.88
June	13-100	13	-20.74	7-31	23	+20.41	4-27	15	-11.25	2-42	5	-29.90
July	10-108	9	-64.47	5-42	12	-22.72	4-24	17	-7.25	1-42	2	-34.50
August	17-101	17	-10.79	5-28	18	-6.63	4-27	15	+4.83	8-46	17	-9.00
September	7-96	7	-25.50	3-39	8	-9.00	1-17	6	-8.00	3-40	8	+0.50
October	4-53	8	-2.00	3-20	15	+21.00	1-11	9	-1.00	0-22	-	-22.00
November	2-35	6	-10.50	0-11	-	-11.00	1-10	10	-6.50	1-14	7	+7.00
December	7-35	20	+8.83	1-9	11	-4.00	4-10	40	+19.83	2-16	13	-7.00

2009

	Overall			Two-year-olds			Three-year-olds			Older horses		
	W-R	%	£1	W-R	%	£1	W-R	%	£1	W-R	%	£1
January	13-47	28	+1.42	0-0	-	+0.00	2-6	33	+3.33	11-41	27	-1.92
February	8-49	16	-31.78	0-0	-	+0.00	3-14	21	-8.39	5-35	14	-23.40
March	6-41	15	-23.20	0-1	-	-1.00	1-10	10	-8.27	5-30	17	-13.92
April	10-68	15	-14.73	1-14	7	-12.60	3-24	13	-8.00	6-30	20	+5.88
May	13-119	11	-34.72	1-19	5	-17.82	6-42	14	+2.30	6-58	10	-19.20
June	11-92	12	+12.00	2-14	14	+22.00	0-28	-	-28.00	9-50	18	+18.00
July	9-104	9	-53.20	2-35	6	-17.00	3-33	9	-11.00	4-36	11	-25.20
August	9-112	8	-64.38	4-34	12	-23.88	1-34	3	-19.00	4-44	9	-21.50
September	8-101	8	-35.93	2-35	6	-29.43	2-26	8	-18.00	4-40	10	+11.50
October	4-78	5	-46.50	3-34	9	-7.50	0-23	-	-23.00	1-21	5	-16.00
November	3-39	8	-29.42	1-15	7	-12.63	0-9	-	-9.00	2-15	13	-7.79
December	2-17	12	+6.75	1-4	25	+17.00	1-8	13	-5.25	0-5	-	-5.00

2008

	Overall			Two-year-olds			Three-year-olds			Older horses		
	W-R	%	£1	W-R	%	£1	W-R	%	£1	W-R	%	£1
January	8-43	19	-19.30	0-0	-	+0.00	1-11	9	-7.00	7-32	22	-12.30
February	4-30	13	-15.13	0-0	-	+0.00	0-10	-	-10.00	4-20	20	-5.13
March	6-42	14	-23.65	0-1	-	-1.00	2-12	17	-6.27	4-29	14	-16.38
April	5-61	8	-23.50	1-7	14	-3.00	3-25	12	+1.50	1-29	3	-22.00
May	7-90	8	-34.89	3-24	13	+0.75	2-31	6	-12.64	2-35	6	-23.00
June	14-106	13	-40.29	5-31	16	-2.00	6-41	15	-17.29	3-34	9	-21.00
July	19-125	15	-6.91	7-41	17	+7.47	7-37	19	+1.13	5-47	11	-15.50
August	15-117	13	+7.16	6-42	14	+12.66	5-46	11	+4.50	4-29	14	-10.00
September	13-120	11	-30.43	5-39	13	-5.16	3-35	9	-15.75	5-46	11	-9.50
October	7-76	9	-27.42	2-32	6	-11.75	1-15	7	-10.67	4-29	14	-5.00
November	7-50	14	-9.33	2-16	13	-8.83	2-11	18	+7.50	3-23	13	-8.00
December	3-29	10	-20.97	0-5	-	-5.00	0-7	-	-7.00	3-17	18	-8.97

By race type – 2010

	Overall			Two-year-olds			Three-year-olds			Older horses		
	W-R	%	£1	W-R	%	£1	W-R	%	£1	W-R	%	£1
Handicap	61-497	12	-70.89	8-53	15	+5.78	33-159	21	+59.04	20-285	7	-135.72
Group 1,2,3	0-17	-	-17.00	0-6	-	-6.00	0-1	-	-1.00	0-10	-	-10.00
Maiden	21-172	12	-40.33	15-124	12	-22.09	3-36	8	-18.47	3-12	25	+0.23

2009

	Overall			Two-year-olds			Three-year-olds			Older horses		
	W-R	%	£1	W-R	%	£1	W-R	%	£1	W-R	%	£1
Handicap	56-517	11	-119.03	2-50	4	-12.00	17-169	10	-57.55	37-298	12	-49.48
Group 1,2,3	1-20	5	-14.00	1-7	14	-1.00	0-7	-	-7.00	0-6	-	-6.00
Maiden	15-165	9	-86.81	11-104	11	-37.29	4-51	8	-39.52	0-10	-	-10.00

2008

	Overall			Two-year-olds			Three-year-olds			Older horses		
	W-R	%	£1	W-R	%	£1	W-R	%	£1	W-R	%	£1
Handicap	57-533	11	-200.89	4-50	8	-34.39	22-207	11	-52.26	31-276	11	-114.25
Group 1,2,3	2-24	8	-5.50	2-11	18	+7.50	0-3	-	-3.00	0-10	-	-10.00
Maiden	27-174	16	-20.40	18-128	14	-19.95	8-45	18	-0.73	1-1	100	+0.29

By jockey – 2010

	Overall			Two-year-olds			Three-year-olds			Older horses		
	W-R	%	£1	W-R	%	£1	W-R	%	£1	W-R	%	£1
Paul Hanagan	16-58	28	+15.91	2-16	13	-9.47	9-21	43	+19.38	5-21	24	+6.00
Neil Callan	14-96	15	-37.33	5-25	20	+6.50	1-18	6	-13.67	8-53	15	-30.16
Jamie Spencer	12-78	15	-22.28	5-26	19	+0.50	0-13	-	-13.00	7-39	18	-9.78
Amy Ryan	9-104	9	-60.97	0-3	-	-3.00	4-20	20	+0.25	5-81	6	-58.22
Phillip Makin	8-56	14	+8.73	3-24	13	-3.00	1-12	8	+0.00	4-20	20	+11.73
P J McDonald	5-26	19	+5.25	2-10	20	-3.63	3-11	27	+13.88	0-5	-	-5.00
S De Sousa	4-27	15	+23.88	2-12	17	+11.88	2-10	20	+17.00	0-5	-	-5.00
Tom Eaves	4-28	14	+0.95	2-10	20	-0.25	1-10	10	-7.80	1-8	13	+9.00
Julie Burke	4-34	12	+0.50	1-6	17	+3.00	2-13	15	+6.00	1-15	7	-8.50
Alan Munro	3-8	38	+15.25	1-2	50	+1.25	2-4	50	+16.00	0-2	-	-2.00
Fergus Sweeney	3-10	30	+9.25	0-1	-	-1.00	3-6	50	+13.25	0-3	-	-3.00
Tony Hamilton	3-17	18	-2.63	2-6	33	+5.50	1-4	25	-1.13	0-7	-	-7.00
Paul Mulrennan	3-30	10	-15.50	2-7	29	+3.50	0-8	-	-8.00	1-15	7	-11.00
Franny Norton	3-32	9	-10.75	0-12	-	-12.00	3-14	21	+7.25	0-6	-	-6.00
Richard Mullen	2-11	18	-1.83	2-10	20	-0.83	0-0	-	+0.00	0-1	-	-1.00

2009

	Overall			Two-year-olds			Three-year-olds			Older horses		
	W-R	%	£1	W-R	%	£1	W-R	%	£1	W-R	%	£1
Neil Callan	33-232	14	-36.23	7-51	14	-5.81	8-63	13	-6.66	18-118	15	-23.76
Amy Ryan	17-114	15	+3.05	0-1	-	-1.00	3-20	15	+3.50	14-93	15	+0.55
Jamie Spencer	15-48	31	+14.01	2-8	25	+5.00	2-7	29	+2.33	11-33	33	+6.67
Phillip Makin	4-41	10	-27.63	3-23	13	-13.13	1-12	8	-8.50	0-6	-	-6.00
Robert Winston	3-17	18	-4.60	1-5	20	-3.17	0-5	-	-5.00	2-7	29	+3.57
Darryll Holland	3-18	17	-6.88	1-6	17	-2.75	0-4	-	-4.00	2-8	25	-0.13
Joe Fanning	3-20	15	-7.20	0-4	-	-4.00	2-7	29	-1.20	1-9	11	-2.00
Paul Mulrennan	3-41	7	-25.75	0-11	-	-11.00	1-17	6	-14.75	2-13	15	+0.00
Fergus Sweeney	2-10	20	+16.00	1-7	14	+10.00	0-2	-	-2.00	1-1	100	+8.00
Richard Hughes	1-3	33	-0.25	0-0	-	+0.00	1-3	33	-0.25	0-0	-	+0.00
Jim Crowley	1-4	25	-2.71	0-0	-	+0.00	0-1	-	-1.00	1-3	33	-1.71

By jockey – 2008

	Overall			Two-year-olds			Three-year-olds			Older horses		
	W-R	%	£1	W-R	%	£1	W-R	%	£1	W-R	%	£1
Neil Callan	39-306	13	-130.69	11-95	12	-32.24	11-83	13	-42.33	17-128	13	-56.13
Fergal Lynch	12-85	14	-0.33	7-25	28	+30.13	3-32	9	-12.70	2-28	7	-17.75
Paul Mulrennan	9-78	12	-21.46	5-21	24	+16.17	3-27	11	-13.13	1-30	3	-24.50
Neil Brown	8-43	19	+26.12	1-5	20	-3.39	3-19	16	+20.50	4-19	21	+9.00
Darryll Holland	6-31	19	+21.66	2-8	25	+12.25	2-14	14	+12.00	2-9	22	-2.59
Jamie Spencer	6-32	19	-3.13	1-7	14	-1.50	0-7	-	-7.00	5-18	28	+5.38
Chris Catlin	5-33	15	-10.51	0-8	-	-8.00	0-6	-	-6.00	5-19	26	+3.49
Franny Norton	4-24	17	-4.59	0-9	-	-9.00	2-12	17	-3.09	2-3	67	+7.50
Robert Winston	3-19	16	+2.70	2-10	20	-1.30	1-4	25	+9.00	0-5	-	-5.00
Royston Ffrench	2-6	33	+14.00	0-2	-	-2.00	2-4	50	+16.00	0-0	-	+0.00
Jamie Moriarty	2-7	29	+2.50	0-1	-	-1.00	2-5	40	+4.50	0-1	-	-1.00

By course – 2007-2010

	Overall			Two-year-olds			Three-year-olds			Older horses		
	W-R	%	£1	W-R	%	£1	W-R	%	£1	W-R	%	£1
Ascot	5-69	7	+6.00	2-16	13	-3.50	0-10	-	-10.00	3-43	7	+19.50
Ayr	14-148	9	-52.28	7-45	16	-12.78	1-32	3	-27.00	6-71	8	-12.50
Bath	0-5	-	-5.00	0-2	-	-2.00	0-2	-	-2.00	0-1	-	-1.00
Beverley	18-129	14	-35.30	6-45	13	-16.88	4-34	12	-10.75	8-50	16	-7.67
Brighton	0-1	-	-1.00	0-0	-	+0.00	0-1	-	-1.00	0-0	-	+0.00
Carlisle	10-50	20	+49.98	4-17	24	+20.38	4-13	31	+39.00	2-20	10	-9.40
Catterick	16-118	14	-22.17	7-38	18	+3.83	4-40	10	-15.00	5-40	13	-11.00
Chepstow	0-2	-	-2.00	0-1	-	-1.00	0-0	-	+0.00	0-1	-	-1.00
Chester	12-84	14	+6.50	4-24	17	+5.00	1-18	6	-12.00	7-42	17	+13.50
Doncaster	7-180	4	-120.70	2-47	4	-28.00	1-38	3	-27.00	4-95	4	-65.70
Epsom	1-27	4	-24.75	0-2	-	-2.00	1-7	14	-4.75	0-18	-	-18.00
Goodwood	2-40	5	-27.00	0-8	-	-8.00	1-9	11	-0.50	1-23	4	-18.50
Hamilton	24-125	19	+3.09	6-34	18	-8.13	10-46	22	+15.23	8-45	18	-4.00
Haydock	13-156	8	-51.50	5-67	7	-20.50	0-32	-	-32.00	8-57	14	+1.00
Kempton (AW)	22-139	16	-20.97	5-24	21	+20.00	5-40	13	-15.67	12-75	16	-25.31
Leicester	15-86	17	+41.76	7-40	18	+12.10	7-34	21	+35.66	1-12	8	-6.00
Lingfield	1-2	50	+2.50	0-0	-	+0.00	1-1	100	+3.50	0-1	-	-1.00
Lingfield (AW)	38-176	22	-1.77	3-19	16	-1.50	7-41	17	-4.19	28-116	24	+3.92
Musselburgh	12-134	9	-79.14	4-35	11	-20.89	6-34	18	-1.75	2-65	3	-56.50
Newbury	2-38	5	-11.50	1-12	8	+9.00	0-12	-	-12.00	1-14	7	-8.50
Newcastle	16-110	15	-26.71	4-31	13	-15.33	6-36	17	-4.63	6-43	14	-6.75
Newmarket	1-49	2	-30.00	1-12	8	+7.00	0-16	-	-16.00	0-21	-	-21.00
Newmarket (J)	2-46	4	-27.00	1-13	8	-1.00	0-14	-	-14.00	1-19	5	-12.00
Nottingham	5-68	7	-27.75	2-37	5	-9.00	1-22	5	-17.50	2-9	22	-1.25
Pontefract	12-75	16	+16.29	5-30	17	+20.79	5-23	22	+9.50	2-22	9	-14.00
Redcar	8-130	6	-70.39	4-58	7	-41.39	2-40	5	-31.00	2-32	6	+2.00
Ripon	23-140	16	-6.89	9-49	18	-5.98	5-42	12	-4.67	9-49	18	+3.75
Salisbury	0-3	-	-3.00	0-1	-	-1.00	0-1	-	-1.00	0-1	-	-1.00
Sandown	0-18	-	-18.00	0-4	-	-4.00	0-12	-	-12.00	0-2	-	-2.00
Southwell	0-4	-	-4.00	0-0	-	+0.00	0-2	-	-2.00	0-2	-	-2.00
Southwell (AW)	44-306	14	-90.81	6-52	12	-11.88	15-92	16	-4.85	23-162	14	-74.08
Thirsk	15-166	9	-58.33	2-39	5	-34.57	5-54	9	-9.26	8-73	11	-14.50
Warwick	1-17	6	-8.00	0-6	-	-6.00	1-6	17	+3.00	0-5	-	-5.00
Windsor	4-17	24	+6.60	1-8	13	-5.13	0-2	-	-2.00	3-7	43	+13.73
Wolves (AW)	62-447	14	-139.15	12-102	12	-33.00	17-129	13	-45.03	33-216	15	-61.12
Yarmouth	2-17	12	-10.63	1-7	14	-3.50	0-5	-	-5.00	1-5	20	-2.13
York	5-136	4	-72.00	3-43	7	-9.00	1-24	4	+2.00	1-69	1	-65.00

Ten-year summary

	Wins	Runs	%	Win prize	Total prize	£1 Stake
2010	107	813	13	£510,410.42	£865,913.67	-155.62
2009	96	867	11	£603,355.68	£1,024,522.80	-313.68
2008	108	889	12	£553,275.27	£955,575.07	-244.64
2007	107	932	11	£628,750.47	£1,111,861.68	-218.21
2006	95	827	11	£621,912.82	£1,314,626.82	-195.53
2005	82	643	13	£722,268.12	£1,030,981.10	-35.89
2004	67	489	14	£371,653.22	£640,902.62	+13.03
2003	41	418	10	£252,725.31	£372,798.16	-69.64
2002	54	429	13	£253,441.70	£358,217.73	+11.42
2001	22	447	5	£88,579.50	£178,986.25	-236.67

ARGANIL: got among the winners again last season for Kevin Ryan

John Gosden

It took 17 years but Gosden finally recorded his first century since 1993 last year as he finished on 105.

There had been much interest in his surprise decision to part with Jimmy Fortune, but his faith in young rider William Buick was rewarded as he rode Arctic Cosmos to win the St Leger.

By month – 2010

	Overall			Two-year-olds			Three-year-olds			Older horses		
	W-R	%	£1	W-R	%	£1	W-R	%	£1	W-R	%	£1
January	0-3	-	-3.00	0-0	-	+0.00	0-0	-	+0.00	0-3	-	-3.00
February	1-2	50	+1.00	0-0	-	+0.00	1-1	100	+2.00	0-1	-	-1.00
March	6-18	33	+6.02	0-0	-	+0.00	6-17	35	+7.02	0-1	-	-1.00
April	10-41	24	+8.20	0-0	-	+0.00	7-34	21	+0.50	3-7	43	+7.70
May	10-64	16	-16.92	1-7	14	-2.50	8-49	16	-18.42	1-8	13	+4.00
June	10-69	14	-20.52	2-11	18	+13.25	7-48	15	-26.27	1-10	10	-7.50
July	7-47	15	-3.65	0-6	-	-6.00	5-32	16	-8.65	2-9	22	+11.00
August	24-70	34	+33.64	6-27	22	+2.41	17-37	46	+31.23	1-6	17	+0.00
September	22-100	22	+5.01	12-46	26	+4.55	7-47	15	-5.38	3-7	43	+5.83
October	11-72	15	-16.85	5-41	12	-22.23	5-26	19	+6.38	1-5	20	-1.00
November	1-21	5	-19.09	1-14	7	-12.09	0-7	-	-7.00	0-0	-	+0.00
December	3-11	27	-2.55	2-8	25	-0.75	1-3	33	-1.80	0-0	-	+0.00

2009

	Overall			Two-year-olds			Three-year-olds			Older horses		
	W-R	%	£1	W-R	%	£1	W-R	%	£1	W-R	%	£1
January	0-0	-	+0.00	0-0	-	+0.00	0-0	-	+0.00	0-0	-	+0.00
February	0-0	-	+0.00	0-0	-	+0.00	0-0	-	+0.00	0-0	-	+0.00
March	7-24	29	-0.02	0-0	-	+0.00	6-19	32	+0.65	1-5	20	-0.67
April	14-64	22	-4.35	0-1	-	-1.00	11-52	21	-8.10	3-11	27	+4.75
May	17-80	21	+11.44	0-7	-	-7.00	12-60	20	+3.73	5-13	38	+14.72
June	4-64	6	-43.30	0-5	-	-5.00	1-43	2	-36.00	3-16	19	-2.30
July	11-64	17	-11.14	3-14	21	-7.48	6-39	15	-4.67	2-11	18	+1.00
August	9-55	16	-25.30	5-22	23	-10.55	3-23	13	-11.25	1-10	10	-3.50
September	6-50	12	-20.38	4-20	20	+0.25	1-22	5	-19.63	1-8	13	-1.00
October	12-83	14	+1.13	7-51	14	+1.13	5-28	18	+4.00	0-4	-	-4.00
November	7-27	26	-2.47	3-12	25	-5.82	3-13	23	-4.15	1-2	50	+7.50
December	1-5	20	-3.17	1-1	100	+0.83	0-4	-	-4.00	0-0	-	+0.00

2008

	Overall			Two-year-olds			Three-year-olds			Older horses		
	W-R	%	£1	W-R	%	£1	W-R	%	£1	W-R	%	£1
January	0-2	-	-2.00	0-0	-	+0.00	0-1	-	-1.00	0-1	-	-1.00
February	0-0	-	+0.00	0-0	-	+0.00	0-0	-	+0.00	0-0	-	+0.00
March	2-6	33	-0.88	0-0	-	+0.00	2-5	40	+0.13	0-1	-	-1.00
April	13-46	28	+19.16	0-0	-	+0.00	10-39	26	+19.00	3-7	43	+0.16
May	6-61	10	-32.81	0-4	-	-4.00	5-46	11	-22.81	1-11	9	-6.00
June	10-76	13	-31.35	2-14	14	-8.13	7-55	13	-23.23	1-7	14	+0.00
July	13-73	18	-2.49	4-21	19	+0.79	7-40	18	-1.27	2-12	17	-2.00
August	14-57	25	+19.19	2-13	15	-7.50	9-36	25	+9.19	3-8	38	+17.50
September	17-64	27	+27.39	9-32	28	-3.56	7-27	26	+24.94	1-5	20	+6.00
October	16-81	20	+42.22	9-41	22	+32.76	6-35	17	-11.54	1-5	20	+21.00
November	3-29	10	-19.64	2-18	11	-13.64	1-11	9	-6.00	0-0	-	+0.00
December	1-3	33	+0.50	1-2	50	+1.50	0-1	-	-1.00	0-0	-	+0.00

By race type – 2010

	Overall			Two-year-olds			Three-year-olds			Older horses		
	W-R	%	£1	W-R	%	£1	W-R	%	£1	W-R	%	£1
Handicap	31-175	18	+2.46	3-20	15	+10.38	25-133	19	+0.58	3-22	14	-8.50
Group 1,2,3	7-40	18	+9.25	1-5	20	-1.75	3-18	17	+6.00	3-17	18	+5.00
Maiden	59-256	23	-24.39	23-126	18	-26.62	33-123	27	-13.97	3-7	43	+16.20

2009

	Overall			Two-year-olds			Three-year-olds			Older horses		
	W-R	%	£1	W-R	%	£1	W-R	%	£1	W-R	%	£1
Handicap	25-155	16	-13.44	3-10	30	-1.07	15-115	13	-29.41	7-30	23	+17.03
Group 1,2,3	6-58	10	-21.25	1-7	14	-4.00	0-25	-	-25.00	5-26	19	+7.75
Maiden	49-253	19	-40.70	18-108	17	-23.18	27-133	20	-19.13	4-12	33	+1.62

2008

	Overall			Two-year-olds			Three-year-olds			Older horses		
	W-R	%	£1	W-R	%	£1	W-R	%	£1	W-R	%	£1
Handicap	24-147	16	+36.76	0-7	-	-7.00	18-112	16	+9.51	6-28	21	+34.25
Group 1,2,3	12-50	24	+2.11	3-9	33	-3.60	6-27	22	+2.71	3-14	21	+3.00
Maiden	51-256	20	-48.21	24-119	20	-25.17	26-132	20	-23.04	1-5	20	+0.00

By jockey – 2010

	Overall			Two-year-olds			Three-year-olds			Older horses		
	W-R	%	£1	W-R	%	£1	W-R	%	£1	W-R	%	£1
William Buick	54-258	21	+9.97	15-76	20	-2.64	32-153	21	-1.09	7-29	24	+13.70
Nicky Mackay	18-73	25	+20.83	7-28	25	+17.63	10-40	25	-2.80	1-5	20	+6.00
Robert Havlin	12-86	14	-39.85	1-25	4	-23.09	11-52	21	-7.76	0-9	-	-9.00
Richard Hills	5-20	25	-0.42	2-7	29	+0.75	1-6	17	+0.00	2-7	29	-1.17
Ryan Moore	4-7	57	+8.35	1-1	100	+1.38	3-6	50	+6.98	0-0	-	+0.00
Frankie Dettori	4-9	44	+5.00	0-0	-	+0.00	3-7	43	+4.50	1-2	50	+0.50
Tadhg O'Shea	4-14	29	+1.69	1-4	25	-2.09	3-9	33	+4.78	0-1	-	-1.00
Paul Hanagan	2-3	67	+1.80	1-1	100	+0.80	1-2	50	+1.00	0-0	-	+0.00
Neil Callan	2-7	29	+4.91	1-2	50	-0.09	0-4	-	-4.00	1-1	100	+9.00
Dane O'Neill	0-1	-	-1.00	0-0	-	+0.00	0-1	-	-1.00	0-0	-	+0.00
Eddie Ahern	0-1	-	-1.00	0-0	-	+0.00	0-0	-	+0.00	0-1	-	-1.00
J-P Guillambert	0-1	-	-1.00	0-1	-	-1.00	0-0	-	+0.00	0-0	-	+0.00
Jimmy Fortune	0-1	-	-1.00	0-0	-	+0.00	0-1	-	-1.00	0-0	-	+0.00
Martin Dwyer	0-1	-	-1.00	0-0	-	+0.00	0-1	-	-1.00	0-0	-	+0.00
Patrick Hills	0-1	-	-1.00	0-0	-	+0.00	0-1	-	-1.00	0-0	-	+0.00

2009

	Overall			Two-year-olds			Three-year-olds			Older horses		
	W-R	%	£1	W-R	%	£1	W-R	%	£1	W-R	%	£1
J Fortune	43-244	18	-29.22	12-64	19	-1.07	19-130	15	-50.70	12-50	24	+22.55
Robert Havlin	14-63	22	+6.17	4-27	15	-11.42	8-28	29	+13.08	2-8	25	+4.50
Richard Mullen	9-79	11	-41.45	1-11	9	-7.75	6-60	10	-33.90	2-8	25	+0.20
Richard Hills	8-37	22	-1.20	0-7	-	-7.00	7-26	27	+6.55	1-4	25	-0.75
Nicky Mackay	8-41	20	-2.88	3-10	30	-2.32	5-27	19	+3.43	0-4	-	-4.00
Ryan Moore	4-12	33	-2.46	2-3	67	+0.42	2-8	25	-1.88	0-1	-	-1.00
Frankie Dettori	1-5	20	+3.00	0-0	-	+0.00	1-2	50	+6.00	0-3	-	-3.00
Tadhg O'Shea	1-21	5	-15.50	1-5	20	+0.50	0-15	-	-15.00	0-1	-	-1.00
Franny Norton	0-1	-	-1.00	0-1	-	-1.00	0-0	-	+0.00	0-0	-	+0.00
Jack Mitchell	0-1	-	-1.00	0-0	-	+0.00	0-1	-	-1.00	0-0	-	+0.00
Kieren Fallon	0-1	-	-1.00	0-1	-	-1.00	0-0	-	+0.00	0-0	-	+0.00

By jockey – 2008

	Overall			Two-year-olds			Three-year-olds			Older horses		
	W-R	%	£1	W-R	%	£1	W-R	%	£1	W-R	%	£1
J Fortune	50-239	21	-14.99	11-60	18	-16.99	34-149	23	+5.25	5-30	17	-3.25
Robert Havlin	13-94	14	-41.84	6-36	17	-12.43	6-50	12	-24.41	1-8	13	-5.00
Richard Hills	8-30	27	+42.73	4-14	29	+2.98	2-12	17	+8.75	2-4	50	+31.00
Richard Mullen	4-14	29	+20.50	1-3	33	+0.00	3-11	27	+20.50	0-0	-	+0.00
Frankie Dettori	4-17	24	-4.63	2-7	29	-3.08	2-7	29	+1.44	0-3	-	-3.00
Martin Dwyer	3-13	23	+30.25	2-3	67	+33.25	1-7	14	+0.00	0-3	-	-3.00
Steve Drowne	3-13	23	+2.00	1-3	33	+6.00	2-10	20	-4.00	0-0	-	+0.00
Ted Durcan	2-6	33	+0.41	0-1	-	-1.00	1-3	33	+1.50	1-2	50	-0.09
L-P Beuzelin	2-8	25	+14.00	0-2	-	-2.00	0-4	-	-4.00	2-2	100	+20.00
David Kinsella	2-16	13	+3.88	0-5	-	-5.00	2-10	20	+9.88	0-1	-	-1.00
Darryll Holland	1-5	20	-0.50	0-1	-	-1.00	1-4	25	+0.50	0-0	-	+0.00

By course – 2007-2010

	Overall			Two-year-olds			Three-year-olds			Older horses		
	W-R	%	£1	W-R	%	£1	W-R	%	£1	W-R	%	£1
Ascot	10-91	11	-43.25	4-18	22	-3.68	2-47	4	-38.67	4-26	15	-0.90
Ayr	0-5	-	-5.00	0-2	-	-2.00	0-3	-	-3.00	0-0	-	+0.00
Bath	2-21	10	-16.13	0-6	-	-6.00	2-13	15	-8.13	0-2	-	-2.00
Beverley	2-5	40	-0.58	1-2	50	-0.20	1-3	33	-0.38	0-0	-	+0.00
Brighton	7-13	54	+24.16	3-4	75	+6.91	4-9	44	+17.25	0-0	-	+0.00
Catterick	1-4	25	+1.50	0-1	-	-1.00	1-3	33	+2.50	0-0	-	+0.00
Chepstow	4-13	31	-2.84	1-3	33	+0.75	2-8	25	-3.20	1-2	50	-0.39
Chester	6-35	17	-4.71	0-4	-	-4.00	5-26	19	-7.71	1-5	20	+7.00
Doncaster	20-94	21	+19.87	4-34	12	-24.42	10-48	21	+14.46	6-12	50	+29.83
Epsom	3-33	9	-18.05	0-5	-	-5.00	2-17	12	-11.05	1-11	9	-2.00
Ffos Las	2-8	25	+1.25	0-3	-	-3.00	2-5	40	+4.25	0-0	-	+0.00
Folkestone	0-5	-	-5.00	0-0	-	+0.00	0-5	-	-5.00	0-0	-	+0.00
Goodwood	15-117	13	-39.51	2-22	9	-12.93	12-74	16	-8.08	1-21	5	-18.50
Hamilton	2-3	67	+0.94	0-0	-	+0.00	2-3	67	+0.94	0-0	-	+0.00
Haydock	6-40	15	-10.09	1-10	10	-8.09	4-23	17	+0.00	1-7	14	-2.00
Kempton (AW)	34-189	18	-16.86	14-64	22	+12.44	17-109	16	-31.80	3-16	19	+2.50
Leicester	11-34	32	+11.98	3-11	27	+6.25	6-19	32	+2.23	2-4	50	+3.50
Lingfield	2-12	17	-1.63	0-2	-	-2.00	2-10	20	+0.38	0-0	-	+0.00
Lingfield (AW)	19-115	17	-47.57	2-31	6	-21.50	16-71	23	-24.07	1-13	8	-2.00
Musselburgh	0-1	-	-1.00	0-0	-	+0.00	0-1	-	-1.00	0-0	-	+0.00
Newbury	15-110	14	-50.78	7-34	21	-10.99	4-62	6	-46.63	4-14	29	+6.83
Newcastle	3-14	21	-3.35	1-2	50	+1.25	2-10	20	-2.60	0-2	-	-2.00
Newmarket	34-223	15	+28.14	8-84	10	+1.63	21-115	18	+6.26	5-24	21	+20.25
Newmarket (J)	29-138	21	+37.70	9-50	18	+11.42	16-68	24	+21.08	4-20	20	+5.20
Nottingham	11-70	16	-8.19	4-19	21	+4.75	7-51	14	-12.94	0-0	-	+0.00
Pontefract	5-17	29	+7.75	0-2	-	-2.00	4-12	33	+6.75	1-3	33	+3.00
Redcar	1-6	17	-3.13	0-2	-	-2.00	1-2	50	+0.88	0-2	-	-2.00
Ripon	5-8	63	+2.01	0-0	-	+0.00	3-6	50	-0.40	2-2	100	+2.41
Salisbury	6-46	13	-20.54	3-10	30	+1.38	3-33	9	-18.92	0-3	-	-3.00
Sandown	24-121	20	-13.36	7-24	29	-4.08	15-78	19	-10.28	2-19	11	+1.00
Southwell (AW)	12-27	44	+9.84	5-10	50	+2.45	6-15	40	+7.78	1-2	50	-0.39
Thirsk	2-6	33	-1.60	0-0	-	+0.00	1-5	20	-3.60	1-1	100	+2.00
Warwick	2-11	18	-8.27	1-1	100	+0.29	1-10	10	-8.56	0-0	-	+0.00
Windsor	9-64	14	-16.50	2-13	15	-7.50	7-47	15	-5.00	0-4	-	-4.00
Wolves (AW)	18-83	22	-41.17	5-30	17	-20.13	13-48	27	-16.04	0-5	-	-5.00
Yarmouth	21-83	25	+39.28	13-40	33	+31.64	4-34	12	-10.56	4-9	44	+18.20
York	5-37	14	-11.00	1-5	20	-2.00	2-19	11	-5.50	2-13	15	-3.50

Ten-year summary

	Wins	Runs	%	Win prize	Total prize	£1 Stake
2010	105	518	20	£1,101,277.72	£1,714,237.43	-28.71
2009	88	516	17	£1,447,841.46	£2,308,709.36	-97.55
2008	95	498	19	£1,843,697.13	£2,596,896.00	+19.30
2007	68	401	17	£1,055,409.41	£1,644,331.67	-75.22
2006	56	299	19	£605,236.89	£848,468.86	-21.24
2005	91	486	19	£1,064,566.17	£1,487,571.10	+95.30
2004	66	458	14	£741,368.45	£1,273,377.98	-88.20
2003	72	391	18	£881,783.33	£1,356,380.42	-77.21
2002	85	375	23	£872,898.95	£1,305,968.18	+58.57
2001	55	335	16	£398,187.49	£736,205.94	-46.62

TAZEEZ: storms home for a tremendous win in the Darley Stakes at Newmarket

Mick Channon

Few trainers are as consistent as Channon, who just managed his seventh century in nine seasons and has now finished with a 10% strike-rate in each of the last four seasons, which is no mean feat given the size of his string even if it lags behind the likes of Johnston, Hannon and Fahey.

By month – 2010

	Overall			Two-year-olds			Three-year-olds			Older horses		
	W-R	%	£1	W-R	%	£1	W-R	%	£1	W-R	%	£1
January	2-10	20	-3.00	0-0	-	+0.00	2-4	50	+3.00	0-6	-	-6.00
February	0-12	-	-12.00	0-0	-	+0.00	0-6	-	-6.00	0-6	-	-6.00
March	4-21	19	+0.75	0-4	-	-4.00	3-12	25	+2.75	1-5	20	+2.00
April	5-88	6	-45.75	1-22	5	-18.25	4-44	9	-5.50	0-22	-	-22.00
May	19-140	14	-44.11	8-45	18	-10.86	8-61	13	-19.25	3-34	9	-14.00
June	15-137	11	-55.69	8-61	13	-30.97	5-45	11	-10.22	2-31	6	-14.50
July	14-161	9	-64.25	8-81	10	-29.13	6-56	11	-11.13	0-24	-	-24.00
August	20-160	13	+17.25	8-84	10	-27.48	10-58	17	+54.50	2-18	11	-9.77
September	9-137	7	-52.97	6-80	8	-17.47	3-47	6	-25.50	0-10	-	-10.00
October	12-95	13	-10.49	7-57	12	-16.49	5-31	16	+13.00	0-7	-	-7.00
November	1-11	9	-6.50	1-9	11	-4.50	0-1	-	-1.00	0-1	-	-1.00
December	0-4	-	-4.00	0-3	-	-3.00	0-1	-	-1.00	0-0	-	+0.00

2009

	Overall			Two-year-olds			Three-year-olds			Older horses		
	W-R	%	£1	W-R	%	£1	W-R	%	£1	W-R	%	£1
January	4-23	17	-3.08	0-0	-	+0.00	4-17	24	+2.92	0-6	-	-6.00
February	4-33	12	-2.00	0-0	-	+0.00	3-23	13	+4.00	1-10	10	-6.00
March	10-51	20	-8.70	1-3	33	+2.00	8-35	23	-4.70	1-13	8	-6.00
April	9-88	10	-60.53	5-22	23	-8.97	3-46	7	-33.67	1-20	5	-17.90
May	12-142	8	-77.76	8-44	18	-10.26	2-67	3	-56.00	2-31	6	-11.50
June	16-150	11	-79.82	9-53	17	-27.07	2-58	3	-52.00	5-39	13	-0.75
July	10-177	6	-102.50	6-83	7	-37.25	2-63	3	-53.75	2-31	6	-11.50
August	17-159	11	-40.04	13-82	16	+13.71	2-52	4	-42.25	2-25	8	-11.50
September	11-150	7	-43.38	5-83	6	-47.88	5-47	11	+18.00	1-20	5	-13.50
October	9-99	9	+1.00	3-46	7	-2.50	3-32	9	+4.00	3-21	14	-0.50
November	6-27	22	+9.63	4-11	36	+9.75	1-7	14	-4.13	1-9	11	+4.00
December	0-20	-	-20.00	0-6	-	-6.00	0-7	-	-7.00	0-7	-	-7.00

2008

	Overall			Two-year-olds			Three-year-olds			Older horses		
	W-R	%	£1	W-R	%	£1	W-R	%	£1	W-R	%	£1
January	1-3	33	+2.50	0-0	-	+0.00	0-1	-	-1.00	1-2	50	+3.50
February	5-15	33	+18.83	0-0	-	+0.00	4-12	33	+6.83	1-3	33	+12.00
March	2-43	5	-31.50	0-4	-	-4.00	2-29	7	-17.50	0-10	-	-10.00
April	4-72	6	-44.00	0-16	-	-16.00	2-37	5	-18.50	2-19	11	-9.50
May	15-135	11	-4.89	10-30	33	+20.62	2-73	3	-58.50	3-32	9	+33.00
June	13-152	9	-41.97	5-58	9	-32.22	6-60	10	+4.75	2-34	6	-14.50
July	13-164	8	-83.63	8-71	11	-22.38	3-56	5	-44.25	2-37	5	-17.00
August	19-154	12	-27.38	10-73	14	+1.38	7-47	15	-3.25	2-34	6	-25.50
September	11-113	10	-16.00	2-53	4	-43.25	8-34	24	+40.25	1-26	4	-13.00
October	7-102	7	-55.11	6-46	13	-5.61	1-39	3	-32.50	0-17	-	-17.00
November	4-19	21	+9.00	2-11	18	-3.50	2-5	40	+15.50	0-3	-	-3.00
December	2-16	13	-0.13	1-12	8	-9.13	1-3	33	+10.00	0-1	-	-1.00

By race type – 2010

	Overall			Two-year-olds			Three-year-olds			Older horses		
	W-R	%	£1	W-R	%	£1	W-R	%	£1	W-R	%	£1
Handicap	44-513	9	-131.03	8-117	7	-65.40	29-258	11	+22.38	7-138	5	-88.00
Group 1,2,3	4-41	10	+0.50	2-14	14	+13.00	2-15	13	-0.50	0-12	-	-12.00
Maiden	35-279	13	-93.51	28-223	13	-81.41	7-54	13	-10.10	0-2	-	-2.00

2009

	Overall			Two-year-olds			Three-year-olds			Older horses		
	W-R	%	£1	W-R	%	£1	W-R	%	£1	W-R	%	£1
Handicap	50-617	8	-224.25	13-108	12	-10.63	21-316	7	-146.38	16-193	8	-67.25
Group 1,2,3	3-45	7	-7.00	1-15	7	+11.00	1-13	8	-6.00	1-17	6	-12.00
Maiden	30-261	11	-119.34	23-191	12	-81.68	7-69	10	-36.66	0-1	-	-1.00

2008

	Overall			Two-year-olds			Three-year-olds			Older horses		
	W-R	%	£1	W-R	%	£1	W-R	%	£1	W-R	%	£1
Handicap	45-538	8	-125.17	9-78	12	-17.00	26-283	9	-58.67	10-177	6	-49.50
Group 1,2,3	4-54	7	-10.25	3-27	11	+3.75	0-5	-	-5.00	1-22	5	-9.00
Maiden	28-246	11	-80.28	20-179	11	-66.53	7-64	11	-15.25	1-3	33	+1.50

By jockey – 2010

	Overall			Two-year-olds			Three-year-olds			Older horses		
	W-R	%	£1	W-R	%	£1	W-R	%	£1	W-R	%	£1
Sam Hitchcott	22-216	10	-47.50	11-112	10	-33.13	9-77	12	-6.88	2-27	7	-7.50
Chris Catlin	19-211	9	-66.67	10-110	9	-39.38	8-70	11	+0.21	1-31	3	-27.50
Alan Munro	14-126	11	-39.45	5-48	10	-27.63	6-50	12	-0.06	3-28	11	-11.77
Kieren Fallon	11-70	16	-31.20	4-24	17	-16.45	6-35	17	-9.25	1-11	9	-5.50
R Hughes	5-32	16	-12.09	4-16	25	-3.59	1-9	11	-1.50	0-7	-	-7.00
Cathy Gannon	5-46	11	-15.75	2-13	15	+3.00	3-23	13	-8.75	0-10	-	-10.00
Ted Durcan	3-19	16	+1.88	1-6	17	-3.00	2-11	18	+6.88	0-2	-	-2.00
Ryan Moore	3-24	13	-10.63	2-12	17	-5.63	0-8	-	-8.00	1-4	25	+3.00
Paul Mulrennan	2-3	67	+14.50	1-1	100	+3.50	1-2	50	+11.00	0-0	-	+0.00
Amy Scott	2-6	33	+8.00	0-1	-	-1.00	2-3	67	+11.00	0-2	-	-2.00
Joe Fanning	2-7	29	+0.00	0-3	-	-3.00	2-4	50	+3.00	0-0	-	+0.00
M Davies	2-17	12	-6.50	1-10	10	-4.00	1-3	33	+1.50	0-4	-	-4.00
Tony Culhane	2-22	9	-8.09	2-11	18	+2.91	0-3	-	-3.00	0-8	-	-8.00
Hayley Turner	1-1	100	+2.50	0-0	-	+0.00	1-1	100	+2.50	0-0	-	+0.00
Julie Burke	1-1	100	+8.00	0-0	-	+0.00	1-1	100	+8.00	0-0	-	+0.00

2009

	Overall			Two-year-olds			Three-year-olds			Older horses		
	W-R	%	£1	W-R	%	£1	W-R	%	£1	W-R	%	£1
Tony Culhane	27-306	9	-129.19	11-86	13	-13.85	12-159	8	-90.34	4-61	7	-25.00
Sam Hitchcott	23-207	11	-76.96	16-99	16	-31.94	5-70	7	-26.13	2-38	5	-18.90
Chris Catlin	10-100	10	-31.21	6-59	10	-20.75	2-23	9	-18.46	2-18	11	+8.00
Darryll Holland	9-71	13	-25.99	6-29	21	-2.49	2-31	6	-18.00	1-11	9	-5.50
Michael Geran	9-89	10	-37.65	2-13	15	+6.00	5-43	12	-20.40	2-33	6	-23.25
Cathy Gannon	6-64	9	+4.63	3-28	11	-10.38	3-32	9	+19.00	0-4	-	-4.00
E Creighton	6-79	8	-35.75	2-26	8	-14.75	1-27	4	-19.00	3-26	12	-2.00
Ryan Moore	3-18	17	-8.39	1-9	11	-7.39	1-6	17	-2.50	1-3	33	+1.50
Charles Eddery	2-3	67	+5.00	0-0	-	+0.00	1-2	50	+3.00	1-1	100	+2.00
Kieren Fallon	2-12	17	+18.00	2-7	29	+23.00	0-2	-	-2.00	0-3	-	-3.00
Paul Hanagan	2-13	15	+0.25	1-7	14	+3.00	1-6	17	-2.75	0-0	-	+0.00

By jockey – 2008

	Overall			Two-year-olds			Three-year-olds			Older horses		
	W-R	%	£1	W-R	%	£1	W-R	%	£1	W-R	%	£1
E Creighton	28-220	13	-32.77	14-102	14	-12.85	11-86	13	-13.92	3-32	9	-6.00
D Holland	21-152	14	-32.56	11-60	18	-0.31	7-57	12	-18.75	3-35	9	-13.50
Tadhg O'Shea	14-136	10	+1.70	6-60	10	-29.80	6-54	11	+14.50	2-22	9	+17.00
Tony Culhane	10-81	12	+3.13	2-30	7	-23.88	8-36	22	+42.00	0-15	-	-15.00
Sam Hitchcott	6-89	7	-38.25	3-42	7	-10.50	2-33	6	-18.25	1-14	7	-9.50
Michael Geran	5-64	8	-24.75	4-21	19	+3.25	0-25	-	-25.00	1-18	6	-3.00
Chris Catlin	5-80	6	-41.75	2-26	8	-17.25	1-33	3	-22.00	2-21	10	-2.50
Joe Fanning	2-4	50	+25.50	0-1	-	-1.00	1-2	50	+1.50	1-1	100	+25.00
M Davies	2-62	3	-51.75	1-6	17	+0.50	1-28	4	-24.25	0-28	-	-28.00
Paul Mulrennan	1-1	100	+7.00	0-0	-	+0.00	1-1	100	+7.00	0-0	-	+0.00
Frankie Dettori	1-6	17	-2.25	1-3	33	+0.75	0-0	-	+0.00	0-3	-	-3.00

By course – 2007-2010

	Overall			Two-year-olds			Three-year-olds			Older horses		
	W-R	%	£1	W-R	%	£1	W-R	%	£1	W-R	%	£1
Ascot	10-173	6	-38.17	6-62	10	+14.83	1-47	2	-34.00	3-64	5	-19.00
Ayr	7-57	12	-2.25	1-25	4	-2.00	4-16	25	+6.75	2-16	13	-7.00
Bath	28-188	15	-58.17	14-85	16	-22.33	7-68	10	-39.58	7-35	20	+3.75
Beverley ·	12-70	17	+30.16	6-29	21	+24.16	5-31	16	+11.50	1-10	10	-5.50
Brighton	15-142	11	-66.16	10-56	18	-9.66	5-64	8	-34.50	0-22	-	-22.00
Carlisle	2-8	25	+4.50	1-2	50	+1.50	1-5	20	+4.00	0-1	-	-1.00
Catterick	12-61	20	-2.51	6-38	16	-3.97	6-20	30	+4.46	0-3	-	-3.00
Chepstow	1-77	1	-69.00	1-28	4	-20.00	0-35	-	-35.00	0-14	-	-14.00
Chester	10-70	14	-8.64	6-30	20	+4.37	2-21	10	-12.00	2-19	11	-1.00
Doncaster	4-80	5	-43.50	1-43	2	-35.00	2-21	10	-7.50	1-16	6	-1.00
Epsom	6-74	8	-18.75	3-27	11	-2.75	2-30	7	-4.00	1-17	6	-12.00
Ffos Las	1-22	5	-9.00	0-11	-	-11.00	1-8	13	+5.00	0-3	-	-3.00
Folkestone	12-106	11	+24.33	3-40	8	-21.17	7-44	16	+44.50	2-22	9	+1.00
Goodwood	19-271	7	-61.25	6-108	6	-33.75	5-86	6	-33.00	8-77	10	+5.50
Hamilton	9-57	16	-18.11	5-19	26	-3.86	3-29	10	-11.75	1-9	11	-2.50
Haydock	8-96	8	-43.06	4-39	10	-9.00	3-35	9	-14.56	1-22	5	-19.50
Kempton (AW)	18-267	7	-173.09	6-101	6	-65.40	10-120	8	-74.19	2-46	4	-33.50
Leicester	16-95	17	-14.48	12-53	23	-3.85	4-30	13	+1.38	0-12	-	-12.00
Lingfield	8-72	11	-36.04	5-30	17	-5.54	3-30	10	-18.50	0-12	-	-12.00
Lingfield (AW)	33-262	13	-13.24	8-56	14	-15.13	19-155	12	+7.88	6-51	12	-6.00
Musselburgh	4-44	9	-26.23	3-19	16	-4.75	1-14	7	-10.50	0-11	-	-11.00
Newbury	13-251	5	-125.75	4-122	3	-97.25	6-82	7	-10.00	3-47	6	-18.50
Newcastle	11-78	14	+5.53	6-35	17	+7.65	2-29	7	-18.13	3-14	21	+16.00
Newmarket	10-127	8	+10.00	3-35	9	+6.50	5-57	9	+6.50	2-35	6	-3.00
Newmarket (J)	16-138	12	-11.25	13-76	17	+26.25	1-37	3	-29.50	2-25	8	-8.00
Nottingham	6-81	7	-40.25	6-37	16	+3.75	0-36	-	-36.00	0-8	-	-8.00
Pontefract	10-85	12	-6.00	5-35	14	+2.50	5-30	17	+11.50	0-20	-	-20.00
Redcar	10-73	14	+18.97	5-40	13	+3.85	3-24	13	-6.39	2-9	22	+21.50
Ripon	9-80	11	-39.65	7-38	18	-3.75	0-22	-	-22.00	2-20	10	-13.90
Salisbury	8-136	6	-72.81	4-59	7	-48.06	4-50	8	+2.25	0-27	-	-27.00
Sandown	12-91	13	-27.72	6-42	14	-16.47	5-32	16	-0.25	1-17	6	-11.00
Southwell	0-1	-	-1.00	0-0	-	+0.00	0-1	-	-1.00	0-0	-	+0.00
Southwell (AW)	2-14	14	-1.50	0-3	-	-3.00	1-7	14	-3.50	1-4	25	+5.00
Thirsk	9-69	13	-34.95	8-30	27	+0.55	1-25	4	-21.50	0-14	-	-14.00
Warwick	8-67	12	-8.75	6-35	17	+13.25	2-19	11	-9.00	0-13	-	-13.00
Windsor	11-148	7	-51.90	7-72	10	-11.40	1-45	2	-32.00	3-31	10	-8.50
Wolves (AW)	24-213	11	-69.53	6-72	8	-37.75	12-102	12	-36.28	6-39	15	+4.50
Yarmouth	10-120	8	-51.27	2-42	5	-31.25	6-55	11	-6.25	2-23	9	-13.77
York	5-71	7	-39.75	2-27	7	-14.50	2-19	11	-7.25	1-25	4	-18.00

Ten-year summary

	Wins	Runs	%	Win prize	Total prize	£1 Stake
2010	101	976	10	£592,916.93	£1,286,154.26	-280.75
2009	108	1119	10	£655,056.88	£1,244,635.23	-427.19
2008	96	988	10	£673,850.59	£1,248,309.95	-274.26
2007	109	1086	10	£986,798.47	£1,703,200.25	-179.17
2006	127	1027	12	£878,648.60	£1,548,625.72	-107.34
2005	103	1041	10	£679,909.99	£1,341,136.21	-275.68
2004	98	1039	9	£899,749.14	£1,738,355.43	-363.78
2003	144	1136	13	£1,174,784.70	£2,029,345.33	-179.41
2002	123	1008	12	£879,674.97	£1,552,270.13	-131.71
2001	67	804	8	£480,011.75	£976,025.24	-452.07

MUSIC SHOW: often frustrated Mick Channon last year but not in the Falmouth Stakes

Tim Easterby

2010 was an astonishing year for Easterby, who kept his string in fine form virtually throughout and finished with 98 winners, an improvement on his previous best of 81 in 2002 and up a whopping 44 on his 2009 total.

More runners helped, but he still took his strike-rate up to a healthy 12%.

By month – 2010

	Overall			Two-year-olds			Three-year-olds			Older horses		
	W-R	%	£1	W-R	%	£1	W-R	%	£1	W-R	%	£1
January	0-0	-	+0.00	0-0	-	+0.00	0-0	-	+0.00	0-0	-	+0.00
February	0-1	-	-1.00	0-0	-	+0.00	0-0	-	+0.00	0-1	-	-1.00
March	2-8	25	+19.00	0-3	-	-3.00	0-1	-	-1.00	2-4	50	+23.00
April	6-68	9	-31.79	2-11	18	-3.92	2-25	8	-11.38	2-32	6	-16.50
May	19-134	14	-42.33	1-33	3	-31.20	3-35	9	-20.25	15-66	23	+9.13
June	13-133	10	-59.25	2-36	6	-27.13	0-37	-	-37.00	11-60	18	+4.88
July	18-143	13	-42.75	2-41	5	-19.50	7-31	23	+2.75	9-71	13	-26.00
August	14-140	10	-58.50	4-49	8	-24.50	3-37	8	-20.00	7-54	13	-14.00
September	14-106	13	+31.03	5-32	16	+17.94	2-23	9	-2.50	7-51	14	+15.58
October	8-86	9	-46.75	3-36	8	-21.25	0-13	-	-13.00	5-37	14	-12.50
November	3-22	14	+10.75	1-7	14	-3.75	1-4	25	+4.50	1-11	9	+10.00
December	1-5	20	+21.00	0-0	-	+0.00	0-3	-	-3.00	1-2	50	+24.00

2009

	Overall			Two-year-olds			Three-year-olds			Older horses		
	W-R	%	£1	W-R	%	£1	W-R	%	£1	W-R	%	£1
January	0-1	-	-1.00	0-0	-	+0.00	0-0	-	+0.00	0-1	-	-1.00
February	0-0	-	+0.00	0-0	-	+0.00	0-0	-	+0.00	0-0	-	+0.00
March	0-2	-	-2.00	0-0	-	+0.00	0-1	-	-1.00	0-1	-	-1.00
April	2-75	3	-56.00	0-12	-	-12.00	1-35	3	-28.00	1-28	4	-16.00
May	6-108	6	-45.75	1-24	4	-17.00	2-38	5	-24.75	3-46	7	-4.00
June	4-106	4	-79.75	2-27	7	-12.50	2-31	6	-19.25	0-48	-	-48.00
July	8-79	10	-27.00	1-22	5	-16.50	2-27	7	-13.75	5-30	17	+3.25
August	11-100	11	-15.13	2-33	6	-8.50	3-22	14	-13.88	6-45	13	+7.25
September	9-75	12	-2.59	0-26	-	-26.00	1-16	6	+1.00	8-33	24	+22.41
October	9-65	14	-10.50	2-14	14	+5.75	2-10	20	-2.00	5-41	12	-14.25
November	4-16	25	+8.33	1-8	13	-6.17	2-3	67	+10.50	1-5	20	+4.00
December	1-1	100	+1.50	0-0	-	+0.00	1-1	100	+1.50	0-0	-	+0.00

2008

	Overall			Two-year-olds			Three-year-olds			Older horses		
	W-R	%	£1	W-R	%	£1	W-R	%	£1	W-R	%	£1
January	0-1	-	-1.00	0-0	-	+0.00	0-1	-	-1.00	0-0	-	+0.00
February	0-4	-	-4.00	0-0	-	+0.00	0-4	-	-4.00	0-0	-	+0.00
March	1-14	7	-8.50	0-1	-	-1.00	0-10	-	-10.00	1-3	33	+2.50
April	2-54	4	-44.67	1-13	8	-8.67	1-26	4	-21.00	0-15	-	-15.00
May	7-106	7	-50.40	2-22	9	-14.90	5-40	13	+8.50	0-44	-	-44.00
June	10-104	10	-35.39	3-27	11	+2.71	3-35	9	-21.93	4-42	10	-16.17
July	8-97	8	-9.70	2-34	6	-20.50	3-20	15	+33.80	3-43	7	-23.00
August	8-71	11	+2.33	2-17	12	-5.67	3-23	13	-0.50	3-31	10	+8.50
September	6-69	9	-16.92	0-28	-	-28.00	2-11	18	+17.00	4-30	13	-5.92
October	6-55	11	+4.50	1-19	5	-9.00	4-15	27	+59.00	1-21	5	+2.00
November	3-15	20	+9.50	0-4	-	-4.00	0-0	-	+0.00	3-11	27	+13.50
December	0-7	-	-7.00	0-0	-	+0.00	0-0	-	+0.00	0-7	-	-7.00

By race type – 2010

	Overall			Two-year-olds			Three-year-olds			Older horses		
	W-R	%	£1	W-R	%	£1	W-R	%	£1	W-R	%	£1
Handicap	78-591	13	-71.54	7-67	10	-15.25	13-151	9	-77.50	58-373	16	+21.21
Group 1,2,3	0-5	-	-5.00	0-2	-	-2.00	0-0	-	+0.00	0-3	-	-3.00
Maiden	16-194	8	-101.67	11-141	8	-83.55	5-50	10	-15.13	0-3	-	-3.00

2009

	Overall			Two-year-olds			Three-year-olds			Older horses		
	W-R	%	£1	W-R	%	£1	W-R	%	£1	W-R	%	£1
Handicap	45-421	11	-86.13	4-40	10	-9.25	13-113	12	-37.63	28-268	10	-39.25
Group 1,2,3	0-7	-	-7.00	0-3	-	-3.00	0-4	-	-4.00	0-0	-	+0.00
Maiden	8-168	5	-111.42	4-103	4	-79.67	3-62	5	-49.75	1-3	33	+18.00

2008

	Overall			Two-year-olds			Three-year-olds			Older horses		
	W-R	%	£1	W-R	%	£1	W-R	%	£1	W-R	%	£1
Handicap	39-397	10	-27.21	3-27	11	-6.50	17-126	13	+60.87	19-244	8	-81.58
Group 1,2,3	0-3	-	-3.00	0-3	-	-3.00	0-0	-	+0.00	0-0	-	+0.00
Maiden	12-164	7	-31.53	6-111	5	-88.53	6-53	11	+57.00	0-0	-	+0.00

By jockey – 2010

	Overall			Two-year-olds			Three-year-olds			Older horses		
	W-R	%	£1	W-R	%	£1	W-R	%	£1	W-R	%	£1
David Allan	55-366	15	-27.53	11-102	11	-32.24	10-92	11	-26.13	34-172	20	+30.83
D Fentiman	13-169	8	-47.75	1-52	2	-47.00	3-51	6	-30.50	9-66	14	+29.75
G Gibbons	7-56	13	-18.00	2-20	10	-10.25	1-10	10	-4.50	4-26	15	-3.25
Ted Durcan	4-17	24	+15.00	0-3	-	-3.00	0-3	-	-3.00	4-11	36	+21.00
David Nolan	4-32	13	-13.75	0-6	-	-6.00	1-9	11	-5.75	3-17	18	-2.00
Paul Hanagan	3-13	23	-6.31	1-4	25	-2.56	1-6	17	-3.38	1-3	33	-0.38
Robert Winston	3-15	20	-2.75	0-5	-	-5.00	1-2	50	+0.88	2-8	25	+1.38
Lance Betts	2-49	4	-27.50	2-20	10	+1.50	0-11	-	-11.00	0-18	-	-18.00
Neil Farley	1-2	50	+11.00	0-0	-	+0.00	0-0	-	+0.00	1-2	50	+11.00
Kieren Fallon	1-4	25	+5.00	0-1	-	-1.00	0-0	-	+0.00	1-3	33	+6.00
Racheal Kneller	1-5	20	-1.75	0-0	-	+0.00	0-1	-	-1.00	1-4	25	-0.75
Tom Eaves	1-7	14	-3.50	1-2	50	+1.50	0-0	-	+0.00	0-5	-	-5.00
P J McDonald	1-13	8	-5.50	0-2	-	-2.00	1-5	20	+2.50	0-6	-	-6.00
Paul Mulrennan	1-15	7	-11.25	1-3	33	+0.75	0-2	-	-2.00	0-10	-	-10.00
Kelly Harrison	1-20	5	-3.00	1-11	9	+6.00	0-5	-	-5.00	0-4	-	-4.00

2009

	Overall			Two-year-olds			Three-year-olds			Older horses		
	W-R	%	£1	W-R	%	£1	W-R	%	£1	W-R	%	£1
David Allan	31-300	10	-101.01	6-87	7	-43.42	6-82	7	-41.75	19-131	15	-15.84
D Fentiman	8-143	6	-82.13	0-31	-	-31.00	6-58	10	-22.13	2-54	4	-29.00
David Nolan	3-27	11	-4.00	0-9	-	-9.00	2-9	22	+1.00	1-9	11	+4.00
Kelly Harrison	2-10	20	+6.00	0-1	-	-1.00	0-3	-	-3.00	2-6	33	+10.00
G Gibbons	2-23	9	+9.00	1-8	13	+9.00	0-1	-	-1.00	1-14	7	-5.00
Franny Norton	1-1	100	+4.00	0-0	-	+0.00	1-1	100	+4.00	0-0	-	+0.00
Richard Mullen	1-1	100	+22.00	0-0	-	+0.00	0-0	-	+0.00	1-1	100	+22.00
Tony Hamilton	1-3	33	+18.00	0-0	-	+0.00	0-1	-	-1.00	1-2	50	+19.00
Barry McHugh	1-5	20	-2.50	0-0	-	+0.00	0-0	-	+0.00	1-5	20	-2.50
P J McDonald	1-5	20	+0.50	1-4	25	+1.50	0-1	-	-1.00	0-0	-	+0.00
John Egan	1-7	14	+0.00	1-3	33	+4.00	0-2	-	-2.00	0-2	-	-2.00

By jockey – 2008

	Overall			Two-year-olds			Three-year-olds			Older horses		
	W-R	%	£1	W-R	%	£1	W-R	%	£1	W-R	%	£1
David Allan	38-314	12	+34.26	10-95	11	-29.03	17-96	18	+115.37	11-123	9	-52.08
D Fentiman	7-150	5	-95.50	1-43	2	-33.00	1-44	2	-35.00	5-63	8	-27.50
Paul Mulrennan	2-19	11	+25.00	0-3	-	-3.00	0-5	-	-5.00	2-11	18	+33.00
Eddie Ahern	1-2	50	+7.00	0-1	-	-1.00	1-1	100	+8.00	0-0	-	+0.00
Miss J Coward	1-2	50	+10.00	0-0	-	+0.00	0-0	-	+0.00	1-2	50	+10.00
Tom Eaves	1-7	14	-2.50	0-1	-	-1.00	1-1	100	+3.50	0-5	-	-5.00
Fergal Lynch	1-8	13	+3.00	0-2	-	-2.00	1-4	25	+7.00	0-2	-	-2.00
Andrew Elliott	0-1	-	-1.00	0-0	-	+0.00	0-1	-	-1.00	0-0	-	+0.00
Barry McHugh	0-1	-	-1.00	0-0	-	+0.00	0-1	-	-1.00	0-0	-	+0.00
Dougie Costello	0-1	-	-1.00	0-0	-	+0.00	0-0	-	+0.00	0-1	-	-1.00
Hayley Turner	0-1	-	-1.00	0-1	-	-1.00	0-0	-	+0.00	0-0	-	+0.00

By course – 2007-2010

	Overall			Two-year-olds			Three-year-olds			Older horses		
	W-R	%	£1	W-R	%	£1	W-R	%	£1	W-R	%	£1
Ascot	0-21	-	-21.00	0-4	-	-4.00	0-2	-	-2.00	0-15	-	-15.00
Ayr	15-93	16	+17.24	1-19	5	+0.00	3-22	14	-13.68	11-52	21	+30.92
Beverley	23-269	9	-139.76	3-76	4	-66.42	8-87	9	-36.75	12-106	11	-36.59
Carlisle	16-92	17	+9.00	2-17	12	-11.13	4-26	15	+8.75	10-49	20	+11.38
Catterick	23-187	12	-46.87	8-46	17	+3.63	5-65	8	-28.50	10-76	13	-22.00
Chester	3-39	8	-29.70	1-8	13	-4.50	2-14	14	-8.20	0-17	-	-17.00
Doncaster	10-136	7	-54.50	1-43	2	-26.00	3-36	8	-12.00	6-57	11	-16.50
Epsom	0-3	-	-3.00	0-0	-	+0.00	0-0	-	+0.00	0-3	-	-3.00
Goodwood	0-7	-	-7.00	0-0	-	+0.00	0-2	-	-2.00	0-5	-	-5.00
Hamilton	9-53	17	-14.17	0-7	-	-7.00	2-15	13	-9.25	7-31	23	+2.08
Haydock	11-133	8	-56.75	2-41	5	-29.50	3-35	9	-11.25	6-57	11	-16.00
Kempton (AW)	1-3	33	+6.00	0-0	-	+0.00	0-1	-	-1.00	1-2	50	+7.00
Leicester	4-26	15	+0.25	0-10	-	-10.00	1-7	14	-3.75	3-9	33	+14.00
Lingfield (AW)	1-2	50	+19.00	0-0	-	+0.00	0-0	-	+0.00	1-2	50	+19.00
Musselburgh	17-87	20	-15.38	5-23	22	-10.67	5-23	22	+4.29	7-41	17	-9.00
Newbury	0-12	-	-12.00	0-5	-	-5.00	0-1	-	-1.00	0-6	-	-6.00
Newcastle	19-201	9	-48.17	4-58	7	-16.17	4-59	7	-30.50	11-84	13	-1.50
Newmarket	1-19	5	-8.00	1-4	25	+7.00	0-4	-	-4.00	0-11	-	-11.00
Newmarket (J)	0-26	-	-26.00	0-6	-	-6.00	0-6	-	-6.00	0-14	-	-14.00
Nottingham	6 68	9	22.50	0-21	-	-21.00	3-24	13	+0.50	3-23	13	-2.00
Pontefract	10-127	8	-12.00	0-30	-	-30.00	3-44	7	+16.50	7-53	13	+1.50
Redcar	21-276	8	-32.13	1-95	1	-88.00	8-106	8	-0.88	12-75	16	+56.75
Ripon	20-254	8	-132.55	7-81	9	-25.83	8-82	10	-46.47	5-91	5	-60.25
Sandown	0-5	-	-5.00	0-0	-	+0.00	0-1	-	-1.00	0-4	-	-4.00
Southwell	0-8	-	-8.00	0-0	-	+0.00	0-7	-	-7.00	0-1	-	-1.00
Southwell (AW)	8-91	9	-13.13	1-21	5	-16.50	5-45	11	+4.00	2-25	8	+3.38
Thirsk	16-225	7	-114.88	4-58	7	-18.00	3-62	5	-47.50	9-105	9	-49.38
Warwick	4-20	20	+7.00	0-1	-	-1.00	2-7	29	+7.00	2-12	17	+1.00
Windsor	0-1	-	-1.00	0-0	-	+0.00	0-0	-	+0.00	0-1	-	-1.00
Wolves (AW)	8-83	10	-17.25	1-18	6	-14.75	0-16	-	-16.00	7-49	14	+13.50
Yarmouth	0-2	-	-2.00	0-1	-	-1.00	0-0	-	+0.00	0-1	-	-1.00
York	15-200	8	-64.38	5-60	8	+8.88	2-37	5	-22.00	8-103	8	-51.25

Ten-year summary

	Wins	Runs	%	Win prize	Total prize	£1 Stake
2010	98	846	12	£551,995.88	£902,812.12	-200.59
2009	54	628	9	£423,561.62	£691,718.70	-229.88
2008	51	597	9	£303,779.45	£515,182.50	-113.74
2007	58	702	8	£321,822.60	£548,335.85	-308.39
2006	54	719	8	£312,565.45	£582,443.23	-220.39
2005	58	756	8	£347,955.85	£685,477.04	-186.36
2004	62	738	8	£561,783.65	£919,052.16	-283.34
2003	58	829	7	£678,868.82	£1,177,970.22	-444.17
2002	81	826	10	£1,034,255.02	£1,462,077.05	-261.97
2001	73	804	9	£531,857.45	£784,244.01	-248.57

HAMISH McGONAGALL: Tim Easterby's stable star winning at York's Ebor meeting

Saeed Bin Suroor

Bin Suroor was always unlikely to match his sensational 2009, when 148 winners came at a 28% strike-rate and a £17 profit to £1 level stakes, especially when several of Godolphin's finest were sent to Mahmood Al Zarooni, so a tally of 90 marked another extremely respectable campaign.

By month – 2010

	Overall			Two-year-olds			Three-year-olds			Older horses		
	W-R	%	£1	W-R	%	£1	W-R	%	£1	W-R	%	£1
January	0-0	-	+0.00	0-0	-	+0.00	0-0	-	+0.00	0-0	-	+0.00
February	0-0	-	+0.00	0-0	-	+0.00	0-0	-	+0.00	0-0	-	+0.00
March	0-0	-	+0.00	0-0	-	+0.00	0-0	-	+0.00	0-0	-	+0.00
April	0-4	-	-4.00	0-0	-	+0.00	0-4	-	-4.00	0-0	-	+0.00
May	2-40	5	-35.05	0-3	-	-3.00	2-18	11	-13.05	0-19	-	-19.00
June	11-42	26	+16.19	4-12	33	-3.43	3-8	38	+3.25	4-22	18	+16.38
July	12-64	19	-15.97	5-14	36	+6.88	3-19	16	-1.00	4-31	13	-21.84
August	21-78	27	+5.49	11-20	55	+6.54	5-29	17	-5.10	5-29	17	+4.04
September	23-75	31	+20.56	10-27	37	-7.29	9-22	41	+23.75	4-26	15	+4.10
October	18-73	25	-11.99	8-29	28	-3.92	6-20	30	+8.83	4-24	17	-16.90
November	3-24	13	-18.00	2-10	20	-4.75	0-4	-	-4.00	1-10	10	-9.25
December	0-0	-	+0.00	0-0	-	+0.00	0-0	-	+0.00	0-0	-	+0.00

2009

	Overall			Two-year-olds			Three-year-olds			Older horses		
	W-R	%	£1	W-R	%	£1	W-R	%	£1	W-R	%	£1
January	0-0	-	+0.00	0-0	-	+0.00	0-0	-	+0.00	0-0	-	+0.00
February	0-0	-	+0.00	0-0	-	+0.00	0-0	-	+0.00	0-0	-	+0.00
March	0-0	-	+0.00	0-0	-	+0.00	0-0	-	+0.00	0-0	-	+0.00
April	2-5	40	+1.75	0-0	-	+0.00	0-2	-	-2.00	2-3	67	+3.75
May	5-52	10	-27.75	2-5	40	+0.25	1-25	4	-21.00	2-22	9	-7.00
June	7-55	13	-22.70	1-9	11	-4.50	5-22	23	+0.30	1-24	4	-18.50
July	19-63	30	+17.55	10-24	42	+7.99	5-21	24	-6.07	4-18	22	+15.63
August	27-97	28	-4.83	14-54	26	-0.11	11-33	33	+0.68	2-10	20	-5.40
September	27-95	28	+12.13	16-59	27	+3.46	8-25	32	+10.26	3-11	27	-1.58
October	42-129	33	+23.67	25-78	32	+15.31	14-38	37	+4.98	3-13	23	+3.38
November	19-34	56	+17.85	10-16	63	+13.58	7-12	58	+3.56	2-6	33	+0.70
December	0-0	-	+0.00	0-0	-	+0.00	0-0	-	+0.00	0-0	-	+0.00

2008

	Overall			Two-year-olds			Three-year-olds			Older horses		
	W-R	%	£1	W-R	%	£1	W-R	%	£1	W-R	%	£1
January	0-0	-	+0.00	0-0	-	+0.00	0-0	-	+0.00	0-0	-	+0.00
February	0-0	-	+0.00	0-0	-	+0.00	0-0	-	+0.00	0-0	-	+0.00
March	0-0	-	+0.00	0-0	-	+0.00	0-0	-	+0.00	0-0	-	+0.00
April	0-0	-	+0.00	0-0	-	+0.00	0-0	-	+0.00	0-0	-	+0.00
May	5-25	20	-3.50	0-1	-	-1.00	2-15	13	-7.50	3-9	33	+5.00
June	7-41	17	-9.38	0-1	-	-1.00	3-23	13	-5.88	4-17	24	-2.50
July	10-61	16	-32.05	4-13	31	-6.18	4-21	19	-4.90	2-27	7	-20.97
August	8-55	15	-3.84	1-14	7	-8.00	4-19	21	-7.71	3-22	14	+11.88
September	7-52	15	-17.32	3-18	17	-0.67	2-12	17	-3.75	2-22	9	-12.90
October	17-59	29	-1.59	9-33	27	-1.68	5-14	36	+4.00	3-12	25	-3.92
November	4-20	20	+11.25	2-9	22	-0.25	1-3	33	+4.50	1-8	13	+7.00
December	0-0	-	+0.00	0-0	-	+0.00	0-0	-	+0.00	0-0	-	+0.00

By race type – 2010

	Overall			Two-year-olds			Three-year-olds			Older horses		
	W-R	%	£1	W-R	%	£1	W-R	%	£1	W-R	%	£1
Handicap	20-100	20	+36.18	4-13	31	+3.60	13-59	22	+6.58	3-28	11	+26.00
Group 1,2,3	10-82	12	-44.52	4-17	24	-7.89	4-16	25	+1.50	2-49	4	-38.13
Maiden	33-91	36	-7.46	28-75	37	-4.81	5-16	31	-2.65	0-0	-	+0.00

2009

	Overall			Two-year-olds			Three-year-olds			Older horses		
	W-R	%	£1	W-R	%	£1	W-R	%	£1	W-R	%	£1
Handicap	26-103	25	+2.47	6-19	32	+8.64	16-64	25	-9.54	4-20	20	+3.38
Group 1,2,3	11-91	12	-44.68	3-21	14	-10.13	4-26	15	+0.10	4-44	9	-34.65
Maiden	77-204	38	+53.06	59-168	35	+43.56	18-36	50	+9.50	0-0	-	+0.00

2008

	Overall			Two-year-olds			Three-year-olds			Older horses		
	W-R	%	£1	W-R	%	£1	W-R	%	£1	W-R	%	£1
Handicap	12-44	27	+26.75	1-4	25	-1.63	4-10	40	+5.38	7-30	23	+23.00
Group 1,2,3	3-62	5	-44.50	0-7	-	-7.00	1-21	5	-11.00	2-34	6	-26.50
Maiden	26-121	21	-19.77	15-68	22	-11.11	11-53	21	-8.66	0-0	-	+0.00

By jockey – 2010

	Overall			Two-year-olds			Three-year-olds			Older horses		
	W-R	%	£1	W-R	%	£1	W-R	%	£1	W-R	%	£1
Frankie Dettori	51-191	27	+0.58	22-63	35	+2.46	16-60	27	+3.98	13-68	19	-5.85
Ted Durcan	32-129	25	-1.77	16-39	41	-3.09	9-43	21	-0.80	7-47	15	+2.13
D O'Donohoe	5-23	22	+10.75	0-5	-	-5.00	3-8	38	+18.50	2-10	20	-2.75
Richard Mullen	1-4	25	-1.00	1-1	100	+2.00	0-0	-	+0.00	0-3	-	-3.00
Kieren Fallon	1-6	17	-4.33	1-2	50	-0.33	0-1	-	-1.00	0-3	-	-3.00
Dane O'Neill	0-1	-	-1.00	0-0	-	+0.00	0-0	-	+0.00	0-1	-	-1.00
Jimmy Fortune	0-1	-	-1.00	0-0	-	+0.00	0-0	-	+0.00	0-1	-	-1.00
Joe Fanning	0-1	-	-1.00	0-0	-	+0.00	0-0	-	+0.00	0-1	-	-1.00
Neil Callan	0-1	-	-1.00	0-0	-	+0.00	0-0	-	+0.00	0-1	-	-1.00
Olivier Peslier	0-1	-	-1.00	0-0	-	+0.00	0-1	-	-1.00	0-0	-	+0.00
P J Smullen	0-1	-	-1.00	0-0	-	+0.00	0-0	-	+0.00	0-1	-	-1.00
Steve Drowne	0-1	-	-1.00	0-1	-	-1.00	0-0	-	+0.00	0-0	-	+0.00
Tony Culhane	0-1	-	-1.00	0-1	-	-1.00	0-0	-	+0.00	0-0	-	+0.00
Tony Hamilton	0-1	-	-1.00	0-0	-	+0.00	0-0	-	+0.00	0-1	-	-1.00
Franny Norton	0-2	-	-2.00	0-0	-	+0.00	0-1	-	-1.00	0-1	-	-1.00

2009

	Overall			Two-year-olds			Three-year-olds			Older horses		
	W-R	%	£1	W-R	%	£1	W-R	%	£1	W-R	%	£1
Frankie Dettori	69-231	30	-12.12	30-90	33	+0.02	27-87	31	+0.09	12-54	22	-12.23
Ted Durcan	52-147	35	+44.19	29-65	45	+40.77	20-60	33	+14.22	3-22	14	-10.80
Ahmed Ajtebi	14-70	20	+17.60	12-49	24	+7.60	0-9	-	-9.00	2-12	17	+19.00
Alan Munro	4-6	67	+13.37	2-3	67	+2.37	0-0	-	+0.00	2-3	67	+11.00
D O'Donohoe	4-31	13	-15.22	2-20	10	-7.67	2-9	22	-5.55	0-2	-	-2.00
Dane O'Neill	3-10	30	-2.90	2-4	50	+1.90	1-3	33	-1.80	0-3	-	-3.00
Royston Ffrench	1-2	50	+3.00	1-2	50	+3.00	0-0	-	+0.00	0-0	-	+0.00
Jamie Spencer	1-5	20	-2.25	0-2	-	-2.00	1-2	50	+0.75	0-1	-	-1.00
Jimmy Fortune	0-1	-	-1.00	0-1	-	-1.00	0-0	-	+0.00	0-0	-	+0.00
Micky Fenton	0-1	-	-1.00	0-1	-	-1.00	0-0	-	+0.00	0-0	-	+0.00
Paul Hanagan	0-1	-	-1.00	0-1	-	-1.00	0-0	-	+0.00	0-0	-	+0.00

By jockey – 2008

	Overall			Two-year-olds			Three-year-olds			Older horses		
	W-R	%	£1	W-R	%	£1	W-R	%	£1	W-R	%	£1
Frankie Dettori	30-165	18	-55.19	10-47	21	-11.98	12-56	21	-9.59	8-62	13	-33.62
Ted Durcan	11-46	24	+16.67	4-15	27	+7.58	2-11	18	-2.25	5-20	25	+11.33
Kerrin McEvoy	7-29	24	-5.09	2-4	50	-0.29	3-16	19	-3.80	2-9	22	-1.00
Jamie Spencer	4-9	44	+8.63	1-3	33	+0.25	1-1	100	+6.50	2-5	40	+1.88
Dane O'Neill	1-1	100	+25.00	0-0	-	+0.00	0-0	-	+0.00	1-1	100	+25.00
T Quinn	1-2	50	-0.33	1-1	100	+0.67	0-1	-	-1.00	0-0	-	+0.00
Darryll Holland	1-4	25	+0.50	0-1	-	-1.00	1-1	100	+3.50	0-2	-	-2.00
Martin Dwyer	1-5	20	+0.00	0-2	-	-2.00	1-1	100	+4.00	0-2	-	-2.00
Chris Catlin	1-8	13	-4.00	1-6	17	-2.00	0-0	-	+0.00	0-2	-	-2.00
D O'Donohoe	1-10	10	-8.60	0-2	-	-2.00	1-3	33	-1.60	0-5	-	-5.00
Eddie Ahern	0-1	-	-1.00	0-1	-	-1.00	0-0	-	+0.00	0-0	-	+0.00

By course – 2007-2010

	Overall			Two-year-olds			Three-year-olds			Older horses		
	W-R	%	£1	W-R	%	£1	W-R	%	£1	W-R	%	£1
Ascot	12-112	11	-8.38	4-19	21	-3.88	4-31	13	-4.50	4-62	6	+0.00
Ayr	3-14	21	-6.38	0-4	-	-4.00	2-4	50	+0.63	1-6	17	-3.00
Bath	6-21	29	-3.29	1-9	11	-7.00	5-10	50	+5.71	0-2	-	-2.00
Beverley	2-8	25	-2.60	1-5	20	-3.60	1-3	33	+1.00	0-0	-	+0.00
Brighton	2-7	29	+0.90	1-6	17	+0.50	1-1	100	+0.40	0-0	-	+0.00
Catterick	0-2	-	-2.00	0-1	-	-1.00	0-1	-	-1.00	0-0	-	+0.00
Chepstow	0-4	-	-4.00	0-3	-	-3.00	0-1	-	-1.00	0-0	-	+0.00
Chester	1-25	4	-20.00	0-3	-	-3.00	0-8	-	-8.00	1-14	7	-9.00
Doncaster	12-77	16	-26.60	8-23	35	+0.65	4-25	16	+1.75	0-29	-	-29.00
Epsom	9-32	28	-5.34	3-8	38	+1.33	2-13	15	-6.63	4-11	36	-0.05
Ffos Las	0-1	-	-1.00	0-1	-	-1.00	0-0	-	+0.00	0-0	-	+0.00
Folkestone	5-16	31	-6.79	2-7	29	-2.79	3-9	33	-4.00	0-0	-	+0.00
Goodwood	16-112	14	-53.68	5-22	23	-3.51	6-37	16	-19.27	5-53	9	-30.90
Hamilton	2-8	25	-0.77	0-0	-	+0.00	0-4	-	-4.00	2-4	50	+3.23
Haydock	6-33	18	-3.99	3-10	30	+1.02	2-6	33	+9.00	1-17	6	-14.00
Kempton (AW)	43-118	36	+17.25	22-55	40	+16.87	15-39	38	+4.76	6-24	25	-4.38
Leicester	14-36	39	+11.81	4-17	24	-4.81	5-14	36	+3.60	5-5	100	+13.02
Lingfield	5-21	24	-7.18	1-7	14	-4.63	3-11	27	-2.05	1-3	33	-0.50
Lingfield (AW)	31-61	51	+45.82	15-27	56	+30.82	11-25	44	+10.27	5-9	56	+4.73
Musselburgh	1-4	25	-2.17	0-2	-	-2.00	0-1	-	-1.00	1-1	100	+0.83
Newbury	19-79	24	+43.33	9-21	43	+12.87	5-27	19	-7.54	5-31	16	+38.00
Newcastle	1-16	6	-12.25	1-8	13	-4.25	0-4	-	-4.00	0-4	-	-4.00
Newmarket	19-144	13	-50.75	6-45	13	-30.97	8-54	15	-16.65	5-45	11	3.13
Newmarket (J)	22-92	24	-13.22	12-37	32	+3.32	7-25	28	+8.05	3-30	10	-24.59
Nottingham	21-43	49	+26.89	7-13	54	+7.14	10-18	56	+20.75	4-12	33	-1.00
Pontefract	12-33	36	+13.75	4-12	33	+4.50	3-11	27	+2.75	5-10	50	+6.50
Redcar	8-25	32	-3.02	4-11	36	+2.22	3-7	43	-0.24	1-7	14	-5.00
Ripon	2-9	22	-4.28	0-2	-	-2.00	2-6	33	-1.28	0-1	-	-1.00
Salisbury	7-31	23	-14.15	1-8	13	-6.27	4-14	29	-2.48	2-9	22	-5.40
Sandown	12-61	20	-7.26	4-11	36	+5.50	6-27	22	+4.62	2-23	9	-17.38
Southwell (AW)	8-16	50	+13.32	6-11	55	+10.70	2-5	40	+2.62	0-0	-	+0.00
Thirsk	5-10	50	+4.75	1-2	50	+1.75	4-8	50	+3.00	0-0	-	+0.00
Warwick	2-16	13	-2.50	1-7	14	+1.00	0-5	-	-5.00	1-4	25	+1.50
Windsor	13-49	27	-4.15	1-12	8	-10.27	8-23	35	-1.73	4-14	29	+7.85
Wolves (AW)	18-49	37	+8.82	13-34	38	+9.84	5-15	33	-1.02	0-0	-	+0.00
Yarmouth	8-39	21	-20.92	6-27	23	-14.37	0-5	-	-5.00	2-7	29	-1.55
York	16-87	18	-9.38	5-11	45	+5.38	2-22	9	-14.50	9-54	17	-0.25

Ten-year summary

	Wins	Runs	%	Win prize	Total prize	£1 Stake
2010	90	400	23	£1,383,089.08	£2,064,698.09	-42.77
2009	148	530	28	£1,743,062.05	£2,765,249.72	+17.67
2008	58	313	19	£758,691.92	£1,268,209.97	-56.42
2007	72	285	25	£1,225,192.68	£1,680,865.13	-20.61
2006	70	247	28	£935,405.65	£1,610,204.02	+13.15
2005	78	407	19	£901,450.30	£1,522,250.25	-52.73
2004	115	455	25	£3,057,921.70	£4,320,171.12	+12.99
2003	23	98	23	£529,431.35	£987,310.75	-8.21
2002	21	88	24	£895,268.79	£1,654,512.49	+5.57
2001	24	84	29	£1,108,782.10	£1,934,729.10	+24.31

POET'S VOICE: earned Frankie Dettori a standing ovation with his win in the QEII

David Evans

Thrust into the spotlight by his first century in 2009, Wales-based Evans had a bigger pool of runners to work with last year and therefore may be slightly disappointed to have slipped below the 100 barrier. Even so, a tally of 88 should prove a good season of consolidation at the top table.

By month – 2010

	Overall			Two-year-olds			Three-year-olds			Older horses		
	W-R	%	£1	W-R	%	£1	W-R	%	£1	W-R	%	£1
January	10-92	11	-60.70	0-0	-	+0.00	2-17	12	-13.55	8-75	11	-47.15
February	10-68	15	-42.85	0-0	-	+0.00	3-18	17	-11.01	7-50	14	-31.84
March	6-67	9	-42.54	0-6	-	-6.00	2-20	10	-13.25	4-41	10	-23.29
April	8-89	9	-25.75	4-32	13	+11.50	2-21	10	-14.75	2-36	6	-22.50
May	14-141	10	-44.01	6-41	15	-18.89	2-38	5	-4.00	6-62	10	-21.13
June	5-95	5	-52.25	2-28	7	-3.00	0-21	-	-21.00	3-46	7	-28.25
July	9-112	8	-59.38	4-35	11	-10.00	2-29	7	-13.00	3-48	6	-36.38
August	6-91	7	-48.13	3-31	10	+0.00	2-28	7	-21.13	1-32	3	-27.00
September	5-73	7	+16.88	3-27	11	+54.50	2-20	10	-11.63	0-26	-	-26.00
October	3-70	4	-35.50	1-24	4	-7.00	1-27	4	-21.50	1-19	5	-7.00
November	4-44	9	-7.67	1-20	5	-5.00	0-7	-	-7.00	3-17	18	+4.33
December	8-77	10	-31.25	2-27	7	-18.25	4-23	17	+2.25	2-27	7	-15.25

2009

	Overall			Two-year-olds			Three-year-olds			Older horses		
	W-R	%	£1	W-R	%	£1	W-R	%	£1	W-R	%	£1
January	5-66	8	-32.25	0-0	-	+0.00	0-17	-	-17.00	5-49	10	-15.25
February	6-47	13	-21.88	0-0	-	+0.00	1-11	9	-8.13	5-36	14	-13.75
March	4-35	11	-14.28	1-2	50	+11.00	0-9	-	-9.00	3-24	13	-16.28
April	9-61	15	-6.57	4-17	24	-4.90	1-14	7	-10.75	4-30	13	+9.08
May	16-100	16	+2.79	4-27	15	-9.88	2-22	9	-0.67	10-51	20	+13.33
June	13-92	14	+25.55	2-15	13	-6.27	5-28	18	+38.50	6-49	12	-6.68
July	13-109	12	-40.56	5-26	19	-8.31	3-25	12	-5.00	5-58	9	-27.25
August	13-105	12	+1.67	4-30	13	-0.79	4-25	16	+22.00	5-50	10	-19.54
September	11-104	11	+74.50	3-34	9	+65.00	3-27	11	-7.00	5-43	12	+16.50
October	7-92	8	-45.25	2-29	7	-5.00	3-22	14	-8.75	2-41	5	-31.50
November	8-68	12	+34.25	3-25	12	+33.50	1-10	10	-6.25	4-33	12	+7.00
December	9-76	12	-21.13	3-22	14	-7.38	1-18	6	-13.00	5-36	14	-0.75

2008

	Overall			Two-year-olds			Three-year-olds			Older horses		
	W-R	%	£1	W-R	%	£1	W-R	%	£1	W-R	%	£1
January	4-56	7	-23.50	0-0	-	+0.00	0-6	-	-6.00	4-50	8	-17.50
February	9-64	14	+11.33	0-0	-	+0.00	0-7	-	-7.00	9-57	16	+18.33
March	6-40	15	+38.41	1-2	50	+7.00	3-7	43	+53.00	2-31	6	-21.59
April	10-64	16	+8.80	5-21	24	+13.88	1-16	6	-6.00	4-27	15	+0.92
May	9-76	12	-28.13	3-28	11	-17.25	2-21	10	-11.13	4-27	15	+0.25
June	8-81	10	-39.42	2-24	8	-15.00	2-17	12	-11.75	4-40	10	-12.67
July	6-96	6	-48.38	0-33	-	-33.00	4-25	16	+3.63	2-38	5	-19.00
August	7-81	9	-25.50	2-20	10	+5.50	2-30	7	-21.50	3-31	10	-9.50
September	6-56	11	+5.50	2-18	11	+7.00	2-17	12	-5.50	2-21	10	+4.00
October	4-75	5	-37.00	1-21	5	-12.00	2-25	8	-13.00	1-29	3	-12.00
November	3-54	6	-29.00	0-15	-	-15.00	2-17	12	+3.50	1-22	5	-17.50
December	10-76	13	+31.50	1-15	7	+14.00	2-20	10	-2.00	7-41	17	+19.50

By race type – 2010

	Overall			Two-year-olds			Three-year-olds			Older horses		
	W-R	%	£1	W-R	%	£1	W-R	%	£1	W-R	%	£1
Handicap	36-628	6	-333.29	6-84	7	+30.00	11-176	6	-95.00	19-368	5	-268.29
Group 1,2,3	0-6	-	-6.00	0-4	-	-4.00	0-1	-	-1.00	0-1	-	-1.00
Maiden	6-129	5	-95.39	6-97	6	-63.39	0-27	-	-27.00	0-5	-	-5.00

2009

	Overall			Two-year-olds			Three-year-olds			Older horses		
	W-R	%	£1	W-R	%	£1	W-R	%	£1	W-R	%	£1
Handicap	62-586	11	-77.46	7-73	10	-13.00	16-148	11	+5.00	39-365	11	-69.46
Group 1,2,3	0-5	-	-5.00	0-4	-	-4.00	0-0	-	+0.00	0-1	-	-1.00
Maiden	10-96	10	+33.35	6-57	11	+45.48	4-31	13	-4.13	0-8	-	-8.00

2008

	Overall			Two-year-olds			Three-year-olds			Older horses		
	W-R	%	£1	W-R	%	£1	W-R	%	£1	W-R	%	£1
Handicap	44-508	9	-98.33	4-39	10	+12.50	8-137	6	-57.50	32-332	10	-53.33
Group 1,2,3	0-3	-	-3.00	0-3	-	-3.00	0-0	-	+0.00	0-0	-	+0.00
Maiden	7-90	8	-2.75	4-64	6	-26.75	2-20	10	+23.00	1-6	17	+1.00

By jockey – 2010

	Overall			Two-year-olds			Three-year-olds			Older horses		
	W-R	%	£1	W-R	%	£1	W-R	%	£1	W-R	%	£1
Cathy Gannon	20-234	9	-97.64	12-109	11	-32.89	6-73	8	-30.25	2-52	4	-34.50
A Heffernan	15-145	10	-74.32	1-25	4	-13.00	3-37	8	-26.52	11-83	13	-34.79
Richard Evans	9-107	8	-55.75	2-11	18	+9.00	1-23	4	-17.50	6-73	8	-47.25
J-P Guillambert	8-28	29	-7.67	0-0	-	+0.00	3-6	50	-0.08	5-22	23	-7.59
Paul Doe	4-46	9	-36.40	0-2	-	-2.00	0-7	-	-7.00	4-37	11	-27.40
S De Sousa	3-16	19	+10.00	3-9	33	+17.00	0-5	-	-5.00	0-2	-	-2.00
George Baker	3-24	13	-4.92	0-1	-	-1.00	0-8	-	-8.00	3-15	20	+4.08
Stevie Donohoe	3-24	13	+4.00	0-8	-	-8.00	2-10	20	+10.00	1-6	17	+2.00
Martin Lane	3-39	8	-13.75	1-10	10	-7.25	1-17	6	+0.00	1-12	8	-6.50
M Cosham	3-43	7	-28.75	1-6	17	+0.00	1-8	13	-4.75	1-29	3	-24.00
Tom Queally	2-11	18	+7.00	0-4	-	-4.00	0-0	-	+0.00	2-7	29	+11.00
Richard Hughes	2-13	15	-7.00	2-3	67	+3.00	0-0	-	+0.00	0-10	-	-10.00
Jimmy Fortune	2-15	13	-1.00	1-7	14	+3.00	1-3	33	+1.00	0-5	-	-5.00
Paul Hanagan	2-21	10	+22.00	2-7	29	+36.00	0-4	-	-4.00	0-10	-	-10.00
Pat Cosgrave	2-25	8	+43.80	1-6	17	+61.00	1-7	14	-5.20	0-12	-	-12.00

2009

	Overall			Two-year-olds			Three-year-olds			Older horses		
	W-R	%	£1	W-R	%	£1	W-R	%	£1	W-R	%	£1
Paul Doe	27-154	18	+27.98	6-35	17	+4.23	4-31	13	-7.63	17-88	19	+31.38
Cathy Gannon	20-136	15	+80.45	10-47	21	+65.82	5-49	10	+4.50	5-40	13	+10.13
Richard Evans	17-180	9	-76.50	5-22	23	+8.50	2-28	7	-20.42	10-130	8	-64.58
A Heffernan	11-79	14	-19.25	0-19	-	-19.00	4-18	22	+5.75	7-42	17	-6.00
Jamie Spencer	4-16	25	-3.18	0-3	-	-3.00	1-3	33	+2.00	3-10	30	-2.18
Paul Hanagan	4-18	22	+14.00	2-7	29	+4.00	0-3	-	-3.00	2-8	25	+13.00
Stevie Donohoe	4-45	9	+35.23	2-9	22	+33.73	2-15	13	+22.50	0-21	-	-21.00
Dean Heslop	2-8	25	+8.00	0-1	-	-1.00	0-0	-	+0.00	2-7	29	+9.00
L-P Beuzelin	2-8	25	+8.50	0-2	-	-2.00	2-6	33	+10.50	0-0	-	+0.00
Richard Hughes	2-10	20	+5.50	0-0	-	+0.00	0-4	-	-4.00	2-6	33	+9.50
J-P Guillambert	2-12	17	-3.25	0-1	-	-1.00	2-6	33	+2.75	0-5	-	-5.00

By jockey – 2008

	Overall			Two-year-olds			Three-year-olds			Older horses		
	W-R	%	£1	W-R	%	£1	W-R	%	£1	W-R	%	£1
Richard Evans	23-186	12	+3.71	0-15	-	-15.00	6-31	19	+19.38	17-140	12	-0.66
S Donohoe	13-98	13	+13.50	2-20	10	-12.50	0-16	-	-16.00	11-62	18	+42.00
T McLaughlin	12-109	11	-25.97	6-39	15	+0.13	4-41	10	-12.00	2-29	7	-14.09
James Doyle	6-48	13	-6.00	0-7	-	-7.00	1-16	6	-3.00	5-25	20	+4.00
Robert Winston	4-20	20	+46.00	2-11	18	+19.00	2-6	33	+30.00	0-3	-	-3.00
Tom Eaves	3-11	27	+8.00	2-4	50	+5.00	1-4	25	+6.00	0-3	-	-3.00
Ryan Moore	2-4	50	+6.00	0-1	-	-1.00	2-2	100	+8.00	0-1	-	-1.00
Neil Callan	2-11	18	-1.00	0-2	-	-2.00	1-3	33	+2.00	1-6	17	-1.00
P Donaghy	2-15	13	+22.00	1-3	33	+26.00	0-1	-	-1.00	1-11	9	-3.00
Pat Cosgrave	2-22	9	-9.00	0-5	-	-5.00	1-7	14	-4.00	1-10	10	+0.00
John Egan	2-29	7	-9.13	1-11	9	+6.00	1-7	14	-4.13	0-11	-	-11.00

By course – 2007-2010

	Overall			Two-year-olds			Three-year-olds			Older horses		
	W-R	%	£1	W-R	%	£1	W-R	%	£1	W-R	%	£1
Ascot	1-33	3	-12.00	0-14	-	-14.00	1-8	13	+13.00	0-11	-	-11.00
Ayr	3-34	9	-10.67	0-7	-	-7.00	1-13	8	+2.00	2-14	14	-5.67
Bath	14-141	10	-19.00	3-41	7	+1.50	1-39	3	-34.67	10-61	16	+14.17
Beverley	2-14	14	-10.21	2-8	25	-4.21	0-3	-	-3.00	0-3	-	-3.00
Brighton	14-100	14	-21.38	1-8	13	-6.50	3-30	10	-18.13	10-62	16	+3.25
Carlisle	1-13	8	-10.00	0-2	-	-2.00	1-6	17	-3.00	0-5	-	-5.00
Catterick	8-58	14	-3.67	4-19	21	+6.00	0-13	-	-13.00	4-26	15	+3.33
Chepstow	12-154	8	-44.39	3-36	8	-3.75	5-52	10	+0.00	4-66	6	-40.64
Chester	10-130	8	-19.77	5-38	13	-2.77	1-30	3	-21.00	4-62	6	+4.00
Doncaster	3-61	5	-9.50	1-19	5	-14.50	1-20	5	+14.00	1-22	5	-9.00
Epsom	4-26	15	-8.00	1-5	20	+2.00	0-1	-	-1.00	3-20	15	-9.00
Ffos Las	5-32	16	-1.51	3-11	27	+4.12	2-12	17	+3.38	0-9	-	-9.00
Folkestone	4-49	8	-33.17	1-12	8	-8.00	1-16	6	-12.50	2-21	10	-12.67
Goodwood	0-34	-	-34.00	0-11	-	-11.00	0-5	-	-5.00	0-18	-	-18.00
Hamilton	0-9	-	-9.00	0-0	-	+0.00	0-3	-	-3.00	0-6	-	-6.00
Haydock	6-62	10	-7.50	2-22	9	+9.50	1-20	5	-14.50	3-20	15	-2.50
Kempton (AW)	28-321	9	-107.72	8-58	14	+23.38	6-81	7	-33.25	14-182	8	-97.84
Leicester	7-116	6	-18.63	2-50	4	+25.00	2-38	5	-27.00	3-28	11	-16.63
Lingfield	2-33	6	-8.00	0-4	-	-4.00	1-12	8	-2.00	1-17	6	-2.00
Lingfield (AW)	28-313	9	-130.52	2-37	5	-22.13	8-87	9	-44.08	18-189	10	-64.32
Musselburgh	1-12	8	-9.00	1-3	33	+0.00	0-5	-	-5.00	0-4	-	-4.00
Newbury	4-55	7	+37.50	4-19	21	+73.50	0-13	-	-13.00	0-23	-	-23.00
Newcastle	1-7	14	-4.13	1-3	33	-0.13	0-2	-	-2.00	0-2	-	-2.00
Nowmarket	2-22	9	-0.50	0-0	-	+0.00	2-12	17	+9.50	0-10	-	-10.00
Newmarket (J)	2-18	11	-4.00	0-6	-	-6.00	0-4	-	-4.00	2-8	25	+6.00
Nottingham	12-70	17	+34.35	6-30	20	+34.73	1-17	6	-10.00	5-23	22	+9.63
Pontefract	2-12	17	+3.00	1-3	33	+4.00	1-3	33	+5.00	0-6	-	-6.00
Redcar	2-49	4	-28.00	2-23	9	-2.00	0-11	-	-11.00	0-15	-	-15.00
Ripon	4-40	10	-6.00	3-14	21	+15.00	1-17	6	-12.00	0-9	-	-9.00
Salisbury	8-74	11	-14.55	2-20	10	-4.00	1-18	6	-1.00	5-36	14	-9.55
Sandown	0-23	-	-23.00	0-10	-	-10.00	0-4	-	-4.00	0-9	-	-9.00
Southwell	0-4	-	-4.00	0-0	-	+0.00	0-3	-	-3.00	0-1	-	-1.00
Southwell (AW)	32-173	18	+50.53	3-37	8	+24.00	10-35	29	+8.43	19-101	19	+18.10
Thirsk	6-44	14	-8.50	3-21	14	-6.50	1-5	20	+0.00	2-18	11	-2.00
Warwick	6-60	10	-18.75	2-16	13	-1.00	2-18	11	-2.00	2-26	8	-15.75
Windsor	22-172	13	+48.96	5-57	9	-26.42	8-49	16	+44.50	9-66	14	+30.88
Wolves (AW)	71-667	11	-187.99	8-129	6	-49.84	19-160	12	-56.90	44-378	12	-81.25
Yarmouth	3-65	5	-47.50	1-30	3	-26.00	0-13	-	-13.00	2-22	9	-8.50
York	2-33	6	-13.00	2-18	11	+2.00	0-3	-	-3.00	0-12	-	-12.00

Ten-year summary

	Wins	Runs	%	Win prize	Total prize	£1 Stake
2010	88	1019	9	£277,361.35	£488,961.34	-433.14
2009	114	955	12	£441,761.95	£674,962.77	-43.14
2008	82	819	10	£279,109.78	£427,300.22	-135.38
2007	53	587	9	£171,771.61	£320,454.87	-105.18
2006	45	465	10	£162,754.00	£285,542.23	-166.34
2005	38	542	7	£180,714.37	£291,886.61	-281.30
2004	62	694	9	£259,826.72	£412,921.05	-146.57
2003	42	536	8	£206,745.80	£331,379.99	-133.25
2002	30	476	6	£140,717.45	£231,713.92	-85.67
2001	48	547	9	£169,077.95	£260,447.75	-89.90

DINGLE VIEW (right): a breakthrough winner for David Evans at the Curragh

David Nicholls

Long known as the king of the sprint handicap, Nicholls took his operation to another level last year as he recorded a personal best of 88 at a 13% strike-rate. The highlights came thick and fast in the usual places – Evens And Odds landing the Stewards' Cup and Redford leading an Ayr Gold Cup one-two.

By month – 2010

	Overall			Two-year-olds			Three-year-olds			Older horses		
	W-R	%	£1	W-R	%	£1	W-R	%	£1	W-R	%	£1
January	2-11	18	+3.25	0-0	-	+0.00	2-6	33	+8.25	0-5	-	-5.00
February	2-9	22	+1.75	0-0	-	+0.00	1-6	17	+2.00	1-3	33	-0.25
March	6-31	19	-6.38	0-0	-	+0.00	3-11	27	-2.25	3-20	15	-4.13
April	11-64	17	+4.00	1-4	25	+1.50	2-17	12	+8.25	8-43	19	-5.75
May	11-89	12	-24.10	1-6	17	+3.00	0-9	-	-9.00	10-74	14	-18.10
June	13-86	15	-7.00	3-9	33	+8.50	3-13	23	+23.50	7-64	11	-39.00
July	11-88	13	+22.48	1-12	8	-10.27	4-14	29	+12.00	6-62	10	+20.75
August	9-67	13	-14.83	0-3	-	-3.00	2-15	13	-2.50	7-49	14	-9.33
September	7-63	11	-9.00	1-4	25	+2.00	0-13	-	-13.00	6-46	13	+2.00
October	1-44	2	-40.00	0-5	-	-5.00	0-12	-	-12.00	1-27	4	-23.00
November	7-29	24	+6.08	2-8	25	-1.50	1-8	13	-4.00	4-13	31	+11.58
December	8-47	17	-7.60	3-11	27	+1.00	1-10	10	-8.60	4-26	15	+0.00

2009

	Overall			Two-year-olds			Three-year-olds			Older horses		
	W-R	%	£1	W-R	%	£1	W-R	%	£1	W-R	%	£1
January	1-4	25	-1.38	0-0	-	+0.00	1-2	50	+0.63	0-2	-	-2.00
February	0-7	-	-7.00	0-0	-	+0.00	0-3	-	-3.00	0-4	-	-4.00
March	7-42	17	-2.92	0-0	-	+0.00	1-5	20	-1.00	6-37	16	-1.92
April	5-69	7	-21.50	1-2	50	+3.00	0-16	-	-16.00	4-51	8	-8.50
May	14-117	12	-20.67	0-11	-	-11.00	3-20	15	+7.33	11-86	13	-17.00
June	11-101	11	-35.93	2-12	17	-2.13	0-14	-	-14.00	9-75	12	-19.81
July	16-103	16	+10.33	2-10	20	-0.75	2-12	17	+13.00	12-81	15	-1.92
August	13-89	15	-9.78	3-14	21	-5.65	2-11	18	+12.00	8-64	13	-16.13
September	7-88	8	+61.63	4-21	19	+101.13	0-6	-	-6.00	3-61	5	-33.50
October	6-51	12	+14.63	3-13	23	+7.13	0-7	-	-7.00	3-31	10	+14.50
November	2-10	20	-3.00	1-4	25	+0.50	0-0	-	+0.00	1-6	17	-3.50
December	2-6	33	+3.00	1-2	50	+2.00	0-0	-	+0.00	1-4	25	+1.00

2008

	Overall			Two-year-olds			Three-year-olds			Older horses		
	W-R	%	£1	W-R	%	£1	W-R	%	£1	W-R	%	£1
January	0-1	-	-1.00	0-0	-	+0.00	0-0	-	+0.00	0-1	-	-1.00
February	0-2	-	-2.00	0-0	-	+0.00	0-0	-	+0.00	0-2	-	-2.00
March	3-41	7	-10.25	0-1	-	-1.00	0-5	-	-5.00	3-35	9	-4.25
April	12-75	16	+37.32	0-0	-	+0.00	2-14	14	-1.25	10-61	16	+38.57
May	14-108	13	+28.68	2-6	33	+36.00	2-14	14	-6.00	10-88	11	-1.33
June	8-79	10	-1.25	0-9	-	-9.00	1-6	17	+3.00	7-64	11	+4.75
July	11-57	19	+4.59	2-9	22	+23.00	0-5	-	-5.00	9-43	21	-13.41
August	10-66	15	+25.75	1-10	10	+2.00	0-6	-	-6.00	9-50	18	+29.75
September	8-70	11	+19.00	2-11	18	-1.00	0-7	-	-7.00	6-52	12	+27.00
October	2-29	7	-17.00	0-5	-	-5.00	0-6	-	-6.00	2-18	11	-6.00
November	0-4	-	-4.00	0-2	-	-2.00	0-1	-	-1.00	0-1	-	-1.00
December	0-0	-	+0.00	0-0	-	+0.00	0-0	-	+0.00	0-0	-	+0.00

By race type – 2010

	Overall			Two-year-olds			Three-year-olds			Older horses		
	W-R	%	£1	W-R	%	£1	W-R	%	£1	W-R	%	£1
Handicap	41-419	10	-57.67	4-18	22	+0.00	9-73	12	+10.50	28-328	9	-68.17
Group 1,2,3	1-12	8	-3.50	0-1	-	-1.00	0-2	-	-2.00	1-9	11	-0.50
Maiden	10-60	17	-2.10	4-24	17	+1.50	6-33	18	-0.60	0-3	-	-3.00

2009

	Overall			Two-year-olds			Three-year-olds			Older horses		
	W-R	%	£1	W-R	%	£1	W-R	%	£1	W-R	%	£1
Handicap	40-443	9	-102.48	6-16	38	+14.60	2-54	4	-43.67	32-373	9	-73.42
Group 1,2,3	1-14	7	+1.00	0-2	-	-2.00	0-0	-	+0.00	1-12	8	+3.00
Maiden	12-84	14	+105.38	7-50	14	+89.38	4-28	14	+16.00	1-6	17	+0.00

2008

	Overall			Two-year-olds			Three-year-olds			Older horses		
	W-R	%	£1	W-R	%	£1	W-R	%	£1	W-R	%	£1
Handicap	35-373	9	+8.38	1-6	17	+6.00	3-43	7	-21.25	31-324	10	+23.63
Group 1,2,3	0-7	-	-7.00	0-1	-	-1.00	0-0	-	+0.00	0-6	-	-6.00
Maiden	4-43	9	+16.50	3-29	10	+28.00	1-8	13	-5.50	0-6	-	-6.00

By jockey – 2010

	Overall			Two-year-olds			Three-year-olds			Older horses		
	W-R	%	£1	W-R	%	£1	W-R	%	£1	W-R	%	£1
A Nicholls	50-272	18	-33.12	7-30	23	+8.73	12-64	19	-4.00	31-178	17	-37.85
Billy Cray	7-69	10	-6.35	2-9	22	+0.75	2-11	18	+3.40	3-49	6	-10.50
M O'Connell	6-41	15	-3.00	0-2	-	-2.00	0-5	-	-5.00	6-34	18	+4.00
Michael Geran	6-62	10	-31.38	1-5	20	-1.25	0-10	-	-10.00	5-47	11	-20.13
Ian Mongan	4-17	24	+6.50	0-5	-	-5.00	1-3	33	+1.00	3-9	33	+10.50
Frankie Dettori	2-5	40	+18.00	0-0	-	+0.00	0-1	-	-1.00	2-4	50	+19.00
Paul Quinn	2-29	7	+9.00	0-2	-	-2.00	1-6	17	+17.00	1-21	5	-6.00
Andrew Mullen	2-47	4	-33.25	0-0	-	+0.00	1-13	8	-2.00	1-34	3	-31.25
David Probert	1-1	100	+28.00	0-0	-	+0.00	0-0	-	+0.00	1-1	100	+28.00
Neil Farley	1-1	100	+1.25	1-1	100	+1.25	0-0	-	+0.00	0-0	-	+0.00
Steve Drowne	1-1	100	+2.25	0-0	-	+0.00	1-1	100	+2.25	0-0	-	+0.00
Tom Queally	1-1	100	+7.00	0-0	-	+0.00	0-0	-	+0.00	1-1	100	+7.00
D O'Donohoe	1-3	33	+2.50	0-0	-	+0.00	0-0	-	+0.00	1-3	33	+2.50
Paul Hanagan	1-3	33	+6.50	0-0	-	+0.00	0-1	-	-1.00	1-2	50	+7.50
P J McDonald	1-4	25	-0.25	1-2	50	+1.75	0-1	-	-1.00	0-1	-	-1.00

2009

	Overall			Two-year-olds			Three-year-olds			Older horses		
	W-R	%	£1	W-R	%	£1	W-R	%	£1	W-R	%	£1
A Nicholls	40-312	13	-92.00	8-49	16	-6.90	2-49	4	-40.67	30-214	14	-44.43
Franny Norton	8-54	15	+0.16	2-5	40	+2.25	2-10	20	+13.00	4-39	10	-15.09
Andrew Mullen	6-53	11	+105.00	3-11	27	+98.50	0-3	-	-3.00	3-39	8	+9.50
S De Sousa	5-31	16	+20.00	0-2	-	-2.00	2-7	29	+16.00	3-22	14	+6.00
Ahmed Ajtebi	4-10	40	+26.25	0-0	-	+0.00	2-2	100	+23.00	2-8	25	+3.25
Paul Quinn	3-34	9	+6.50	0-4	-	-4.00	0-1	-	-1.00	3-29	10	+11.50
Eddie Ahern	2-3	67	+4.13	2-2	100	+5.13	0-0	-	+0.00	0-1	-	-1.00
Richard Hughes	2-3	67	+11.50	0-0	-	+0.00	0-0	-	+0.00	2-3	67	+11.50
William Carson	2-14	14	-7.25	0-0	-	+0.00	0-0	-	+0.00	2-14	14	-7.25
Nicky Lawes	2-36	6	-13.00	0-3	-	-3.00	0-2	-	-2.00	2-31	6	-8.00
Tom Queally	1-1	100	+14.00	1-1	100	+14.00	0-0	-	+0.00	0-0	-	+0.00

By jockey – 2008

	Overall			Two-year-olds			Three-year-olds			Older horses		
	W-R	%	£1	W-R	%	£1	W-R	%	£1	W-R	%	£1
A Nicholls	30-248	12	-44.47	2-29	7	-8.50	2-39	5	-32.75	26-180	14	-3.22
S De Sousa	14-112	13	+47.32	4-15	27	+43.50	1-10	10	-1.00	9-87	10	+4.82
A Mulrennan	5-30	17	+8.75	0-3	-	-3.00	1-4	25	+1.50	4-23	17	+10.25
Ahmed Ajtebi	4-7	57	+29.82	0-0	-	+0.00	0-0	-	+0.00	4-7	57	+29.82
Mark Coumbe	2-3	67	+6.50	0-0	-	+0.00	0-0	-	+0.00	2-3	67	+6.50
William Carson	2-5	40	+17.00	0-0	-	+0.00	0-0	-	+0.00	2-5	40	+17.00
Andrew Mullen	2-9	22	+11.50	0-0	-	+0.00	0-1	-	-1.00	2-8	25	+12.50
Yutaka Take	1-1	100	+3.00	0-0	-	+0.00	0-0	-	+0.00	1-1	100	+3.00
Martin Dwyer	1-2	50	+7.00	0-0	-	+0.00	1-1	100	+8.00	0-1	-	-1.00
Ted Durcan	1-2	50	+3.00	0-0	-	+0.00	0-0	-	+0.00	1-2	50	+3.00
Paul Mulrennan	1-3	33	+31.00	0-0	-	+0.00	0-1	-	-1.00	1-2	50	+32.00

By course – 2007-2010

	Overall			Two-year-olds			Three-year-olds			Older horses		
	W-R	%	£1	W-R	%	£1	W-R	%	£1	W-R	%	£1
Ascot	6-79	8	-18.50	0-4	-	-4.00	0-2	-	-2.00	6-73	8	-12.50
Ayr	14-140	10	-41.58	4-22	18	+9.38	2-16	13	-8.25	8-102	8	-42.71
Bath	0-2	-	-2.00	0-0	-	+0.00	0-1	-	-1.00	0-1	-	-1.00
Beverley	10-84	12	+4.50	0-11	-	-11.00	1-13	8	+4.00	9-60	15	+11.50
Brighton	0-2	-	-2.00	0-0	-	+0.00	0-0	-	+0.00	0-2	-	-2.00
Carlisle	7-53	13	-9.84	0-10	-	-10.00	2-6	33	+12.50	5-37	14	-12.34
Catterick	26-141	18	+30.92	3-24	13	-11.25	5-30	17	-8.88	18-87	21	+51.04
Chepstow	0-1	-	-1.00	0-0	-	+0.00	0-1	-	-1.00	0-0	-	+0.00
Chester	6-93	6	-67.00	2-8	25	+1.25	0-10	-	-10.00	4-75	5	-58.25
Doncaster	7-123	6	-24.88	2-5	40	+18.63	3-18	17	+26.00	2-100	2	-69.50
Epsom	2-61	3	-43.50	0-0	-	+0.00	0-2	-	-2.00	2-59	3	-41.50
Ffos Las	3-3	100	+16.92	0-0	-	+0.00	1-1	100	+14.00	2-2	100	+2.92
Folkestone	1-4	25	-1.50	0-0	-	+0.00	0-0	-	+0.00	1-4	25	-1.50
Goodwood	10-94	11	+70.00	4-10	40	+42.00	0-8	-	-8.00	6-76	8	+36.00
Hamilton	16-76	21	-6.58	2-7	29	+1.10	0-12	-	-12.00	14-57	25	+4.32
Haydock	18-111	16	+41.23	7-18	39	+62.73	2-21	10	-3.00	9-72	13	-18.50
Kempton (AW)	6-46	13	-9.09	0-8	-	-8.00	1-9	11	-6.38	5-29	17	+5.28
Leicester	2-25	8	+5.00	0-1	-	-1.00	0-9	-	-9.00	2-15	13	+15.00
Lingfield (AW)	7-43	16	+1.42	0-3	-	-3.00	1-7	14	-3.75	6-33	18	+8.17
Musselburgh	27-147	18	+27.19	3-9	33	+2.88	4-20	20	+9.13	20-118	17	+15.19
Newbury	1-7	14	+1.50	0-0	-	+0.00	0-1	-	-1.00	1-6	17	+2.50
Newcastle	6-78	8	-39.63	0-7	-	-7.00	1-15	7	-6.00	5-56	9	-26.63
Newmarket	4-33	12	4.63	0-0	-	0.00	0-7	-	-7.00	4-26	15	+2.30
Newmarket (J)	1-31	3	-26.00	0-1	-	-1.00	0-4	-	-4.00	1-26	4	-21.00
Nottingham	3-21	14	+1.50	0-1	-	-1.00	0-5	-	-5.00	3-15	20	+7.50
Pontefract	4-58	7	-26.50	1-4	25	+1.00	0-8	-	-8.00	3-46	7	-19.50
Redcar	14-115	12	-37.60	1-20	5	-17.25	3-24	13	+0.00	10-71	14	-20.35
Ripon	17-116	15	+38.00	2-19	11	-5.00	6-22	27	+43.25	9-75	12	-0.25
Sandown	1-17	6	-12.50	0-0	-	+0.00	0-3	-	-3.00	1-14	7	-9.50
Southwell	1-6	17	-2.25	0-0	-	+0.00	1-1	100	+2.75	0-5	-	-5.00
Southwell (AW)	38-187	20	+143.48	8-21	38	+117.25	9-45	20	+2.15	21-121	17	+24.08
Thirsk	20-151	13	+27.00	4-17	24	+29.25	3-29	10	+6.33	13-105	12	-8.58
Warwick	0-5	-	-5.00	0-0	-	+0.00	0-1	-	-1.00	0-4	-	-4.00
Windsor	0-7	-	-7.00	0-0	-	+0.00	0-1	-	-1.00	0-6	-	-6.00
Wolves (AW)	18-111	16	-7.05	0-6	-	-6.00	1-25	4	-21.00	17-80	21	+19.95
Yarmouth	0-6	-	-6.00	0-0	-	+0.00	0-0	-	+0.00	0-6	-	-6.00
York	11-139	8	+9.00	3-13	23	+19.50	3-9	33	+32.50	5-117	4	-43.00

Ten-year summary

	Wins	Runs	%	Win prize	Total prize	£1 Stake
2010	88	628	14	£693,133.21	£976,234.10	-71.35
2009	84	687	12	£742,938.03	£1,168,438.46	-12.59
2008	68	532	13	£563,945.21	£862,023.95	+79.83
2007	68	577	12	£388,681.98	£627,020.68	+25.12
2006	59	674	9	£421,152.94	£734,690.32	-165.28
2005	67	592	11	£646,033.65	£915,516.85	+28.33
2004	55	681	8	£614,422.77	£874,519.19	-216.28
2003	65	782	8	£450,829.03	£740,891.39	-112.57
2002	65	696	9	£661,545.10	£1,033,390.53	-133.29
2001	47	746	6	£326,617.50	£523,039.80	-336.01

REDFORD: leading a one-two for trainer David Nicholls in the Ayr Gold Cup

Top trainers by winners (Turf)

All runs				First time out			Horses		
Won	Ran	%	Trainer	Won	Ran	%	Won	Ran	%
166	1080	15	**Richard Hannon**	49	267	18	137	267	51
145	1095	13	**Mark Johnston**	38	262	15	121	262	46
143	1088	13	**Richard Fahey**	42	225	19	116	225	52
90	814	11	**Mick Channon**	12	143	8	72	143	50
88	795	11	**Tim Easterby**	6	123	5	54	123	44
74	384	19	**John Gosden**	28	159	18	74	159	47
68	410	17	**Sir Michael Stoute**	21	148	14	57	148	39
66	581	11	**Kevin Ryan**	22	127	17	62	127	49
65	459	14	**B W Hills**	14	133	11	54	133	41
64	283	23	**Michael Jarvis**	31	97	32	59	97	61
62	326	19	**Saeed Bin Suroor**	28	132	21	63	132	48
62	492	13	**David Nicholls**	18	123	15	52	123	42
60	453	13	**Brian Meehan**	8	143	6	52	143	36
53	253	21	**Luca Cumani**	12	94	13	39	94	41
50	243	21	**Henry Cecil**	15	85	18	44	85	52
50	376	13	**Andrew Balding**	18	118	15	57	118	48
46	279	16	**William Haggas**	16	101	16	34	101	34
45	568	8	**David Evans**	6	146	4	52	146	36
44	283	16	**Ralph Beckett**	18	103	17	53	103	51
42	273	15	**Alan Swinbank**	11	77	14	35	77	45
41	319	13	**Bryan Smart**	13	92	14	41	92	45
40	242	17	**Jeremy Noseda**	11	88	13	40	88	45
40	195	21	**Roger Charlton**	9	64	14	29	64	45
39	148	26	**Sir Mark Prescott**	7	61	11	31	61	51
38	313	12	**Michael Bell**	11	92	12	38	92	41
37	301	12	**John Dunlop**	6	79	8	31	79	39
34	234	15	**Mahmood Al Zarooni**	16	103	16	39	103	38
34	403	8	**Jim Goldie**	2	59	3	20	59	34
34	250	14	**David Barron**	8	55	15	33	55	60
33	265	12	**David Simcock**	8	95	8	30	95	32
33	257	13	**Walter Swinburn**	6	77	8	33	77	43
32	311	10	**Michael Dods**	7	68	10	30	68	44
31	251	12	**Hughie Morrison**	7	78	9	37	78	47
27	307	9	**John Quinn**	6	66	9	21	66	32
27	236	11	**Richard Guest**	7	51	14	21	51	41
25	289	9	**Paul Cole**	7	79	9	29	79	37
25	192	13	**Chris Wall**	6	51	12	20	51	39
24	240	10	**Brian Ellison**	7	56	13	29	56	52
24	140	17	**David O'Meara**	2	28	7	15	28	54
23	163	14	**Henry Candy**	8	49	16	18	49	37
23	272	8	**James Given**	1	63	2	15	63	24
22	157	14	**William Knight**	9	51	18	23	51	45
22	285	8	**Ruth Carr**	3	48	6	15	48	31
22	246	9	**Alan McCabe**	7	78	9	20	78	26
22	261	8	**Linda Perratt**	3	34	9	13	34	38
22	181	12	**Declan Carroll**	3	35	9	20	35	57
21	202	10	**Clive Brittain**	9	84	11	27	84	32
21	120	18	**Ed McMahon**	4	38	11	18	38	47

Top trainers by prize money (Turf)

Total prizemoney	Trainer	Win prizemoney	Wins	Class 1-3 Won	Ran	%	Class 4-6 Won	Ran	%
£2,980,338	**Sir Michael Stoute**	£2,232,303	68	31	192	16	37	218	17
£2,934,426	**Richard Hannon**	£1,850,077	166	56	392	14	110	688	16
£2,821,567	**A P O'Brien**	£1,283,570	7	7	89	8	0	0	—
£2,166,767	**Henry Cecil**	£1,567,008	50	24	116	21	26	127	20
£2,072,205	**Mark Johnston**	£1,424,959	145	57	500	11	88	595	15
£1,928,489	**Richard Fahey**	£1,225,735	143	44	487	9	99	601	16
£1,865,143	**Saeed Bin Suroor**	£1,230,291	62	41	262	16	21	64	33
£1,587,440	**John Gosden**	£1,018,447	74	30	168	18	44	216	20
£1,432,868	**B W Hills**	£840,886	65	22	218	10	43	241	18
£1,221,684	**Mick Channon**	£565,430	90	18	207	9	72	607	12
£1,163,966	**Michael Jarvis**	£695,877	64	29	142	20	35	141	25
£1,099,565	**William Haggas**	£882,458	46	19	96	20	27	183	15
£1,067,125	**Brian Meehan**	£628,336	60	23	157	15	37	296	13
£969,907	**Andrew Balding**	£593,085	50	21	190	11	29	186	16
£875,276	**David Nicholls**	£627,447	62	19	220	9	43	272	16
£870,645	**Luca Cumani**	£610,591	53	21	110	19	32	143	22
£838,385	**Tim Easterby**	£495,399	88	18	215	8	70	580	12
£759,001	**Michael Bell**	£473,189	38	11	93	12	27	220	12
£707,031	**Jeremy Noseda**	£377,112	40	11	97	11	29	145	20
£642,303	**Kevin Ryan**	£352,496	66	11	204	5	55	377	15
£593,153	**Mahmood Al Zarooni**	£264,756	34	4	64	6	30	170	18
£588,858	**David Simcock**	£354,774	33	11	115	10	22	150	15
£566,230	**Ed Dunlop**	£333,677	19	7	62	11	12	162	7
£528,139	**Clive Cox**	£283,738	18	10	90	11	8	150	5
£477,525	**Henry Candy**	£278,599	23	5	45	11	18	118	15
£471,776	**John Dunlop**	£330,560	37	11	91	12	26	210	12
£453,147	**Ralph Beckett**	£330,955	44	12	97	12	32	186	17
£451,615	**Roger Charlton**	£327,856	40	13	66	20	27	129	21
£429,384	**Clive Brittain**	£293,547	21	6	92	7	15	110	14
£427,639	**Sir Mark Prescott**	£323,092	39	7	35	20	32	113	28
£416,481	**Paul Cole**	£204,513	25	7	118	6	18	171	11
£397,782	**Jim Goldie**	£210,159	34	9	111	8	25	292	9
£395,963	**Chris Wall**	£259,173	25	9	55	16	16	137	12
£380,316	**James Fanshawe**	£121,951	15	5	41	12	10	90	11
£371,687	**Hughie Morrison**	£150,824	31	5	73	7	26	178	15
£368,227	**David Barron**	£250,593	34	12	80	15	22	170	13
£357,518	**Bryan Smart**	£204,315	41	8	95	8	33	224	15
£333,700	**Michael Dods**	£243,957	32	13	93	14	19	218	9
£332,328	**Ed McMahon**	£271,151	21	8	32	25	13	88	15
£330,155	**A Fabre**	£255,465	1	1	2	50	0	0	—
£316,477	**David Evans**	£186,162	45	7	86	8	38	482	8
£310,988	**Walter Swinburn**	£223,584	33	11	85	13	22	172	13
£307,146	**David Elsworth**	£179,888	19	7	75	9	12	95	13
£276,682	**Alan Swinbank**	£172,334	42	5	58	9	37	215	17
£259,169	**William Knight**	£174,295	22	4	47	9	18	110	16
£253,611	**Tom Tate**	£123,969	19	4	73	5	15	100	15
£240,195	**James Given**	£160,473	23	4	34	12	19	238	8
£234,276	**M Delzangles**	£227,080	1	1	6	17	0	0	—

Top trainers by winners (AW)

All runs				First time out			Horses		
Won	Ran	%	Trainer	Won	Ran	%	Won	Ran	%
66	363	18	Mark Johnston	38	262	15	121	262	46
44	261	17	Richard Hannon	49	267	18	137	267	51
43	451	10	David Evans	6	146	4	52	146	36
41	232	18	Kevin Ryan	22	127	17	62	127	49
38	268	14	Richard Fahey	42	225	19	116	225	52
34	245	14	J S Moore	1	69	1	31	69	45
31	134	23	John Gosden	28	159	18	74	159	47
28	74	38	Saeed Bin Suroor	28	132	21	63	132	48
28	135	21	Andrew Balding	18	118	15	57	118	48
27	352	8	Ronald Harris	2	69	3	23	69	33
27	120	23	Brian Ellison	7	56	13	29	56	52
26	136	19	David Nicholls	18	123	15	52	123	42
26	117	22	Ralph Beckett	18	103	17	53	103	51
26	281	9	Paul Howling	2	42	5	15	42	36
25	138	18	George Baker	11	56	20	25	56	45
23	151	15	Marco Botti	13	69	19	27	69	39
22	66	33	Michael Jarvis	31	97	32	59	97	61
22	95	23	David Barron	8	55	15	33	55	60
22	123	18	Tom Dascombe	9	86	10	30	86	35
22	234	9	Jim Boyle	5	64	8	21	64	33
22	207	11	Gary Moore	10	100	10	35	100	35
21	111	19	Sir Mark Prescott	7	61	11	31	61	51
21	132	16	Bryan Smart	13	92	14	41	92	45
21	170	12	Dean Ivory	4	37	11	20	37	54
21	184	11	Derek Shaw	2	38	5	14	38	37
21	144	15	Stuart Williams	6	59	10	23	59	39
20	105	19	Clive Brittain	9	84	11	27	84	32
20	260	8	Alan McCabe	7	78	9	20	78	26
20	124	16	Ed Dunlop	10	91	11	29	91	32
20	122	16	Hughie Morrison	7	78	9	37	78	47
20	196	10	John Jenkins	5	57	9	16	57	28
20	188	11	Tony Carroll	5	65	8	15	65	23
20	138	14	Michael Easterby	4	65	6	23	65	35
19	141	13	Walter Swinburn	6	77	8	33	77	43
19	187	10	Sylvester Kirk	7	64	11	24	64	30
18	130	14	Jeremy Glover	6	43	14	19	43	44
18	191	9	Jeff Pearce	3	44	7	16	44	36
18	167	11	Conor Dore	2	27	7	12	27	44
17	121	14	Ian Williams	8	63	13	22	63	35
16	142	11	David Simcock	8	95	8	30	95	32
16	93	17	Michael Bell	11	92	12	38	92	41
16	171	9	Reg Hollinshead	5	56	9	19	56	34
15	95	16	Julia Feilden	3	35	9	11	35	31
15	86	17	Jeremy Noseda	11	88	13	40	88	45
15	200	8	Mark Brisbourne	0	39	—	16	39	41
15	111	14	Willie Musson	2	35	6	14	35	40
15	130	12	Michael Quinlan	4	58	7	18	58	31
14	125	11	Alan Bailey	2	32	6	16	32	50

Top trainers by prize money (AW)

Total prizemoney	Trainer	Win prizemoney	Wins	Class 1-3 Won	Ran	%	Class 4-6 Won	Ran	%
£347,513	Mark Johnston	£232,554	66	8	74	11	58	289	20
£284,149	Richard Hannon	£203,982	44	9	45	20	35	215	16
£223,610	Kevin Ryan	£157,914	41	6	46	13	35	185	19
£199,555	Saeed Bin Suroor	£152,798	28	9	28	32	19	46	41
£189,709	Marco Botti	£108,000	23	5	37	14	18	114	16
£172,485	David Evans	£91,199	43	2	38	5	41	409	10
£147,436	Richard Fahey	£99,655	38	2	35	6	35	231	15
£146,902	Andrew Balding	£114,911	28	4	15	27	24	120	20
£136,399	Michael Jarvis	£121,460	22	4	14	29	18	52	35
£126,798	John Gosden	£82,831	31	1	14	7	30	120	25
£123,374	Clive Brittain	£92,505	20	4	18	22	16	87	18
£122,231	David Barron	£97,955	22	3	19	16	19	76	25
£121,250	J S Moore	£76,418	34	0	6	—	34	238	14
£109,256	Gerard Butler	£81,591	13	5	24	21	8	49	16
£108,519	Clive Cox	£82,304	11	4	12	33	7	65	11
£103,922	Ronald Harris	£55,498	27	0	10	—	27	332	8
£100,959	David Nicholls	£65,686	26	1	23	4	25	113	22
£100,380	Henry Cecil	£86,683	12	1	5	20	11	50	22
£99,436	Walter Swinburn	£55,379	19	1	15	7	18	126	14
£98,724	Alan Bailey	£51,375	14	2	28	7	12	97	12
£98,250	Tom Dascombe	£78,870	22	1	13	8	21	110	19
£97,003	Alan McCabe	£54,910	20	1	11	9	19	242	8
£95,438	Jim Boyle	£52,841	22	2	21	10	20	212	9
£95,012	Sir Mark Prescott	£75,359	21	1	3	33	20	108	19
£92,481	Luca Cumani	£57,352	13	1	9	11	12	71	17
£91,658	Ralph Beckett	£66,245	26	0	11	—	26	106	25
£91,525	Bryan Smart	£67,262	21	2	13	15	19	114	17
£88,239	Jeremy Glover	£53,967	18	2	17	12	16	111	14
£87,448	Ed Dunlop	£64,268	20	1	10	10	19	114	17
£86,995	Mike Murphy	£57,624	9	2	14	14	6	39	15
£86,929	Hughie Morrison	£57,000	20	1	9	11	19	113	17
£85,016	John Jenkins	£49,657	20	0	5	—	19	180	11
£84,975	Jeremy Gask	£50,446	12	3	28	11	9	115	8
£84,799	Gary Moore	£47,095	22	0	13	—	21	190	11
£84,358	Brian Ellison	£55,440	27	0	6	—	26	112	23
£81,853	William Haggas	£60,091	13	2	8	25	11	74	15
£80,843	David Simcock	£49,306	16	2	34	6	14	108	13
£79,595	Michael Attwater	£54,577	8	1	13	8	6	121	5
£75,414	Julia Feilden	£69,632	15	3	5	60	12	88	14
£72,590	Tony Carroll	£49,419	20	1	10	10	16	159	10
£72,217	Dean Ivory	£46,068	21	0	0	—	21	170	12
£71,473	Derek Shaw	£52,163	21	2	16	13	17	161	11
£70,945	Paul Howling	£50,198	26	0	6	—	23	267	9
£70,648	William Knight	£48,307	12	3	17	18	9	69	13
£69,039	John Best	£34,658	14	0	9	—	14	192	7
£67,529	Jeremy Noseda	£42,798	15	0	8	—	15	78	19
£66,929	David Elsworth	£41,141	8	1	12	8	7	51	14
£66,216	Stuart Williams	£49,339	21	1	15	7	20	128	16

Top jockeys (Turf)

Won	Ran	%	Jockey	Best Trainer	Won	Ran
168	950	18	**Paul Hanagan**	Richard Fahey	101	567
135	749	18	**Richard Hughes**	Richard Hannon	113	556
118	666	18	**Ryan Moore**	Sir Michael Stoute	40	248
111	661	17	**Kieren Fallon**	Luca Cumani	40	173
96	567	17	**Silvestre De Sousa**	David O'Meara	18	78
89	449	20	**Frankie Dettori**	Saeed Bin Suroor	51	191
77	517	15	**Jamie Spencer**	Michael Bell	13	95
73	459	16	**William Buick**	John Gosden	54	258
70	519	13	**Tom Queally**	Henry Cecil	39	190
68	505	13	**Seb Sanders**	Sir Mark Prescott	39	162
65	512	13	**David Allan**	Tim Easterby	55	366
65	544	12	**P J McDonald**	Alan Swinbank	42	220
63	554	11	**Joe Fanning**	Mark Johnston	84	542
63	448	14	**Steve Drowne**	Roger Charlton	28	136
62	441	14	**Ted Durcan**	Saeed Bin Suroor	32	129
58	514	11	**Jim Crowley**	Ralph Beckett	46	251
56	448	13	**Jimmy Fortune**	Andrew Balding	31	181
55	593	9	**Paul Mulrennan**	James Given	20	214
52	634	8	**Tom Eaves**	Bryan Smart	27	258
50	452	11	**Graham Gibbons**	David Barron	19	86
49	445	11	**Robert Winston**	B W Hills	13	73
48	400	12	**Eddie Ahern**	John Dunlop	8	57
47	508	9	**Neil Callan**	Michael Jarvis	18	73
47	590	8	**Phillip Makin**	Michael Dods	21	187
47	308	15	**Adrian Nicholls**	David Nicholls	50	272
46	345	13	**Richard Hills**	Michael Jarvis	9	39
43	451	10	**Dane O'Neill**	Henry Candy	18	119
43	367	12	**Shane Kelly**	Walter Swinburn	17	96
43	347	12	**Pat Dobbs**	Richard Hannon	31	244
43	442	10	**Liam Keniry**	J S Moore	21	130
42	247	17	**Philip Robinson**	Michael Jarvis	36	152
41	479	9	**Chris Catlin**	Mick Channon	19	211
40	317	13	**Martin Dwyer**	Brian Meehan	26	162
39	315	12	**George Baker**	Gary Moore	19	157
39	414	9	**Franny Norton**	Richard Guest	8	66
39	330	12	**Greg Fairley**	Mark Johnston	39	297
37	305	12	**Michael Hills**	B W Hills	37	249
36	305	12	**Richard Mullen**	Ed McMahon	12	41
36	401	9	**Barry McHugh**	Brian Ellison	14	41
35	393	9	**Hayley Turner**	Michael Bell	30	191
35	320	11	**Alan Munro**	Mick Channon	14	126
35	349	10	**Ian Brennan**	John Quinn	17	163
34	337	10	**Tadhg O'Shea**	John Gosden	4	14
33	285	12	**Martin Lane**	David Simcock	10	85
33	351	9	**Cathy Gannon**	David Evans	20	234
32	322	10	**Pat Cosgrave**	James Fanshawe	13	67
32	458	7	**James Sullivan**	Michael Easterby	10	149
31	390	8	**David Probert**	Andrew Balding	25	151

Top jockeys (AW)

Won	Ran	%	Jockey	Best Trainer	Won	Ran
63	378	17	George Baker	Gary Moore	19	157
59	314	19	Neil Callan	Michael Jarvis	18	73
57	349	16	Richard Hughes	Richard Hannon	113	556
57	341	17	Joe Fanning	Mark Johnston	84	542
54	505	11	Jimmy Quinn	Paul Howling	7	78
49	360	14	Adam Kirby	Walter Swinburn	21	158
48	636	8	Luke Morris	Clive Cox	11	93
48	402	12	David Probert	Andrew Balding	25	151
47	444	11	Liam Keniry	J S Moore	21	130
46	295	16	Graham Gibbons	David Barron	19	86
43	343	13	Jim Crowley	Ralph Beckett	46	251
40	263	15	Stevie Donohoe	Ian Williams	13	66
39	533	7	Chris Catlin	Mick Channon	19	211
38	414	9	Dane O'Neill	Henry Candy	18	119
38	365	10	Hayley Turner	Michael Bell	30	191
38	357	11	Kieren Fox	John Best	14	125
37	299	12	Robert Winston	B W Hills	13	73
37	264	14	Paul Hanagan	Richard Fahey	101	567
35	349	10	Steve Drowne	Roger Charlton	28	136
34	92	37	Frankie Dettori	Saeed Bin Suroor	51	191
34	254	13	Seb Sanders	Sir Mark Prescott	39	162
31	278	11	Tom Queally	Henry Cecil	39	190
31	175	18	Jamie Spencer	Michael Bell	13	95
31	323	10	Shane Kelly	Walter Swinburn	17	96
30	342	9	Fergus Sweeney	Jamie Osborne	8	95
30	218	14	Ian Mongan	Henry Cecil	13	44
29	160	18	Kieren Fallon	Luca Cumani	40	173
29	272	11	Tom Eaves	Bryan Smart	27	258
28	179	16	Phillip Makin	Michael Dods	21	187
28	161	17	Martin Dwyer	Brian Meehan	26	162
28	224	13	Andrea Atzeni	Pat Eddery	8	40
28	180	16	Richard Kingscote	Tom Dascombe	30	242
28	243	12	William Carson	Stuart Williams	18	153
28	266	11	Cathy Gannon	David Evans	20	234
27	193	14	Tony Culhane	Paul D'Arcy	11	61
26	125	21	William Buick	John Gosden	54	258
26	126	21	Ted Durcan	Saeed Bin Suroor	32	129
26	228	11	Andrew Heffernan	David Evans	15	145
24	143	17	Barry McHugh	Brian Ellison	14	41
22	197	11	J-P Guillambert	Luca Cumani	15	92
22	156	14	Jack Mitchell	Ralph Beckett	6	35
21	164	13	Jimmy Fortune	Andrew Balding	31	181
21	190	11	Nicky Mackay	John Gosden	18	73
20	118	17	Ryan Moore	Sir Michael Stoute	40	248
20	222	9	Eddie Ahern	John Dunlop	8	57
20	174	11	Pat Cosgrave	James Fanshawe	13	67
20	141	14	Matthew Davies	George Baker	21	127
19	222	9	Franny Norton	Richard Guest	8	66

Outlook

Group One records

Year	Winner	Age (if appropriate)	Trainer	Jockey	SP	draw/ran

2,000 Guineas (1m) Newmarket

Year	Winner		Trainer	Jockey	SP	draw/ran
2001	**Golan**		Sir M Stoute	K Fallon	11-1	19/18
2002	**Rock Of Gibraltar**		A O'Brien	J Murtagh	9-1	22/22
2003	**Refuse To Bend**		D Weld	P Smullen	9-2	18/20
2004	**Haafhd**		B Hills	R Hills	11-2	4/14
2005	**Footstepsinthesand**		A O'Brien	K Fallon	13-2	17/19
2006	**George Washington**		A O'Brien	K Fallon	6-4f	6/14
2007	**Cockney Rebel**		G Huffer	O Peslier	25-1	15/24
2008	**Henrythenavigator**		A O'Brien	J Murtagh	11-1	10/15
2009	**Sea The Stars**		J Oxx	M Kinane	8-1	1/15
2010	**Makfi**		M Delzangles	C-P Lemaire	33-1	15/19

THIS HAS increasingly become a specialist miler's race rather than a stepping stone to the Derby, as prior to the mighty Sea The Stars only Golan had gone on to any success over middle distances in recent times. Most winners had proven themseles at two, with 11 of the last 19 winners having won a Group race, including six at the highest level. The Dewhurst tends to be a far better guide than the Racing Post Trophy, with High Top the last horse to complete that double in 1973. Favourites have a desperate record, with Xaar, One Cool Cat and St Nicholas Abbey among the most high-profile failures. Haafhd, who followed up a win in the Craven Stakes over course and distance in 2004, was the only winner to have come via a domestic trial since Mystiko in 1991.

1,000 Guineas (1m) Newmarket

Year	Winner		Trainer	Jockey	SP	draw/ran
2001	**Ameerat**		M Jarvis	P Robinson	11-1	10/18
2002	**Kazzia**		S bin Suroor	L Dettori	14-1	12/17
2003	**Russian Rhythm**		Sir M Stoute	K Fallon	12-1	2/19
2004	**Attraction**		M Johnston	K Darley	11-2	8/16
2005	**Virginia Waters**		A O'Brien	K Fallon	12-1	1/20
2006	**Speciosa**		Mrs P Sly	M Fenton	10-1	3/13
2007	**Finsceal Beo**		J Bolger	K Manning	5-4f	8/21
2008	**Natagora**		P Bary	C Lemaire	11-4f	13/15
2009	**Ghanaati**		B Hills	R Hills	20-1	8/14
2010	**Special Duty**		C Head-Maarek	S Pasquier	9-2f	1/17

COURSE FORM is the key factor in this race. The Rockfel has become the key trial, throwing up five of the last nine winners with Finsceal Beo, Lahan and Speciosa all doing the double, but Special Duty, Natagora and Attraction had won the Cheveley Park, Russian Rhythm had come second in that race, and Speciosa also won the Nell Gwyn. Punters have hit back in recent years with three of the last four favourites obliging, though Ghanaati became the seventh winner out of ten priced in double figures when winning in 2009.

Lockinge (1m) Newbury

2001	Medicean	4	Sir M Stoute	K Fallon	3-1	5/7
2002	Keltos	4	C Laffon-Parias	O Peslier	9-1	7/10
2003	Hawk Wing	4	A O'Brien	M Kinane	2-1f	4/6
2004	Russian Rhythm	4	Sir M Stoute	K Fallon	3-1f	3/15
2005	Rakti	6	M Jarvis	P Robinson	7-4f	5/8
2006	Soviet Song	6	J Fanshawe	J Spencer	7-2f	10/10
2007	Red Evie	4	M Bell	J Spencer	8-1	7/8
2008	Creachadoir	4	S bin Suroor	L Dettori	3-1f	7/11
2009	Virtual	4	J Gosden	J Fortune	6-1	10/11
2010	Paco Boy	5	R Hannon	R Hughes	8-11f	3/9

OFTEN QUITE weak for a Group 1, the Lockinge has been a good race for favourites, with six of the last eight obliging, and fillies, who have been successful in three of the last seven years. However, the strongest trend is the age, as 16 of the last 24 winners were four. Paco Boy ended a dreadful run for winners of the Sandown Mile when coming out on top last year – the previous 11 to attempt to follow up had all been beaten.

Coronation Cup (1m4f) Epsom

2001	Mutafaweq	5	S bin Suroor	L Dettori	11-2	1/6
2002	Boreal	4	P Schiergen	K Fallon	4-1	3/6
2003	Warrsan	5	C Brittain	P Robinson	9-2	4/9
2004	Warrsan	5	C Brittain	D Holland	7-1	5/11
2005	Yeats	4	A O'Brien	K Fallon	5-1	9/7
2006	Shirocco	5	A Fabre	C Soumillon	8-11f	5/6
2007	Scorpion	5	A O'Brien	M Kinane	8-1	2/7
2008	Soldier Of Fortune	5	A O'Brien	J Murtagh	9-4	7/11
2009	Ask	6	Sir M Stoute	R Moore	5-1	8/8
2010	Fame And Glory	4	A O'Brien	J Murtagh	5-6f	8/9

THIS race almost always features a small field, and bearing that in mind the record of favourites is very poor with only three successful in the last 13 years. The combination of a false pace and the tricky course could be responsible for some funny results and punters have perhaps been too easily seduced by youngsters as Yeats and Fame And Glory are the only winning four-year-olds in the last eight years.

The Oaks (1m4f) Epsom

2001	Imagine	A O'Brien	M Kinane	3-1f	10/14
2002	Kazzia	S bin Suroor	L Dettori	100-30f	13/14
2003	Casual Look	A Balding	Martin Dwyer	10-1	7/15
2004	Ouija Board	E Dunlop	K Fallon	7-2	3/7
2005	Eswarah	M Jarvis	R Hills	11-4jf	2/12
2006	Alexandrova	A O'Brien	K Fallon	9-4f	1/10
2007	Light Shift	H Cecil	T Durcan	13-2	11/14

2008	**Look Here**	R Beckett	S Sanders	33-1	13/16
2009	**Sariska**	M Bell	J Spencer	9-4f	5/10
2010	**Snow Fairy**	E Dunlop	R Moore	9-1	15/15

BREEDING is critical since so few three-year-old fillies stay so far at this time of the year and there seem few clues from the racecourse performances of the winners – Shahtoush, Imagine, Kazzia and Casual Look had never run beyond a mile previously, but Ramruma, Love Divine, Ouija Board, Eswarah, Light Shift, Sariska and Snow Fairy had all won over at least 1m2f. It rarely pays to look beyond the market principles – though Look Here won at 33-1 in 2008, only four winners since 1999 have been bigger than 7-2.

The Derby (1m4f) Epsom

2001	**Galileo**	A O'Brien	M Kinane	11-4j	10/12
2002	**High Chaparral**	A O'Brien	J Murtagh	7-2	9/12
2003	**Kris Kin**	Sir M Stoute	K Fallon	6-1	4/20
2004	**North Light**	Sir M Stoute	K Fallon	7-2jf	6/14
2005	**Motivator**	M Bell	J Murtagh	3-1f	5/13
2006	**Sir Percy**	M Tregoning	M Dwyer	6-1	10/18
2007	**Authorized**	P Chapple-Hyam	L Dettori	5-4f	14/17
2008	**New Approach**	J Bolger	K Manning	5-1	3/16
2009	**Sea The Stars**	J Oxx	M Kinane	11-4	4/12
2010	**Workforce**	Sir M Stoute	R Moore	6-1	8/12

MANY HIGH-CLASS colts are beaten here due to lack of stamina. It's important to have a top-class sire plus a staying pedigree on the dam's side. Despite Sea The Stars's heroics last year, only two horses since Mill Reef in 1971 have won the 2,000 Guineas and the Derby, with Nashwan being the other. It still looks wiser to follow one of the recognised trials, the route taken by ten of the last 13 winners with four Dante winners (Benny The Dip, North Light, Motivator and Authorized) and a runner-up (Workforce), three Leopardstown winners (Sinndar, Galileo and High Chaparral), two Chester winners (Oath and Kris Kin) and one Lingfield winner (High-Rise). This is a race for fancied runners from the first four in the betting – 20-1 hero High-Rise in 1998 is the biggest-priced winner in 37 years.

Queen Anne Stakes (1m) Royal Ascot

2001	**Medicean**	4	Sir M Stoute	K Fallon	11-2	8/10
2002	**No Excuse Needed**	4	Sir M Stoute	J Murtagh	13-2	11/12
2003	**Dubai Destination**	4	S bin Suroor	L Dettori	9-2	10/10
2004	**Refuse To Bend**	4	S bin Suroor	L Dettori	12-1	1/16
2005	**Valixir**	4	A Fabre	C Soumillon	4-1	1/10*
2006	**Ad Valorem**	4	A O'Brien	K Fallon	13-2	2/7
2007	**Ramonti**	5	S bin Suroor	L Dettori	5-1	2/8
2008	**Haradasun**	5	A O'Brien	J Murtagh	5-1	10/11
2009	**Paco Boy**	4	R Hannon	R Hughes	10-3	3/9
2010	**Goldikova**	5	F Head	O Peslier	11-8f	1/10

Formerly Group 3. Group 2 from 1985, Group 1 from 2003.
*Note – all Royal Ascot races were run at York in 2005

FOUR-YEAR-OLDS once considered Classic contenders fit the bill and this age group has taken 17 of the last 22 runnings, though just one of the last four. The Lockinge was a key race but is becoming a slightly unreliable guide. Medicean won both in 2001 and Ramonti had been second at Newbury, but Paco Boy, Haradasun and No Excuse Needed were well-beaten there before landing this and two outstanding Newbury winners, Hawk Wing and Rakti, lost when well fancied to follow up.

St James's Palace Stakes (1m) Royal Ascot

2001	Black Minnaloushe		A O'Brien	J Murtagh	8-1	1/11
2002	Rock Of Gibraltar		A O'Brien	M Kinane	4-5f	4/9
2003	Zafeen		M Channon	D Holland	8-1	5/11
2004	Azamour		J Oxx	M Kinane	9-2	1/11
2005	Shamardal		S bin Suroor	K McEvoy	7-4f	2/8
2006	Araafa		J Noseda	A Munro	2-1f	2/11
2007	Excellent Art		A O'Brien	J Spencer	8-1	1/8
2008	Henrythenavigator		A O'Brien	J Murtagh	4-7f	6/8
2009	Mastercraftsman		A O'Brien	J Murtagh	5-6f	8/10
2010	Canford Cliffs		R Hannon	R Hughes	11-4j	6/9

GUINEAS form holds the key to this prize with winners and also-rans from the Irish, French and English versions forming the vast majority of the line-up. Nine of the last 13 winners had made the frame at Newmarket, while eight of the last 11 also ran in the Irish Guineas – Canford Cliffs, Mastercraftsman, Henrythenavigator, Rock Of Gibraltar and Black Minnaloushe won at the Curragh, while Giant's Causeway, Azamour and Araafa took second. Shamardal had won a French Classic double and Excellent Art was the moral winner at Longchamp. The profile adds up to an out-and-out miler proven at the top level.

Prince Of Wales's Stakes (1m2f) Royal Ascot

2001	Fantastic Light	5	S bin Suroor	L Dettori	100-30	8/9
2002	Grandera	4	S bin Suroor	L Dettori	4-1	3/12
2003	Nayef	5	M Tregoning	R Hills	5-1	6/10
2004	Rakti	5	M Jarvis	P Robinson	3-1	10/10
2005	Azamour	4	J Oxx	M Kinane	11-8f	3/8*
2006	Ouija Board	5	E Dunlop	O Peslier	8-1	5/7
2007	Manduro	5	A Fabre	S Pasquier	15-8f	4/6
2008	Duke Of Marmalade	4	A O'Brien	J Murtagh	Evsf	13/12
2009	Vision D'Etat	4	E Libaud	O Peslier	4-1	7/8
2010	Byword	4	A Fabre	M Guyon	5-2f	8/12

Formerly Group 2, Group 1 from 2000.

A RACE that has altered hugely since gaining Group 1 status in 2000, when Dubai Millennium provided one of the outstanding moments in Royal Ascot history. With the quality getting better and better, traditional trials like the Brigadier Gerard Stakes, the Gordon Richards Stakes and the Tattersalls Gold Cup are largely being eschewed in favour of international preparations, a route taken by Grandera, Nayef, Rakti, Ouija Board and, of course, French trio Manduro, Vision D'Etat and Byword.

Gold Cup (2m4f) Royal Ascot

2001	Royal Rebel	5	M Johnston	J Murtagh	8-1	10/12
2002	Royal Rebel	6	M Johnston	J Murtagh	16-1	8/15
2003	Mr Dinos	4	P Cole	K Fallon	3-1	6/12
2004	Papineau	4	S bin Suroor	L Dettori	5-1	4/13
2005	Westerner	6	E Lellouche	O Peslier	7-4f	4/17
2006	Yeats	5	A O'Brien	K Fallon	7-1	8/12

2007	**Yeats**	6	A O'Brien	M Kinane	8-13f	2/14
2008	**Yeats**	7	A O'Brien	J Murtagh	11-8f	4/10
2009	**Yeats**	8	A O'Brien	J Murtagh	6-4f	6/9
2010	**Rite Of Passage**	6	D Weld	P Smullen	20-1	13/12

THE ONLY British Group One race run over 2m4f understandably attracts plenty of real specialists. Yeats became the first ever four-time winner in 2009, but many others have followed up from the year before, including Royal Rebel in 2002. The best trial is Sandown's Henry II Stakes, the route taken by eight of the 13 winners prior to Yeat's reign and both placed horses in 2009, with Mr Dinos and Papineau the last to pull off the double.

Coronation Stakes (1m) Royal Ascot

2001	**Banks Hill**	A Fabre	O Peslier	4-1j	4/13
2002	**Sophisticat**	A O'Brien	M Kinane	11-2	3/11
2003	**Russian Rhythm**	Sir M Stoute	K Fallon	4-7f	11/9
2004	**Attraction**	M Johnston	K Darley	6-4f	10/11
2005	**Maids Causeway**	B Hills	M Hills	9-2	9/10
2006	**Nannina**	J Gosden	J Fortune	6-1jf	13/15
2007	**Indian Ink**	R Hannon	R Hughes	8-1	2/13
2008	**Lush Lashes**	J Bolger	K Manning	5-1	3/11
2009	**Ghanaati**	B Hills	R Hills	2-1f	6/10
2010	**Lillie Langtry**	A O'Brien	J Murtagh	7-2f	11/13

A CHAMPIONSHIP race for three-year-old fillies. The English 1,000 Guineas was a dreadful guide for many years, with no winner following up from 1980 to 2002, but Russian Rhythm bucked that trend and both Attraction and Ghanaati have done the double since. Nonetheless, this still looks a race to avoid short-priced favourites as Harayir, Las Meninas, Shadayid, Sleepytime, Ameerat, Speciosa and Finsceal Beo have been among several expensive flops since the mid-Nineties. Crimplene and Attraction had won the Irish Guineas, while Banks Hill and Sophisticat followed up fine efforts in the French Guineas.

Golden Jubilee Stakes (6f) Royal Ascot

2001	**Harmonic Way**	6	R Charlton	S Drowne	10-1	1/21
2002	**Malhub**	4	J Gosden	K Darley	16-1	12/12
2003	**Choisir**	4	P Perry	J Murtagh	13-2	20/17
2004	**Fayr Jag**	4	T Easterby	W Supple	12-1	9/14
2005	**Cape of Good Hope**	7	D Oughton	M Kinane	6-1	2/15
2006	**Les Arcs**	6	T Pitt	J Egan	33-1	4/18
2007	**Soldier's Tale**	6	J Noseda	J Murtagh	9-1	11/21
2008	**Kingsgate Native**	3	J Best	S Sanders	33-1	3/17
2009	**Art Connoisseur**	3	M Bell	T Queally	20-1	4/14
2010	**Starspangledbanner**	4	A O'Brien	J Murtagh	13-2j	4/24

Formerly Group 3. Group 2 from 1999, Group 1 from 2002.

A RACE whose profile has been steadily on the rise and has now reached fever pitch with its inauguration into the Global Sprint Challenge alongside the King's Stand Stakes, attracting the best sprinters from around the world. Its essence hasn't changed, though, as this is a fiercely competitive sprint which throws up more than its share of shocks, with Les Arcs and Kingsgate Native winning at 33-1 in the last five years and Art Connoisseur going in at 20-1 in 2009. The latter pair are among a host of big-priced three-year-olds to run well including Society Rock (second at 50-1 last year), Balthazaar's Gift (second at 50-1 in 2006), Baron's Pit (third at 50-1 in 2004), Indian Country (fourth at 50-1 in 2003) and Freud (third at 25-1 in 2001), but five of the last 11 winners have been six or older.

Eclipse (1m2f) Sandown

2001	Medicean	4	Sir M Stoute	K Fallon	7-2	7/8
2002	Hawk Wing	3	A O'Brien	M Kinane	8-15f	6/5
2003	Falbrav	5	L Cumani	D Holland	8-1	14/15
2004	Refuse To Bend	4	S bin Suroor	L Dettori	15-2	9/12
2005	Oratorio	3	A O'Brien	K Fallon	12-1	1/7
2006	David Junior	4	B Meehan	J Spencer	9-4	2/9
2007	Notnowcato	5	Sir M Stoute	R Moore	7-1	1/8
2008	Mount Nelson	4	A O'Brien	J Murtagh	7-2	1/8
2009	Sea The Stars	3	J Oxx	M Kinane	4-7f	5/10
2010	Twice Over	5	H Cecil	T Queally	13-8f	5/5

THREE-YEAR-OLDS have tended to struggle in the last 20 years, with a spell of three winners in four years around the turn of the century very much the exception. Oratorio and Sea The Stars proved that good ones can still do it, but overall Derby winners still have a poor record, with Authorized, Motivator, Benny The Dip and Erhaab the latest to get turned over. If you want to back a three-year-old, rather look to the 2,000 Guineas, the stepping stone for 11 of the 16 three-year-old winners since 1965. Fillies are to be avoided – Pebbles, in the mid-Eighties, was the first filly to succeed since the 19th century, and Bosra Sham and Ouija Board were beaten favourites. Royal Ascot form is the key. Twice Over, David Junior, Falbrav and Daylami, all beaten in the Prince of Wales's Stakes, kept up the good record of runners from that race, Giant's Causeway had won the St James's Palace, and Medicean and Refuse To Bend won the Queen Anne.

July Cup (6f) Newmarket

2001	Mozart	3	A O'Brien	M Kinane	4-1f	19/18
2002	Continent	5	D Nicholls	D Holland	12-1	2/14
2003	Oasis Dream	3	J Gosden	R Hughes	9-2	11/16
2004	Frizzante	5	J Fanshawe	J Murtagh	14-1	18/20
2005	Pastoral Pursuits	4	H Morrison	J Egan	22-1	10/19
2006	Les Arcs	6	T Pitt	J Egan	10-1	15/15
2007	Sakhee's Secret	3	H Morrison	S Drowne	9-2	16/18
2008	Marchand d'Or	5	F Head	D Bonilla	5-2f	9/13
2009	Fleeting Spirit	4	J Noseda	T Queally	12-1	9/13
2010	Starspangledbanner	4	A O'Brien	J Murtagh	2-1f	11/14

THOUGH a race for specialist sprinters with the Golden Jubilee (Starspangledbanner and Les Arcs have doubled up in the last five years) and the Duke of York (York, May) giving the most helpful clues, horses dropping down in trip have more of a chance here – greats like Ajdal and Soviet Song achieved the seemingly impossible in the late Eighties, while Mozart had won the 7f Jersey Stakes and been second in the Irish Guineas in 2001 and Pastoral Pursuits was a Guineas horse until his stamina limitations were exposed in 2004.

King George VI and Queen Elizabeth Stakes (1m4f) Ascot

2001	Galileo	3	A O'Brien	M Kinane	1-2f	7/12
2002	Golan	4	Sir M Stoute	K Fallon	11-2	8/9
2003	Alamshar	3	J Oxx	J Murtagh	13-2	5/12
2004	Doyen	4	S bin Suroor	L Dettori	11-10f	5/11

2005	**Azamour**	4	J Oxx	M Kinane	5-2f	12/12*
2006	**Hurricane Run**	4	A Fabre	C Soumillon	5-6f	4/6
2007	**Dylan Thomas**	4	A O'Brien	J Murtagh	5-4f	5/7
2008	**Duke Of Marmalade**	4	A O'Brien	J Murtagh	4-6f	4/8
2009	**Conduit**	4	Sir M Stoute	R Moore	13-8f	2/9
2010	**Harbinger**	4	Sir M Stoute	O Peslier	4-1	6/6

*Run at Newbury

THIS RACE has suffered from a lack of three-year-old representation in recent years, and the way Harbinger crushed Cape Blanco and Workforce last year might not help in that regard. It still takes a top-class older horse to win, though, as Harbinger was only the second winner (after Doyen) who hadn't previously won a Group 1 since Belmez in 1990 and just the third not to have been first or second in a Group 1 at the trip.

Sussex Stakes (1m) Goodwood

2001	**Noverre**	3	S Bin Suroor	L Dettori	9-2	11/10
2002	**Rock Of Gibraltar**	3	A O'Brien	M Kinane	8-13f	3/5
2003	**Reel Buddy**	5	R Hannon	Pat Eddery	20-1	7/9
2004	**Soviet Song**	5	J Fanshawe	J Murtagh	3-1	5/11
2005	**Proclamation**	3	J Noseda	M Kinane	3-1	7/12
2006	**Court Masterpiece**	6	E Dunlop	E Dunlop	15-2	5/7
2007	**Ramonti**	5	Sir M Stoute	L Dettori	9-2	8/8
2008	**Henrythenavigator**	3	A O'Brien	J Murtagh	4-11f	3/6
2009	**Rip Van Winkle**	3	A O'Brien	J Murtagh	6-4f	2/8
2010	**Canford Cliffs**	3	R Hannon	R Hughes	4-6f	1/7

THIS IS a great race for glamorous three-year-olds with Canford Cliffs, Rip Van Winkle and Henrythenavigator reinforcing the dominance they enjoyed at the turn of the century when four won in a row from 1999 to 2002 – and six of the last eight three-year-old winners were favourites. No prizes for guessing the key trials – seven of the last 11 winning three-year-olds were first or second in the St James's Palace Stakes, while five of the last seven successful older horses had contested the Queen Anne.

Nassau Stakes (1m1f192yds) Goodwood

2001	**Lailani**	3	E Dunlop	L Dettori	5-4f	5/7
2002	**Islington**	3	Sir M Stoute	K Fallon	100-30	6/10
2003	**Russian Rhythm**	3	Sir M Stoute	K Fallon	4-5f	7/8
2004	**Favourable Terms**	4	Sir M Stoute	K Fallon	11-2	2/6
2005	**Alexander Goldrun**	4	J Bolger	K Manning	13-8f	9/11
2006	**Ouija Board**	5	E Dunlop	L Dettori	Evensf	7/7
2007	**Peeping Fawn**	3	A O'Brien	J Murtagh	2-1f	4/8
2008	**Halfway To Heaven**	3	A O'Brien	J Murtagh	5-1	4/9
2009	**Midday**	3	H Cecil	T Quealy	11-2	1/10
2010	**Midday**	4	H Cecil	T Quealy	15-8f	2/7

AN AMAZINGLY good race for favourites, with six of the last ten winners being the market leader and Lush Lashes desperately unlucky not to make it another in 2008, while three-year-olds have also dominated but for a blip between 2004 and 2006. However, it's those dropping down in trip who tend to be worth following far more than those stepping up, with Russian Rhythm the first Guineas winner to triumph for many a year in 2003.

Juddmonte International Stakes (1m2f85yds) York

2001	Sakhee	4	S bin Suroor	L Dettori	7-4f	5/8
2002	Nayef	4	M Tregoning	R Hills	6-4f	5/7
2003	Falbrav	5	L Cumani	D Holland	5-2	2/8
2004	Sulamani	5	S bin Suroor	L Dettori	3-1	9/9
2005	Electrocutionist	4	V Valiani	M Kinane	9-2	5/7
2006	Notnowcato	4	Sir M Stoute	R Moore	8-1	5/7
2007	Authorized	3	P Chapple-Hyam	L Dettori	6-4f	1/7
2008	Duke Of Marmalade	4	A O'Brien	J Murtagh	4-6f	4/9*
2009	Sea The Stars	3	J Oxx	M Kinane	1-4f	3/4
2010	Rip Van Winkle	4	A O'Brien	J Murtagh	7-4f	7/9

*Note – this race and following two York races all run at Newmarket in 2008

FAMOUS FOR its many upsets since Brigadier Gerard suffered his only defeat to Roberto in 1972, the race has turned in punters' favour in recent times. Halling twice won as favourite in the mid-Nineties and no winner has returned bigger than 8-1 since then. Favourites won four in a row before 2003, Falbrav, Sulamani and Electrocutionist were all well fancied, and Rip Van Winkle became the fourth successive jolly to prevail last year. Older horses, especially lightly-raced ones such as the subsequent Arc winner Sakhee, have mostly kept on top of the three-year-olds, though three great ones – Sea The Stars, Authorized and Giant's Causeway – bucked the trend. Note the previous year's running and the Eclipse.

Yorkshire Oaks (1m3f195yds) York

2001	Super Tassa	5	V Valiani	K Darley	25-1	7/9
2002	Islington	3	Sir M Stoute	K Fallon	2-1	9/11
2003	Islington	4	Sir M Stoute	K Fallon	8-11f	5/8
2004	Quiff	3	Sir M Stoute	K Fallon	7-2	3/8
2005	Punctilious	4	S bin Suroor	K McEvoy	13-2	5/11
2006	Alexandrova	3	A O'Brien	M Kinane	4-9f	4/6
2007	Peeping Fawn	3	A O'Brien	J Murtagh	4-9f	8/8
2008	Lush Lashes	3	J Bolger	K Manning	Evsf	2/6*
2009	Dar Re Mi	4	J Gosden	J Fortune	11-2	4/6
2010	Midday	4	H Cecil	T Queally	11-4	6/8

ALWAYS A top-class race, this has generally seen the Classic generation hold sway with eight winners in the last 12 years, but the last two Oaks heroines, Sariska and Snow Fairy, were both beaten favourites. The five-year-old Super Tassa was the ultimate trend-buster in 2001 – the first Italian winner in Britain for 41 years and consequently sent off at 25-1.

Nunthorpe Stakes (5f) York

2001	Mozart	3	A O'Brien	M Kinane	4-9f	4/10
2002	Kyllachy	4	H Candy	J Spencer	3-1f	15/17
2003	Oasis Dream	3	J Gosden	R Hughes	4-9f	2/8
2004	Bahamian Pirate	9	D Nicholls	S Sanders	16-1	5/12
2005	La Cucaracha	4	B Hills	M Hills	7-1	8/16
2006	Reverence	5	E Ahern	K Darley	5-1	6/14
2007	Kingsgate Native	2	J Best	J Quinn	12-1	13/16
2008	Borderlescott	6	R Bastiman	P Cosgrave	12-1	12/14
2009	Borderlescott	7	R Bastiman	N Callan	9-1	2/16
2010	Sole Power	3	E Lynam	W Lordan	100-1	11/12

BIZARRELY, even though he was 100-1, Sole Power marked a return to the trends that had been prevalent in this race for many years prior to a run of older winners following Bahamian Pirate's win in 2004, during which time Borderlescott became the first back-to-back winner since Sharpo in the early 1980s and only the third horse aged six or older to win since 1945. What you really need is a relatively young horse still on the upgrade as eight out of nine winners prior to Borderlescott had been aged five or less and all but two were winning at the highest level for the first time.

Sprint Cup (6f) Haydock

2001	Nuclear Debate	6	J Hammond	G Mosse	11-2	9/12
2002	Invincible Spirit	5	J Dunlop	J Carroll	25-1	10/14
2003	Somnus	3	T Easterby	T Durcan	12-1	7/10
2004	Tante Rose	4	R Charlton	R Hughes	10-1	14/19
2005	Goodricke	3	D Loder	J Spencer	14-1	4/17
2006	Reverence	5	E Alston	K Darley	5-1	6/14
2007	Red Clubs	4	B Hills	M Hills	33-1	4/18
2008	African Rose	3	Mme C Head	S Pasquier	7-2f	12/15
2009	Regal Parade	5	D Nicholls	A Nicholls	14-1	13/14
2010	Markab	7	H Candy	P Cosgrave	12-1	14/13

THIS CAN often be run on ground with plenty of give, so there have been a string of upsets as midsummer form proves misleading, with seven of the last nine winners returned in double figures up to the 33-1 of Red Clubs in 2007. In fact no July Cup winner has followed up at Haydock since Ajdal in 1987, with Starspangledbanner, Sakhee's Secret and Fleeting Spirit the latest to be beaten favourites in the last three years, and African Rose is the only winning jolly since Godolphin hotpot Diktat in 1999.

St Leger (1m6f127yds) Doncaster

2001	Milan		A O'Brien	M Kinane	13-8f	7/10
2002	Bollin Eric		T Easterby	K Darley	7-1	3/8
2003	Brian Boru		A O'Brien	J Spencer	5-4f	9/12
2004	Rule Of Law		S bin Suroor	K McEvoy	3-1f	9/9
2005	Scorpion		A O'Brien	L Dettori	10-11f	2/6
2006	Sixties Icon		J Noseda	L Dettori	11-8f	11/11*
2007	Lucarno		J Gosden	J Fortune	11-8f	11/11
2008	Conduit		Sir M Stoute	L Dettori	8-1	5/14
2009	Mastery		S bin Suroor	T Durcan	14-1	7/8
2010	Arctic Cosmos		J Gosden	W Buick	12-1	8/10

Run at York

THE OLDEST of the five Classics, first run in 1776, but it has rather suffered in recent years from a move to keep class horses to shorter trips. Only three of the last 14 winners came via the traditional route of stepping up on strong Epsom Derby form – Silver Patriarch and Rule Of Law were second at Epsom, and Lucarno was third – although nine of the last 12 winners had run in a European Derby of some sort. The key race has been the Great Voltigeur at York, with 2009 hero Mastery (second to Leger third Monitor Closely at York) becoming the seventh winner to use that as a prep since 1999. Bollin Eric led a repeat of the York 1-2-3 in 2002, while Lucarno, Rule Of Law and Milan won both races.

Queen Elizabeth II Stakes (1m) Ascot

2001	Summoner	4	S bin Suroor	R Hills	33-1	7/8

2002	Where Or When	3	T Mills	K Darley	7-1	3/5
2003	Falbrav	5	L Cumani	D Holland	6-4f	4/8
2004	Rakti	5	M Jarvis	P Robinson	9-2	13/11
2005	Starcraft	3	L Cumani	C Lemaire	7-2	2/6
2006	George Washington	3	A O'Brien	K Fallon	13-8f	7/8
2007	Ramonti	5	S bin Suroor	L Dettori	5-1	8/7
2008	Raven's Pass	3	J Gosden	J Fortune	3-1	1/7
2009	Rip Van Winkle	3	A O'Brien	J Murtagh	8-13f	1/4
2010	Poet's Voice	3	S Bin Suroor	L Dettori	9-2	2/8

KNOWN AS the mile championship of Europe, and one in which the Classic generation have firmly held sway with 14 of the last 22 winners. That has made the St James's Palace Stakes the key trial, as six of the last 11 winning three-year-olds ran there. The top form isn't always upheld, though, and there have been some short-priced horses turned over such as Hawk Wing at 1-2 in 2002 and Giant's Causeway in 2000.

Prix de l'Arc De Triomphe (1m4f) Longchamp

2001	Sakhee	4	S bin Suroor	L Dettori	22-10f	15/17
2002	Marienbard	5	S bin Suroor	L Dettori	158-10	3/16
2003	Dalakhani	3	A de Royer-Dupre	C Soumillon	9-4	14/13
2004	Bago	3	J Pease	T Gillet	10-1	5/20
2005	Hurricane Run	3	A Fabre	K Fallon	11-4	6/15
2006	Rail Link	3	A Fabre	S Pasquier	8-1	4/8
2007	Dylan Thomas	4	A O'Brien	K Fallon	11-2	6/12
2008	Zarkava	3	A de Royer-Dupre	C Soumillon	13-8f	1/16
2009	Sea The Stars	3	J Oxx	M Kinane	4-6f	6/19
2010	Workforce	3	Sir M Stoute	R Moore	6-1	8/19

THIS RACE has restored its reputation as the premier middle-distance championship of Europe, with top-class 1m4f horses now trained specifically for the race from the summer. Dylan Thomas, Sea The Stars and Workforce have broken France's dominance, but it generally pays to follow the domestic horses, looking for a lightly-raced, progressive three-year-old preferably trained by Andre Fabre (five of the last 18 winners) and having run in the Prix Niel (ten of the last 17). Zarkava was the first winning filly since Akiyda in 1982.

Dubai Champion Stakes (1m2f) Newmarket

2001	Nayef	3	M Tregoning	R Hills	3-1	1/12
2002	Storming Home	4	B Hills	M Hills	8-1	4/11
2003	Rakti	4	M Jarvis	P Robinson	11-1	3/12
2004	Haafhd	3	B Hills	R Hills	12-1	9/11
2005	David Junior	3	B Meehan	J Spencer	25-1	13/15
2006	Pride	6	A de Royer-Dupre	C Lemaire	7-2	2/8
2007	Literato	3	J-C Rouget	C Lemaire	7-2	5/12
2008	New Approach	3	J Bolger	K Manning	6-5f	10/11
2009	Twice Over	4	H Cecil	T Queally	14-1	8/14
2010	Twice Over	5	H Cecil	T Queally	7-2	7/10

THE FINAL major contest of the year but a clash with the Breeders' Cup means the quality is dipping. Three-year-olds have the edge, with 17 winners since 1980. Twelve of those had won Classics but just two over 1m4f courtesy of Time Charter and New Approach, so look for horses with their best form over 1m and don't miss any Guineas winners who take their chance, with Haafhd the latest to follow up in 2004.

Outlook

Big handicap records

Lincoln Handicap (1m) Doncaster

Year	Winner	Age	Weight	Trainer	Jockey	SP	Draw/ran
2001	**Nimello**	5	8-9	P Cole	J Fortune	9-2f	1/23
2002	**Zucchero**	6	8-13	D Arbuthnot	S Whitworth	33-1	7/23
2003	**Pablo**	4	8-11	B Hills	M Hills	5-1	6/24
2004	**Babodana**	4	9-10	M Tompkins	P Robinson	20-1	23/24
2005	**Stream of Gold**	4	9-0	Sir M Stoute	R Winston	5-1f	13/22
2006	**Blythe Knight**	6	8-10	J Quinn	G Gibbons	22-1	9/30*
2007	**Very Wise**	5	8-11	W Haggas	J Fanning	9-1	16/20
2008	**Smokey Oakey**	4	8-9	M Tompkins	J Quinn	10-1	12/21
2009	**Expresso Star**	4	8-12	J Gosden	J Fortune	10-3f	9/20
2010	**Penitent**	4	9-2	W Haggas	J Murtagh	3-1f	1/21

*Run at Redcar

THE perennial question is what effect the draw will have – Penitent won from stall one from last year after high numbers had generally been doing best, and the best advice is to watch the Spring Mile, run a day earlier. Weight was traditionally a major barrier to success but has become less so since Hunters Of Brora's victory in 1998. At the time he was the first winner to carry 9st or more since 1985, but since then Right Wing, Babodana, Stream Of Gold and Penitent have followed suit. Turf horses having their first run of the year remain far preferable to race-fit all-weather types, even though Very Wise was having his seventh run since December in 2007. Northern-based trainers no longer dominate, with Paul Cole, Mark Tompkins and William Haggas all dual winners in the last 11 years.

Royal Hunt Cup Handicap (1m) Royal Ascot

2001	**Surprise Encounter**	5	8-9	E Dunlop	L Dettori	8-1	29/30
2002	**Norton**	5	8-9	T Mills	J Fortune	25-1	10/30
2003	**Macadamia**	4	8-13	J Fanshawe	D O'Neill	8-1	6/32
2004	**Mine**	6	9-5	J Bethell	T Quinn	16-1	8/31
2005	**New Seeker**	5	9-0	C Cox	P Robinson	11-1	6/22*
2006	**Cesare**	5	8-8	J Fanshawe	J Spencer	14-1	3/30
2007	**Royal Oath**	4	9-0	J Gosden	J Fortune	9-1	14/26
2008	**Mr Aviator**	4	9-5	R Hannon	R Hughes	25-1	4/29
2009	**Forgotten Voice**	4	9-1	J Noseda	J Murtagh	4-1f	1/25
2010	**Invisible Man**	4	8-9	S Bin Suroor	L Dettori	28-1	23/29

*Royal Hunt Cup and the Wokingham run at York in 2005

A GREAT betting race in which there are few pointers and plots are thick on the ground, so most winners go off at a decent price – Forgotten Voice in 2009 was the first winning favourite since Yeast 13 years earlier. Low numbers tend to be favoured – in 2006 the first seven came from the bottom 11 stalls, the first four came from the bottom six in 2008 and the first three came from the bottom five in 2009 – but the best finisher from a single-figure berth last year was 17th so check on previous races at the royal meeting. Weight trends have changed markedly – Mine, in 2004, was the first horse since 1989 to carry more than 9st to victory, but Mr Aviator and Forgotten Voice have followed him.

Wokingham Handicap (6f) Royal Ascot

2001	Nice One Clare	5	9-3	J Payne	J Murtagh	7-1f	4/30
2002	Capricho	5	8-11	J Akehurst	T Quinn	20-1	21/28
2003	Fayr Jag	4	9-6	T Easterby	W Supple	10-1	13/29
	Ratio	5	9-3	J Hammond	L Dettori	14-1	22/29
2004	Lafi	5	8-13	D Nicholls	E Ahern	6-1f	30/29
2005	Iffraaj	4	9-6	M Jarvis	P Robinson	9-4f	6/17
2006	Baltic King	6	9-10	H Morrison	J Fortune	10-1	6/28
2007	Dark Missile	4	8-6	A Balding	W Buick	22-1	27/26
2008	Big Timer	4	9-2	Miss L Perrett	T Eaves	20-1	28/27
2009	High Standing	4	8-12	W Haggas	R Moore	6-1	28/26
2010	Laddies Poker Two	5	8-11	J Noseda	J Murtagh	9-2f	2/27

ANY draw bias in the Hunt Cup has often been completely changed by this race, with eight of the last 15 winners drawn 20 or higher yet Laddies Poker Two winning from stall two last year when the Hunt Cup had gone the other way. Class horses have been increasingly successful since the turn of the century, with eight of the last 14 winners carrying at least 9st 2lb to victory and four winning favourites in ten years. A key trial is the Victoria Cup at the same track in May. Only two winners have been older than six in the race's history.

Northumberland Plate (2m) Newcastle

2001	Archduke Ferdinand	3	8-4	P Cole	F Norton	12-1	17/18
2002	Bangalore	6	9-5	A Perrett	S Sanders	8-1	9/16
2003	Unleash	4	8-11	P Hobbs	J Spencer	10-1	1/20
2004	Mirjan	8	8-3	L Lungo	P Hanagan	25-1	5/19
2005	Sergeant Cecil	6	8-8	D Millman	A Munro	14-1	7/20
2006	Toldo	4	8-2	G Moore	N de Souza	33-1	16/20
2007	Juniper Girl	4	8-11	M Bell	L Morris	5-1f	13/20
2008	Arc Bleu	7	8-2	A Martin	A Nicholls	14-1	6/18
2009	Som Tala	6	8-8	M Channon	T Culhane	16-1	4/17
2010	Overturn	6	8-7	D McCain	E Ahern	14-1	21/19

A RACE traditionally identified with providing an opportunity for older, experienced stayers to grind out victory, though in recent years age doesn't seem to have had any bearing. Younger, less exposed types took over around the turn of the century, since when seven out of 11 winners have been six or older (including a couple of eight-year-olds) but the other four have been three or four. The first bend comes shortly after the start, so those drawn high can be disadvantaged, with eight of the last 12 winners drawn seven or lower, and Overturn used controversial tactics to overcome that last year.

Bunbury Cup (7f) Newmarket

2001	Atavus	4	8-9	G Margarson	J Mackay (3)	10-1	14/19
2002	Mine	4	8-12	J Bethell	K Fallon	5-1f	3/17
2003	Patavellian	5	9-1	R Charlton	S Drowne	4-1f	2/20

2004	**Material Witness**	7	9-3	W Muir	M Dwyer	25-1	6/19
2005	**Mine**	7	9-9	J Bethell	T Quinn	16-1	6/18
2006	**Mine**	8	9-10	J Bethell	M Kinane	10-1	14/19
2007	**Giganticus**	4	8-8	B Hills	P Robinson	16-1	3/18
2008	**Little White Lie**	4	9-0	J Jenkins	D Holland	14-1	19/18
2009	**Plum Pudding**	6	9-10	R Hannon	R Moore	12-1	5/19
2010	**St Moritz**	4	9-1	M Johnston	L Dettori	4-1f	16/19

THE AWESOME figure of Mine stands tall over the other winners of this race as he picked up the prize on three occasions between 2002 and 2006. Mine's last two wins were further evidence that weight is no barrier to success with eight out of the last 12 winners carrying 9st 1lb or more and Plum Pudding defying 9-10 in 2009. Course management have struggled with the fairness of the draw in recent years with huge biases either way. No three-year-old has won since Ho Leng defied a welter burden in 1998.

John Smith's Cup (1m2f85yds) York

2001	**Foreign Affairs**	3	8-6	Sir M Prescott	G Duffield	5-2f	8/19
2002	**Vintage Premium**	5	9-9	R Fahey	P Hanagan	20-1	9/20
2003	**Far Lane**	4	9-4	B Hills	M Hills	7-1	4/20
2004	**Arcalis**	4	9-2	H Johnson	R Winston	20-1	18/21
2005	**Mullins Bay**	4	9-7	A O'Brien	K Fallon	4-1f	19/20
2006	**Fairmile**	4	8-12	W Swinburn	A Kirby	6-1j	9/20
2007	**Charlie Tokyo**	4	8-9	R Fahey	J Moriarty	11-1	4/17
2008	**Flying Clarets**	5	8-12	R Fahey	F Tylicki (7)	12-1	12/16
2009	**Sirvino**	4	8-8	T Brown	N Brown (3)	16-1	16/18
2010	**Wigmore Hall**	3	8-5	M Bell	M Lane (3)	5-1	13/19

YOUTH seems to be the key to this race, with only one horse aged five or older successful since Vintage Premium in 2002, and even though three-year-olds had ensured an even longer drought prior to Wigmore Hall's win last year that's because they struggle to get a run thes days – indeed, Wigmore Hall was the only runner from that age group.

Stewards' Cup (6f) Goodwood

2001	**Guinea Hunter**	5	9-0	T Easterby	J Spencer	33-1	19/30
2002	**Bond Boy**	5	8-2	B Smart	C Catlin	14-1	29/28
2003	**Patavellian**	5	8-11	R Charlton	S Drowne	4-1	27/29
2004	**Pivotal Point**	4	8-11	P Makin	S Sanders	7-1c	1/28
2005	**Gift Horse**	5	9-7	D Nicholls	K Fallon	9-2	19/27
2006	**Borderlescott**	4	9-5	R Bastiman	R Ffrench	10-1	19/27
2007	**Zidane**	5	9-1	J Fanshawe	J Spencer	6-1f	11/27
2008	**Conquest**	4	8-9	W Haggas	D O'Neill	40-1	14/26
2009	**Genki**	5	9-1	R Charlton	S Drowne	14-1	10/26
2010	**Evens And Odds**	6	9-3	D Nicholls	B Cray (5)	20-1	18/28

THIS is a major betting heat with a strong ante-post market, though that's not helped by the importance of the draw – even a casual glance at the results proves the point, with Patavellian's win in 2003 (leading home a 1-2-3 for the widest four stalls) fairly typical. However, Pivotal Point managed a scorching win from stall one in 2004, and since then Genki, Conquest and Zidane have triumphed from central draws. Horses aged four and five have dominated in recent years, while the betting offers few clues with an equal number of favourites and rags winning. The Wokingham has the most bearing, with ten of the last 14 winners having previously run in the big Royal Ascot handicap.

Ebor Handicap (1m6f) York

2001	Mediterranean	3	8-4	A O'Brien	M Kinane	16-1	20/22
2002	Hugs Dancer	5	8-5	J Given	D McKeown	25-1	20/22
2003	Saint Alebe	4	8-8	D Elsworth	T Quinn	20-1	17/22
2004	Mephisto	4	9-4	L Cumani	D Holland	6-1	3/19
2005	Sergeant Cecil	6	8-12	B Millman	A Munro	11-1	18/20
2006	Mudawin	5	8-4	J Chapple-Hyam	J Egan	100-1	13/22
2007	Purple Moon	4	9-4	L Cumani	J Spencer	7-2f	14/19
2008	All The Good	5	9-0	S bin Suroor	D O'Neill	25-1	7/20
2009	Sesenta	5	8-8	W Mullins	G Carroll (5)	25-1	16/19
2010	Dirar	5	9-1	G Elliott	J Spencer	14-1	22/20

*Run at Newbury as the Newburgh Handicap in 2008

ONE OF the oldest and most famous handicaps, first run in 1847, again with an extremely strong ante-post market. Sea Pigeon brought the house down when lumping top-weight home in 1979, but low weights are massively favoured and all five winners to carry more than 8st 8lb to victory since 1998 did so in the last seven years when the weights have become more and more condensed. Watch out for three-year-olds – they had a tremendous record around the turn of the century and have simply found it increasingly tough to get a run since then, with two of the three to run since 2006, Honolulu and Changingoftheguard, finishing honourable seconds. Watch the Northumberland Plate (Newcastle, June) and the Duke of Edinburgh Handicap (Royal Ascot, June).

Ayr Gold Cup Handicap (6f) Ayr

2001	Continent	4	8-10	D Nicholls	D Holland	10-1	22/28
2002	Funfair Wane	3	9-3	D Nicholls	A Nicholls	16-1	16/28
2003	Quito	6	8-6	D Chapman	A Culhane	20-1	10/26
2004	Funfair Wane	5	8-6	D Nicholls	P Doe	33-1	8/24
2005	Presto Shinko	4	9-2	R Hannon	S Sanders	12-1	2/27
2006	Fonthill Road	6	9-2	R Fahey	P Hanagan	16-1	6/28
2007	Advanced	4	9-9	K Ryan	J Spencer	20-1	22/28
2008	Regal Parade	4	8-10	D Nicholls	W Carson (5)	18-1	20/27
2009	Jimmy Styles	5	9-2	C Cox	L Dettori	14-1	15/26
2010	Redford	5	9-2	D Nicholls	L Dettori	14-1	17/26

A HISTORIC race first run in 1804, but punters are still struggling to get to grips with it – Continent was the most fancied winner of the last 13 years at 10-1. There seems little clues from the draw in recent runnings, but the effect can be gleaned from the consolation races – the Bronze Cup was run for the first time in 2009 the day before the real thing, with the Silver Cup moved to the Saturday. A horse with good recent form who can settle in large fields and come from off the pace is required. Key races are the Wokingham, the Stewards' Cup and the Portland (Doncaster, September). Take a close look at David Nicholls' runners – there are a few but his record is brilliant, particularly with less fancied runners, and he's even saddled the first and second in two of the last three years.

Cambridgeshire Handicap (1m1f) Newmarket

2001	I Cried For You	6	8-6	J Given	M Fenton	33-1	11/35
2002	Beauchamp Pilot	4	9-5	G Butler	E Ahern	9-1	26/30
2003	Chivalry	4	8-1	Sir M Prescott	G Duffield	14-1	17/34
2004	Spanish Don	6	8-7	D Elsworth	L Keniry	100-1	3/32
2005	Blue Monday	4	9-3	R Charlton	S Drowne	5-1f	28/30

2006	**Formal Decree**	3	8-9	G Swinbank	J Spencer	9-1	17/33
2007	**Pipedreamer**	3	8-12	J Gosden	J Fortune	5-1f	11/34
2008	**Tazeez**	4	9-2	J Gosden	R Hills	25-1	21/28
2009	**Supaseus**	6	9-1	H Morrison	T Block	16-1	26/32
2010	**Credit Swap**	5	8-7	M Wigham	J Crowley	14-1	33/35

THE FIRST leg of the Autumn Double. Because of its unusual distance and its straight course, this has thrown up a number of specialists down the years so consider horses who have run well in the race before. Only two three-year-olds have won in 11 years, but if looking to that age group make it one bred to find improvement over longer trips which hadn't been attempted until the weights came out. The heritage handicap at Newbury in September has become the key trial, throwing up four of the last seven winners.

Cesarewitch Handicap (2m2f) Newmarket

2001	**Distant Prospect**	4	8-8	I Balding	M Dwyer	14-1	32/31
2002	**Miss Fara**	7	8-0	M Pipe	R Moore	12-1	36/36
2003	**Landing Light**	8	9-4	N Henderson	Pat Eddery	12-1	36/36
2004	**Contact Dancer**	5	8-2	M Johnston	R Ffrench	16-1	18/34
2005	**Sergeant Cecil**	6	9-8	B Millman	A Munro	10-1	28/34
2006	**Detroit City**	4	9-1	P Hobbs	J Spencer	9-2f	29/32
2007	**Leg Spinner**	6	8-11	A Martin	J Murtagh	14-1	23/33
2008	**Caracciola**	11	9-6	N Henderson	E Ahern	50-1	11/32
2009	**Darley Sun**	3	8-6	D Simcock	A Atzeni (3)	9-2f	25/32
2010	**Aaim To Prosper**	7	8-2	B Meehan	L-P Beuzelin (3)	16-1	30/32

THE SECOND leg of the Autumn Double. This is another race in which a long sweeping bend makes the draw far more important than you would think from the trip with Caracciola the only winner drawn lower than 17 since Turnpole in 1997. It generally takes a fair amount of experience to win this race, and Darley Sun was only the third winning three-year-old in 20 years. Seven of the last 13 winners had been hurdling the previous winter with jumps legends Nicky Henderson and Martin Pipe (twice), Mary Reveley, Philip Hobbs and Tony Martin all successful, and David Pipe's Mamlook was second to Darley Sun.

November Handicap (1m4f) Doncaster

2001	**Royal Cavalier**	4	7-10	R Hollinshead	P Quinn	50-1	5/14
2002	**Red Wine**	3	8-1	J Osborne	M Dwyer	16-1	20/23
2003	**Turbo**	4	9-2	G Balding	A Clark	25-1	14/24
2004	**Carte Diamond**	4	9-6	D Ellison	K Fallon	12-1	3/24
2005	**Come On Jonny**	3	8-0	R Beckett	N de Souza	14-1	18/21
2006	**Group Captain**	4	9-5	R Charlton	R Hughes	10-1	20/20
2007	**Malt Or Mash**	3	8-10	R Hannon	R Moore	5-1	13/21
2008	**Tropical Strait**	5	8-13	D Arbuthnot	M Dwyer	20-1	22/21
2009	**Charm School**	4	8-12	J Gosden	J Fortune	17-2	14/23
2010	**Times Up**	4	8-13	J Dunlop	D O'Neill	14-1	9/22

THE LAST big betting heat of the season. Lightly-raced, progressive three-year-olds are most likely to succeed, with 11 of the last 21 winners aged three and four of the last eight among those unraced at two. Weights of the winners vary, but nine of the last 11 were returned at double-figure odds and favourites have a desperate record, which makes the colossal gamble on Scriptwriter in 2006 (down to 2-1 in a 20-runner race) all the more amazing. Only Royal Cavalier and Carte Diamond have won from single-figure draws in the last 12 years. The 1m4f handicap run on Racing Post Trophy day is worth studying.

Big Race Dates, Fixtures and Track Facts

Fixtures

Key - Flat, **Jumps**

March

30	Wednesday	Catterick, **Hereford**, Lingfield, Wolverhampton
31	Thursday	Leicester, **Ludlow**, Wolverhampton

April

1	Friday	Musselburgh, **Newcastle, Stratford**, Wolverhampton
2	Saturday	**Chepstow**, Doncaster, Kempton, **Uttoxeter**
3	Sunday	Doncaster, **Market Rasen**
4	Monday	Folkestone, **Kelso**, Windsor
5	Tuesday	**Exeter**, Kempton, Pontefract
6	Wednesday	Beverley, Kempton, Lingfield, Nottingham
7	Thursday	**Aintree, Hereford**, Kempton, Ripon
8	Friday	**Aintree, Fontwell**, Newcastle, Wolverhampton
9	Saturday	**Aintree, Bangor, Chepstow**, Lingfield, Thirsk, Wolverhampton
10	Sunday	**Ascot, Ludlow, Wincanton**
11	Monday	**Ffos Las, Hexham, Plumpton**, Windsor, Wolverhampton
12	Tuesday	Folkestone, Southwell, **Towcester, Taunton**, Wolverhampton
13	Wednesday	Catterick, **Cheltenham**, Kempton, Newmarket, **Southwell**
14	Thursday	Beverley, **Cheltenham**, Kempton, Newmarket, **Sedgefield**
15	Friday	Ayr, Brighton, **Chepstow**, Newbury, Wolverhampton
16	Saturday	**Ayr**, Doncaster, Haydock, Leicester, Newbury, Ripon
17	Sunday	**Stratford, Wetherby**
18	Monday	**Exeter**, Redcar, **Towcester**, Windsor
19	Tuesday	Bath, **Fontwell**, Pontefract, Southwell, Wolverhampton
20	Wednesday	Epsom, **Hereford**, Kempton, Newcastle, Southwell
21	Thursday	Folkestone, **Ludlow, Wincanton**
23	Saturday	**Carlisle, Haydock, Kelso**, Musselburgh, **Newton Abbot**, Nottingham, **Sandown**
24	Sunday	Musselburgh, **Plumpton**, Sandown, **Towcester**
25	Monday	**Fakenham, Ffos Las, Huntingdon, Market Rasen, Plumpton**, Redcar, Warwick, Yarmouth
26	Tuesday	**Exeter**, Lingfield, **Sedgefield**, Wolverhampton, Yarmouth
27	Wednesday	Ascot, Kempton, Newcastle, **Perth**, Pontefract
28	Thursday	Bath, Brighton, **Hereford, Perth, Southwell**
29	Friday	**Bangor**, Doncaster, **Fontwell**, Leicester, **Perth**
30	Saturday	Doncaster, Goodwood, **Hexham**, Newmarket, Thirsk, **Uttoxeter**

May

1	Sunday	Hamilton, Newmarket, Salisbury
2	Monday	Beverley, Chepstow, Kempton, Warwick, Windsor
3	Tuesday	Bath, Catterick, **Exeter, Fakenham**, Newcastle
4	Wednesday	**Cheltenham**, Chester, **Kelso, Sedgefield**, Southwell
5	Thursday	Ffos Las, Goodwood, **Newton Abbot, Wetherby, Wincanton**
6	Friday	**Aintree**, Ascot, Chester, Hamilton, Lingfield, Nottingham, Ripon
7	Saturday	Ascot, **Haydock, Hexham**, Lingfield, Nottingham, Thirsk, Warwick
8	Sunday	**Plumpton, Uttoxeter, Worcester**

 9 Monday.........................Brighton, Redcar, **Towcester**, Windsor, Wolverhampton
10 Tuesday...........................Beverley, **Sedgefield**, Southwell, Warwick, Yarmouth
11 Wednesday ....**Fontwell**, Kempton, **Perth**, **Wincanton**, York
12 Thursday ....**Folkestone**, **Ludlow**, Newmarket, **Perth**, Salisbury, York
13 Friday.......................**Aintree**, Hamilton, Newbury, Newcastle, Newmarket, York
14 Saturday ....**Bangor**, Doncaster, Newbury, Newmarket, Thirsk, **Uttoxeter**
15 Sunday ....**Market Rasen**, Ripon, **Stratford**
16 Monday ....Bath, Leicester, **Newton Abbot**, Windsor, Wolverhampton
17 Tuesday......................Brighton, Kempton, Nottingham, **Southwell**, **Towcester**
18 Wednesday ....Goodwood, Kempton, Lingfield, **Sedgefield**, **Worcester**
19 Thursday ....Haydock, Salisbury, Sandown, Southwell, **Wetherby**
20 Friday................Bath, Catterick, Haydock, Musselburgh, **Towcester**, Yarmouth
21 Saturday ....Haydock, Chester, Goodwood, Haydock, Lingfield, Newbury,
    ....York
22 Sunday..**Fakenham**, Kelso
23 Monday...Carlisle, Leicester, Thirsk, Windsor
24 Tuesday ....Chepstow, **Hexham**, **Huntingdon**, Lingfield, Ripon
25 Wednesday ....Ayr, Beverley, **Newton Abbot**, Sedgefield, **Southwell**
26 Thursday...............Ayr, Brighton, Folkestone, Newcastle, Sandown, **Wetherby**
27 Friday...........Brighton, Haydock, Newcastle, Newmarket, Pontefract, **Stratford**
28 Saturday.............Beverley, **Cartmel**, Catterick, Haydock, Newmarket, **Stratford**
29 Sunday...**Fontwell**, Nottingham, **Uttoxeter**
30 Monday ....Carlisle, **Cartmel**, Goodwood, Chepstow, Leicester, Redcar,
    ....**Towcester**
31 Tuesday...**Ffos Las**, Leicester, Redcar, Yarmouth

June

 1 Wednesday...........................**Cartmel**, **Fontwell**, Kempton, Nottingham, Ripon
 2 Thursday ....Hamilton, Lingfield, Sandown, Southwell, **Uttoxeter**, **Wetherby**
 3 Friday ....Bath, Catterick, Doncaster, Epsom, Goodwood, Musselburgh
 4 Saturday.......Doncaster, Epsom, **Hexham**, Lingfield, Musselburgh, Newcastle,
    ....**Worcester**
 5 Sunday ....**Perth**, **Worcester**
 6 Monday.................................Folkestone, **Newton Abbot**, Pontefract, Windsor
 7 Tuesday ....**Ffos Las**, Redcar, Salisbury, **Southwell**
 8 Wednesday ....Beverley, Hamilton, Haydock, **Kempton**, Yarmouth
 9 Thursday........**Fontwell**, Haydock, Newbury, Nottingham, **Uttoxeter**, Yarmouth
10 Friday ....**Aintree**, Chepstow, Goodwood, **Market Rasen**, Sandown, York
11 Saturday ....Bath, Chester, **Hexham**, Leicester, Lingfield, Sandown, York
12 Sunday...Doncaster, Salisbury
13 Monday................................Carlisle, **Sedgefield**, Warwick, Windsor
14 Tuesday ....Brighton, **Newton Abbot**, Royal Ascot, Thirsk
15 Wednesday ....Royal Ascot, Hamilton, **Kempton**, Ripon, **Worcester**
16 Thursday...............Beverley, **Ffos Las**, Leicester, Ripon, Royal Ascot, Warwick
17 Friday.............Ayr, Goodwood, Musselburgh, Newmarket, Redcar, Royal Ascot
18 Saturday ....Ayr, Haydock, Lingfield, Newmarket, Redcar, Royal Ascot
19 Sunday ....**Hexham**, **Hereford**, Pontefract
20 Monday......................................Chepstow, Kempton, Windsor, Wolverhampton
21 Tuesday ....Beverley, Brighton, Newbury, **Newton Abbot**
22 Wednesday.............................Bath, Carlisle, Kempton, Salisbury, **Worcester**
23 Thursday ....**Ffos Las**, Hamilton, Leicester, Newcastle, Warwick
24 Friday ....Chester, Doncaster, Folkestone, **Market Rasen**, Newcastle,
    ....Newmarket

25 Saturday ....Chester, Doncaster, Lingfield, Newcastle, Newmarket, Windsor
26 Sunday ....Salisbury, **Uttoxeter**, Windsor
27 Monday..............................Musselburgh, Pontefract, Windsor, Wolverhampton
28 Tuesday ....Brighton, Hamilton, Southwell, **Stratford**
29 Wednesday ....Catterick, Chepstow, Kempton, **Perth**, **Worcester**
30 Thursday ....Epsom, Haydock, Newbury, **Perth**, Yarmouth

July

1 Friday ....Beverley, Doncaster, Haydock, Sandown, Warwick
2 Saturday ....Beverley, Carlisle, Haydock, Leicester, Nottingham, Sandown
3 Sunday..Ayr, **Market Rasen**
4 Monday ....Brighton, **Newton Abbot**, Ripon, Windsor
5 Tuesday ....Pontefract, Southwell, **Uttoxeter**, Wolverhampton
6 Wednesday.............................Bath, Catterick, Kempton, Lingfield, **Worcester**
7 Thursday.......................Doncaster, Epsom, Folkestone, Newmarket, Warwick
8 Friday ....Ascot, Chepstow, Chester, Newbury, Newmarket, York
9 Saturday........................Ascot, Chester, Hamilton, Newmarket, Salisbury, York
10 Sunday ....**Perth**, **Southwell**, **Stratford**
11 Monday ....Ayr, Ffos Las, Windsor, Wolverhampton
12 Tuesday ....Beverley, Brighton, Southwell, Yarmouth
13 Wednesday.....................Catterick, Lingfield, Sandown, **Uttoxeter**, **Worcester**
14 Thursday ....Bath, **Cartmel**, Doncaster, Epsom, Hamilton, Leicester
15 Friday.......................Hamilton, Haydock, Newbury, Newmarket, Nottingham,
....Pontefract
16 Saturday ....Haydock, Lingfield, **Market Rasen**, Newbury, Newmarket,
....Ripon
17 Sunday ....**Newton Abbot**, Redcar, **Stratford**
18 Monday ....Ayr, Beverley, Windsor, Yarmouth
19 Tuesday ....**Bangor**, Musselburgh, Southwell, Yarmouth
20 Wednesday ....Catterick, Leicester, Lingfield, Sandown, **Worcester**
21 Thursday ....Bath, Doncaster, Epsom, Folkestone, Sandown, **Uttoxeter**
22 Friday............................Ascot, Chepstow, Newmarket, **Southwell**, Thirsk, York
23 Saturday ....Ascot, Lingfield, Newcastle, Newmarket, Salisbury, York
24 Sunday...Ascot, Carlisle, Pontefract
25 Monday ....Ayr, **Uttoxeter**, Windsor, Yarmouth
26 Tuesday ....Beverley, Goodwood, Perth, **Worcester**
27 Wednesday ....Goodwood, Leicester, **Perth**, Redcar, Sandown
28 Thursday........................Epsom, Ffos Las, Goodwood, Nottingham, **Stratford**
29 Friday.................**Bangor**, Bath, Goodwood, Musselburgh, Newmarket, Thirsk
30 Saturday ....Doncaster, Goodwood, Hamilton, Lingfield, Newmarket, Thirsk
31 Sunday...Chester, **Market Rasen**, Newbury

August

1 Monday...Carlisle, **Newton Abbot**, Ripon, Windsor
2 Tuesday...............................Bath, Catterick, Ffos Las, Southwell
3 Wednesday ....Brighton, Kempton, Newcastle, Pontefract, Yarmouth
4 Thursday.......................Brighton, Chepstow, Folkestone, Haydock, Sandown,
....Yarmouth
5 Friday ....Brighton, Haydock, Lingfield, Newmarket, **Worcester**
6 Saturday.......................Ascot, Ayr, Haydock, Lingfield, Newmarket, Redcar
7 Sunday..Leicester, Windsor
8 Monday.............................Lingfield, Thirsk, Windsor, Wolverhampton
9 Tuesday ....Ayr, Ffos Las, **Newton Abbot**, Nottingham

10	Wednesday	Beverley, Kempton, Salisbury, Wolverhampton, Yarmouth
11	Thursday	Beverley, Chepstow, Goodwood, Newmarket, Salisbury, **Stratford**
12	Friday	Catterick, Kempton, Newbury, Newcastle, Newmarket, Nottingham
13	Saturday	Doncaster, Lingfield, **Market Rasen**, Newbury, Newmarket, Ripon
14	Sunday	Pontefract, **Southwell**
15	Monday	Kempton, Thirsk, Windsor, Yarmouth
16	Tuesday	Brighton, Kempton, Musselburgh, **Worcester**
17	Wednesday	Carlisle, Folkestone, **Hereford**, Nottingham, York
18	Thursday	Epsom, **Fontwell**, Hamilton, Southwell, **Stratford**, York
19	Friday	**Bangor**, Salisbury, Sandown, Wolverhampton, York
20	Saturday	Bath, Chester, **Market Rasen**, **Newton Abbot**, **Perth**, Sandown, York
21	Sunday	Folkestone, **Newton Abbot**
22	Monday	Hamilton, **Hereford**, Kempton, Windsor
23	Tuesday	Leicester, **Sedgefield**, Warwick, Yarmouth
24	Wednesday	Catterick, Chepstow, Kempton, Wolverhampton, **Worcester**
25	Thursday	Carlisle, **Cartmel**, **Ffos Las**, Lingfield, Wolverhampton
26	Friday	Brighton, Ffos Las, Hamilton, Newcastle, Newmarket, Thirsk
27	Saturday	Beverley, **Cartmel**, Goodwood, Newmarket, Redcar, Windsor
28	Sunday	Beverley, Goodwood, Yarmouth
29	Monday	**Bangor**, **Cartmel**, Chepstow, Epsom, **Huntingdon**, Newcastle, Ripon, Warwick
30	Tuesday	Epsom, Goodwood, Ripon, Southwell, Wolverhampton
31	Wednesday	Bath, Carlisle, Folkestone, **Hereford**, Kempton

September

1	Thursday	Kempton, **Newton Abbot**, Redcar, Salisbury
2	Friday	Brighton, Chepstow, Haydock, Kempton
3	Saturday	Ascot, Haydock, Kempton, Musselburgh, **Stratford**, Thirsk, Wolverhampton
4	Sunday	**Fontwell**, York,
5	Monday	Bath, Newcastle, **Newton Abbot**
6	Tuesday	Leicester, Lingfield, **Sedgefield**
7	Wednesday	Carlisle, Doncaster, Kempton, **Uttoxeter**
8	Thursday	Chepstow, Doncaster, Epsom, Wolverhampton
9	Friday	Chester, Doncaster, Sandown, Wolverhampton
10	Saturday	Bath, Chester, Doncaster, Goodwood, Kempton
11	Sunday	Ffos Las, Goodwood
12	Monday	Brighton, Kempton, Musselburgh
13	Tuesday	Folkestone, Haydock, Yarmouth
14	Wednesday	Beverley, Kempton, Sandown, Yarmouth
15	Thursday	Ayr, Kempton, Pontefract, Yarmouth
16	Friday	Ayr, Lingfield, Newbury, Wolverhampton
17	Saturday	Ayr, Catterick, Newbury, Newmarket, Wolverhampton
18	Sunday	Hamilton, **Plumpton**, **Uttoxeter**
19	Monday	Hamilton, Kempton, Leicester
20	Tuesday	Beverley, Folkestone, **Newton Abbot**
21	Wednesday	Goodwood, Kempton, **Perth**, Redcar
22	Thursday	Newmarket, **Perth**, Pontefract, Wolverhampton
23	Friday	Haydock, Newmarket, Wolverhampton, **Worcester**

24 Saturday ....Chester, Haydock, **Market Rasen**, Newmarket, Ripon,
....Wolverhampton
25 Sunday...Epsom, Musselburgh
26 Monday ....Bath, Ffos Las, Hamilton
27 Tuesday..Ayr, Chepstow, **Sedgefield**
28 Wednesday ....Kempton, Newcastle, Nottingham, Salisbury
29 Thursday ....**Bangor**, Kempton, Warwick, Wolverhampton
30 Friday ....Ascot, Fontwell, **Hexham**, Wolverhampton

October

1 Saturday...........................Ascot, **Fontwell**, Redcar, Wolverhampton
2 Sunday...**Huntingdon**, **Kelso**, **Uttoxeter**
3 Monday.....................................Pontefract, Warwick, Windsor
4 Tuesday.....................................Catterick, Leicester, Southwell
5 Wednesday.........................Kempton, **Ludlow**, Nottingham, **Towcester**
6 Thursday ....Ayr, **Exeter**, Wolverhaampton, **Worcester**
7 Friday ....**Carlisle**, Newmarket, Wolverhampton, York
8 Saturday ....**Chepstow**, **Hexham**, Newmarket, Wolverhampton, York
9 Sunday...**Ffos Las**, Goodwood
10 Monday ....Salisbury, Windsor, Yarmouth
11 Tuesday...........................**Huntingdon**, Leicester, Newcastle
12 Wednesday.........................Kempton, Lingfield, Nottingham, **Wetherby**
13 Thursday.........................Brighton, Kempton, **Uttoxeter**, **Wincanton**
14 Friday ....**Cheltenham**, Haydock, Redcar, Wolverhampton
15 Saturday ....Ascot, Catterick, **Cheltenham**, **Kelso**, Wolverhampton
16 Sunday...Bath, **Kempton**
17 Monday ....**Plumpton**, Pontefract, Windsor
18 Tuesday ....**Exeter**, Lingfield, Yarmouth
19 Wednesday ....**Fontwell**, Kempton, Newmarket, **Worcester**
20 Thursday.........................Brighton, **Carlisle**, **Ludlow**, Wolverhampton
21 Friday...........................Doncaster, **Fakenham**, Newbury, Wolverhampton
22 Saturday...........................**Aintree**, **Chepstow**, Doncaster, Newbury, **Stratford**,
....Wolverhampton
23 Sunday...**Aintree**, **Wincanton**
24 Monday...........................Leicester, Redcar, Leicester, Southwell
25 Tuesday.....................................Catterick, **Taunton**, Yarmouth
26 Wednesday ....**Haydock**, Kempton, Musselburgh, Nottingham
27 Thursday ....**Fontwell**, Kempton, Lingfield, **Stratford**
28 Friday...........................Newmarket, **Uttoxeter**, **Wetherby**, Wolverhampton
29 Saturday...........................**Ascot**, Ayr, Newmarket, **Wetherby**, Wolverhampton
30 Sunday ....**Carlisle**, **Huntingdon**
31 Monday...........................**Kempton**, **Plumpton**, Wolverhampton

November

1 Tuesday...**Exeter**, Kempton, Redcar
2 Wednesday ....**Chepstow**, Kempton, Nottingham, **Warwick**
3 Thursday ....**Musselburgh**, Southwell, **Towcester**, Wolverhampton
4 Friday...........................Ffos Las, **Fontwell**, **Hexham**, Wolverhampton
5 Saturday...........................Doncaster, **Kelso**, **Sandown**, **Wincanton**
6 Sunday ....**Ffos Las**, **Market Rasen**
7 Monday ....**Carlisle**, **Hereford**, **Southwell**
8 Tuesday...........................**Huntingdon**, **Lingfield**, **Sedgefield**
9 Wednesday ....**Bangor**, **Exeter**, Kempton, Southwell

10	Thursday	Kempton, **Ludlow**, Southwell, **Taunton**
11	Friday	**Cheltenham**, Lingfield, **Newcastle**, Wolverhampton
12	Saturday	**Cheltenham**, Lingfield, **Uttoxeter**, **Wetherby**, Wolverhampton
13	Sunday	**Cheltenham**, **Fontwell**
14	Monday	**Leicester**, **Plumpton**, Wolverhampton
15	Tuesday	**Fakenham**, **Folkestone**, Southwell
16	Wednesday	**Hexham**, Kempton, Lingfield, **Warwick**
17	Thursday	**Hereford**, Kempton, **Market Rasen**, **Wincanton**
18	Friday	**Ascot**, **Haydock**, Kempton, Wolverhampton
19	Saturday	**Ascot**, **Haydock**, **Huntingdon**, Lingfield, Wolverhampton
20	Sunday	**Exeter**, **Towcester**
21	Monday	**Ffos Las**, **Kempton**, **Ludlow**
22	Tuesday	**Lingfield**, **Sedgefield**, Southwell
23	Wednesday	**Fontwell**, Kempton, Lingfield, **Wetherby**
24	Thursday	Kempton, **Newbury**, **Taunton**, **Uttoxeter**
25	Friday	**Doncaster**, **Musselburgh**, **Newbury**, Wolverhampton
26	Saturday	**Bangor**, **Newbury**, **Newcastle**, **Towcester**, Wolverhampton
27	Sunday	**Carlisle**, **Leicester**
28	Monday	**Ffos Las**, **Folkestone**, Wolverhampton
29	Tuesday	**Ayr**, Lingfield, **Southwell**
30	Wednesday	**Catterick**, **Hereford**, Kempton, **Uttoxeter**

December

1	Thursday	**Leicester**, **Market Rasen**, **Wincanton**, Wolverhampton
2	Friday	**Exeter**, Lingfield, **Sandown**, Wolverhampton
3	Saturday	**Aintree**, **Chepstow**, **Sandown**, **Wetherby**, Wolverhampton
4	Sunday	**Kelso**, **Warwick**
5	Monday	Lingfield, **Musselburgh**, **Plumpton**
6	Tuesday	**Fontwell**, **Sedgefield**, Southwell
7	Wednesday	**Hexham**, Kempton, **Leicester**, Lingfield
8	Thursday	**Huntingdon**, Kempton, **Ludlow**, **Taunton**
9	Friday	**Cheltenham**, **Doncaster**, Southwell, Wolverhampton
10	Saturday	**Cheltenham**, **Doncaster**, **Lingfield**, Southwell, Wolverhampton
11	Sunday	**Hereford**, Southwell
12	Monday	**Fakenham**, Wolverhampton
13	Tuesday	**Catterick**, **Folkestone**, Southwell
14	Wednesday	**Bangor**, Kempton, Lingfield, **Newbury**
15	Thursday	**Exeter**, Kempton, Southwell, **Towcester**
16	Friday	**Ascot**, Southwell, **Uttoxeter**, Wolverhampton
17	Saturday	**Ascot**, **Haydock**, Lingfield, **Newcastle**
18	Sunday	**Carlisle**, Kempton
19	Monday	**Bangor**, **Plumpton**, Wolverhampton
20	Tuesday	Kempton, **Musselburgh**, **Taunton**
21	Wednesday	**Ffos Las**, Kempton, **Ludlow**, Wolverhampton
22	Thursday	**Hereford**, **Sedgefield**, Southwell
26	Monday	**Ffos Las**, **Fontwell**, **Huntingdon**, **Kempton**, **Market Rasen**, **Towcester**, **Wetherby**, **Wincanton**, Wolverhampton
27	Tuesday	**Chepstow**, **Kempton**, Southwell, **Wetherby**
28	Wednesday	**Catterick**, **Leicester**, Lingfield, Wolverhampton
29	Thursday	**Doncaster**, **Kelso**, Kempton, Southwell
30	Friday	**Haydock**, Lingfield, **Taunton**, Wolverhampton
31	Saturday	Lingfield, **Newbury**, **Uttoxeter**, **Warwick**

Big-race dates

April

2 Apr	Doncaster	Lincoln (Heritage Handicap)
13 Apr	Newmarket	Nell Gwyn Stakes (Group 3)
14 Apr	Newmarket	Earl of Sefton Stakes (Group 3)
14 Apr	Newmarket	Craven Stakes (Group 3)
16 Apr	Newbury	Fred Darling Stakes (Group 3)
16 Apr	Newbury	Greenham Stakes (Group 3)
16 Apr	Newbury	John Porter Stakes (Group 3)
24 Apr	Sandown Park	Gordon Richards Stakes (Group 3)
24 Apr	Sandown Park	bet365 Mile (Group 2)
24 Apr	Sandown Park	Classic Trial (Group 3)
27 Apr	Ascot	Sagaro Stakes (Group 3)
30 Apr	Newmarket	2,000 Guineas (Group 1)
30 Apr	Newmarket	Dahlia Stakes (Group 3)

May

1 May	Newmarket	1,000 Guineas (Group 1)
1 May	Newmarket	Jockey Club Stakes (Group 2)
4 May	Chester	Chester Cup (Heritage Handicap)
5 May	Chester	Chester Vase (Group 3)
5 May	Chester	Huxley Stakes (Group 3)
6 May	Chester	Ormonde Stakes (Group 3)
6 May	Chester	Dee Stakes (Group 3)
7 May	Ascot	Victoria Cup (Heritage Handicap)
7 May	Lingfield Park	Derby Trial (Group 3)
11 May	York	Duke of York Stakes (Group 2)
11 May	York	Musidora Stakes (Group 3)
12 May	York	Dante Stakes (Group 2)
12 May	York	Middleton Stakes (Group 3)
13 May	York	Yorkshire Cup (Group 2)
14 May	Newbury	Lockinge Stakes (Group 1)
21 May	Haydock Park	Temple Stakes (Group 2)
26 May	Sandown Park	Henry II Stakes (Group 2)
26 May	Sandown Park	Brigadier Gerard Stakes (Group 3)
28 May	Haydock Park	John Of Gaunt Stakes (Group 3)

June

3 Jun	Epsom	Coronation Cup (Group 1)
3 Jun	Epsom	Oaks (Group 1)
4 Jun	Epsom	The Derby (Group 1)
4 Jun	Epsom	Princess Elizabeth Stakes (Group 3)
14 Jun	Royal Ascot	King's Stand Stakes (Group 1)
14 Jun	Royal Ascot	Queen Anne Stakes (Group 1)
14 Jun	Royal Ascot	St James's Palace Stakes (Group 1)
14 Jun	Royal Ascot	Coventry Stakes (Group 2)
15 Jun	Royal Ascot	Prince of Wales's Stakes (Group 1)
15 Jun	Royal Ascot	Queen Mary Stakes (Group 2)
15 Jun	Royal Ascot	Windsor Forest Stakes (Group 2)
15 Jun	Royal Ascot	Jersey Stakes (Group 3)
15 Jun	Royal Ascot	Royal Hunt Cup (Heritage Handicap)
16 Jun	Royal Ascot	Gold Cup (Group 1)
16 Jun	Royal Ascot	Ribblesdale Stakes (Group 2)
16 Jun	Royal Ascot	Norfolk Stakes (Group 2)

17 Jun	Royal Ascot	Coronation Stakes (Group 1)
17 Jun	Royal Ascot	King Edward VII Stakes (Group 2)
17 Jun	Royal Ascot	Albany Stakes (Group 3)
17 Jun	Royal Ascot	Queen's Vase (Group 3)
18 Jun	Royal Ascot	Golden Jubilee Stakes (Group 1)
18 Jun	Royal Ascot	Hardwicke Stakes (Group 2)
18 Jun	Royal Ascot	Wokingham (Heritage Handicap)
25 Jun	Newcastle	Northumberland Plate (Heritage Handicap)
25 Jun	Newmarket	Criterion Stakes (Group 3)

July

2 Jul	Haydock Park	Lancashire Oaks (Group 2)
2 Jul	Haydock Park	Old Newton Cup (Heritage Handicap)
2 Jul	Sandown Park	Coral-Eclipse Stakes (Group 1)
6 Jul	Newmarket	Falmouth Stakes (Group 1)
6 Jul	Newmarket	Cherry Hinton Stakes (Group 2)
7 Jul	Newmarket	Princess of Wales's Stakes (Group 2)
7 Jul	Newmarket	July Stakes (Group 2)
8 Jul	Newmarket	July Cup (Group 1)
8 Jul	Newmarket	Superlative Stakes (Group 2)
8 Jul	Newmarket	Bunbury Cup (Heritage Handicap)
8 Jul	York	Summer Stakes (Group 3)
9 Jul	Ascot	Summer Mile (Group 2)
9 Jul	York	John Smith's Cup (Heritage Handicap)
11 Jul	Ayr	Giles Insurance Brokers (Heritage Handicap)
16 Jul	Newbury	Weatherbys Super Sprint
23 Jul	Ascot	King George VI and Queen Elizabeth Stakes (Group 1)
23 Jul	Ascot	totesport International (Heritage Handicap)
23 Jul	York	York Stakes (Group 2)
26 Jul	Goodwood	Betfair Cup (registered as the Lennox Stakes) (Group 2)
26 Jul	Goodwood	Gordon Stakes (Group 3)
26 Jul	Goodwood	Molecomb Stakes (Group 3)
27 Jul	Goodwood	Sussex Stakes (Group 1)
27 Jul	Goodwood	Vintage Stakes (Group 2)
28 Jul	Goodwood	Goodwood Cup (Group 2)
28 Jul	Goodwood	King George Stakes (Group 3)
28 Jul	Goodwood	Lillie Langtry Fillies' Stakes (Group 3)
29 Jul	Goodwood	Richmond Stakes (Group 2)
29 Jul	Goodwood	Oak Tree Stakes (Group 3)
29 Jul	Goodwood	totesport Mile (Heritage Handicap)
30 Jul	Goodwood	Nassau Stakes (Group 1)
30 Jul	Goodwood	Stewards' Cup (Heritage Handicap)

August

6 Aug	Ascot	Shergar Cup Day
6 Aug	Haydock Park	Rose of Lancaster Stakes (Group 3)
6 Aug	Newmarket	Sweet Solera Stakes (Group 3)
11 Aug	Salisbury	Sovereign Stakes (Group 3)
13 Aug	Newbury	Hungerford Stakes (Group 2)
13 Aug	Newbury	Geoffrey Freer Stakes (Group 3)
17 Aug	York	Juddmonte International (Group 1)
17 Aug	York	Great Voltigeur Stakes (Group 2)
17 Aug	York	Acomb Stakes (Group 3)
18 Aug	York	Yorkshire Oaks (Group 1)
18 Aug	York	Lowther Stakes (Group 2)
18 Aug	York	Gimcrack Stakes (Group 2)
19 Aug	York	Nunthorpe Stakes (Group 1)

20 Aug	York	Lonsdale Cup (Group 2)
20 Aug	York	Ebor (Heritage Handicap)
20 Aug	Sandown Park	Solario Stakes (Group 3)
27 Aug	Windsor	Winter Hill Stakes (Group 3)
27 Aug	Goodwood	Celebration Mile (Group 2)
27 Aug	Goodwood	Prestige Stakes (Group 3)

September

3 Sep	Haydock Park	Sprint Cup (Group 1)
3 Sep	Kempton Park	Sirenia Stakes (Group 3)
3 Sep	Kempton Park	September Stakes (Group 3)
6 Sep	Goodwood	Supreme Stakes (Group 3)
8 Sep	Doncaster	May Hill Stakes (Group 2)
8 Sep	Doncaster	Park Hill Stakes (Group 2)
9 Sep	Doncaster	Doncaster Cup (Group 2)
9 Sep	Doncaster	Flying Childers Stakes (Group 2)
10 Sep	Doncaster	St Leger (Group 1)
10 Sep	Doncaster	Park Stakes (Group 2)
10 Sep	Doncaster	Champagne Stakes (Group 2)
10 Sep	Doncaster	Portland (Heritage Handicap)
11 Sep	Goodwood	Select Stakes (Group 3)
16 Sep	Newbury	Arc Trial (Group 3)
17 Sep	Ayr	Firth Of Clyde Stakes (Group 3)
17 Sep	Ayr	Ayr Gold Cup (Heritage Handicap)
17 Sep	Newbury	Mill Reef Stakes (Group 2)
17 Sep	Newbury	World Trophy (Group 3)
22 Sep	Newmarket	Somerville Tattersall Stakes (Group 3)
22 Sep	Newmarket	Oh So Sharp Stakes (Group 3)
23 Sep	Newmarket	Joel Stakes (Group 3)
24 Sep	Newmarket	Cheveley Park Stakes (Group 1)
24 Sep	Newmarket	Fillies' Mile (Group 1)
24 Sep	Newmarket	Royal Lodge Stakes (Group 2)
24 Sep	Newmarket	Sun Chariot Stakes (Group 1)
24 Sep	Newmarket	Cambridgeshire (Heritage Handicap)
26 Sep	Ascot	Cumberland Lodge Stakes (Group 3)

October

1 Oct	Ascot	Cumberland Lodge Stakes (Group 3)
1 Oct	Ascot	Bengough Stakes (Group 3)
7 Oct	Newmarket	Cornwallis Stakes (Group 3)
7 Oct	Newmarket	Darley Stakes (Group 3)
8 Oct	Newmarket	Middle Park Stakes (Group 1)
8 Oct	Newmarket	Dewhurst Stakes (Group 1)
8 Oct	Newmarket	Rockfel Stakes (Group 2)
8 Oct	Newmarket	Challenge Stakes (Group 2)
8 Oct	Newmarket	Autumn Stakes (Group 3)
8 Oct	Newmarket	Cesarewitch (Heritage Handicap)
15 Oct	Ascot	Queen Elizabeth II Stakes (Group 1)
15 Oct	Ascot	Champion Stakes (Group 1)
15 Oct	Ascot	Diadem Stakes (Group 2)
15 Oct	Ascot	Pride Stakes (Group 2)
15 Oct	Ascot	Jockey Club Cup (Group 3)
22 Oct	Doncaster	Racing Post Trophy (Group 1)
22 Oct	Newbury	Horris Hill Stakes (Group 3)
22 Oct	Newbury	St Simon Stakes (Group 3)

November

5 Nov	Doncaster	November (Heritage Handicap)

Track Facts

WANT TO size up the layout and undulations of the course where your fancy's about to line up? Over the next 30-odd pages, we bring you three-dimensional maps of all Britain's Flat tracks, allowing you to see at a glance the task facing your selection. The maps come to you courtesy of the *Racing Post*'s website (www.racingpost.com).

We've listed the top dozen trainers and jockeys at each course, ranked by strike-rate, with a breakdown of their relevant statistics over the last five years. The record of favourites is here as well and underline a basic fact of racing – that favourites generally offer very little in the way of value. Market leaders generated a profit (to level stakes of £1) at only four tracks and run up colossal losses on the All-Weather.

We've included addresses, phone numbers, directions and fixture lists for each track, together with Time Test's standard times for all you clock-watchers.

And Graham Wheldon has chipped in with his views on the draw at every course – see page 226. As his analysis has repeatedly shown, most tracks feature a bias of some kind, so check whether the beast on your betting slip is running on the right side before you hand it over.

ASCOT

Ascot, Berkshire SL5 7JX
0870 7227 227

How to get there
Road: M4 junction 6
or M3 junction 3 on
to A332. Rail:
Frequent service
from Reading or
Waterloo
Features RH

2011 Fixtures
April 27, May 6-7,
June 14-18, July 8-9, 22-24, August 6,
September 3, 30, October 1, 15

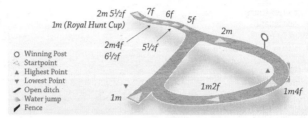

O Winning Post
⌐ Startpoint
▲ Highest Point
▼ Lowest Point
╱ Open ditch
≈ Water jump
╱ Fence

Time Test standard times

5f	58.85	1m2f	2min3.2
6f	1min12.3	1m4f	2min27.8
6f110yds	1min18.7	2m	3min23.5
7f	1min25.2	2m4f	4min18.7
1m (str)	1min37.9	2m5f195yds	4min41
1m (rnd)	1min38.6		

Trainers	Wins-Runs	%	2yo	3yo+	£1 level stks
Sir Michael Stoute	24-140	17	2-7	22-133	-37.49
Mark Johnston	22-227	10	5-35	17-192	-51.62
A P O'Brien	20-117	17	3-30	17-87	-35.37
Richard Hannon	17-259	7	7-112	10-147	-108.38
William Haggas	17-94	18	3-15	14-79	+75.80
Andrew Balding	12-143	8	0-20	12-123	-54.00
Saeed Bin Suroor	12-112	11	4-19	8-93	-8.38
Michael Jarvis	12-82	15	2-18	10-64	-13.04
Michael Bell	12-72	17	2-15	10-57	+45.93
B W Hills	11-130	8	2-28	9-102	-38.50
Brian Meehan	11-117	9	7-38	4-79	+8.18
Mick Channon	10-173	6	6-62	4-111	-38.17
John Gosden	10-91	11	4-18	6-73	-43.25

Jockeys	Wins-Rides	%	£1 level stks	Best Trainer	W-R
Ryan Moore	27-257	11	-122.31	Sir Michael Stoute	20-98
Richard Hughes	26-219	12	-24.01	Richard Hannon	11-116
Richard Hills	25-160	16	+12.95	William Haggas	7-28
Jamie Spencer	23-160	14	+17.71	James Fanshawe	7-24
J Murtagh	23-120	19	+70.77	A P O'Brien	15-56
Frankie Dettori	22-193	11	-56.40	Saeed Bin Suroor	11-77
Jimmy Fortune	20-191	10	-55.75	John Gosden	8-50
William Buick	10-110	9	+28.75	Andrew Balding	4-41
Steve Drowne	10-97	10	+126.50	Hughie Morrison	4-27
Eddie Ahern	9-107	8	-28.00	Gerard Butler	2-8
Michael Hills	9-94	10	-33.27	B W Hills	6-70
Tom Queally	9-81	11	+48.80	Henry Cecil	5-26
Joe Fanning	9-78	12	+0.30	Mark Johnston	8-59

Favourites

2yo	30.9%	-21.30	3yo	31.6%	-2.52	TOTAL	30.2%	-57.00

Whitletts Road Ayr KA8 0JE.
Tel 01292 264 179

AYR

How to get there
Road: south from
Glasgow on A77 or
A75, A70, A76. Rail:
Ayr, bus service
from station on big
race days

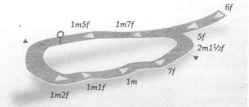

○ Winning Post
⊙ Startpoint
▲ Highest Point
▼ Lowest Point
✓ Open ditch
≋ Water jump
✦ Fence

2011 Fixtures
April 15, May
25-26, June 17-18,
July 3, 11, 18, 25, August 6, 9,
September 15-17, 27, October 6, 29

Time Test standard times

5f	57.7	1m2f	2min4.4
6f	1min9.7	1m2f192yds	2min14.3
7f	1min25	1m5f13yds	2min45.4
7f50yds	1min28	1m7f	3min13.2
1m	1min37.7	2m1f105yds	3min46
1m1f20yds	1min50	2m4f90yds	4min25

Trainers	Wins-Runs	%	2yo	3yo+	£1 level stks
Richard Fahey	44-244	18	16-65	28-179	+10.10
Jim Goldie	35-405	9	0-36	35-369	-130.83
Michael Dods	17-187	9	3-30	14-157	-66.88
Tim Easterby	15-93	16	1-19	14-74	+17.24
Kevin Ryan	14-148	9	7-45	7-103	-52.28
David Nicholls	14-140	10	4-22	10-118	-41.58
Linda Perratt	11-201	5	0-20	11-181	-28.50
Mark Johnston	11-121	9	7-61	4-60	-80.67
I Semple	11-108	10	3-24	8-84	-21.25
David Barron	11-100	11	3-13	8-87	-10.57
Alan Swinbank	11-71	15	5-21	6-50	-19.25
Eric Alston	10-69	14	0-2	10-67	-15.00
Bryan Smart	9-82	11%	7–32	2–50	-19.49

Jockeys	Wins-Rides	%	£1 level stks	Best Trainer	W-R
Paul Hanagan	34-216	16	-33.95	Richard Fahey	27-112
Phillip Makin	28-207	14	+62.62	Michael Dods	10-92
David Allan	23-136	17	-3.21	Tim Easterby	13-67
Tony Hamilton	19-157	12	+4.23	Richard Fahey	6-38
Tom Eaves	18-223	8	-72.13	Bryan Smart	6-58
P J McDonald	17-142	12	+38.88	Alan Swinbank	8-40
Paul Mulrennan	15-156	10	-65.00	Edwin Tuer	2-2
Adrian Nicholls	12-105	11	-27.33	David Nicholls	11-79
Andrew Elliott	11-117	9	-29.62	K R Burke	3-31
Greg Fairley	11-81	14	+4.00	Mark Johnston	3-32
Gary Bartley	10-140	7	-68.50	Jim Goldie	7-111
Graham Gibbons	10-68	15	+2.00	James Bethell	3-6
Royston Ffrench	9-143	6	-92.33	Mark Johnston	4-23

Favourites

2yo	41.9%	-10.33	3yo	31.6%	-9.36	TOTAL	30.6% -56.02

BATH

Lansdown, Bath, Glos BA1 9BU
Tel 01291 622 260

How to get there
Road: M4, Jctn 18,
then A46 south.
Rail: Bath Spa,
special bus service
to course on race
days
Features LH oval,
uphill straight of 4f

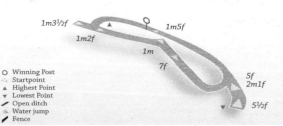

○ Winning Post
⟁ Startpoint
▲ Highest Point
▼ Lowest Point
⟋ Open ditch
⟁ Water jump
⟋ Fence

2011 Fixtures
April 19, 28, May 3, 16, 20, June 3, 11,
22, July 6, 14, 21, 29, August 2, 20, 31,
September 5, 10, 26, October 16

Time Test standard times

5f11yds	1min0.5	1m3f144yds	2min26
5f161yds	1min9	1m5f22yds	2min47.3
1m5yds	1min38	2m1f34yds	3min44
1m2f46yds	2min6.2		

Trainers	Wins-Runs	%	2yo	3yo+	£1 level stks
Mick Channon	28-188	15	14-85	14-103	-58.17
Richard Hannon	19-135	14	11-80	8-55	-44.23
Brian Meehan	18-80	23	13-45	5-35	+12.38
Andrew Balding	15-95	16	4-23	11-72	-2.04
Ronald Harris	14-186	8	2-32	12-154	-82.50
David Evans	14-141	10	3-41	11-100	-19.00
Andrew Haynes	14-123	11	1-31	13-92	+8.25
Milton Bradley	13-191	7	0-7	13-184	-84.92
Roger Charlton	12-47	26	4-14	8-33	+7.52
Mark Johnston	11-40	28	3-17	8-23	-2.08
B W Hills	10-52	19	2-18	8-34	-10.93
Peter Makin	10-48	21	1-11	9-37	+6.13
Ron Hodges	9-141	6	0-14	9-127	-96.59

Jockeys	Wins-Rides	%	£1 level stks	Best Trainer	W-R
Liam Keniry	21-142	15	-13.04	Andrew Balding	7-20
Martin Dwyer	19-84	23	+30.64	Brian Meehan	8-15
Chris Catlin	17-164	10	-81.27	Mick Channon	4-29
Steve Drowne	17-163	10	-61.37	Hughie Morrison	5-18
David Probert	16-130	12	-0.50	Bryn Palling	4-14
Seb Sanders	15-89	17	-0.28	Ralph Beckett	2-16
Tadhg O'Shea	15-83	18	+1.38	Denis Coakley	4-16
Dane O'Neill	13-126	10	-10.78	Henry Candy	2-16
Jim Crowley	13-117	11	-15.88	Amanda Perrett	4-19
Richard Hughes	13-84	15	-25.64	Richard Hannon	5-36
Darryll Holland	13-66	20	+0.10	Mick Channon	6-16
Tom McLaughlin	12-93	13	-32.50	Malcolm Saunders	5-40
Eddie Ahern	12-53	23	+15.38	Brian Meehan	3-8

Favourites

2yo	43.9% +8.90	3yo	33%	-19.63	TOTAL 34.5% -35.67

York Road, Beverley, E Yorkshire
HU17 8QZ. Tel 01482 86/ 488

BEVERLEY

How to get there
Road: Course is
signposted from the
M62. Rail: Beverley,
bus service to
course on race days
Features RH,
uphill finish

2011 Fixtures
April 6, 14, May 2,
10, 25, 28, June 8, 16, 21, July 1-2, 12,
18, 26, August 10-11, 27-28, September
14, 20

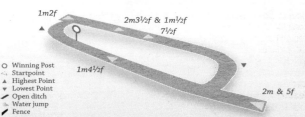

1m2f
2m3½f & 1m½f
7½f
1m4½f
2m & 5f

O Winning Post
◁ Startpoint
▲ Highest Point
▼ Lowest Point
✐ Open ditch
⊾ Water jump
✐ Fence

Time Test standard times

5f	1min0.5	1m3f216yds	2min30.6
7f100yds	1min29.5	1m4f16yds	2min32
1m100yds	1min42.4	2m35yds	3min29.5
1m1f207yds	2min0	2m3f100yds	4min16.7

Trainers	Wins-Runs	%	2yo	3yo+	£1 level stks
Richard Fahey	37-265	14	9-56	28-209	-84.41
Mark Johnston	35-149	23	12-40	23-109	+17.83
Tim Easterby	23-269	9	3-76	20-193	-139.76
Kevin Ryan	18-129	14	6-45	12-84	-35.30
Paul Midgley	13-172	8	1-43	12-129	-85.65
Bryan Smart	13-95	14	5-29	8-66	+44.10
John Quinn	12-133	9	1-25	11-108	-48.88
Richard Whitaker	12-97	12	3-17	9-80	-18.63
Mick Channon	12-70	17	6-29	6-41	+30.16
Michael Dods	12-68	18	0-6	12-62	-1.92
Ann Duffield	10-97	10	5-35	5-62	-8.92
Brian Ellison	10-88	11	1-10	9-78	+4.91
David Nicholls	10-84	12	0-11	10-73	+4.50

Jockeys	Wins-Rides	%	£1 level stks	Best Trainer	W-R
Paul Hanagan	35-238	15	-74.27	Richard Fahey	21-129
Silvestre De Sousa	19-138	14	-48.28	Mel Brittain	4-5
Graham Gibbons	18-165	11	-43.72	Tim Walford	5-18
David Allan	18-165	11	-49.38	Tim Easterby	15-113
Joe Fanning	18-116	16	+10.02	Mark Johnston	12-58
Neil Callan	17-86	20	-4.25	Kevin Ryan	4-32
Phillip Makin	16-120	13	+5.20	Michael Dods	8-29
Tony Hamilton	15-160	9	-72.91	Ollie Pears	5-8
Royston Ffrench	15-150	10	-58.15	Mark Johnston	5-21
Franny Norton	14-95	15	+75.41	Richard Hannon	2-3
Robert Winston	12-81	15	-8.79	Alan Swinbank	3-7
Tom Eaves	11-179	6	-41.00	Bryan Smart	3-48
Paul Mulrennan	11-168	7	-104.26	Kevin Ryan	4-16

Favourites

2yo	39.3%	-13.19	3yo	37.7%	-15.10	TOTAL 35.6%	-17.46

BRIGHTON

Freshfield Road, Brighton, E Sussex
BN2 2XZ. Tel 01273 603 580

How to get there
Road: Signposted
from A23
London Road and
A27. Rail: Brighton,
bus to course on
race days
Features LH,
undulating and
sharp

○ Winning Post
↖ Startpoint
▲ Highest Point
▼ Lowest Point
⟋ Open ditch
⟍ Water jump
⟋ Fence

2011 Fixtures April 15, 28, May 9, 17,
26-27, June 14, 21, 28, July 4, 12,
August 3-5, 16, 26, September 2, 12,
October 13, 20

Time Test standard times

5f59yds	59.5	7f214yds	1min32
5f213yds	1min7.5	1m1f209yds	1min57.5
6f209yds	1min19.6	1m3f196yds	2min26

Trainers	Wins-Runs	%	2yo	3yo+	£1 level stks
Richard Hannon	18-72	25	11-44	7-28	+23.54
Mick Channon	15-142	11	10-56	5-86	-66.16
Jeremy Noseda	15-30	50	2-9	13-21	+21.06
David Evans	14-100	14	1-8	13-92	-21.38
Gary Moore	13-143	9	2-19	11-124	-80.70
Simon Dow	12-64	19	0-5	12-59	+9.20
David Simcock	12-41	29	2-7	10-34	+12.56
Hughie Morrison	11-46	24	1-7	10-39	+54.68
Sir Mark Prescott	11-38	29	3-14	8-24	-2.10
Mark Johnston	11-36	31	5-16	6-20	+39.07
Andrew Haynes	10-121	8	1-15	9-106	-54.19
Jim Best	10-32	31	0-0	10-32	+62.00
Ronald Harris	9-104	9	0-8	9-96	-36.13

Jockeys	Wins-Rides	%	£1 level stks	Best Trainer	W-R
Seb Sanders	34-163	21	-31.75	Sir Mark Prescott	9-25
Jim Crowley	22-177	12	-28.23	Patrick Chamings	4-14
Chris Catlin	21-163	13	-15.33	Peter Hiatt	5-23
Ryan Moore	20-73	27	-8.85	Jeremy Noseda	4-6
Paul Doe	19-72	26	+133.63	Jim Best	5-8
Liam Keniry	14-134	10	-57.90	Alan Coogan	3-6
George Baker	14-123	11	-62.00	Patrick Chamings	3-13
Neil Callan	14-56	25	+28.00	Gay Kelleway	3-5
Richard Hughes	13-58	22	+4.65	Richard Hannon	8-20
David Probert	12-108	11	+1.00	Sylvester Kirk	2-5
Fergus Sweeney	12-103	12	-12.75	Tony Newcombe	2-5
Liam Jones	12-51	24	+51.49	William Haggas	6-10
Steve Drowne	10-81	12	-34.69	Andrew Haynes	3-10

Favourites

2yo	43.8% +1.17	3yo	39% -4.47	TOTAL	35.2% -24.76

Durdar Road, Carlisle, Cumbria,
CA2 4IS. Tel 01228 554 700

CARLISLE

How to get there
Road: M6 Jctn 42,
follow signs on
Dalston Road. Rail:
Carlisle, 66 bus to
course on race days
Features RH,
undulating, uphill
finish

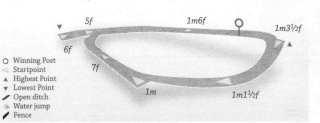

O Winning Post
⊙ Startpoint
▲ Highest Point
▼ Lowest Point
╱ Open ditch
≈ Water jump
╱ Fence

2011 Fixtures
May 23, 30, June 13, 22, July 2, 24,
August 1, 17, 25, 31, September 7

Time Test standard times

5f	59.6	1m1f61yds	1min55
5f193yds	1min11.8	1m3f107yds	2min23
6f192yds	1min24.7	1m6f32yds	2min59.2
7f200yds	1min37.6	2m1f52yds	3min42

Trainers	Wins-Runs	%	2yo	3yo+	£1 level stks
Richard Fahey	21-122	17	4-32	17-90	-6.63
Tim Easterby	16-92	17	2-17	14-75	+9.00
Kevin Ryan	10-50	20	4-17	6-33	+49.98
Alan Swinbank	8-80	10	1-15	7-65	-0.84
Bryan Smart	8-34	24	4-12	4-22	+10.75
David Nicholls	7-53	13	0-10	7-43	-9.84
Michael Dods	6-70	9	2-9	4-61	-20.30
Brian Ellison	6-44	14	0-2	6-42	+13.95
Howard Johnson	6-42	14	4-13	2-29	-5.19
K R Burke	6-37	16	3-11	3-26	+58.00
Jim Goldie	5-52	10	0-2	5-50	-9.00
Ann Duffield	5-45	11	3-16	2-29	+27.38
Mark Johnston	5-41	12	2-14	3-27	-27.05

Jockeys	Wins-Rides	%	£1 level stks	Best Trainer	W-R
Paul Hanagan	21-109	19	-9.41	Richard Fahey	14-69
David Allan	17-92	18	+0.09	Tim Easterby	13-59
Royston Ffrench	11-74	15	+56.88	Ann Duffield	4-20
Phillip Makin	9-87	10	+15.20	Michael Dods	4-32
P J McDonald	8-70	11	-17.47	Alan Swinbank	5-34
Tom Eaves	7-97	7	-50.00	Bryan Smart	3-19
Jamie Moriarty	7-44	16	+7.50	Ollie Pears	2-3
Tony Hamilton	6-97	6	-53.63	Richard Fahey	3-17
Paul Mulrennan	6-81	7	-46.05	Howard Johnson	4-10
Andrew Elliott	6-59	10	+12.38	John Weymes	2-7
Graham Gibbons	6-49	12	+16.00	Brian Baugh	1-1
Adrian Nicholls	5-44	11	-5.50	David Nicholls	3-31
Neil Brown	5-35	14	+54.00	Bruce Mactaggart	1-1

Favourites

2yo	40.5%	+0.19	3yo	32.3%	-9.54	TOTAL	27.6%	-48.65

CATTERICK

Catterick Bridge, Richmond, N Yorks
DL10 7PE. Tel 01748 811 478

How to get there
Road: A1, exit 5m
south of Scotch
Corner. Rail:
Darlington or
Northallerton and
bus
Features: LH,
undulating, tight

O Winning Post
⌐ Startpoint
▲ Highest Point
▼ Lowest Point
✓ Open ditch
🔺 Water jump
✦ Fence

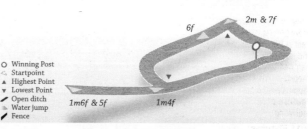

2011 Fixtures
March 30, April 13, May 3, 20, 28, June
3, 29, July 6, 13, 20, August 2, 12, 24,
September 17, October 4, 15, 25

Time Test standard times

5f	57.5	1m3f214yds	2min31
5f212yds	1min10.5	1m5f175yds	2min55.3
7f	1min23.2	1m7f177yds	3min21.2

Trainers	Wins-Runs	%	2yo	3yo+	£1 level stks
Mark Johnston	28-130	22	12-53	16-77	-2.61
David Nicholls	26-141	18	3-24	23-117	+30.92
Tim Easterby	23-187	12	8-46	15-141	-46.87
Kevin Ryan	16-118	14	7-38	9-80	-22.17
Richard Fahey	16-116	14	8-45	8-71	-39.26
Geoffrey Harker	14-67	21	1-8	13-59	+31.38
John Quinn	12-112	11	4-22	8-90	-45.33
Mick Channon	12-61	20	6-38	6-23	-2.51
Ann Duffield	11-109	10	5-41	6-68	-30.50
Brian Ellison	11-68	16	0-4	11-64	-6.70
D W Barker	10-96	10	0-10	10-86	+46.60
Alan Swinbank	9-88	10	1-11	8-77	-20.63
Paul Green	9-40	23	1-3	8-37	+51.83

Jockeys	Wins-Rides	%	£1 level stks	Best Trainer	W-R
Silvestre De Sousa	36-169	21	+142.36	Geoffrey Harker	10-41
Greg Fairley	30-164	18	+12.59	Mark Johnston	18-82
Paul Hanagan	25-171	15	-18.50	Richard Fahey	7-43
Paul Mulrennan	19-164	12	-24.33	Howard Johnson	5-14
David Allan	19-161	12	-44.87	Tim Easterby	15-97
Tom Eaves	15-192	8	-76.07	Brian Ellison	3-13
Adrian Nicholls	15-88	17	-14.71	David Nicholls	15-67
Graham Gibbons	13-108	12	+102.95	John Quinn	4-34
P J McDonald	12-147	8	-40.42	Alan Swinbank	4-45
Tony Hamilton	12-129	9	-38.88	D W Barker	5-34
Duran Fentiman	12-127	9	+14.00	Tim Easterby	4-45
Phillip Makin	10-121	8	-49.13	Michael Dods	5-32
Jamie Moriarty	9-67	13	-5.20	Richard Fahey	3-17

Favourites

2yo	42%	+3.76		3yo	32.2%	-19.83	
					TOTAL	34.4%	-35.68

Chepstow, Monmouthshire,
NP16 6BE. Tel 01291 622 260

CHEPSTOW

How to get there
Road: M4 Jct 22 on
west side of Severn
Bridge, A48 north,
then A446. Rail:
Chepstow, bus to
course on race days
Features LH,
undulating

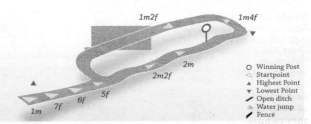

2011 Fixtures
May 2, 24, 30, June 10, 20, 29, July 8,
22, August 4, 11, 24, 29, September 2,
8, 27

Time Test standard times

5f16yds	57	1m4f23yds	2min31.3
6f16yds	1min8.8	2m49yds	3min28
7f16yds	1min20.5	2m1f40yds	3min41
1m14yds	1min32.6	2m2f	3min52
1m2f36yds	2min4.2		

Trainers	Wins-Runs	%	2yo	3yo+	£1 level stks
Richard Hannon	14-88	16	7-33	7-55	-25.81
David Evans	12-154	8	3-36	9-118	-44.39
Bryn Palling	11-113	10	1-16	10-97	+41.67
Ralph Beckett	11-46	24	4-14	7-32	+34.31
Ronald Harris	10-141	7	3-15	7-126	-51.00
Tony Carroll	10-106	9	0-3	10-103	-45.29
Rod Millman	10-80	13	2-11	8-69	-15.50
Milton Bradley	7-164	4	0-4	7-160	-111.25
Malcolm Saunders	7-31	23	1-3	6-28	+64.07
John Spearing	7-26	27	2-3	5-23	+13.75
Mark Johnston	7-23	30	1-9	6-14	+10.75
J S Moore	6-41	15	1-14	5-27	+13.00
Stuart Kittow	5-45	11	1-4	4-41	-10.75

Jockeys	Wins-Rides	%	£1 level stks	Best Trainer	W-R
Richard Hughes	12-46	26	+13.46	Richard Hannon	5-19
Tom McLaughlin	11-62	18	+50.25	Malcolm Saunders	4-10
Luke Morris	9-102	9	+22.00	J S Moore	3-10
David Probert	9-81	11	-19.67	Andrew Balding	3-13
Jim Crowley	9-53	17	+4.35	Ralph Beckett	5-10
Seb Sanders	9-39	23	+15.41	Tony Carroll	2-8
Fergus Sweeney	8-87	9	-32.50	Stuart Kittow	4-17
Cathy Gannon	7-75	9	+42.00	Bryn Palling	2-28
Chris Catlin	7-70	10	-24.50	David Simcock	1-1
Eddie Ahern	7-43	16	-6.07	Andrew Price	2-3
Kirsty Milczarek	7-31	23	+36.00	Tony Carroll	4-7
Steve Drowne	6-62	10	-19.83	Bryn Palling	2-4
Dane O'Neill	6-56	11	-1.63	N A Callaghan	2-2

Favourites

2yo	43.5% -0.41		3yo	30.3% -24.27		TOTAL	29.1% -56.74

CHESTER

Steam Mill Street, Chester, CH1 2LY
Tel 01244 304 600

How to get there
Road: Join Inner
Ring Road and A458
Queensferry Road.
Rail: Chester
General, bus to city
centre
Features LH, flat,
almost circular

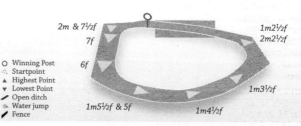

O Winning Post
⌐ Startpoint
▲ Highest Point
▼ Lowest Point
✔ Open ditch
≈ Water jump
✔ Fence

2011 Fixtures
May 4-6, 21, June 11, 24-25, July 8-9,
31, August 20, September 8-10, 24

Time Test standard times

5f16yds	59.8	1m3f79yds	2min22.7
6f18yds	1min13	1m4f66yds	2min35
7f2yds	1min24.7	1m5f89yds	2min48.6
7f122yds	1min31.2	1m7f195yds	3min22
1m1f70yds	1min55	2m2f147yds	4min1
1m2f75yds	2min8		

Trainers	Wins-Runs	%	2yo	3yo+	£1 level stks
Mark Brisbourne	14-151	9	3-22	11-129	-12.75
Richard Fahey	14-129	11	2-25	12-104	-15.42
Mark Johnston	14-109	13	1-16	13-93	-30.25
B W Hills	14-91	15	5-22	9-69	-33.12
Sir Michael Stoute	13-52	25	0-2	13-50	-13.23
Kevin Ryan	12-84	14	4-24	8-60	+6.50
David Evans	10-130	8	5-38	5-92	-19.77
Mick Channon	10-70	14	6-30	4-40	-8.64
Richard Hannon	9-47	19	7-26	2-21	-10.71
Mark H Tompkins	9-37	24	1-8	8-29	+2.31
Andrew Balding	8-37	22	0-1	8-36	+21.95
William Haggas	7-18	39	3-5	4-13	+10.00
David Nicholls	6-93	6	2-8	4-85	-67.00

Jockeys	Wins-Rides	%	£1 level stks	Best Trainer	W-R
Franny Norton	17-124	14	-9.17	Alan Bailey	4-16
Richard Mullen	12-59	20	+14.24	Bryan Smart	2-3
Eddie Ahern	12-45	27	+50.73	Donald McCain	1-1
William Buick	11-51	22	+20.63	John Gosden	3-5
J-P Guillambert	10-66	15	-13.63	Mark Johnston	7-27
Paul Mulrennan	10-57	18	+9.16	Ann Duffield	1-1
Liam Jones	10-52	19	+42.75	Mark Brisbourne	5-27
Pat Cosgrave	10-49	20	+45.57	Jim Boyle	2-2
Silvestre De Sousa	9-63	14	-2.00	Paul Green	4-16
Richard Hills	9-30	30	+7.04	Sir Michael Stoute	3-5
Jamie Spencer	8-52	15	-10.68	David Barron	1-1
Ryan Moore	8-33	24	-10.15	Sir Michael Stoute	6-23
Stevie Donohoe	7-77	9	-40.77	Ed McMahon	2-3

Favourites

2yo	39.2% -12.93		3yo	42.7% +28.48		TOTAL	34.6%	-4.90

Grand Stand, Leger Way, Doncaster
DN2 6BB. Tel 01302 320066/7

DONCASTER

How to get there
Road: M18 Jct 3,
A638, A18 to Hull.
Rail: Doncaster
Central
Features: LH, flat

2011 Fixtures
April 2-3, 16, 29-30,
May 14, June 3-4,
12, 24-25, July 1, 7,
14, 21, 30, August 13, September 7-10,
October 21-22, November 5

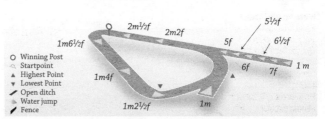

O Winning Post
⊙ Startpoint
▲ Highest Point
▼ Lowest Point
✔ Open ditch
▶ Water jump
✦ Fence

Time Test standard times

5f	58.7	1m (Rnd)	1min 37.2
5f140yds	1min7.4	1m2f60yds	2min6
6f	1min11.5	1m4f	2min30
6f110yds	1min18	1m6f132yds	3min3
7f	1min24.3	2m110yds	3min32
1m (Str)	1min36.8	2m2f	3min53

Trainers	*Wins-Runs*	%	*2yo*	*3yo+*	*£1 level stks*
Richard Fahey	24-241	10	9-59	15-182	-60.27
Richard Hannon	23-134	17	10-75	13-59	+64.08
John Gosden	20-94	21	4-34	16-60	+19.87
B W Hills	19-154	12	9-72	10-82	-32.51
Mark Johnston	18-168	11	6-62	12-106	-59.32
Michael Jarvis	17-78	22	6-25	11-53	+5.37
Jeremy Noseda	15-70	21	5-15	10-55	+9.95
Sir Michael Stoute	13-70	19	3-19	10-51	-4.41
Luca Cumani	13-59	22	0-7	13-52	+14.58
Saeed Bin Suroor	12-77	16	8-23	4-54	-26.60
Henry Cecil	11-38	29	5-15	6-23	+32.00
Tim Easterby	10-136	7	1-43	9-93	-54.50
William Haggas	10-64	16	2-20	8-44	-27.15

Jockeys	*Wins-Rides*	%	*£1 level stks*	*Best Trainer*	*W-R*
Ryan Moore	26-115	23	+21.96	Richard Hannon	10-27
Paul Hanagan	22-194	11	2.68	Richard Fahey	13-122
Jamie Spencer	18-133	14	-1.17	Michael Bell	3-22
William Buick	18-81	22	+30.03	John Gosden	6-16
Frankie Dettori	16-92	17	-27.77	Saeed Bin Suroor	9-39
Joe Fanning	12-125	10	+16.35	Mark Johnston	7-75
Kieren Fallon	12-76	16	-13.76	Luca Cumani	5-16
Neil Callan	11-166	7	-92.45	Michael Jarvis	2-14
Tom Queally	11-87	13	+22.67	Henry Cecil	6-17
Ted Durcan	11-80	14	-0.20	Henry Cecil	3-9
Philip Robinson	11-67	16	+15.70	Michael Jarvis	9-40
Jimmy Quinn	10-104	10	-14.59	Harry Dunlop	2-5
David Allan	10-101	10	+8.00	Tim Easterby	7-68

Favourites

2yo	38.3%	+0.54	3yo	26.8%	-45.34	TOTAL 30.5% -62.05

EPSOM

Epsom Downs, Surrey, KT18 5LQ
Tel 01372 726 311

How to get there
Road: M25 Jct 8
(A217) or 9 (A24),
2m south of Epsom
on B290
Rail: Epsom and
bus, Epsom Downs
or Tattenham Corner
Features LH, un-
dulating, downhill 5f

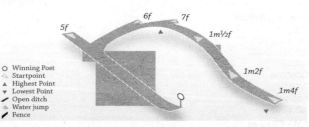

○ Winning Post
◁ Startpoint
▲ Highest Point
▼ Lowest Point
✔ Open ditch
≋ Water jump
✔ Fence

2011 Fixtures April 20, June 3-4, 30,
July 7, 14, 21, 28, August 18, 28-29,
September 8, 25

Time Test standard times

5f	53.8	1m114yds	1min41.6
6f	1min8	1m2f18yds	2min3.5
7f	1min20.2	1m4f10yds	2min33.6

Trainers	Wins-Runs	%	2yo	3yo+	£1 level stks
Andrew Balding	11-42	26	6-12	5-30	+39.45
Mark Johnston	10-86	12	2-17	8-69	-39.10
Richard Hannon	9-83	11	3-27	6-56	-46.53
Saeed Bin Suroor	9-32	28	3-8	6-24	-5.34
Pat Phelan	7-43	16	0-8	7-35	-13.00
Mick Channon	6-74	8	3-27	3-47	-18.75
Sir Mark Prescott	6-12	50	1-3	5-9	+11.23
Simon Dow	5-37	14	0-0	5-37	-0.50
Sir Michael Stoute	5-23	22	0-0	5-23	+1.63
Ralph Beckett	5-23	22	1-4	4-19	+36.00
Gary Moore	4-42	10	0-1	4-41	-18.00
David Evans	4-26	15	1-5	3-21	-8.00
Henry Cecil	4-24	17	0-3	4-21	+0.20

Jockeys	Wins-Rides	%	£1 level stks	Best Trainer	W-R
Seb Sanders	12-40	30	+86.35	Sir Mark Prescott	5-6
Ryan Moore	10-49	20	+9.20	Sir Michael Stoute	3-13
Frankie Dettori	8-47	17	-21.42	Saeed Bin Suroor	6-18
Jim Crowley	7-41	17	+17.42	John Gallagher	2-5
David Probert	6-27	22	+7.75	Andrew Balding	4-13
Jack Mitchell	6-26	23	+32.85	Stuart Williams	2-2
Richard Hughes	5-57	9	-33.55	Richard Hannon	3-33
Ian Mongan	5-43	12	-24.30	Pat Phelan	2-16
Jimmy Fortune	5-35	14	+0.95	Andrew Balding	3-8
Tom Queally	5-35	14	+13.50	Simon Dow	2-4
Darryll Holland	5-27	19	+8.50	Conor Dore	1-1
Kieren Fallon	5-13	38	+19.00	Mark Johnston	4-7
Alan Munro	4-35	11	-11.17	Chris Wall	3-8

Favourites

2yo	34.3% -5.44	3yo	34.5% -5.97	TOTAL 33%	-27.17

Trimsaran, Carmarthenshire, SA17 4DE
Tel: 01554 811092

FFOS LAS

How to get there
Road: M4 Jctn 48
and follow the
A4138 to Llanelli.
Rail: Llanelli,
Kidwelly or
Carmarthen
Features LH, flat,
galloping

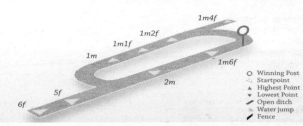

○ Winning Post
◁ Startpoint
▲ Highest Point
▼ Lowest Point
✔ Open ditch
≈ Water jump
✔ Fence

2011 Fixtures
May 5, July 11, 28, August 2, 9, 26,
September 11, 26, November 4

Time Test standard times

5f	56.1	1m2f	2min1.7
6f	1min7.4	1m4f	2min29
1m	1min38	1m6f	2min54
1m1f	1min49.7	2m	3min23

Trainers	Wins-Runs	%	2yo	3yo+	£1 level stks
Mark Johnston	7-29	24	1-4	6-25	+1.50
David Simcock	6-18	33	0-3	6-15	+8.91
David Evans	5-32	16	3-11	2-21	-1.51
William Haggas	4-9	44	3-3	1-6	+8.71
Richard Hannon	3-20	15	0-9	3-11	-5.89
Brian Meehan	3-11	27	1-5	2-6	+2.40
David Nicholls	3-3	100	0-0	3-3	+16.92
Rod Millman	2-21	10	1-5	1-16	-10.75
B W Hills	2-18	11	2-6	0-12	-12.59
William Knight	2-12	17	0-2	2-10	-4.25
Hughie Morrison	2-11	18	0-1	2-10	+1.00
Roger Charlton	2-10	20	2-5	0-5	-6.07
Ralph Beckett	2-9	22	1-4	1-5	+2.00

Jockeys	Wins-Rides	%	£1 level stks	Best Trainer	W-R
Joe Fanning	6-18	33	+8.63	Mark Johnston	4-12
Tadhg O'Shea	6-15	40	+128.25	John Gallagher	2-4
Cathy Gannon	5-24	21	-7.51	David Evans	3-16
Richard Hughes	5-21	24	-2.14	Patrick Morris	1-1
David Probert	4-31	13	-9.00	Chris Dwyer	1-1
Martin Lane	4-22	18	+35.50	David Simcock	2-9
Steve Drowne	4-21	19	-5.57	Roger Charlton	2-6
Shane Kelly	4-17	24	-2.84	William Knight	2-6
Martin Dwyer	4-12	33	+9.40	Brian Meehan	3-5
Jim Crowley	2-18	11	-7.00	Ralph Beckett	2-7
Royston Ffrench	2-9	22	+3.00	Brian Ellison	1-1
Andrew Heffernan	2-8	25	+4.00	Bernard Llewellyn	2-3
Liam Keniry	2-7	29	+19.50	J S Moore	1-1

Favourites

2yo	30%	-6.17		3yo	42.1%	+4.37		TOTAL	35.3%	-5.23

FOLKESTONE

Westenhanger, Hythe, Kent,
CT21 4HX. Tel 01303 266 407

How to get there
Road: M20 Jctn 11,
A20 south.
Rail: Westenhanger
from Charing Cross
or Victoria
Features RH,
sharp turns

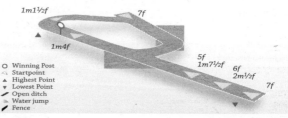

○ Winning Post
⊸ Startpoint
▲ Highest Point
▼ Lowest Point
╱ Open ditch
≈ Water jump
╱ Fence

2011 Fixtures
April 4, 12, 21, May
26, June 6, 24, July 7, 21, August 4, 17,
21, 31, September 13, 20

Time Test standard times

5f	58.6	1m1f149yds	2min0.2
6f	1min11	1m4f	2min33.6
6f189yds (rnd)	1min21.8	1m7f92yds	3min19.4
7f (str)	1min24	2m93yds	3min32.7

Trainers	Wins-Runs	%	2yo	3yo+	£1 level stks
Richard Hannon	15-68	22	9-28	6-40	-4.88
John Dunlop	13-48	27	6-21	7-27	+20.18
Mick Channon	12-106	11	3-40	9-66	+24.33
Luca Cumani	10-31	32	1-9	9-22	+15.77
John Best	8-106	8	2-29	6-77	-53.50
William Muir	8-39	21	0-6	8-33	+16.63
B W Hills	8-30	27	2-6	6-24	+9.26
Rod Millman	8-28	29	0-5	8-23	+21.87
Jim Boyle	7-55	13	0-10	7-45	-17.63
Brendan Powell	7-46	15	0-11	7-35	+5.83
Jamie Osborne	7-25	28	2-6	5-19	-3.65
Hughie Morrison	7-23	30	0-0	7-23	+6.88
John Jenkins	6-64	9	0-13	6-51	-38.00

Jockeys	Wins-Rides	%	£1 level stks	Best Trainer	W-R
Richard Hughes	19-60	32	-3.12	Richard Hannon	9-26
Steve Drowne	15-93	16	+1.53	Hughie Morrison	7-12
Seb Sanders	15-93	16	-25.51	Brendan Powell	2-3
Dane O'Neill	13-77	17	-20.11	Henry Candy	4-11
Jim Crowley	12-96	13	-50.84	Amanda Perrett	3-29
Ian Mongan	11-68	16	+41.10	Harry Dunlop	2-5
Alan Munro	11-47	23	+0.13	Peter Chapple-Hyam	3-7
Tom Queally	10-62	16	+9.78	Simon Dow	2-2
Liam Keniry	9-68	13	+23.60	Andrew Balding	3-9
Darryll Holland	9-60	15	+5.88	Rod Millman	2-3
Eddie Ahern	9-60	15	-6.38	John Dunlop	6-9
Richard Hills	9-18	50	+6.22	B W Hills	3-3
Chris Catlin	8-93	9	-27.38	B W Hills	1-1

Favourites

2yo	40.5%	-8.56	3yo	40.4%	-6.07	TOTAL	38.5%	+1.98

Chichester, W Sussex,
PO18 OPS. Tel 01243 755 022

GOODWOOD

How to get there

Road: signposted
from A27 south and
A285 north
Rail: Chichester, bus
to course on race
days
Features RH,
undulating

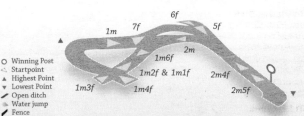

○ Winning Post
◁ Startpoint
▲ Highest Point
▼ Lowest Point
✦ Open ditch
≋ Water jump
✦ Fence

2011 Fixtures

April 30, May 5, 18, 21, 30, June 3, 10,
17, 24, July 26-30, August 11, 27-28,
30, September 10-11, 21

Time Test standard times

5f	56.4	1m3f	2min20
6f	1min10	1m4f	2min32.7
7f	1min24.4	1m6f	2min59
1m	1min36.8	2m	3min22
1m1f	1min52	2m4f	4min13
1m1f192yds	2min2.2	2m5f	4min27.3

Trainers	Wins-Runs	%	2yo	3yo+	£1 level stks
Richard Hannon	60-417	14	38-190	22-227	-35.38
Sir Michael Stoute	27-113	24	1-11	26-102	+21.39
Mark Johnston	25-161	16	4-38	21-123	+78.70
Luca Cumani	20-89	22	2-6	18-83	+5.70
Mick Channon	19-271	7	6-108	13-163	-61.25
John Dunlop	17-157	11	4-46	13-111	-22.17
Amanda Perrett	17-146	12	2-30	15-116	-13.88
Saeed Bin Suroor	16-112	14	5-22	11-90	-53.68
John Gosden	15-117	13	2-22	13-95	-39.51
Brian Meehan	15-104	14	9-42	6-62	-14.77
Jeremy Noseda	14-68	21	3-9	11-59	-4.64
Clive Cox	12-105	11	3-22	9-83	-7.58
Gary Moore	10-164	6	0-19	10-145	-92.75

Jockeys	Wins-Rides	%	£1 level stks	Best Trainer	W-R
Ryan Moore	49-236	21	+23.30	Sir Michael Stoute	18-70
Richard Hughes	41-273	15	-46.99	Richard Hannon	32-172
Frankie Dettori	26-169	15	-78.98	Saeed Bin Suroor	11-75
Jimmy Fortune	23-183	13	-22.55	John Gosden	7-57
Jim Crowley	22-237	9	-48.79	Amanda Perrett	9-84
George Baker	18-110	16	+5.25	Gary Moore	5-36
Tom Queally	16-110	15	+81.03	Henry Cecil	7-27
Darryll Holland	16-106	15	+14.00	Mick Channon	5-32
Dane O'Neill	14-158	9	-7.75	Luca Cumani	4-15
Seb Sanders	14-130	11	-30.91	John Dunlop	2-7
Pat Dobbs	14-115	12	-41.57	Richard Hannon	10-64
Jamie Spencer	14-94	15	-16.80	James Fanshawe	3-6
Martin Dwyer	13-187	7	-107.92	Brian Meehan	3-22

Favourites

2yo	36.1% +0.68	3yo	33.7% -11.18	TOTAL	29.9% -63.03

HAMILTON

Bothwell Road, Hamilton, Lanarkshire
ML3 0DW. Tel 01698 283 806

How to get there
Road: M74 Jct 5, off
the A74. Rail:
Hamilton West
Features RH,
undulating, dip can
become testing in
wet weather

2011 Fixtures
May 1, 6, 13, June
2, 8, 15, 23, 28, July 9, 14-15, 30,
August 18, 22, 26, September 18-19, 26

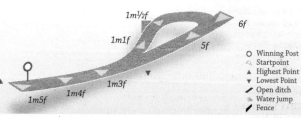

Time Test standard times

5f4yds	58.2	1m1f36yds	1min54.3
5f200yds	1min9.2	1m3f16yds	2min19.2
6f5yds	1min10	1m4f17yds	2min32.2
1m65yds	1min43.5	1m5f9yds	2min45.4

Trainers	Wins-Runs	%	2yo	3yo+	£1 level stks
Mark Johnston	44-192	23	14-48	30-144	+22.00
Richard Fahey	42-193	22	8-33	34-160	+4.35
Kevin Ryan	24-125	19	6-34	18-91	+3.09
Jim Goldie	21-201	10	0-3	21-198	-63.25
Linda Perratt	19-246	8	0-4	19-242	-68.00
Bryan Smart	18-76	24	5-22	13-54	-6.18
David Nicholls	16-76	21	2-7	14-69	-6.58
I Semple	12-153	8	0-15	12-138	-78.05
Sir Mark Prescott	12-25	48	1-2	11-23	+9.23
Alan Swinbank	11-86	13	0-5	11-81	-13.75
Michael Dods	11-59	19	0-2	11-57	-7.59
K R Burke	9-59	15	5-19	4-40	-28.09
Mick Channon	9-57	16	5-19	4-38	-18.11

Jockeys	Wins-Rides	%	£1 level stks	Best Trainer	W-R
Paul Hanagan	37-160	23	+31.17	Richard Fahey	27-87
Tom Eaves	30-245	12	-102.90	Bryan Smart	9-45
Joe Fanning	30-112	27	+24.83	Mark Johnston	23-77
Paul Mulrennan	20-176	11	-91.32	Eric Alston	2-2
Tony Hamilton	17-154	11	-28.21	Richard Fahey	7-43
Greg Fairley	17-126	13	-49.55	Mark Johnston	15-73
Andrew Elliott	14-99	14	+33.46	K R Burke	3-17
Adrian Nicholls	14-71	20	-10.33	David Nicholls	13-46
P J McDonald	13-151	9	-72.00	Alan Swinbank	5-37
Silvestre De Sousa	13-78	17	+41.99	Geoffrey Harker	2-7
Phillip Makin	12-106	11	-48.09	Michael Dods	5-24
David Allan	11-69	16	-3.94	Tim Easterby	7-26
Royston Ffrench	10-110	9	-18.50	Mark Johnston	4-14

Favourites

2yo	47.8%	-0.92	3yo	44.1%	+16.67	TOTAL 37.4% -22.89

Newton-Le-Willows, Merseyside,
WA12 0HQ. Tel 01942 725 963

HAYDOCK

How to get there
Road: M6 Jct 23,
A49 to Wigan. Rail:
Wigan & 320 bus or
Newton-le-Willows
Features LH, flat,
easy turns, suits the
galloping type

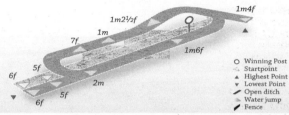

O Winning Post
↘ Startpoint
▲ Highest Point
▼ Lowest Point
✂ Open ditch
≈ Water jump
✦ Fence

2011 Fixtures
April 16, May
19-21, 27-28, June 8-9, 18, 30, July
1-2, 15-16, August 4-6, September 2-3,
13, 23-24, October 14

Time Test standard times

5f	59	1m3f200yds	2min28
6f	1min11.3	1m6f	2min54
7f30yds	1min27.4	2m45yds	3min28
1m30yds	1min40.2	2m1f130yds	3min47
1m2f95yds	2min8.6	2m3f	4min7

Trainers	Wins-Runs	%	2yo	3yo+	£1 level stks
B W Hills	31-123	25	15-40	16-83	+39.46
Michael Jarvis	20-68	29	3-16	17-52	+33.13
David Nicholls	18-111	16	7-18	11-93	+41.23
Richard Fahey	17-192	9	6-46	11-146	-83.16
Mark Johnston	17-172	10	4-49	13-123	-79.88
Alan Swinbank	14-80	18	3-12	11-68	+6.50
Richard Hannon	14-76	18	6-33	8-43	-30.94
Kevin Ryan	13-156	8	5-67	8-89	-51.50
Michael Dods	12-89	13	1-15	11-74	-26.30
Michael Bell	12-58	21	3-12	9-46	+19.38
Tim Easterby	11-133	8	2-41	9-92	-56.75
Ian Williams	11-71	15	1-11	10-60	+16.50
Brian Meehan	11-67	16	1-21	10-46	+37.30

Jockeys	Wins-Rides	%	£1 level stks	Best Trainer	W-R
Michael Hills	19-74	26	+10.19	B W Hills	15-53
Neil Callan	17-153	11	-73.57	Michael Jarvis	5-13
Jamie Spencer	17-80	21	-0.81	Paul Green	2-5
Paul Hanagan	15-164	9	-57.39	Richard Fahey	8-92
Philip Robinson	13-70	19	+1.78	Michael Jarvis	10-40
Tom Eaves	12-128	9	-45.84	Bryan Smart	4-31
P J McDonald	12-75	16	+23.50	Alan Swinbank	8-32
Robert Winston	12-68	18	+21.25	B W Hills	5-11
Graham Gibbons	11-103	11	+60.88	Ed McMahon	2-11
Adrian Nicholls	11-69	16	+26.48	David Nicholls	10-50
Steve Drowne	11-69	16	+11.99	Roger Charlton	4-19
Franny Norton	10-119	8	-30.92	Peter Niven	1-1
Paul Mulrennan	10-100	10	-34.33	Sir Mark Prescott	2-2

Favourites

2yo	43.5% +11.33	3yo	40.3% +7.93	TOTAL	37.4% +28.31

KEMPTON

Staines Rd East, Sunbury-On-Thames,
Middlesex, TW16 5AQ. Tel 01932 782 292

How to get there
Road: M3 Jct 1,
A308 towards
Kingston-on-
Thames. Rail:
Kempton Park from
Waterloo
Features RH,
sharp, all-weather,
inside jumps course

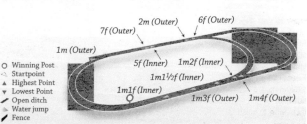

O Winning Post
⚐ Startpoint
▲ Highest Point
▼ Lowest Point
╱ Open ditch
≋ Water jump
╱ Fence

2011 Fixtures April 2, 5-7, 13-14, 20,
27, May 2, 11, 17-18, June 1, 20, 22,
29, July 6, August 3, 10, 12, 15-16, 22,
24, 31, September 1-3, 7, 10, 12, 14-15,
19, 21, 28-29, October 5, 12-13, 19, 26-
27, November 1-2, 9-10, 16-18, 23-24,
30, December 7-8, 14-15, 18, 20-21, 29

Time Test standard times

5f	59.5	1m2f	2min3.7
6f	1min11.5	1m3f	2min17.8
7f	1min24.2	1m4f	2min30.5
1m	1min37.6	2m	3min27
1m1f	1min50.5		

Trainers	Wins-Runs	%	2yo	3yo+	£1 level stks
Richard Hannon	82-633	13	38-281	44-352	-189.52
Gary Moore	50-380	13	3-32	47-348	-100.69
Andrew Balding	48-278	17	9-60	39-218	+6.17
Mark Johnston	43-294	15	8-77	35-217	-94.28
Saeed Bin Suroor	43-118	36	22-55	21-63	+17.25
Tony Carroll	39-325	12	0-10	39-315	-31.63
Jim Boyle	37-319	12	5-47	32-272	-13.48
John Gosden	34-189	18	14-64	20-125	-16.86
Paul Howling	33-369	9	1-12	32-357	-130.13
Michael Jarvis	33-149	22	5-29	28-120	+17.11
Dean Ivory	32-244	13	2-44	30-200	+71.00
Marco Botti	32-200	16	5-46	27-154	+84.00
Walter Swinburn	30-229	13	5-55	25-174	-38.76

Jockeys	Wins-Rides	%	£1 level stks	Best Trainer	W-R
Richard Hughes	88-523	17	-39.41	Richard Hannon	43-230
Jim Crowley	86-740	12	-150.40	Ralph Beckett	13-45
Neil Callan	71-414	17	+47.38	Kevin Ryan	14-53
George Baker	65-476	14	-87.89	Gary Moore	21-145
Adam Kirby	59-525	11	-97.63	Walter Swinburn	20-144
Dane O'Neill	58-599	10	-239.02	David Elsworth	5-31
Jamie Spencer	55-307	18	-76.10	Jane Chapple-Hyam	4-8
Seb Sanders	53-427	12	-168.70	Sir Mark Prescott	16-74
Chris Catlin	49-667	7	-197.75	E J O'Neill	3-16
Liam Keniry	47-609	8	-219.25	Andrew Balding	10-64
Ryan Moore	47-275	17	-85.45	Sir Michael Stoute	12-56
Steve Drowne	46-601	8	-282.27	Hughie Morrison	11-72
Jimmy Quinn	45-541	8	-111.46	Paul Howling	18-122

Favourites

2yo	41.1%	+19.45	3yo	33.8% -95.24	TOTAL	32.8% -193.85

London Road, Oadby, Leicester,
LE2 4QH. Tel 0116 271 6515

LEICESTER

How to get there
Road: M1 Jct 21,
A6, 2m south of
city. Rail: Leicester,
bus
Features RH,
straight mile is
downhill for first 4f,
then uphill to finish

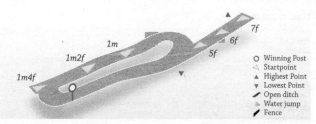

○ Winning Post
⌐ Startpoint
▲ Highest Point
▼ Lowest Point
✎ Open ditch
≈ Water jump
✔ Fence

2011 Fixtures
March 31, April 16, 29, May 16, 23,
30-31, June 11, 16, 23, July 2, 14, 20,
27, August 7, 23, September 6, 19,
October 4, 11, 24

Time Test standard times

5f2yds	58.3	1m60yds	1min41.9
5f218yds	1min10.2	1m1f218yds	2min2.7
7f9yds	1min22.3	1m3f183yds	2min28.6

Trainers	Wins-Runs	%	2yo	3yo+	£1 level stks
Mark Johnston	26-104	25	12-43	14-61	+39.05
Mick Channon	16-95	17	12-53	4-42	-14.48
Richard Hannon	15-97	15	12-56	3-41	-3.98
Kevin Ryan	15-86	17	7-40	8-46	+41.76
John Dunlop	14-72	19	2-29	12-43	-10.23
Michael Jarvis	14-66	21	1-18	13-48	+17.11
Saeed Bin Suroor	14-36	39	4-17	10-19	+11.81
Paul Cole	13-62	21	6-20	7-42	+21.76
Luca Cumani	13-52	25	4-13	9-39	+35.62
B W Hills	11-69	16	8-30	3-39	-11.36
Henry Cecil	11-47	23	2-16	9-31	-4.03
John Gosden	11-34	32	3-11	8-23	+11.98
Reg Hollinshead	10-78	13	1-11	9-67	+5.00

Jockeys	Wins-Rides	%	£1 level stks	Best Trainer	W-R
Jamie Spencer	23-93	25	-7.32	Michael Bell	3-19
Ted Durcan	20-105	19	+75.31	Henry Cecil	4-11
Frankie Dettori	18-51	35	-1.17	Saeed Bin Suroor	10-25
Philip Robinson	15-60	25	+33.68	Michael Jarvis	12-37
Richard Hills	15-56	27	-4.79	John Dunlop	6-14
Neil Callan	14-115	12	-14.40	Kevin Ryan	8-37
Ryan Moore	13-55	24	-16.22	Sir Michael Stoute	4-21
Dane O'Neill	12-99	12	-12.80	Luca Cumani	3-12
Richard Hughes	12-53	23	-3.30	Mick Channon	3-4
Jimmy Fortune	11-50	22	-8.22	Richard Hannon	3-7
Jack Mitchell	11-39	28	+42.25	Ralph Beckett	4-8
Steve Drowne	10-93	11	-37.58	Roger Charlton	6-20
Martin Dwyer	10-69	14	-26.30	Peter Chapple-Hyam	2-2

Favourites

2yo	37.4%	-23.55	3yo	41%	+13.18	TOTAL 38.4% -0.07

LINGFIELD turf

Racecourse Road, Lingfield
RH7 6PQ. Tel 01342 834 800

How to get there
Road: M25 Jctn 6,
south on A22, then
B2029. Rail:
Lingfield from
London Bridge or
Victoria
Features LH,
undulating, straight
runs downhill

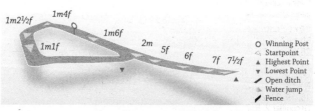

○ Winning Post
◁ Startpoint
▲ Highest Point
▼ Lowest Point
╱ Open ditch
⬩ Water jump
╱ Fence

2011 Fixtures May 7, 18, June 2, 4,
11, 18, 25, July 6, 13, 16, 23, 30,
August 6, 8, 13, 25, September 6, 16

Time Test standard times

5f	56.3	1m2f	2min5.4
6f	1min9	1m3f106yds	2min24.4
7f	1min20.7	1m6f	2min58.6
7f140yds	1min28.2	2m	3min24.6
1m1f	1min52.5		

Trainers	Wins-Runs	%	2yo	3yo+	£1 level stks
Richard Hannon	15-70	21	9-38	6-32	+9.99
Mick Channon	8-72	11	5-30	3-42	-36.04
Rod Millman	8-52	15	2-15	6-37	+0.38
Henry Cecil	8-33	24	1-3	7-30	-11.87
Michael Jarvis	8-24	33	0-3	8-21	-1.74
Gary Moore	6-47	13	1-8	5-39	-12.13
Ralph Beckett	6-37	16	2-13	4-24	+20.45
Chris Wall	6-23	26	1-2	5-21	+35.21
John Dunlop	5-53	9	1-18	4-35	-36.00
Ronald Harris	5-38	13	0-2	5-36	+1.50
Brian Meehan	5-30	17	1-10	4-20	-3.23
Andrew Balding	5-27	19	1-4	4-23	-3.38
William Knight	5-25	20	0-4	5-21	+14.35

Jockeys	Wins-Rides	%	£1 level stks	Best Trainer	W-R
Richard Hughes	15-55	27	+35.29	Richard Hannon	7-17
Seb Sanders	12-61	20	-2.90	Ralph Beckett	3-6
Liam Keniry	9-108	8	-49.00	Conor Dore	1-1
Dane O'Neill	9-71	13	-43.54	Simon Callaghan	2-2
Adam Kirby	9-61	15	+1.38	Walter Swinburn	4-26
Pat Cosgrave	9-45	20	+13.21	Michael Scudamore	2-2
Ryan Moore	8-44	18	-15.53	Richard Hannon	3-8
Richard Hills	8-33	24	-5.72	Marcus Tregoning	2-3
Tom Queally	8-33	24	-10.62	Henry Cecil	7-15
Eddie Ahern	7-65	11	-43.00	John Dunlop	2-7
Steve Drowne	7-60	12	-12.33	Roger Charlton	4-10
Chris Catlin	6-57	11	-3.92	Mick Channon	2-5
Shane Kelly	6-33	18	-14.94	Pat Eddery	2-3

Favourites

2yo	54.1% +14.15	3yo	43.2% +18.77	TOTAL	43.8% +62.86

LINGFIELD sand

Features LH, all-weather, tight

2011 Fixtures
March 30, April 6, 9, 26, May 6, 21, 24, July 20, August 5, October 12, 18, 27, November 11, 12, 16, 19, 23, 29, December 2, 5, 7, 14, 17, 28, 30, 31

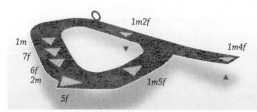

1m2f

1m

7f

6f
2m

5f

1m5f

1m4f

O Winning Post
◁ Startpoint
▲ Highest Point
▼ Lowest Point
✒ Open ditch
▨ Water jump
✔ Fence

Time Test standard times

5f	58	1m2f	2min3
6f	1min11	1m4f	2min29.6
7f	1min23.2	1m5f	2min43
1m	1min36.6	2m	3min21.5

Trainers	*Wins-Runs*	*%*	*2yo*	*3yo+*	*£1 level stks*
Gary Moore	71-523	14	4-34	67-489	-120.57
Mark Johnston	64-330	19	10-69	54-261	-82.06
Richard Hannon	63-448	14	21-147	42-301	-112.56
J S Moore	45-337	13	8-92	37-245	-28.50
John Best	40-499	8	6-81	34-418	-246.20
Jim Boyle	38-332	11	2-35	36-297	-40.50
Kevin Ryan	38-176	22	3-19	35-157	-1.77
Jeremy Noseda	38-147	26	14-43	24-104	-11.19
Mick Channon	33-262	13	8-56	25-206	-13.24
Saeed Bin Suroor	31-61	51	15-27	16-34	+45.82
Tom Dascombe	29-113	26	11-39	18-74	+69.21
David Evans	28-313	9	2-37	26-276	-130.52
Sir Mark Prescott	28-142	20	3-44	25-98	-20.16

Jockeys	*Wins-Rides*	*%*	*£1 level stks*	*Best Trainer*	*W-R*
George Baker	92-532	17	-48.63	Gary Moore	33-172
Jim Crowley	81-660	12	-21.54	Amanda Perrett	13-79
Seb Sanders	71-396	18	-59.77	Sir Mark Prescott	21-80
Neil Callan	70-432	16	-5.40	Kevin Ryan	22-73
Chris Catlin	60-680	9	-268.75	Tor Sturgis	5-19
Liam Keniry	57-560	10	-103.22	J S Moore	19-109
Joe Fanning	56-270	21	+1.06	Mark Johnston	38-141
Jamie Spencer	54-303	18	-86.58	Michael Easterby	4-7
Dane O'Neill	53-496	11	-101.50	Peter Hedger	4-7
Steve Drowne	51-499	10	-115.82	John Best	8-69
Richard Hughes	50-346	14	-113.83	Richard Hannon	28-159
Ryan Moore	50-234	21	-45.79	Richard Hannon	9-41
Hayley Turner	43-418	10	-143.81	Michael Bell	7-47

Favourites

2yo	37.4%	-43.36		3yo	39.3% -21.45	TOTAL	35.3% -120.89

MUSSELBURGH

Linkfield Road EH21 7RG
Tel 0131 665 2859

How to get there
Road: M8 Jct 2, A8 east, follow Ring Road, A1 east.
Rail: Musselburgh from Edinburgh Waverley
Features RH, flat, tight

2011 Fixtures
April 1, 23-24, May 20, June 3-4, 17, 27, July 19, 29, August 16, September 3, 12, 25, October 26

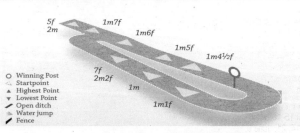

O Winning Post
⚐ Startpoint
▲ Highest Point
▼ Lowest Point
✦ Open ditch
♨ Water jump
✦ Fence

Time Test standard times

5f	57.6	1m4f100yds	2min38.7
7f15yds	1min26.3	1m6f	2min58.4
1m	1min38.3	1m7f16yds	3min11.3
1m1f	1min50.7	2m	3min25
1m3f32yds	2min20		

Trainers	Wins-Runs	%	2yo	3yo+	£1 level stks
Jim Goldie	34-339	10	3-23	31-316	-97.83
David Nicholls	27-147	18	3-9	24-138	+27.19
Mark Johnston	26-128	20	7-37	19-91	-11.25
Bryan Smart	25-105	24	14-35	11-70	+77.26
Richard Fahey	23-180	13	8-25	15-155	-82.63
Alan Swinbank	23-102	23	3-11	20-91	-5.03
David Barron	19-106	18	3-13	16-93	+12.71
Tim Easterby	17-87	20	5-23	12-64	-15.38
Linda Perratt	16-220	7	0-7	16-213	-21.13
Paul Midgley	13-104	13	1-22	12-82	-19.63
Kevin Ryan	12-134	9	4-35	8-99	-79.14
I Semple	9-88	10	0-10	9-78	-35.25
Michael Dods	9-67	13	3-17	6-50	-23.15

Jockeys	Wins-Rides	%	£1 level stks	Best Trainer	W-R
Tom Eaves	39-274	14	+31.01	Bryan Smart	17-71
Paul Hanagan	37-215	17	-48.41	Richard Fahey	16-95
Phillip Makin	25-173	14	-77.82	David Barron	10-31
P J McDonald	24-181	13	-44.51	Alan Swinbank	11-48
Gary Bartley	19-129	15	-5.42	Jim Goldie	16-101
Adrian Nicholls	19-109	17	+0.49	David Nicholls	19-94
Tony Hamilton	16-166	10	-72.00	Richard Fahey	4-26
Daniel Tudhope	15-119	13	-6.54	Jim Goldie	10-81
David Allan	15-114	13	-41.08	Tim Easterby	13-54
Silvestre De Sousa	15-104	14	-31.36	Geoffrey Harker	4-14
Joe Fanning	15-85	18	-0.43	Mark Johnston	12-47
Paul Mulrennan	14-137	10	-33.33	Linda Perratt	2-4
Greg Fairley	12-85	14	-19.55	Mark Johnston	9-34

Favourites

2yo	41.2% -8.92	3yo	38.5% +7.82	TOTAL	36.8% +10.36

Newbury, Berkshire, RG14 7NZ
Tel: 01635 400 15 or 01635 550 354

NEWBURY

How to get there
Road: M4 Jct 13
and A34 south
Rail: Newbury
Racecourse
Features LH,
wide, flat

Rowley Mile

(track diagram with labels: 1m1f, 1m2f, 1m3f, 1m4f, 1m5f, 1m (Rnd) 7½f, 2m, 5f, 6f, 6½f, 7f, 1m)

O Winning Post
⌇ Startpoint
▲ Highest Point
▼ Lowest Point
∕ Open ditch
▨ Water jump
✦ Fence

2011 Fixtures
April 15-16, May
13-14, 21, June 9,
21, 30, July 8, 15-16, 31, August 12-13,
September 16-17, October 21-22

Time Test standard times

5f34yds	1min0	1m1f	1min49.7
6f110yds	1min16.6	1m2f6yds	2min2
7f	1min23	1m3f5yds	2min15.8
7f64yds (rnd)	1min26.4	1m4f4yds	2min29.3
1m (str)	1min36	1m5f61yds	2min45.8
1m7yds (rnd)	1min35.3	2m	3min23

Trainers	Wins-Runs	%	2yo	3yo+	£1 level stks
Richard Hannon	52-470	11	34-273	18-197	-163.61
Brian Meehan	25-222	11	15-116	10-106	-13.38
Sir Michael Stoute	21-118	18	3-29	18-89	-32.57
Saeed Bin Suroor	19-79	24	9-21	10-58	+43.33
Michael Jarvis	16-72	22	4-14	12-58	+14.44
John Gosden	15-110	14	7-34	8-76	-50.78
Henry Cecil	15-65	23	1-5	14-60	+38.38
B W Hills	14-181	8	5-86	9-95	-63.88
Roger Charlton	14-129	11	3-49	11-80	+1.63
Mick Channon	13-251	5	4-122	9-129	-125.75
Mark Johnston	13-80	16	6-30	7-50	-8.88
Jeremy Noseda	12-56	21	1-15	11-41	+26.28
John Dunlop	11-130	8	2-54	9-76	-44.08

Jockeys	Wins-Rides	%	£1 level stks	Best Trainer	W-R
Richard Hughes	48-307	16	+14.04	Richard Hannon	32-190
Ryan Moore	46-281	16	-57.88	Sir Michael Stoute	15-81
Steve Drowne	23-225	10	+8.38	Roger Charlton	10-75
Richard Hills	22-159	14	-61.18	B W Hills	4-30
Frankie Dettori	22-103	21	-13.16	Saeed Bin Suroor	13-42
Jimmy Fortune	21-208	10	-59.63	John Gosden	4-46
Jamie Spencer	20-145	14	-3.50	Brian Meehan	4-25
Ted Durcan	18-129	14	-3.75	Henry Cecil	8-19
Martin Dwyer	15-145	10	+25.75	Brian Meehan	6-48
Jim Crowley	14-151	9	-24.63	Ralph Beckett	4-18
Tom Queally	12-100	12	+2.88	Henry Cecil	4-33
Eddie Ahern	11-106	10	-26.67	John Dunlop	3-22
Philip Robinson	11-66	17	-13.48	Michael Jarvis	9-34

Favourites

2yo	30.5%	-31.31	3yo	30.3%	-30.68	TOTAL	30.4%	-66.61

NEWCASTLE

High Gosforth Park NE3 5HP
Tel: 0191 236 2020 or 236 5508

How to get there
– Road: Signposted
from A1. Rail:
Newcastle Central,
metro to Regent
Centre or Four Lane
End and bus
Features: LH,
galloping, half-mile
straight is all uphill

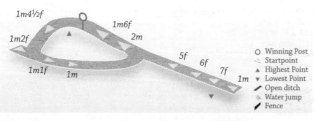

2011 Fixtures April 8, 20, 27, May 3,
13, 26-27, June 4, 23-25, July 23,
August 3, 12, 26, 29, September 5, 28,
October 11

Time Test standard times

5f	59	1m1f9yds	1min52.5
6f	1min11.8	1m2f32yds	2min6.7
7f	1min24.2	1m4f93yds	2min37
1m (rnd)	1min39.7	1m6f97yds	3min2
1m3yds (str)	1min37.2	2m19yds	3min23.7

Trainers	Wins-Runs	%	2yo	3yo+	£1 level stks
Richard Fahey	31-197	16	11-42	20-155	-33.87
Michael Dods	22-161	14	4-29	18-132	+26.10
Mark Johnston	21-125	17	8-41	13-84	-46.29
Tim Easterby	19-201	9	4-58	15-143	-48.17
Kevin Ryan	16-110	15	4-31	12-79	-26.71
Alan Swinbank	14-96	15	3-26	11-70	+29.75
Brian Ellison	12-127	9	1-15	11-112	-39.25
Mick Channon	11-78	14	6-35	5-43	+5.53
Bryan Smart	10-92	11	7-31	3-61	-14.90
Michael Easterby	9-109	8	3-26	6-83	-30.75
David Barron	9-107	8	1-14	8-93	-42.25
Paul Midgley	9-82	11	0-25	9-57	-6.63
Richard Guest	8-31	26	0-4	8-27	+75.50

Jockeys	Wins-Rides	%	£1 level stks	Best Trainer	W-R
Paul Hanagan	30-206	15	-38.07	Richard Fahey	15-91
Tom Eaves	21-247	9	-33.08	Bryan Smart	7-61
David Allan	21-164	13	+8.83	Tim Easterby	16-107
Phillip Makin	20-196	10	-31.78	Michael Dods	15-82
P J McDonald	15-139	11	-18.38	Alan Swinbank	8-58
Tony Hamilton	14-155	9	-51.28	Richard Fahey	5-44
Joe Fanning	13-104	13	-32.33	Mark Johnston	6-45
Neil Callan	13-81	16	-1.59	Kevin Ryan	5-30
Paul Mulrennan	11-157	7	-59.09	James Given	2-17
Silvestre De Sousa	11-88	13	+21.30	Ann Duffield	2-6
Royston Ffrench	10-135	7	-93.48	Mark Johnston	4-31
Andrew Elliott	9-104	9	+71.50	Mrs K Burke	3-6
Micky Fenton	9-81	11	+51.50	Paul Midgley	4-18

Favourites

2yo	40.7% -5.28	3yo	35.9% -6.40	TOTAL	33.9% -7.91

Westfield House, The Links,
Newmarket, Suffolk. CB8 0TG

NEWMARKET

How to get there
Road: from south
M11 Jct 9, then
A11, from east or
west A45, from
north A1 or A45.
Rail: Newmarket
Features RH,
wide, galloping,
uphill finish

2011 Fixtures April 13-14, 30, May 1,
12-14, 27-28, September 17, 22-24,
October 7-8, 19, 28-29

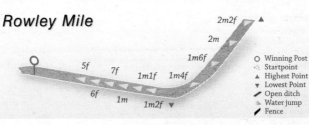

Rowley Mile

2m2f
2m
1m6f
5f 7f 1m1f 1m4f
6f 1m 1m2f ▼

O Winning Post
◁ Startpoint
▲ Highest Point
▼ Lowest Point
◢ Open ditch
≋ Water jump
⚋ Fence

Time Test standard times

5f	57.5	1m2f	2min1.4
6f	1min10.5	1m4f	2min27.7
7f	1min22.7	1m6f	2min54.4
1m	1min35.7	2m	3min20.3
1m1f	1min48.6	2m2f	3min48

Trainers	Wins-Runs	%	2yo	3yo+	£1 level stks
B W Hills	35-258	14	11-112	24-146	+0.37
John Gosden	34-223	15	8-84	26-139	+28.14
Richard Hannon	31-275	11	18-136	13-139	-9.20
Sir Michael Stoute	24-166	14	7-45	17-121	-60.31
Henry Cecil	24-115	21	9-31	15-84	+7.15
Saeed Bin Suroor	19-144	13	6-45	13-99	-50.75
William Haggas	19-117	16	5-47	14-70	+13.73
Mark Johnston	16-164	10	4-35	12-129	-69.03
Michael Jarvis	15-105	14	2-37	13-68	-27.17
Brian Meehan	14-177	8	8-90	6-87	-15.58
Andrew Balding	14-105	13	3-33	11-72	+85.00
John Dunlop	13-125	10	1-40	12-85	-53.09
Luca Cumani	13-88	15	1-15	12-73	+12.78

Jockeys	Wins-Rides	%	£1 level stks	Best Trainer	W-R
Ryan Moore	39-266	15	+10.54	Sir Michael Stoute	15-103
Richard Hills	36-189	19	+36.47	B W Hills	10-45
Jimmy Fortune	34-220	15	+28.76	John Gosden	19-86
Frankie Dettori	30-192	16	-51.75	Saeed Bin Suroor	11-92
Richard Hughes	21-208	10	-47.07	Richard Hannon	15-123
Ted Durcan	20-175	11	-2.75	Henry Cecil	8-32
Michael Hills	19-177	11	-38.75	B W Hills	18-133
Jamie Spencer	19-175	11	-26.26	Michael Bell	7-39
William Buick	18-150	12	-36.11	Andrew Balding	6-27
Tom Queally	16-146	11	+2.92	Henry Cecil	9-49
Kieren Fallon	14-105	13	-9.09	Mick Channon	3-8
Seb Sanders	13-75	17	+118.12	Ralph Beckett	4-14
Kerrin McEvoy	11-82	13	-12.77	Sir Michael Stoute	3-14

Favourites

2yo	37.1%	-6.52	3yo	33.2% -9.42	TOTAL 31%	-71.25

NEWMARKET

Westfield House, The Links,
Newmarket, Suffolk CB8 0TG

How to get there
See previous page
Features RH,
wide, galloping,
uphill finish

2011 Fixtures
June 17-18, 24-25,
July 7-9, 15-16,
22-23, 29-30,
August 5-6, 11-13,
26-27

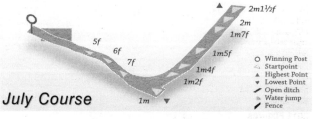

July Course

Time Test standard times

5f	57.7	1m4f	2min26.7
6f	1min10	1m5f	2min39
7f	1min22.8	1m6f175yds	3min3
1m	1min35.7	2m24yds	3min21.2
1m110yds	1min42	2m1f65yds	3min36
1m2f	2min1		

Trainers	Wins-Runs	%	2yo	3yo+	£1 level stks
Richard Hannon	40-265	15	26-152	14-113	+11.47
John Gosden	29-138	21	9-50	20-88	+37.70
Saeed Bin Suroor	22-92	24	12-37	10-55	-13.22
Mark Johnston	17-143	12	2-40	15-103	-10.25
David Elsworth	17-129	13	4-31	13-98	-2.38
Mick Channon	16-138	12	13-76	3-62	-11.25
Jeremy Noseda	16-83	19	6-31	10-52	+6.11
Sir Michael Stoute	15-106	14	7-40	8-66	-20.79
B W Hills	12-155	8	3-64	9-91	-60.67
John Dunlop	12-122	10	2-57	10-65	-19.25
Henry Cecil	11-76	14	3-19	8-57	-17.95
Chris Wall	11-47	23	0-4	11-43	+28.22
Brian Meehan	10-131	8	8-81	2-50	-84.05

Jockeys	Wins-Rides	%	£1 level stks	Best Trainer	W-R
Ryan Moore	30-188	16	+16.35	Richard Hannon	11-42
Ted Durcan	28-226	12	-72.52	Saeed Bin Suroor	9-34
Richard Hughes	28-140	20	+16.21	Richard Hannon	15-78
Jimmy Fortune	26-151	17	+24.60	John Gosden	11-43
Richard Hills	25-163	15	+4.94	Mark Johnston	6-17
Frankie Dettori	23-100	23	+0.73	Saeed Bin Suroor	12-36
Jamie Spencer	20-154	13	-35.69	David Elsworth	2-6
Tom Queally	14-137	10	+39.07	Henry Cecil	4-29
Eddie Ahern	14-102	14	+6.79	John Dunlop	3-14
George Baker	12-65	18	+49.21	Chris Wall	3-9
Dane O'Neill	11-130	8	-1.50	Henry Candy	3-27
Chris Catlin	11-94	12	+33.75	Chris Wall	2-3
Robert Havlin	11-89	12	+57.83	John Gosden	6-29

Favourites

2yo	37.9% -5.84	3yo	32.1% -14.49	TOTAL	30.6% -70.26

Colwick Park, Nottingham,
NG2 4BE. Tel 0115 958 0620

NOTTINGHAM

How to get there
Road: M1 Jct 25,
A52 east to B686,
signs for Trent
Bridge, then Colwick
Park. Rail:
Nottingham
Features LH, flat,
easy turns

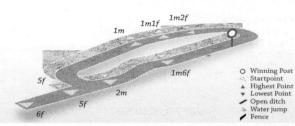

O	Winning Post
⟡	Startpoint
▲	Highest Point
▼	Lowest Point
✓	Open ditch
⟍	Water jump
✓	Fence

2011 Fixtures
April 6, 23, May 6-7, 17, 29, June 1, 9,
July 2, 15, 28, August 9, 12, 17,
September 28, October 5, 12, 26,
November 2

Time Test standard times

5f13yds	58.7	1m6f15yds	2min58.5
6f15yds	1min11.3	2m9yds	3min24.3
1m75yds	1min41.5	2m2f18yds	3min52.3
1m2f50yds	2min5.6		

Trainers	*Wins-Runs*	%	*2yo*	*3yo+*	*£1 level stks*
Saeed Bin Suroor	21-43	49	7-13	14-30	+26.89
Sir Michael Stoute	16-60	27	6-19	10-41	-7.46
Richard Hannon	14-83	17	6-42	8-41	-13.74
Michael Jarvis	13-54	24	5-21	8-33	-11.36
David Evans	12-70	17	6-30	6-40	+34.35
Michael Bell	11-82	13	2-27	9-55	-4.01
John Gosden	11-70	16	4-19	7-51	-8.19
Ralph Beckett	11-53	21	5-23	6-30	+5.26
Roy Bowring	10-51	20	0-4	10-47	+62.50
Roger Charlton	10-42	24	2-16	8-26	-9.90
Mark Johnston	9-98	9	5-42	4-56	-49.25
Ed Dunlop	8-65	12	3-34	5-31	-30.00
Brian Meehan	8-47	17	2-14	6-33	+20.50

Jockeys	*Wins-Rides*	%	*£1 level stks*	*Best Trainer*	*W-R*
Ted Durcan	18-119	15	-16.21	Saeed Bin Suroor	6-11
Frankie Dettori	18-42	43	+15.82	Saeed Bin Suroor	10-20
Jamie Spencer	16-102	16	-36.81	Michael Bell	4-19
Steve Drowne	16-87	18	+10.98	Roger Charlton	8-23
Ryan Moore	15-86	17	-28.49	Sir Michael Stoute	6-31
Dane O'Neill	13-96	14	+28.00	Henry Candy	4-17
Richard Mullen	13-77	17	+35.75	Bryan Smart	2-2
Seb Sanders	11-97	11	-11.62	Ralph Beckett	3-9
Paul Hanagan	11-89	12	+12.38	Richard Fahey	4-24
Philip Robinson	11-60	18	-19.94	Michael Jarvis	8-31
Pat Dobbs	10-52	19	+18.00	Richard Hannon	9-35
Kerrin McEvoy	10-31	32	+16.13	Saeed Bin Suroor	3-4
Neil Callan	9-94	10	-52.13	Chris Wall	1-1

Favourites

2yo	27.3% -40.50	3yo	35.8% -11.50	TOTAL	31.7% -61.44

PONTEFRACT

33 Ropergate, Pontefract,
WF8 1LE. Tel 01977 703 224

How to get there
Road: M62 Jct 32,
then A539. Rail:
Pontefract Monkhill
or Pontefract Baghill
from Leeds
Features LH,
undulating, sharp
home turn, last half-
mile is all uphill

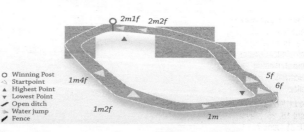

O Winning Post
△ Startpoint
▲ Highest Point
▼ Lowest Point
✓ Open ditch
⌇ Water jump
✔ Fence

2011 Fixtures April 5, 19, 27, May 27,
June 6, 19, 27, July 5, 15, 24, August 3,
14, September 15, 22, October 3, 17

Time Test standard times

5f	1min1.3	1m4f8yds	2min34.5
6f	1min14.2	2m1f22yds	3min42.2
1m4yds	1min41.8	2m1f216yds	3min52
1m2f6yds	2min7.2	2m5f122yds	4min48

Trainers	Wins-Runs	%	2yo	3yo+	£1 level stks
Richard Fahey	23-172	13	5-37	18-135	-4.44
Mark Johnston	17-144	12	5-37	12-107	-49.07
Kevin Ryan	12-75	16	5-30	7-45	+16.29
Michael Jarvis	12-37	32	4-10	8-27	-0.53
Saeed Bin Suroor	12-33	36	4-12	8-21	+13.75
John Quinn	11-112	10	3-23	8-89	-9.50
Tim Easterby	10-127	8	0-30	10-97	-12.00
Mick Channon	10-85	12	5-35	5-50	-6.00
Alan Swinbank	9-74	12	2-7	7-67	+6.25
Micky Hammond	9-71	13	0-7	9-64	+26.13
David Barron	9-56	16	1-12	8-44	+29.50
B W Hills	9-34	26	3-16	6-18	+5.86
Henry Cecil	8-27	30	0-3	8-24	+2.06

Jockeys	Wins-Rides	%	£1 level stks	Best Trainer	W-R
Paul Hanagan	30-183	16	+0.65	Richard Fahey	16-93
Jimmy Fortune	13-38	34	+37.58	John Gosden	3-5
Jamie Spencer	12-64	19	-5.02	B W Hills	2-3
Neil Callan	11-74	15	-6.88	Kevin Ryan	6-24
Tom Queally	11-63	17	+24.80	Henry Cecil	3-13
Jimmy Quinn	10-69	14	+21.00	Jeff Pearce	2-2
Ted Durcan	10-62	16	-22.80	Saeed Bin Suroor	5-8
Philip Robinson	10-42	24	-8.58	Michael Jarvis	8-23
Tom Eaves	9-140	6	-77.25	Julie-Ann Camacho	2-6
Paul Mulrennan	9-119	8	-12.25	Howard Johnson	2-12
Richard Hills	9-33	27	-5.63	Michael Jarvis	2-3
Graham Gibbons	8-91	9	-40.00	David Barron	2-3
Kieren Fallon	8-37	22	+12.88	Ollie Pears	1-1

Favourites

2yo	34.9% -18.17		3yo	39.7% -0.53	TOTAL	34.7% +5.51

Redcar, Teesside,
TS10 2BY. Tel 01642 484 068

REDCAR

How to get there
Road: A1, A168,
A19, then A174
Rail: Redcar Central
from Darlington
Features LH, flat,
galloping
2011 Fixtures
April 18, 25, May 9,
30, 31, June 7,
17-18, July 17, 27, August 6, 27,
September 1, 21, October 1, 14, 24,
November 1

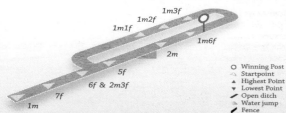

Time Test standard times

5f	56.7	1m3f	2min17
6f	1min9.4	1m4f	2min30
7f	1min22	1m5f135yds	2min54.7
1m	1min34.7	1m6f19yds	3min0
1m1f	1min49.3	2m4yds	3min25
1m2f	2min2.6	2m3f	4min5.3

Trainers	Wins-Runs	%	2yo	3yo+	£1 level stks
Richard Fahey	30-178	17	10-61	20-117	-13.53
Tim Easterby	21-276	8	1-95	20-181	-32.13
Mark Johnston	19-122	16	8-54	11-68	+19.19
Bryan Smart	16-127	13	7-49	9-78	-27.42
David Barron	16-126	13	4-26	12-100	+51.13
David Nicholls	14-115	12	1-20	13-95	-37.60
Michael Dods	13-106	12	2-16	11-90	+36.88
Alan Swinbank	12-118	10	0-20	12-98	-36.07
Ron Barr	11-111	10	0-5	11-106	+64.50
Mick Channon	10-73	14	5-40	5-33	+18.97
Neville Bycroft	9-124	7	0-19	9-105	-39.25
John Quinn	9-91	10	0-20	9-71	-29.42
Kevin Ryan	8-130	6	4-58	4-72	-70.39

Jockeys	Wins-Rides	%	£1 level stks	Best Trainer	W-R
Tom Eaves	22-245	9	-38.25	Bryan Smart	8-73
Paul Hanagan	21-150	14	39.26	Richard Fahey	10-61
Silvestre De Sousa	19-151	13	-2.17	J Hetherton	4-6
Paul Mulrennan	18-225	8	-61.04	Howard Johnson	3-16
Tony Hamilton	18-158	11	-13.32	Richard Fahey	9-45
Phillip Makin	18-132	14	+9.00	David Barron	6-29
David Allan	16-187	9	-18.92	Tim Easterby	9-122
Graham Gibbons	13-103	13	-30.94	John Quinn	4-27
Greg Fairley	13-79	16	+35.43	Mark Johnston	11-39
P J McDonald	11-154	7	-23.00	Alan Swinbank	4-49
Neil Brown	11-84	13	+22.22	David Barron	3-30
Neil Callan	11-77	14	-1.52	Michael Jarvis	2-9
Ted Durcan	10-60	17	-0.01	Saeed Bin Suroor	3-6

Favourites

2yo	37.5%	-0.04		3yo	31.9%	-23.28		TOTAL	33.9%	-9.18

RIPON

77 North Street, Ripon, N Yorkshire
HG4 1DS. Tel 01765 602 156 or 01765 603 696

How to get there
Road: A1, then
B6265. Rail:
Harrogate, bus to
Ripon centre, 1m
walk
Features RH,
sharp

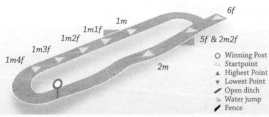

2011 Fixtures
April 7, 16, May 6,
15, 24, June 1, 15-16, July 4, 16,
August 1, 13, 29-30, September 24

Time Test standard times

5f	57.8	1m2f	2min3.3
6f	1min10.6	1m4f10yds	2min31
1m	1min37.8	2m	3min27
1m1f170yds	2min0.4	2m1f203yds	3min52

Trainers	Wins-Runs	%	2yo	3yo+	£1 level stks
Kevin Ryan	23-140	16	9-49	14-91	-6.89
Tim Easterby	20-254	8	7-81	13-173	-132.55
Richard Fahey	18-174	10	5-48	13-126	-64.50
David Nicholls	17-116	15	2-19	15-97	+38.00
Tom Tate	15-65	23	3-10	12-55	+25.71
Mark Johnston	12-123	10	2-30	10-93	-68.57
B W Hills	10-32	31	1-5	9-27	+8.38
Mick Channon	9-80	11	7-38	2-42	-39.65
Alan Swinbank	9-60	15	0-8	9-52	-2.25
K R Burke	8-51	16	6-17	2-34	+22.88
William Haggas	8-26	31	1-7	7-19	+22.75
Michael Jarvis	8-19	42	1-2	7-17	+6.73
Paul Midgley	7-110	6	1-45	6-65	-26.13

Jockeys	Wins-Rides	%	£1 level stks	Best Trainer	W-R
Neil Callan	23-103	22	+7.51	Kevin Ryan	12-46
Paul Hanagan	18-178	10	-49.88	Richard Fahey	10-90
Micky Fenton	17-94	18	+17.71	Tom Tate	14-46
Paul Mulrennan	16-141	11	-72.63	Kevin Ryan	4-20
David Allan	15-171	9	-91.45	Tim Easterby	11-130
P J McDonald	14-83	17	+94.00	Alan Swinbank	7-26
Robert Winston	13-66	20	-0.13	Ruth Carr	2-2
Silvestre De Sousa	11-74	15	-1.25	David O'Meara	3-7
Graham Gibbons	10-94	11	-39.09	John Quinn	3-38
Adrian Nicholls	9-72	13	+11.75	David Nicholls	9-56
Joe Fanning	8-82	10	-37.46	Mark Johnston	4-46
Tadhg O'Shea	8-39	21	+13.88	Brian Meehan	2-4
Eddie Ahern	8-29	28	+1.05	B W Hills	1-1

Favourites

2yo	39.8% -2.34	3yo	37%	-11.41	TOTAL 35.2%	-20.17

Netherhampton, Salisbury, Wilts
SP2 8PN. Tel 01722 326 461

SALISBURY

How to get there
Road: 2m west of
Salisbury on A3094
Rail: Salisbury, bus

Features RH,
uphill finish

2011 Fixtures
May 1, 12, 19, June
1, 12, 22, 26, July
9, 23, August
10-11, 19, September 1, 28, October 10

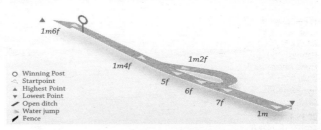

O Winning Post
⌒ Startpoint
▲ Highest Point
▼ Lowest Point
↗ Open ditch
≈ Water jump
✓ Fence

Time Test standard times

5f	59.6	1m1f209yds	2min5
6f	1min12	1m4f	2min32
6f212yds	1min25.2	1m6f21yds	2min58.6
1m	1min39.2		

Trainers	Wins-Runs	%	2yo	3yo+	£1 level stks
Richard Hannon	53-356	15	24-163	29-193	-70.55
Andrew Balding	20-103	19	12-37	8-66	+32.56
Ralph Beckett	15-136	11	5-61	10-75	-35.63
Hughie Morrison	13-102	13	1-18	12-84	-12.28
Sir Michael Stoute	12-60	20	1-11	11-49	-18.25
John Dunlop	10-108	9	4-46	6-62	-13.25
Amanda Perrett	9-85	11	1-30	8-55	-4.63
Brian Meehan	9-68	13	7-40	2-28	+23.54
Henry Candy	9-51	18	3-10	6-41	+15.08
Roger Charlton	9-49	18	4-19	5-30	-16.29
Mick Channon	8-136	6	4-59	4-77	-72.81
David Evans	8-74	11	2-20	6-54	-14.55
Luca Cumani	8-32	25	1-1	7-31	+6.50

Jockeys	Wins-Rides	%	£1 level stks	Best Trainer	W-R
Richard Hughes	39-186	21	-6.12	Richard Hannon	29-136
Ryan Moore	23-114	20	-23.58	Sir Michael Stoute	7-27
Steve Drowne	20-159	13	+2.32	Hughie Morrison	9-50
Dane O'Neill	17-120	14	+40.88	Henry Candy	5-25
Jim Crowley	14-126	11	+12.63	Amanda Perrett	6-41
Jimmy Fortune	14-87	16	-20.83	John Gosden	4-15
Richard Kingscote	11-91	12	-0.68	Tom Dascombe	6-32
Seb Sanders	11-88	13	-27.50	Ralph Beckett	6-41
Martin Dwyer	11-81	14	+40.53	Brian Meehan	3-12
Pat Dobbs	10-92	11	-15.38	Richard Hannon	9-54
Adam Kirby	10-56	18	+29.93	Walter Swinburn	5-24
Liam Keniry	8-105	8	-37.50	Andrew Balding	5-28
Ted Durcan	8-74	11	+11.29	John Dunlop	3-13

Favourites

2yo	42.9%	-3.19	3yo	32.2% -15.86	TOTAL 34.5%	-22.24

SANDOWN

Esher, Surrey, KT10 9AJ.
Tel 01372 463 072 or 01372 464 348

How to get there
Road: M25 Jct 10
then A3. Rail: Esher
from Waterloo
Features RH, last
7f uphill

2011 Fixtures
April 24, May 19,
26, June 2, 10-11,
July 1-2, 13, 20-21,
27, August 4, 19-20, September 9, 14

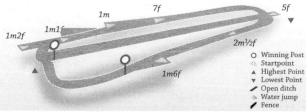

O Winning Post
Startpoint
▲ Highest Point
▼ Lowest Point
Open ditch
Water jump
Fence

Time Test standard times

5f6yds	59.2	1m2f7yds	2min5
7f16yds	1min27	1m3f91yds	2min21.7
1m14yds	1min40	1m6f	2min57
1m1f	1min52	2m78yds	3min30.4

Trainers	Wins-Runs	%	2yo	3yo+	£1 level stks
Richard Hannon	39-283	14	22-122	17-161	-7.96
Sir Michael Stoute	35-153	23	2-21	33-132	+8.29
John Gosden	24-121	20	7-24	17-97	-13.36
Mark Johnston	14-157	9	6-39	8-118	-49.57
William Haggas	13-52	25	2-6	11-46	+20.50
Mick Channon	12-91	13	6-42	6-49	-27.72
Walter Swinburn	12-83	14	2-13	10-70	-10.03
Michael Jarvis	12-80	15	3-12	9-68	-28.88
Saeed Bin Suroor	12-61	20	4-11	8-50	-7.26
Andrew Balding	11-106	10	3-28	8-78	-42.42
John Dunlop	11-83	13	4-20	7-63	-3.90
Henry Cecil	10-55	18	3-8	7-47	-11.79
Jeremy Noseda	10-28	36	1-6	9-22	+8.33

Jockeys	Wins-Rides	%	£1 level stks	Best Trainer	W-R
Ryan Moore	49-242	20	-32.29	Sir Michael Stoute	20-97
Richard Hughes	32-192	17	-43.66	Richard Hannon	22-115
Frankie Dettori	27-144	19	-10.78	Saeed Bin Suroor	8-36
Ted Durcan	19-132	14	+30.67	Henry Cecil	4-21
Jimmy Fortune	17-180	9	-61.76	John Gosden	6-52
William Buick	17-94	18	+5.73	John Gosden	9-22
Adam Kirby	16-125	13	+25.63	Walter Swinburn	10-61
Martin Dwyer	16-104	15	+23.24	Marcus Tregoning	3-8
Darryll Holland	15-89	17	+2.63	Mick Channon	5-19
Jim Crowley	14-165	8	+29.75	Amanda Perrett	3-47
Richard Hills	14-111	13	-43.01	John Dunlop	4-17
Seb Sanders	14-61	23	+29.36	Sir Mark Prescott	6-13
Steve Drowne	11-101	11	+28.08	Roger Charlton	4-24

Favourites

2yo	38.3% -8.02	3yo 32.6% -28.77	TOTAL 33.1% -38.33

Rolleston, Newark, Notts
NG25 0TS. Tel 01636 814 481

SOUTHWELL

How to get there
Road: A1 to Newark,
then A617 or M1 to
Nottingham, then
A612. Rail:
Rolleston
Features LH, all-
weather, sharp

2011 Fixtures
April 12, 19-20,
May 4, 10, 19, June 2, 28, July 5, 12,
19, August 2, 18, 30, October 4, 24,
November 3, 9-10, 15, 22, December 6,
9-11, 13, 15-16, 22, 27, 29

**NB: Due to the shortage of turf
meetings all our stats relate to AW
racing only**

Legend:
○ Winning Post
⋯ Startpoint
▲ Highest Point
▼ Lowest Point
✎ Open ditch
≈ Water jump
✦ Fence

Time Test standard times

5f	57.7	1m4f	2min34
6f	1min13.5	1m5f	2min47.4
7f	1min27	1m6f	3min1.7
1m	1min40	2m	3min30
1m3f	2min21.6	2m2f	3min58

Trainers	*Wins-Runs*	%	2yo	3yo+	£1 level stks
Mark Johnston	58-224	26	9-50	49-174	+19.97
Kevin Ryan	44-306	14	6-52	38-254	-90.81
Richard Fahey	42-272	15	5-33	37-239	-21.84
David Barron	42-189	22	7-21	35-168	+92.64
Alan McCabe	38-408	9	5-50	33-358	-152.64
David Nicholls	38-187	20	8-21	30-166	+143.48
David Evans	32-173	18	3-37	29-136	+50.53
Brian Ellison	31-133	23	3-12	28-121	+45.35
Hughie Morrison	30-128	23	2-15	28-113	+30.78
Paul Midgley	28-269	10	3-39	25-230	+1.75
Bryan Smart	28-189	15	5-29	23-160	+26.07
P A Blockley	25-124	20	1-4	24-120	+10.07
Peter Hiatt	24-153	16	0-1	24-152	+28.82

Jockeys	*Wins-Rides*	%	£1 level stks	*Best Trainer*	*W-R*
Chris Catlin	70-555	13	-106.76	Peter Hiatt	9-53
Robert Winston	58-329	18	+59.16	Hughie Morrison	6-11
Joe Fanning	47-221	21	-3.78	Mark Johnston	28-91
Neil Callan	45-307	15	-115.19	Kevin Ryan	18-101
Phillip Makin	45-258	17	-33.45	David Barron	16-60
Graham Gibbons	35-255	14	+13.53	David Barron	6-13
Tom Eaves	34-324	10	-98.43	Bryan Smart	8-103
Greg Fairley	33-189	17	-4.09	Mark Johnston	21-84
Seb Sanders	33-147	22	-3.31	Sir Mark Prescott	17-51
Stevie Donohoe	31-221	14	-0.49	P A Blockley	7-22
Pat Cosgrave	30-180	17	-2.17	Jim Boyle	11-42
Paul Hanagan	29-288	10	-141.20	Richard Fahey	21-123
Hayley Turner	28-259	11	-83.07	Reg Hollinshead	4-20

Favourites

2yo	39.4% -8.54	3yo 40.1% -26.47	TOTAL 35.9% -117.83

THIRSK

Station Road, Thirsk, N Yorkshire,
YO7 1QL. Tel 01845 522 276

How to get there
Road: A61 from A1
in the west or A19 in
the east. Rail:
Thirsk, 10min walk
Features LH,
sharp, tight turns
2011 Fixtures
April 9, 30, May 7,
14, 23, June 14,
July 22, 29-30, August 8, 15, 26,
September 3

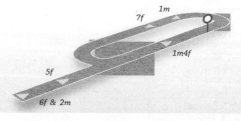

○ Winning Post
⇄ Startpoint
▲ Highest Point
▼ Lowest Point
╱ Open ditch
╲ Water jump
╱ Fence

Time Test standard times

5f	57.4	1m	1min35.8
6f	1min9.5	1m4f	2min30
7f	1min23	2m	3min22.6

Trainers	Wins-Runs	%	2yo	3yo+	£1 level stks
David Nicholls	20-151	13	4-17	16-134	+27.00
Richard Fahey	19-126	15	7-34	12-92	-5.09
Mark Johnston	17-112	15	5-30	12-82	+15.47
Tim Easterby	16-225	7	4-58	12-167	-114.88
Kevin Ryan	15-166	9	2-39	13-127	-58.33
Michael Dods	13-124	10	0-11	13-113	-28.00
Alan Swinbank	13-87	15	2-14	11-73	-9.52
David Barron	10-93	11	0-23	10-70	-38.00
Mick Channon	9-69	13	8-30	1-39	-34.95
Jim Goldie	8-45	18	0-1	8-44	-8.38
Michael Easterby	7-92	8	0-21	7-71	-16.63
Richard Whitaker	7-52	13	0-9	7-43	+18.75
Bryan Smart	6-93	6	0-23	6-70	-34.25

Jockeys	Wins-Rides	%	£1 level stks	Best Trainer	W-R
Silvestre De Sousa	18-116	16	-9.75	David Nicholls	5-29
Paul Hanagan	17-148	11	-65.09	Richard Fahey	10-53
David Allan	15-160	9	-29.38	Tim Easterby	11-112
Phillip Makin	15-150	10	-51.75	Michael Dods	8-64
P J McDonald	12-108	11	+5.63	Alan Swinbank	6-46
Paul Mulrennan	11-161	7	-83.79	Paul Green	2-4
Tom Eaves	11-159	7	-69.62	Paul Cole	2-5
Joe Fanning	11-79	14	-10.24	Mark Johnston	9-42
Adrian Nicholls	10-73	14	+2.50	David Nicholls	9-57
Tony Hamilton	9-110	8	-58.25	Richard Fahey	7-30
Neil Callan	9-88	10	-26.85	Kevin Ryan	5-59
Robert Winston	8-53	15	-6.35	B W Hills	2-5
Graham Gibbons	7-97	7	-3.25	Tim Easterby	2-11

Favourites

2yo	42%	-3.59	3yo	32.8%	-14.55	TOTAL	34.7%	-0.32

6 Hampton Street, Warwick
CV34 6HN. Tel 01926 491 553

WARWICK

How to get there
Road: M40 Jct 14,
A429. Rail: Warwick
Features LH,
sharp turns

2011 Fixtures
April 25, May 2, 7,
10, June 13, 16, 23,
July 1, 7, August
23, 29, September
29, October 3

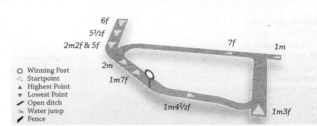

O Winning Post
◠ Startpoint
▲ Highest Point
▼ Lowest Point
✔ Open ditch
➤ Water jump
✔ Fence

Time Test standard times

5f	58	1m4f134yds	2min34.6
5f110yds	1min4	1m6f213yds	3min6
6f	1min10.6	2m39yds	3min24
7f26yds	1min22.2	2m2f214yds	3min58
1m22yds	1min35.3	2m3f13yds	4min0
1m2f 188yds	2min12		

Trainers	Wins-Runs	%	2yo	3yo+	£1 level stks
Richard Hannon	12-67	18	7-35	5-32	+4.58
Reg Hollinshead	9-67	13	1-12	8-55	-7.40
Mick Channon	8-67	12	6-35	2-32	-8.75
Mark Johnston	8-55	15	2-20	6-35	+6.46
Andrew Balding	8-34	24	2-10	6-24	+19.75
William Haggas	8-31	26	1-13	7-18	-9.29
B W Hills	7-43	16	1-15	6-28	+6.50
Ed McMahon	7-24	29	5-11	2-13	+9.75
Henry Cecil	7-21	33	3-6	4-15	+8.73
Michael Jarvis	7-15	47	1-4	6-11	+6.07
David Evans	6-60	10	2-16	4-44	-18.75
Andrew Haynes	6-35	17	2-15	4-20	+23.63
Ralph Beckett	5-40	13	2-13	3-27	-6.63

Jockeys	Wins-Rides	%	£1 level stks	Best Trainer	W-R
Eddie Ahern	14-64	22	+16.25	Henry Cecil	2-2
Jamie Spencer	13-41	32	+6.38	Sir Michael Stoute	2-2
Chris Catlin	12-107	11	-11.25	Paul Webber	2-4
Richard Hughes	9-51	18	+14.73	Richard Hannon	3-18
David Probert	9-50	18	-7.75	Andrew Balding	4-14
Tom Queally	9-43	21	+2.13	Henry Cecil	4-10
Stevie Donohoe	8-61	13	+23.50	Ed McMahon	2-4
Richard Kingscote	8-53	15	-3.25	Tom Dascombe	5-17
Liam Jones	7-60	12	-16.64	William Haggas	4-13
James Doyle	7-56	13	+21.00	Richard Price	2-6
Jim Crowley	7-54	13	+23.50	Amanda Perrett	3-11
Richard Mullen	7-53	13	-22.63	Ed McMahon	3-10
Martin Dwyer	6-53	11	+26.60	William Muir	3-10

Favourites

2yo	27.7%	-26.53	3yo	39.5%	+4.59	TOTAL	32.2%	-29.80

WINDSOR

Maidenhead Road, Windsor, Berks
SL4 5JJ. Tel 01753 498 400

How to get there
Road: M4 Jctn 6,
A355, A308. Rail:
Windsor Central
from Paddington or
Windsor Riverside
from Waterloo
Features Figure of
eight, flat, easy
turns, long straight

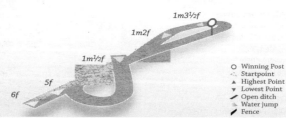

○ Winning Post
∴ Startpoint
▲ Highest Point
▼ Lowest Point
╱ Open ditch
◢ Water jump
╱ Fence

2011 Fixtures April 4, 11, 18, May 2,
9, 16, 23, June 6, 13, 20, 25-27, July 4,
11, 18, 25, August 1, 7-8, 15, 22, 27,
October 3, 10, 17

Time Test standard times

5f10yds	58	1m2f7yds	2min3.6
5f217yds	1min10.2	1m3f135yds	2min22.6
1m67yds	1min41.6		

Trainers	Wins-Runs	%	2yo	3yo+	£1 level stks
Richard Hannon	77-472	16	35-210	42-262	-61.56
Sir Michael Stoute	26-95	27	2-7	24-88	+4.41
David Evans	22-172	13	5-57	17-115	+48.96
B W Hills	20-108	19	9-43	11-65	-16.37
Walter Swinburn	15-134	11	2-21	13-113	-37.00
Ralph Beckett	15-106	14	5-38	10-68	+4.03
Jeremy Noseda	13-57	23	0-7	13-50	+8.65
Michael Jarvis	13-51	25	1-8	12-43	+35.63
Saeed Bin Suroor	13-49	27	1-12	12-37	-4.15
Rod Millman	12-118	10	1-24	11-94	-15.63
Mick Channon	11-148	7	7-72	4-76	-51.90
Brian Meehan	9-121	7	2-47	7-74	-48.70
Clive Cox	9-74	12	2-15	7-59	+1.18

Jockeys	Wins-Rides	%	£1 level stks	Best Trainer	W-R
Richard Hughes	66-337	20	-12.25	Richard Hannon	53-221
Ryan Moore	53-238	22	-26.72	Sir Michael Stoute	20-56
Jim Crowley	27-233	12	+40.53	Peter Winkworth	5-16
Steve Drowne	21-216	10	-57.84	Roger Charlton	6-44
Jimmy Fortune	18-157	11	-65.65	John Gosden	6-38
Seb Sanders	18-131	14	-22.14	Ralph Beckett	5-26
Jamie Spencer	17-115	15	-40.04	Michael Bell	7-25
Michael Hills	16-77	21	+7.78	B W Hills	14-59
Adam Kirby	15-145	10	-32.00	Walter Swinburn	12-81
Ted Durcan	15-127	12	-15.00	Saeed Bin Suroor	3-7
Dane O'Neill	14-184	8	-90.28	Henry Candy	5-40
Eddie Ahern	14-141	10	-54.70	Clive Cox	3-4
Martin Dwyer	13-151	9	+14.75	William Muir	5-39

Favourites

2yo	36.1%	-14.56	3yo	35%	-21.06	TOTAL 33.7%	-45.26

Dunstall Park, Gorsebrook Road, Wolverhampton,
West Midlands. WV6 0PE. Tel 08702 202 442

WOLVES

How to get there
Road: off A449,
close to M6, M42
and M54. Rail:
Wolverhampton, bus
Features LH, all-
weather, very sharp

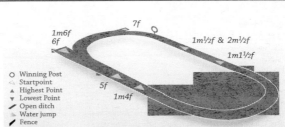

O Winning Post
▵ Startpoint
▲ Highest Point
▾ Lowest Point
✎ Open ditch
⌇ Water jump
✐ Fence

2011 Fixtures
March 30-31, April
1, 8-9, 11-12, 15,
19, 26, May 9, 16, June 20, 27, July 5,
11, August 8, 10, 19, 24-25, 30,
September 3, 8-9, 16-17, 22-24, 29-30,
October 1, 7-8, 14-15, 20-22, 28-29, 31,
November 3-4, 11-12, 14, 18-19, 24-26,
28, December 1-3, 9-10, 12, 16, 19, 21,
26, 28, 30

Time Test standard times

5f20yds	1min0.2	1m1f103yds	1min57.5
5f216yds	1min13.1	1m4f50yds	2min35.2
7f32yds	1min26.9	1m5f194yds	3min
1m141yds	1min46.7	2m119yds	3min36.6

Trainers	Wins-Runs	%	2yo	3yo+	£1 level stks
David Evans	71-667	11	8-129	63-538	-187.99
Mark Johnston	71-348	20	23-109	48-239	-43.16
Reg Hollinshead	70-562	12	9-69	61-493	-44.94
Kevin Ryan	62-447	14	12-102	50-345	-139.15
Mark Brisbourne	55-628	9	4-38	51-590	-276.72
Derek Shaw	51-521	10	0-45	51-476	-156.38
Richard Fahey	40-399	10	7-72	33-327	-27.86
Ronald Harris	39-499	8	3-73	36-426	-112.55
Tom Dascombe	38-190	20	10-60	28-130	-23.38
Paul Howling	36-362	10	2-24	34-338	-96.83
Marco Botti	30-187	16	8-62	22-125	+25.83
David Barron	30-142	21	2-11	28-131	+50.70
Jeff Pearce	29-248	12	2-9	27-239	-27.92

Jockeys	Wins-Rides	%	£1 level stks	Best Trainer	W-R
Jamie Spencer	88-327	27	-7.46	Kevin Ryan	12-28
Chris Catlin	87-918	9	-269.82	E J O'Neill	9-42
Neil Callan	82-382	21	+41.60	Kevin Ryan	18-107
Jimmy Quinn	80-697	11	-53.82	James Bethell	8-36
Graham Gibbons	63-529	12	+151.26	Reg Hollinshead	14-106
Adam Kirby	57-467	12	-80.54	Walter Swinburn	13-71
George Baker	56-333	17	+171.15	Gary Moore	10-40
Tom Queally	55-398	14	-24.93	James Given	9-66
Paul Hanagan	51-471	11	-75.47	Richard Fahey	16-160
Seb Sanders	51-343	15	-91.05	Sir Mark Prescott	13-72
Stevie Donohoe	50-450	11	-24.59	David Evans	11-70
Luke Morris	47-559	8	-93.92	J S Moore	7-32
Hayley Turner	47-436	11	-137.98	Michael Bell	10-43

Favourites

2yo	40.6% -19.26	3yo	35.7% -81.17	TOTAL	34.3% -251.34

YARMOUTH

North Denes, Great Yarmouth, Norfolk
NR30 4AU. Tel 01493 842 527

How to get there
Road: A47 to end,
A1064. Rail: Great
Yarmouth, bus
Features LH, flat

2011 Fixtures
April 25-26, May
10, 20, 31, June
8-9, 30, July 12,
18-19, 25, August
3-4, 10, 15, 23, 28, September 13-15,
October 10, 18, 25

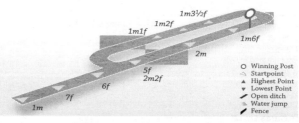

| 1m3½f |
| 1m2f |
| 1m1f |
| 1m6f |
| 2m |
| 5f |
| 2m2f |
| 6f |
| 7f |
| 1m |

O Winning Post
Startpoint
▲ Highest Point
▼ Lowest Point
Open ditch
Water jump
Fence

Time Test standard times

5f43yds	1min0.4	1m3f101yds	2min23
6f3yds	1min10.7	1m6f17yds	2min58
7f3yds	1min23	2m	3min25
1m3yds	1min35.5	2m1f170yds	3min48
1m1f	1min48.4	2m2f51yds	3min54
1m2f21yds	2min3.3		

Trainers	Wins-Runs	%	2yo	3yo+	£1 level stks
Mark H Tompkins	25-214	12	3-66	22-148	+40.25
Chris Wall	23-114	20	3-19	20-95	+49.78
John Gosden	21-83	25	13-40	8-43	+39.28
Michael Bell	19-107	18	8-47	11-60	-30.85
James Fanshawe	18-100	18	3-18	15-82	+17.75
Michael Jarvis	16-57	28	8-25	8-32	+13.21
Sir Michael Stoute	15-64	23	8-31	7-33	-25.19
Sir Mark Prescott	14-49	29	0-12	14-37	-6.88
William Haggas	12-85	14	5-40	7-45	-33.58
Andrew Haynes	12-73	16	2-15	10-58	-1.27
Peter Chapple-Hyam	12-59	20	3-25	9-34	+36.03
Christine Dunnett	11-235	5	0-36	11-199	-71.67
Clive Brittain	11-98	11	6-31	5-67	-60.20

Jockeys	Wins-Rides	%	£1 level stks	Best Trainer	W-R
Jamie Spencer	41-168	24	+4.97	James Fanshawe	9-23
Ryan Moore	31-126	25	-19.78	Sir Michael Stoute	13-43
Seb Sanders	27-112	24	+14.86	Sir Mark Prescott	8-19
Jimmy Quinn	19-250	8	-46.09	Mark H Tompkins	8-66
Darryll Holland	18-122	15	+15.38	Mick Channon	3-18
Richard Hills	18-80	23	-16.43	Michael Jarvis	5-10
Hayley Turner	17-158	11	-82.15	Michael Bell	11-49
Richard Mullen	16-175	9	-7.35	David Simcock	3-13
Ted Durcan	16-133	12	-38.68	Henry Cecil	3-17
Tom Queally	15-147	10	-48.68	Henry Cecil	3-30
Chris Catlin	15-143	10	-22.85	Chris Wall	2-4
Alan Munro	14-90	16	+12.31	Chris Wall	4-23
Jack Mitchell	14-72	19	+31.88	Peter Chapple-Hyam	5-9

Favourites

2yo	49.3% +11.85		3yo	35.6% -25.29		TOTAL	36.4% -43.98

York, YO23 1EX
Tel 01904 620 911

YORK

How to get there
Road: Course south
of city on
Knavesmire Road.
From north, A1, A59
to York, northern by-
pass from A19 to
A64. Otherwise,
A64. Rail: York, bus 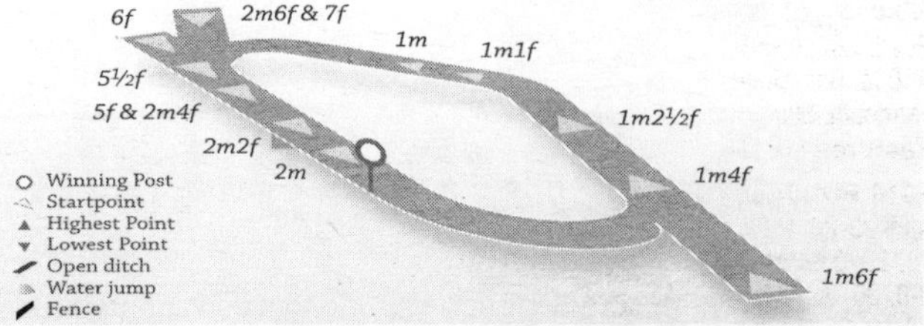
Features LH, flat

6f   2m6f & 7f
   1m   1m1f
5½f
5f & 2m4f
2m2f
2m   1m2½f
   1m4f
   1m6f

○ Winning Post
↘ Startpoint
▲ Highest Point
▼ Lowest Point
✏ Open ditch
≈ Water jump
❘ Fence

2011 Fixtures May 11-13, 21, June
10-11, July 8-9, 22-23, August 17-20,
September 4, October 7-8

Time Test standard times

5f	56.6	1m2f88yds	2min7.2
5f89yds	1min1.2	1m4f	2min27.7
6f	1min9.2	1m6f	2min54.5
7f	1min22	2m88yds	3min26.5
1m	1min36.4	2m2f	3min49.7
1m208yds	1min48.2		

Trainers	Wins-Runs	%	2yo	3yo+	£1 level stks
Richard Fahey	42-368	11	12-80	30-288	-31.06
Saeed Bin Suroor	16-87	18	5-11	11-76	-9.38
Tim Easterby	15-200	8	5-60	10-140	-64.38
Sir Michael Stoute	13-85	15	1-5	12-80	-15.94
David Nicholls	11-139	8	3-13	8-126	+9.00
Mark Johnston	10-164	6	5-45	5-119	-84.50
B W Hills	10-103	10	4-25	6-78	-34.75
John Dunlop	10-34	29	1-3	9-31	+49.00
John Quinn	9-79	11	1-7	8-72	-7.00
David Barron	7-69	10	0-5	7-64	+28.50
Mark H Tompkins	7-63	11	0-8	7-55	-5.00
William Haggas	7-43	16	1-6	6-37	+2.50
Henry Cecil	7-32	22	1-3	6-29	-8.42

Jockeys	Wins-Rides	%	£1 level stks	Best Trainer	W-R
Paul Hanagan	28-227	12	+14.94	Richard Fahey	25-189
Ryan Moore	22-111	20	+13.53	Sir Michael Stoute	9-50
Frankie Dettori	19-105	18	-25.47	Saeed Bin Suroor	11-46
David Allan	15-137	11	+12.88	Tim Easterby	11-108
Jamie Spencer	15-97	15	-4.47	Michael Bell	4-13
Eddie Ahern	11-78	14	+2.25	John Dunlop	5-13
Neil Callan	10-135	7	-44.50	Kevin Ryan	3-60
Graham Gibbons	10-76	13	+42.00	David Barron	3-6
Silvestre De Sousa	10-67	15	+52.00	Nigel Tinkler	2-8
Jimmy Quinn	10-63	16	+24.00	Mark H Tompkins	4-13
Richard Hills	10-62	16	+2.38	Ed Dunlop	3-8
John Egan	9-49	18	+49.63	Paul Cole	3-7
Jimmy Fortune	8-85	9	-17.17	John Gosden	4-17

Favourites

2yo	33.3% -5.90	3yo	27.6% -17.00	TOTAL	27.7% -42.48

Graham Wheldon

DRAW ANALYSIS is a vital part of Flat racing. Most races (outside festival meetings) are restricted to 20 runners, and as many courses can accommodate more than that number it is simply impossible for punters to assess the chances of any runner with any accuracy until they have sized up the effect of the draw.

It's fundamental – on some courses, a particular draw is almost impossible to overcome, while on others there are draws that confer a tremendous advantage.

The picture has been clouded this season by the BHA's decision to have low stalls on the inside at all right-handed tracks. This means that traditional biases, such as Beverley's high-number advantage, will now be a low-number bias. It will therefore be tricky for punters to work out stats-based systems, but hopefully the following pages, which form my outline of the factors you need to consider when betting on the Flat in Britain, will make things a lot clearer.

Course by course: your guide to Britain's draw biases

ASCOT (right-handed)
Following extensive redevelopment there have been some pretty exaggerated draw biases. Watering often seems to be the deciding factor and far too much has been applied on more than one occasion.

Stalls: Usually go up the stands' side (used to be low but will be high from this season).

Biases: One side or other was often favoured last season but the middle can also ride best, and biases remain very hard to predict.

Splits: Are common in big-field handicaps and occasionally will occur on soft ground in round-course races, when some head for the outside rail (covered by trees).

AYR (left)
Throughout the Nineties high numbers were massively favoured in the Gold and Silver Cups but things have become less clear-cut since. Traditionally the centre of the course has ridden slower here but the strip is nothing like the disadvantage it once was.

Stalls: Usually go up the stands' side (high) in sprints, but occasionally go on the other side. It isn't uncommon for jockeys to switch from the far side to race down the centre or even come right across to the stands' rail.

Biases: There's ultimately not a lot between the two sides in big fields now.

Splits: Are becoming more common, having only usually occurred in the Silver and Gold Cups in the past.

BATH (left)
The draw is of less importance than the pace at which races are run. In big fields, runners drawn low are often inclined to go off too fast to hold a rail position (the course turns left most of the way, including one major kink) and this can see hold-up horses drawn wide coming through late. Conversely, in smaller fields containing little pace, up front and on the inside is often the place to be.

Stalls: Always go on the inside (low).

Splits: Fields almost always stick together, but soft ground can see a split, with the outside rail (high) then favoured.

BEVERLEY (right)
A high draw (low from this season) used to be essential on good to soft or faster ground over 5f and also on the round course, particularly in races of 7f100y and 1m100y. However, things were far less clear-cut last year, presumably down to watering, and a lot of races developed towards the centre. The course management experimented with moving stalls to the stands' side over 5f in 2002 (unsuccessfully, as it led to a huge low bias) and haven't done so since.

Stalls: Go on the inside (was high but now low) at all distances.

Biases: High numbers are traditionally best on good to soft or faster ground but watering looked to play a big part last year.

Splits: Splits are rare and only likely over 5f on soft ground.

BRIGHTON (left)

Much depends on the going and time of year. On good to soft or slower ground runners often head for the outside rail, while in late season it's usually just a case of whichever jockey finds the least cut-up strip of ground. Otherwise, low-drawn prominent-racers tend to hold sway in fast-ground sprints, with double figures always facing an uphill task over 5f59yds.

Stalls: Always go on the inside (low) in sprints.

Splits: These occur frequently, as jockeys look for a fresh strip on ground that seems to churn up easily.

CARLISLE (right)

Runners racing with the pace and hardest against the inside rail (was high but now low) do well in big fields on decent ground. This is largely down to the fact that the Flat course and jumps course are the same, and that those racing nearest the fence are running where the hurdle wings were positioned, while those wider out are on the raced-on surface. On soft ground, the bias swings completely, with runners racing widest (was low but now high) and grabbing the stands' rail in the straight favoured at all distances.

Stalls: Normally go on the inside (was high but now low) but can go down the middle in sprints (usually on slow ground).

Biases: High numbers (now low) have been best in fast-ground sprints. Look to back low numbers (now high) on soft/heavy ground.

Splits: Rarely will two groups form but, on easy ground, runners often spread out.

CATTERICK (left)

When the ground is testing, the stands' rail is definitely the place to be, which suits high numbers in 5f races and high-drawn prominent-racers at all other distances. However, when the ground is good to firm or faster, horses drawn on the inside (low) often hold the edge, and there have been several meetings over the last few seasons in which those racing prominently hardest against the inside rail have dominated (over all distances).

Stalls: Go on the inside (low) at all distances these days (they often used to go on the outer over 5f212yds).

Biases: Low numbers are best in sprints on fast ground (particularly watered firm going) but the stands' rail (high) rides faster under slower conditions.

Splits: Are common over 5f.

BEVERLEY: will be much affected by the BHA's new rules on stall numbering

CHEPSTOW (left)

High numbers enjoyed a massive advantage in straight-course races in 2000 and the course management duly took steps to eradicate the faster strip, using the same 'earthquake' machine as had been employed at Goodwood in the late Nineties. This has led to little in the way of a draw bias since.

Stalls: Always go on the stands' side (high) on the straight course.

Biases: Have become hard to predict in recent times.

Splits: Splits are common as jockeys drawn low often head far side.

CHESTER (left)

It's well known that low numbers are favoured at all distances here, even in the 2m2f Chester Cup, and the bias is factored into the prices these days. That said sprints (and in particular handicaps) are still playable, as it often pays to stick to a runner drawn 1-3.

Stalls: Go on the inside (low) at all distances bar

1m2f75yds and 2m2f117yds (same starting point) when they go on the outside. Certain starters ask for the stalls to come off the inside rail slightly in sprints.

Biases: Low numbers are favoured at all distances. Soft ground seems to accentuate the bias until a few races have been staged, when a higher draw becomes less of a disadvantage as the ground on the inside becomes chewed up.

DONCASTER (left)

There's been very little between the two sides since the course reopened. Jockeys now tend to swerve the stands' rail (high) on good or slower ground, instead preferring to head for the centre.

Stalls: Can go either side but tend to go up the stands' side (high) whenever possible.

Biases: Runners down the centre are usually worst off. The longer the trip on the straight course the better chance the far side (low) has against the stands' side in big fields.

TED SPREAD: helped by a stall-one berth at Chester, even in the Vase over 1m4f

EPSOM (left)

When the going is on the soft side, jockeys tack over to the stands' side for the better ground (this strip rides quicker in such conditions as the course cambers away from the stands' rail). In 5f races, the stalls are invariably placed on the stands' side, so when the going is soft the majority of the runners are on the best ground from the outset. Prominent-racers drawn low in round-course races are able to take the shortest route around Tattenham Corner, and on faster ground have a decisive edge over 6f, 7f and 1m114yds. Over 5f, high numbers used to hold quite an advantage, but the bias is not so great these days.

Stalls: Always go on the outside (high) over 5f and 6f (races over the latter trip start on a chute) and inside (low) at other distances, bar 1m4f10yds (centre).
Biases: Low-drawn prominent racers are favoured at between 6f and 1m114yds.
Splits: Good to soft ground often leads to a few trying the stands' side route.

FOLKESTONE (right)

Prior to 1998, Folkestone was never thought to have much in the way of a bias, but nowadays the draw is often crucial on the straight course (up to 7f). On very soft ground, the far rail (was high but now low) rides faster than the stands' rail. However, on good to soft or faster ground runners tend to stay up the near side now (the ambulance used to go this side of the far rail but now goes the other side of the fence) and those racing on the pace hardest against the fence often enjoy a major advantage.

Stalls: Usually go up the stands' side (was low but now high) on the straight track, but occasionally down the centre.
Biases: High numbers (now low) are favoured over 6f and 7f, and also over the minimum trip when 14 or more line up. However, very low numbers (now very high) have a good record in smaller fields over 5f. Front-runners are well worth considering at all distances.
Splits: Often occur.

GOODWOOD (right)

The course management took steps to end the major high bias (now low) seen in the Stewards' Cup throughout the late 90s by breaking up the ground by machine in 1998. This led to the stands' side dominating the race in 1999 before the far side gradually took over again.

Stalls: Invariably go on the stands' side (was low but now high).
Biases: High numbers (now low) are best at between 7f-1m1f, and the faster the ground, the more pronounced the bias (keep an eye out for the rail on the home turn being moved during Glorious Goodwood week, usually after the Thursday).
Splits: Although fields tend not to break into groups in most sprints, runners often spread out to about two-thirds of the way across in fields of around 20.

HAMILTON (right)

Extensive drainage work was carried out in the winter of 2002 in a bid to level up the two sides of the track but, after encouraging early results, the natural bias in favour of the far side (was high but now low) kicked in again. This can be altered by watering on faster going, though, and low numbers (now high) were definitely favoured under such conditions in 2008 before a less clearcut pattern last year when jockeys more often than not headed for the centre. High numbers (now low) have been best over 1m65yds, thanks to runners encountering a tight right-handed loop soon after the start.

Stalls: It's not uncommon for the ground to become too soft for the use of stalls, but otherwise they go either side.
Biases: High draws (now low) have been best in soft/heavy-ground sprints, but the bias has become middle to high (now low) otherwise, often switching to low (now high) on watered fast ground. Front-runners do particularly well at all distances.
Splits: Rarely happen now.

HAYDOCK (left)

High numbers used to enjoy a major advantage in soft-ground sprints but runners usually head for the centre these days and the draw rarely makes much of a difference.

Stalls: Usually go down the centre in the straight.

KEMPTON (right)

High numbers (now low) are best over 5f and preferable over 6f, while those drawn very low (now very high) over 7f often have a bit to do. Otherwise, pace of races counts for a lot and this is one of the fairest courses around in that respect.

LEICESTER (right)

There was a four-year spell between 1998 and 2001 when the centre-to-far-side strip (was middle to high but now middle to low) enjoyed a decisive advantage over the stands' rail, jockeys eventually choosing to avoid the near side. However, that's changed recently, with very low numbers (now very high) more than holding their own.

Stalls: Invariably go up the stands' side (was low but now high).
Splits: Still occur occasionally.

LINGFIELD (left)
Turf

Following a less predictable spell, the stands' rail (high) has taken over again in the past couple of years. The one factor that can have a massive effect on the draw is heavy rainfall on to firm ground. Presumably because of the undulating nature of the track and the fact that the far rail on the straight course is towards the bottom of a slope where it joins the round course, rainfall seems to make the middle and far side ride a deal slower. In these conditions, the top three or four stalls have a massive edge.

Stalls: Go up the stands' side (high) at between 5f and 7f and down the middle over 7f140yds.

Biases: High numbers are favoured unless the ground is genuinely soft.

Splits: It's unusual to see two distinct groups, but runners often fan out centre to stands' side in big fields.

All-Weather

There is little bias over most trips, but it is an advantage to be drawn low over 6f and 1m2f, with both starts being situated very close to the first bend. A low to middle draw is preferable over 5f, even with a safety limit of just ten, though the very inside stall has a poor recent record. No horse managed to win from stall one over that trip in 2004, which suggests the ground right against the inside rail is slower than elsewhere.

Stalls: Are against the outside rail (high) over 5f and 1m, but against the inside rail (low) for all other distances.

Splits: Fields never split but runners usually come wide off the home turn.

MUSSELBURGH (right)

The bias in favour of low numbers (now high) over 5f isn't as pronounced as many believe, apart from on soft ground, while the bias in favour of high numbers (now high) at 7f and 1m also isn't that great.

Stalls: Usually go up the stands' side (was low but now high) over 5f nowadays, but they can be rotated.

Splits: Look out for runners drawn very high in big-field 5f races on fast ground, as they occasionally go right to the far rail.

NEWBURY (left)

There's basically little between the two sides these days, apart from on soft ground, in which case the stands' rail (high) is often the place to be. When the ground is testing it's not uncommon to see runners race wide down the back straight and down the side at between 1m3f56yds and 2m (particularly over 1m5f61yds). In such circumstances, a high draw becomes an advantage.

Stalls: Can go anywhere for straight-course races.

Splits: Are pretty rare.

NEWCASTLE (left)

It used to be a case of high numbers best at up to and including 7f on good or firmer, and low numbers having the advantage when the ground is good to soft or softer. However, now things depend largely on the positioning of the stands' rail. If the course is at its widest high numbers are almost always best off, while if the rail is further in things are less clear-cut.

Stalls: Invariably go on the stands' side (high), only being switched to the inside under exceptional circumstances.

Splits: Two groups are usually formed when 14+ go to post, and often when 8-13 line up.

NEWMARKET (right)
July Course

The major draw biases seen under the former clerk of the course have become a thing of the past and now only the occasional meeting will be affected. The course is permanently divided into two halves by a rail (the Racing Post now carry information regarding which side is to be used) and, as a rule of thumb, the two outside rails (stands' rail when they're on the stands' side half, far rail when they're on the far-side half) ride faster than the dividing rail. When they're on the stands' side half, on fast ground (particularly watered) very high numbers (now very low) are often favoured at up to 1m, when there's a narrow strip hard against the fence that rides quicker. However, on good to soft or slower ground, runners racing down the centre are favoured. On the far side half, there's rarely much in the draw, apart from on slow ground, when the far side (was low but now high) rides faster.

Stalls: Can go either side on either half of the track.

Splits: Runners just about tend to form two groups in capacity fields, but are more likely to run to their draw here than at tracks such as Newcastle.

Rowley Mile

Similarly to the July Course, the draw seems to have been evened out since the clerk of the course changed, although it's still generally a case of the further away from the stands' rail the better.

Stalls: Can go anywhere and are rotated.

Biases: High numbers (now low) have dominated the 2m2f Cesarewitch in recent years, the logic here being that those on the inside can be switched off early, while low numbers (now high) have to work to get into position before the sole right-handed turn.

Splits: It's not unusual for jockeys to come stands' side on slow ground in round-course races.

NOTTINGHAM (left)

Biases are far harder to predict now on the both the inner (spring/autumn) and outer (summer) course.

Stalls: Tend to go on the stands' side (high) unless the ground is very soft.

Splits: Fields usually split in sprints when 14+ line up.

PONTEFRACT (left)

Low numbers have always been considered best here for the same reason as at Chester, in that the course has several distinct left-hand turns with a short home straight, but this is not always true. High numbers at least hold their own over 6f now, whatever the ground, but massively so on soft/heavy. Drainage work was carried out in the late Nineties to try to eradicate the outside-rail bias on slow ground, and this worked immediately afterwards, but during the last few seasons there have been definite signs that it's now riding much faster.

Stalls: Go on the inside (low) unless the ground is very soft, when they're switched to the outside rail.

Splits: Although it's uncommon to see distinct groups, high numbers usually race wide these days on good to soft/heavy ground.

REDCAR (left)

It's not unusual to see big fields throughout the season but the draw rarely makes a difference.

Stalls: Go towards the stands' side (high).

Splits: Unusual.

RIPON (right)

The draw is often the sole deciding factor in big-field sprints and watering plays a major part. As a general rule, low numbers (now high) are best when the ground is good to firm or faster, while the far side is always best on softer going but, ultimately, the best guide here these days is the most recent meeting.

Stalls: Go on the stands' side (was low but now high) apart from under exceptional circumstances.

Biases: Front-runners, particularly from high draws (now low) over 1m, have an excellent record, and any horse trying to make ground from behind and out wide is always facing a tough task.

Splits: Fields tend to stay together in races of 12 or fewer, but a split is near guaranteed when 15 or more line up. Look for 'draw' jockeys who might chance

going far side in fields of 13-14.

SALISBURY (right)

For most of last year those racing against the inside rail (was high but now low) on fast ground looked worst off if anything (centre often best), which is the opposite of how things have been in the past. Presumably this was down to watering. On slower ground jockeys invariably head towards the stands' rail (good to soft seems to be the cut-off point) and whoever grabs the fence in front can prove hard to pass.

Stalls: Go on the far side (was high but now low) unless the ground is soft, when they're often moved to the near side.

Biases: Low numbers are always best on soft/heavy ground.

Splits: Fields only tend to divide on good to soft ground; otherwise they all converge towards either rail, dependant upon going.

SANDOWN (right)

On the 5f chute, when the going is on the soft side and the stalls are on the far side (was high but now low),

CASTLES IN THE AIR: wins at Pontefract, where the bias isn't quite as great as many believe

far-side runners enjoy a decisive advantage. On the rare occasions that the stalls are placed on the stands' side, low numbers (now high) enjoy a slight advantage when all the runners stay towards the stands' rail, but when a few break off and go to the far side high numbers (now low) comfortably hold the upper hand again. High numbers (now low) enjoy a decent advantage in double-figure fields over 7f and 1m on good going or faster, but jockeys invariably head for the stands' side on slow ground.

Stalls: Usually go far side (was high but now low) over 5f, as the course is more level that side.

Splits: It's unusual for runners to split over 5f, with capacity fields rare and jockeys all inclined to head for the far rail.

SOUTHWELL (left)
All-Weather

Over most trips on the round track it is preferable to be drawn away from the extreme inside or outside. The exceptions are over 6f and 1m3f, which both start close to the first bend, making it better to be drawn low to middle. At most meetings the centre of the track rides faster than against either rail, though that can change in extreme weather when power-harrowing can even out the bias. A low to middle draw is preferable over 5f.

Stalls: Are placed next to the inside rail (low), except over 5f where they are placed next to the stands' rail (high).

Splits: The fields do not tend to split into groups as such, but can fan right out and take varied routes once into the home straight. Even in big fields over the straight 5f, the runners basically stick to their draw and race as straight as they can from start to finish.

THIRSK (left)

This used to be the biggest draw course in the country, back in the days of the old watering system (which was badly affected by the wind), but while biases still often show up, they're not as predictable as used to be the case. Field sizes, watering and going always have to be taken into account when 12 or more line up (11 or fewer runners and it's rare to see anything bar one group up the stands' rail, with high numbers best). Otherwise, either rail can enjoy the edge on watered fast ground (the one place not to be under any circumstances is down the middle). Low-drawn prominent-racers are well worth considering whatever the distance.

Stalls: Always go up the stands' side (high).

Biases: High numbers are best in sprints when 11 or fewer line up, but it's hard to know which side is likely to do best in bigger fields on fast ground. The far (inside) rail is always best on slow going (the softer the ground, the greater the advantage).

Splits: Runners invariably stay towards the stands' side in sprints containing 12 or fewer runners (unless the ground is soft) and frequently when 13-14 line up. Any more and it becomes long odds-on two groups.

WARWICK (left)

Low numbers are no longer favoured, whatever the ground, and jockeys rarely if ever stick to the inside rail now. Presumably this is down to watering (hold-up runners are not as badly off as they used to be).

Stalls: Always go on the inside (low).

WINDSOR (figure of eight)

The bias in favour of high numbers on fast ground is nothing like as predictable as it used to be, presumably because of watering. On slower ground, jockeys head centre to far side, and right over to the far rail (low) on genuine soft/heavy.

Stalls: Can be positioned anywhere for sprints.

Biases: High-drawn prominent-racers are favoured in fast-ground sprints, and also over 1m67yds. On good to soft going, there's rarely much between the two sides, but it's a case of nearer to the far rail (low) the better on bad ground.

Splits: Splits only occur on good to soft ground, and even then it's rare to see two defined groups.

WOLVERHAMPTON (left)

A low draw is a big advantage over 5f20yds and 5f216yds, and low to middle is preferable over 7f32yds. Beyond that it doesn't seem to matter, although it's never a good idea to race too wide on the home bend, as those that do rarely seem to make up the lost ground.

Stalls: Are placed against the outside rail (high) over 7f and against the inside rail (low) at all other distances.

YARMOUTH (left)

High numbers enjoyed a major advantage for much of the Nineties, but this was put to an end by the course switching from pop-up sprinklers (which were affected by the off-shore breeze) to a Briggs Boom in 1999. These days a bias will appear occasionally but it's hard to predict, and runners often head for the centre whatever the going.

Stalls: Go one side or the other.

Splits: It's common to see groups form, often including one down the centre, in big fields.

YORK (left)

The draw is nothing like as unpredictable in sprints as many believe, although things are never quite as clearcut in September/October as earlier in the season. Essentially, on good or faster ground, the faster strip is to be found centre to far side, which means in capacity fields, the place to be is stall 6-12, while in fields of 12-14 runners drawn low are favoured (the course is only wide enough to house 20 runners). On soft/heavy ground, the stands' side (high) becomes the place to be.

Stalls: Can go anywhere.

Biases: Prominent racers in the centre are favoured in fast-ground sprints, but high numbers take over on genuine soft/heavy ground.

Splits: Defined groups are rare.

Win – free form!

THIS YEAR'S QUIZ could hardly be more simple, and the prize should prove invaluable to our lucky winner. We're offering a free subscription to Raceform, the BHA's official form book – every week from May to November, you could be getting the previous week's results in full, together with note-book comments highlighting future winners, adjusted Official Ratings and Raceform's *Performance* ratings. The winner will also get a copy of last year's complete form book.

All you have to do is this: identify the two potential Classic hopes for 2011 pictured on the following pages. And here's a clue – they were both first-time Group 1 winners for their trainers in France last year. If you think you know the answer, write their names in the box below in the order in which they appear.

Send your answers along with your details on the entry form below, to:

**2011 Flat Annual Competition, Racing & Football Outlook,
Floor 23, 1 Canada Square, London, E14 5AP.**

Entries must reach us no later than first post on April 15. The winner's name and the right answers will be printed in the RFO's April 19 edition.

Six runners-up will each receive a copy of last year's form book.

Name

Address

Town

Postcode

In the event of more than one correct entry, the winner will be drawn at random from the correct entries. The Editor's decision is final and no correspondence will be entered into.

BETTING CHART

ON	ODDS	AGAINST
50	Evens	50
52.4	11-10	47.6
54.5	6-5	45.5
55.6	5-4	44.4
58	11-8	42
60	6-4	40
62	13-8	38
63.6	7-4	36.4
65.3	15-8	34.7
66.7	2-1	33.3
68	85-40	32
69.2	9-4	30.8
71.4	5-2	28.6
73.4	11-4	26.6
75	3-1	25
76.9	100-30	23.1
77.8	7-2	22.2
80	4-1	20
82	9-2	18
83.3	5-1	16.7
84.6	11-2	15.4
85.7	6-1	14.3
86.7	13-2	13.3
87.5	7-1	12.5
88.2	15-2	11.8
89	8-1	11
89.35	100-12	10.65
89.4	17-2	10.6
90	9-1	10
91	10-1	9
91.8	11-1	8.2
92.6	12-1	7.4
93.5	14-1	6.5
94.4	16-1	5.6
94.7	18-1	5.3
95.2	20-1	4.8
95.7	22-1	4.3
96.2	25-1	3.8
97.2	33-1	2.8
97.6	40-1	2.4
98.1	50-1	1.9
98.5	66-1	1.3
99.0	100-1	0.99

The table above (often known as the 'Field Money Table') shows both bookmakers' margins and how much a backer needs to invest to win £100. To calculate a bookmaker's margin, simply add up the percentages of all the odds on offer. The sum by which the total exceeds 100% gives the 'over-round' on the book. To determine what stake is required to win £100 (includes returned stake) at a particular price, just look at the relevant row, either odds-against or odds-on.

RULE 4 DEDUCTIONS

When a horse is withdrawn before coming under starter's orders, but after a market has been formed, bookmakers are entitled to make the following deductions from win and place returns (excluding stakes) in accordance with Tattersalls' Rule 4(c).

	Odds of withdrawn horse	*Deduction from winnings*
(1)	3-10 or shorter	75p in the £
(2)	2-5 to 1-3	70p in the £
(3)	8-15 to 4-9	65p in the £
(4)	8-13 to 4-7	60p in the £
(5)	4-5 to 4-6	55p in the £
(6)	20-21 to 5-6	50p in the £
(7)	Evens to 6-5	45p in the £
(8)	5-4 to 6-4	40p in the £
(9)	13-8 to 7-4	35p in the £
(10)	15-8 to 9-4	30p in the £
(11)	5-2 to 3-1	25p in the £
(12)	100-30 to 4-1	20p in the £
(13)	9-2 to 11-2	15p in the £
(14)	6-1 to 9-1	10p in the £
(15)	10-1 to 14-1	5p in the £
(16)	longer than 14-1	no deductions

(17) ....When more than one horse is withdrawn without coming under starter's orders, total deductions shall not exceed 75p in the £.

*Starting-price bets are affected only when there was insufficient time to form a new market.

Feedback!

If you have any comments or criticism about this book, or suggestions for future editions, please tell us.

Write   Nick Watts/Dylan Hill
2011 Flat Annual
Racing & Football Outlook
Floor 23,
1 Canada Square,
London E14 5AP

email   rfo@rfoutlook.com

Fax   FAO Nick Watts, 0207 510 6457

Horse index

*All horses discussed, with page numbers, except for references in the Group 1
and two-year-old form sections (pages 87-113), which have their own indexes.*